Oh, the doors you will open!

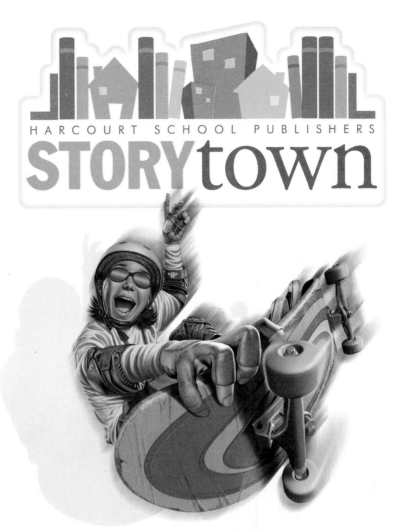

HARCOURT SCHOOL PUBLISHERS

STORYtown

Ride the Edge

Senior Authors

Isabel L. Beck • Roger C. Farr • Dorothy S. Strickland

Authors

Alma Flor Ada • Roxanne F. Hudson • Margaret G. McKeown
Robin C. Scarcella • Julie A. Washington

Consultants

F. Isabel Campoy • Tyrone C. Howard • David A. Monti

HOUGHTON
MIFFLIN
HARCOURT
School Publishers

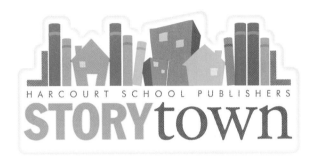

Ride the Edge

HOUGHTON
MIFFLIN
HARCOURT
School Publishers

Theme 1
Finding a Way

Contents

Theme 2
Common Goals

Theme 3
Go with the Flow

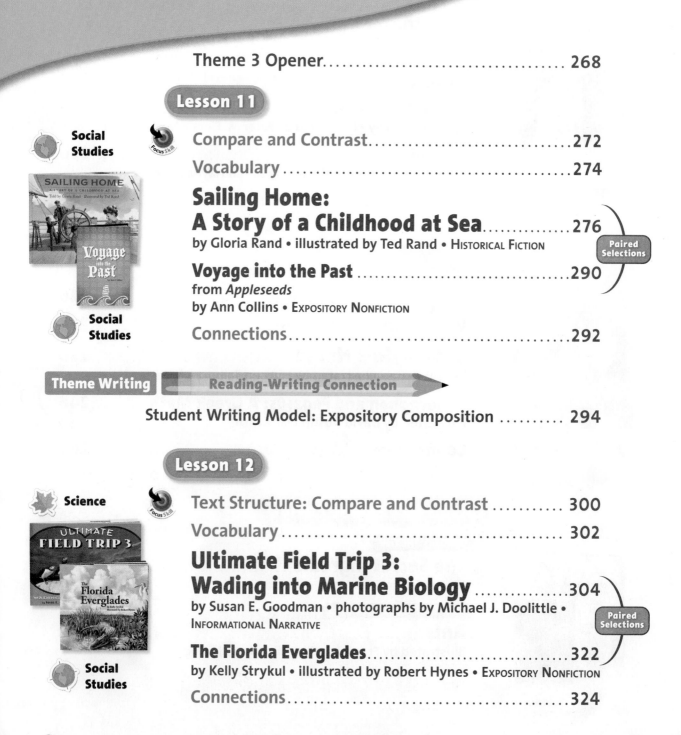

Theme 4
Dare to Be Great

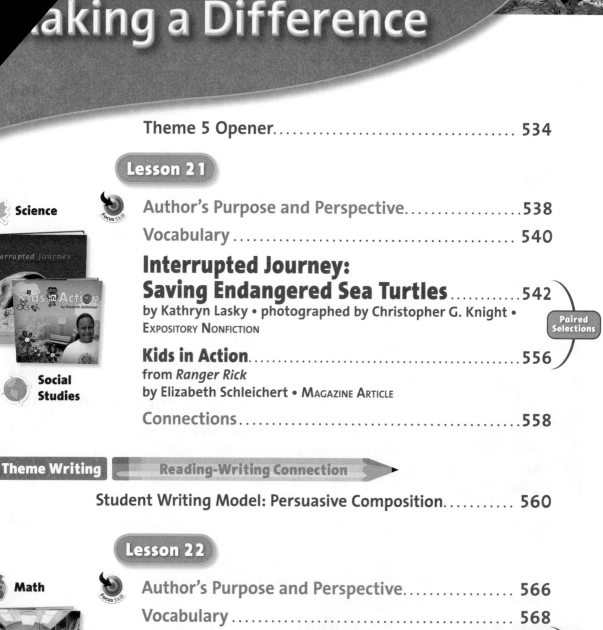

5
aking a Difference

Theme 6
Feats of Daring

Comprehension Strategies

Strategies for Reading

A **strategy** is a plan for doing something well. You can use strategies before, during, and after reading.

Before You Read

- **Preview the text** by looking at the title, headings, and photographs or illustrations.
- **Access prior knowledge** by thinking about what you already know about the topic or genre.
- **Predict** what the text will be about and what you might learn from reading it. Then **set a purpose** for reading.

While You Read

Think about what you understand and do not understand. Use the comprehension strategies on page 17 to help you understand the text and remember it later.

After You Read

Talk with a classmate about which strategies you used and why you used them.

Strategies To Use When Reading

- **Use Story Structure** Keep track of the characters, setting, and plot events to help you understand how a story is organized.

- **Summarize** Pause as you read to identify the most important ideas in the text.

- **Ask and Answer Questions** Ask yourself questions about what you do not understand in the text. Look for answers to questions as you read.

- **Use Graphic Organizers** Make charts and diagrams as you read to show how important ideas in the text are related.

- **Monitor Comprehension** When you do not understand a section of text, use one of these strategies to clarify the information.
  - **Reread**
  - **Read Ahead**
  - **Adjust Reading Rate**
  - **Self-Correct**

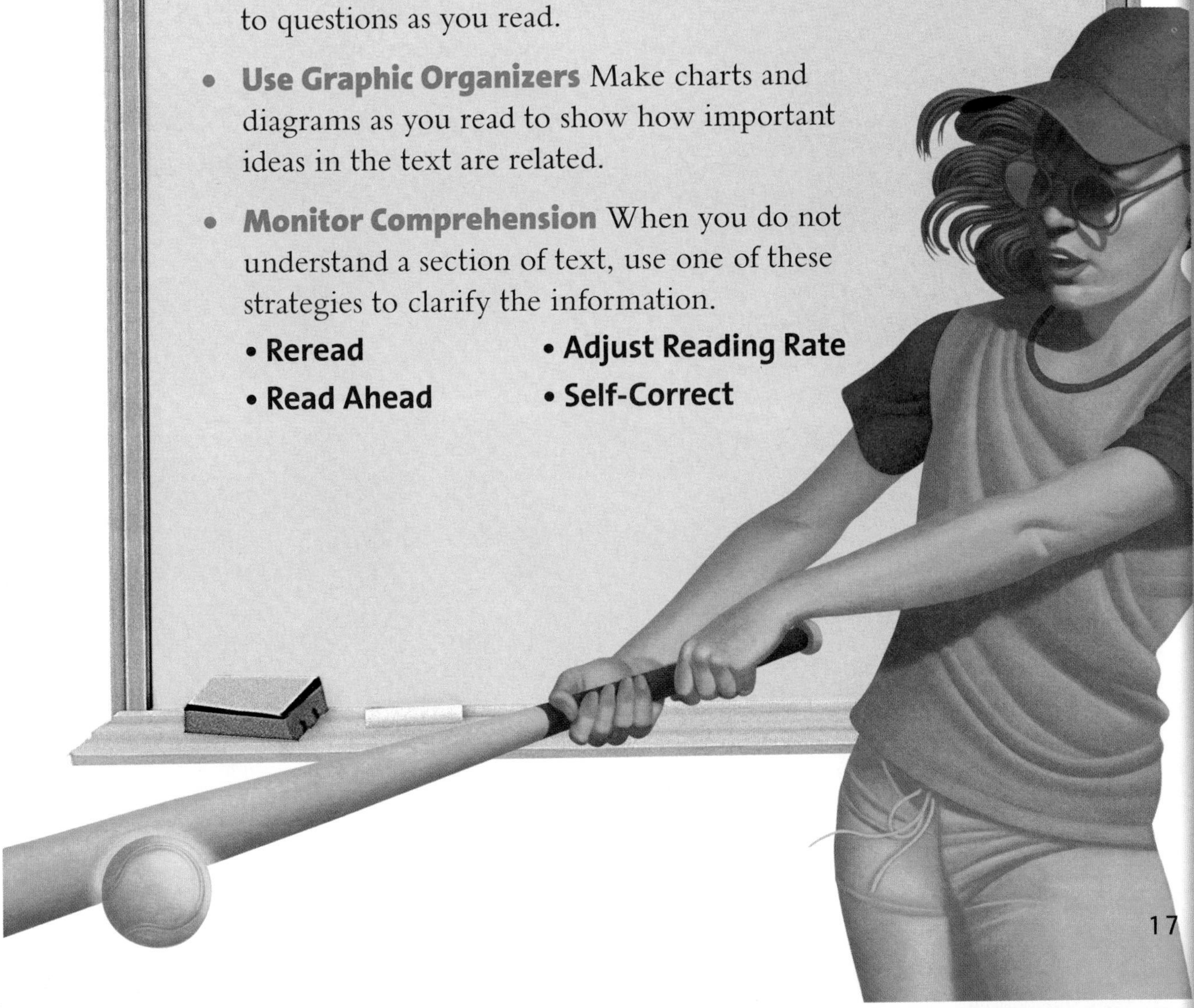

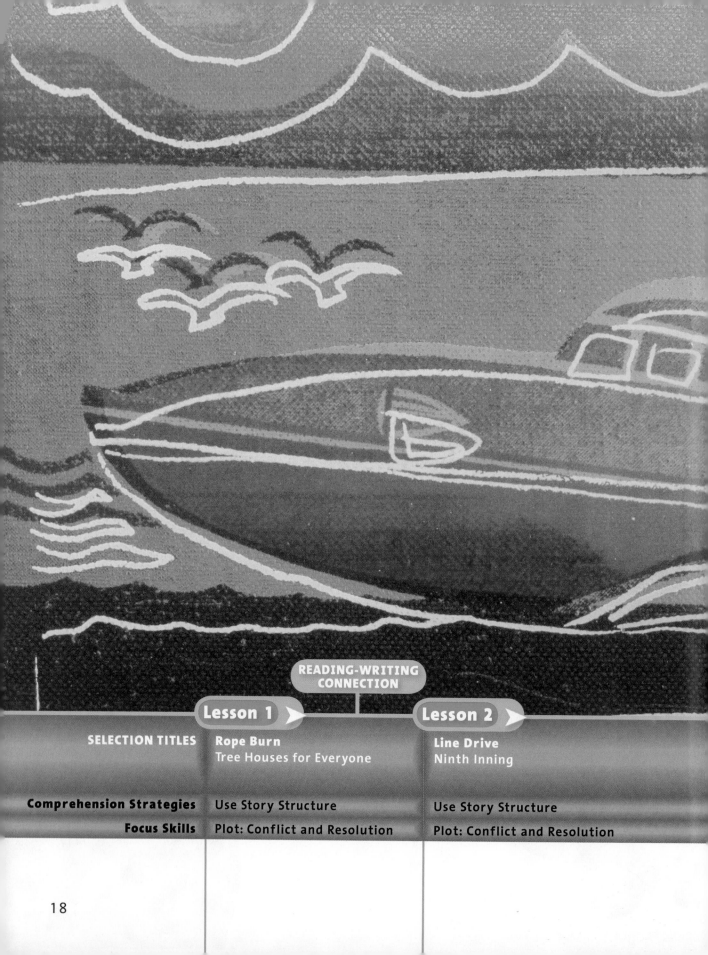

READING-WRITING
CONNECTION

	Lesson 1 ▷	**Lesson 2** ▷
SELECTION TITLES	**Rope Burn** Tree Houses for Everyone	**Line Drive** Ninth Inning
Comprehension Strategies	Use Story Structure	Use Story Structure
Focus Skills	Plot: Conflict and Resolution	Plot: Conflict and Resolution

Theme 1 Finding a Way

Speedboat, Andy Warhol

Lesson 3	Lesson 4	Lesson 5 Review
Chang and the Bamboo Flute Evren Ozan, Musician	**The Daring Nellie Bly: America's Star Reporter** Around the World in Seventy-two Days	**It Takes Talent!** **The Alligator Race**
Monitor Comprehension: Reread	Monitor Comprehension: Reread	Review Skills and Strategies
Character's Motives	Character's Motives	

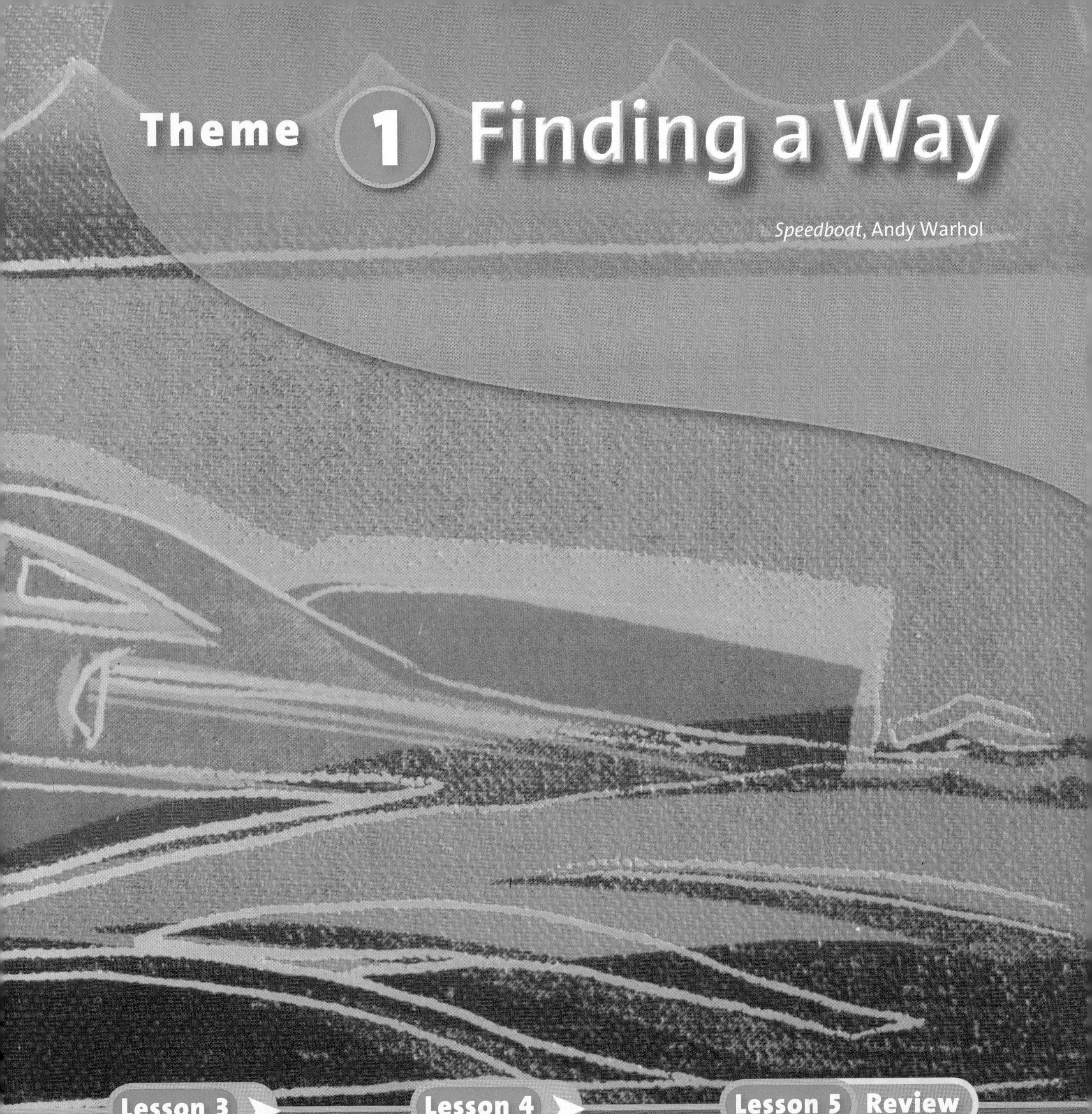

Big Idea
The characters of realistic fiction face challenges.

Enduring ! Understanding
The story plot is based on events that determine the conflict and lead to the resolution.

Essential ? Question
How do readers identify the conflict and resolution?

Spelling Words

Words with Closed Syllables: Short Vowel Patterns

bandage	scrap
chest	shift
drift	smash
dull	switch
dusk	swept
stretch	threat
flock	timid
fond	plaid
measure	trust
cactus	twist

Challenge

rustic	absence
frantic	clasp
biscuit	

Fluency

Accuracy

Robust Vocabulary

- humiliation
- expectations
- fringes
- hesitating
- sincere
- coaxed

Comprehension

 Plot: Conflict and Resolution

 Use Story Structure

Writing

- Character Description Paragraph
- Voice

Lesson 1

Genre: Realistic Fiction

Rope Burn

Jan Sieb

Tree Houses for Everyone

by Tiffany Sommers

Genre: Magazine Article

Focus Skill

Plot: Conflict and Resolution

All stories have a **plot**, or a series of story events. Most plots contain a **conflict**, or problem, that occurs early in the story. Plot events throughout the story lead to a **resolution**, or solution to the problem, near the end. Recognizing the conflict and the resolution in a story can help you better understand what you read.

Conflict

↓

Plot Events

↓

Resolution

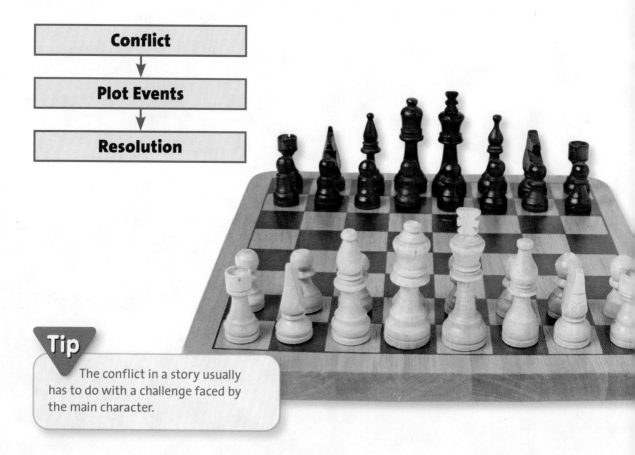

Tip

The conflict in a story usually has to do with a challenge faced by the main character.

Read the story below. Then look at the graphic organizer. The plot conflict is stated in the first sentence. The plot events lead to the story's resolution.

Freddy had trouble making friends at his new school. One day, he saw a poster about a meeting of the chess club, and he decided to go. At the meeting, Freddy met a boy named Dennis who lived on his block.

"I didn't know you played chess. You should come over after school so we can play a game," Dennis said. Freddy was glad to meet someone who liked chess as much as he did.

Conflict
Freddy has trouble making friends at his new school.

Plot Events
• Freddy sees a poster for the chess club meeting.
• Freddy goes to the meeting.

Resolution
Freddy meets Dennis, who also likes to play chess.

Try This!

Look back at the story. What other action might Freddy have taken to resolve the conflict?

www.harcourtschool.com/storytown

Vocabulary

Build Robust Vocabulary

humiliation

fringes

expectations

coaxed

sincere

hesitating

Gym Class Blues

October 14

I have suffered enough **humiliation** in gym class. I'm tired of always being on the **fringes** of the basketball court. It's all we ever play, and it's just not my best sport.

October 16

I'm worried that if Coach Thomas sees nothing but my poor basketball skills, she'll have low **expectations** of me. Maybe I can convince her to let us try volleyball. Then I could show her what I've got!

October 17

Today was a great day! I **coaxed** three other students to talk to Coach Thomas with me. It turns out I'm not the only one who'd like to play a different sport. We explained our concerns to the coach. She saw that we were **sincere** in wanting to try something new. Coach Thomas listened to us, and then without **hesitating** she said, "I'm glad you spoke up. I didn't realize everyone was tired of basketball. We'll start on volleyball today."

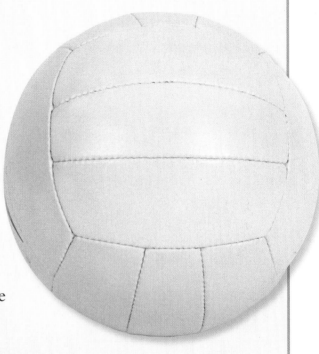

 www.harcourtschool.com/storytown

Word Scribe

This week your task is to use Vocabulary Words in your writing. In your vocabulary journal, write sentences to show the meanings of the words. For example, you could write about something you coaxed a friend to do, or things you do to show you are sincere. Use as many of the Vocabulary Words as you can. Share your writing with your classmates.

Award Winner

Rope Burn
Jan Siebold

Realistic Fiction

Genre Study

Realistic fiction has characters and events that are like people and events in real life. As you read, look for

- characters who have feelings that real people have.

- a main character who overcomes a challenge.

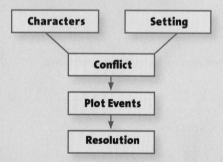

Characters → Setting
↓
Conflict
↓
Plot Events
↓
Resolution

Comprehension Strategy

Use story structure to identify and remember a story's conflict and resolution.

One of the worst things that can happen to a kid is having to move to a new school. You don't know where you're going, you don't know any of the teachers, and you don't have any friends. It's an open invitation for humiliation.

I figured that the best way to survive was to blend in like a chameleon. If you're new, the minute you stand out or call attention to yourself, you're dead. That first week of school, I was careful to wear the standard uniform of most kids my age: jeans, a T-shirt, and sneakers. I have shaggy blond hair and brown eyes. I guess I'm pretty average-looking.

The first few days went by without any major problems. The routine was pretty much the same as in my old school. The teachers gave their beginning-of-the-year speeches about homework and expectations and stuff, and handed out books. The other kids were still getting used to the shock of being back in school, so they didn't even seem to notice me.

Things were going along well until Friday. That was the day I had my first gym class. Right away, the gym teacher, Mr. Reynolds, announced that we would be starting the year with a basic physical education test. He said that he wanted to see where we all stood. The test was to be made up of four stations: sit-ups, push-ups, laps, and rope-climbing.

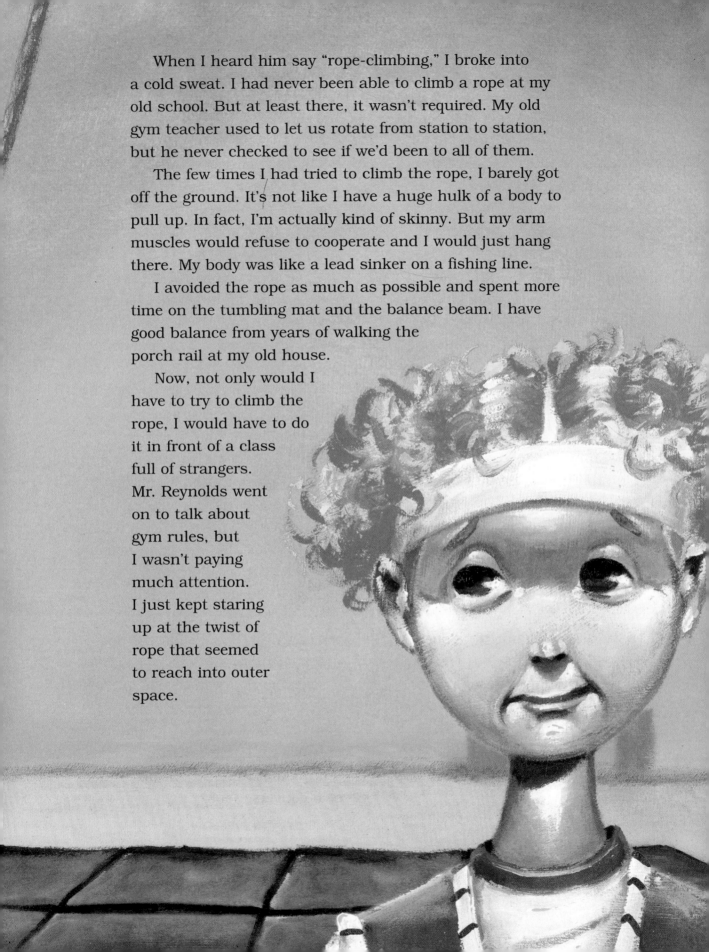

When I heard him say "rope-climbing," I broke into
a cold sweat. I had never been able to climb a rope at my
old school. But at least there, it wasn't required. My old
gym teacher used to let us rotate from station to station,
but he never checked to see if we'd been to all of them.

The few times I had tried to climb the rope, I barely got
off the ground. It's not like I have a huge hulk of a body to
pull up. In fact, I'm actually kind of skinny. But my arm
muscles would refuse to cooperate and I would just hang
there. My body was like a lead sinker on a fishing line.

I avoided the rope as much as possible and spent more
time on the tumbling mat and the balance beam. I have
good balance from years of walking the
porch rail at my old house.

Now, not only would I
have to try to climb the
rope, I would have to do
it in front of a class
full of strangers.
Mr. Reynolds went
on to talk about
gym rules, but
I wasn't paying
much attention.
I just kept staring
up at the twist of
rope that seemed
to reach into outer
space.

After Mr. Reynolds's announcements, we counted off by fours. I was a four. Rope-climbing started with the threes. Luckily, we only had enough time left for one station that day. That meant I probably wouldn't get to that station until my next gym class. Maybe I could be sick that day.

After gym, I went to my locker to get my lunch. As I was dialing my combination, I heard someone say, "You're not too crazy about rope-climbing, are you?"

I turned to see a dark-skinned boy looking at me through thick glasses.

"Actually, I hate rope-climbing," I admitted. "How did you guess?"

"You looked like you were going to pass out when Mr. Reynolds was talking about it," explained the boy. He was wearing black jeans and a bright yellow T-shirt with a picture of a lizard coming out of its pocket.

"Every time I looked at you after that, you were just staring up at that rope like you were in a trance."

I laughed and said, "We never had to climb ropes at my old school. I tried a few times, but I wasn't very good at it."

We started to walk toward the cafeteria.

"I'm James," said the boy.

"I'm Richard."

"You live in the old Miller place on Pine Street, don't you?" asked James.

"How did you know?"

"I've seen you in the backyard. I live on the street behind you, one house away. When I'm up in my tree house, I can see right into your yard."

I wasn't too crazy about the idea of someone spying on me, but I let it pass. "That's your tree house?" I asked. I had seen the back of it from my yard. It sat high in the branches of a big oak tree.

"Yeah. My dad and I built it a few years ago. Do you want to come over after school today and see it?"

"Sure," I said. "Thanks."

By this time, we had reached the cafeteria. I paused at the door and looked around. Students could sit anywhere, but most had already staked out their regular tables. For the first few days, I had moved around, sitting on the fringes of groups that were caught up in their own conversations.

James must have noticed that I was hesitating because he said, "Want to come and eat at my table?" He pointed to a table where two boys were already sitting.

"Okay," I said, relieved. James introduced me to his friends Michael and Roland. At lunch, we compared schedules. It turned out that James was in two of my afternoon classes. He told me all about the good teachers and the bad ones, and about the subjects that he liked least and most. Roland teased him about being a "brain," but James just laughed.

"If I'm a brain, then you're a spleen," he told Roland.

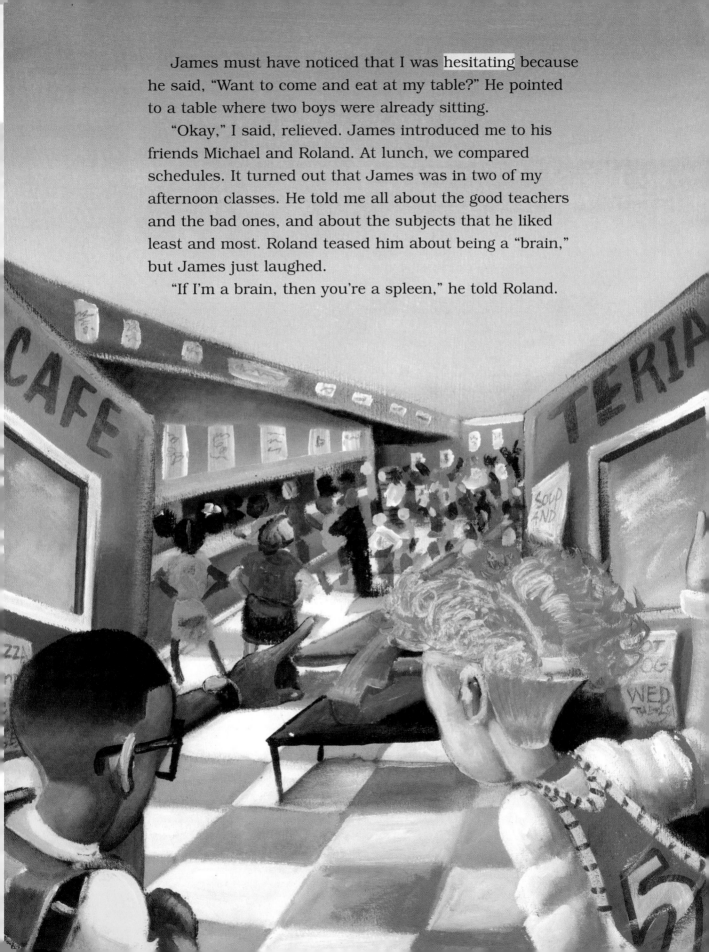

After school, I grabbed a handful of chocolate chip cookies and cut across the backyard to James's tree house.

"Hi," called a voice from somewhere above me. James poked his head out of the doorway and looked down. "Come on up."

I studied the tree. As far as I could tell, the only way to get up to the tree house was by climbing a rope that was tied to a nearby branch.

"Thanks a lot," I said. "I suppose this is your idea of a joke?" I turned to walk back home.

"Wait a minute!" James shouted. "I just wanted to help you. I figured maybe I could teach you to climb it."

He sounded pretty sincere. I went back to the base of the tree. "Do you think you could?" I asked.

"We can try," said James. He caught hold of the rope and slid to the ground. "Let's see what you can do."

I wiped my hands on my pants. Then I reached up and grabbed the rope. I bent my knees and lifted my feet from the ground. As much as I strained, I could not pull myself up any farther. I just hung there while James studied me.

"I see your first mistake right away," he announced. I stood up and let go of the rope.

"First of all, you're expecting your arms to do all of the work," said James. "Didn't you ever watch anyone climb a rope? Their legs do a lot of the work. Watch."

He took hold of the rope with his hands and wrapped his legs around the bottom of it. The rope was clenched between his sneakers. James reached higher with his hands and pulled himself up. At the same time, his feet pushed downward. He repeated this movement over and over, like an inchworm, until he had reached the top of the rope. Then, hand over hand, he lowered himself to the ground.

"Your arms can rest a little while your feet are gripping the rope," explained James. "Try it. And don't put your hands so high this time."

I took the rope in my hands and wrapped my legs around it. I tried to clasp the bottom with my sneakers. The rope kept slipping through my feet. I let go.

33

"You can't use the bottom of your feet to grab the rope," said James. "You've got to use the sides."

This time, while I held the rope with my hands, James tried to position my feet.

"Okay," he said. "Try straightening your legs."

I pushed down, and managed to raise myself several inches.

"Good," said James. "Now hold on with your feet and move your hands up."

I was able to move them up an inch or so. I repeated the motion, inching my way up the rope. After I had climbed a foot or so, I stopped to rest.

"Try not to stop," James advised. "It will only tire out your arms more."

James was right. I shouldn't have stopped. When I tried to climb higher, my arms refused to cooperate. I jumped down, falling to my knees.

I tried again and again. After a while, I was able to climb halfway up the rope before I stopped.

"Keep going!" yelled James.

"I can't. My arms are getting shaky. I need to rest for a while." I let go of the rope and jumped down.

"You always get to the same spot and freeze," James commented. "The rope in the gym is twice as high as this one. You'll never make it to the top at this rate."

"Thanks a lot, coach."

James grinned. "No problem. We can try again tomorrow."

After that, we went back to my house for a while. I showed James my room. He looked at my books and was excited to find *Hatchet* by Gary Paulsen. He said that he had been wanting to read it. I let him borrow it. He was especially interested in my baseball card collection. It turned out that he collects, too. He admired my poster of Ryne Sandberg.

"He's my favorite player," I explained. "He was born on my birthday."

"Don't you mean you were born on *his* birthday?" James asked.

When he left to go home for dinner, he said, "See you tomorrow at the top of the rope."

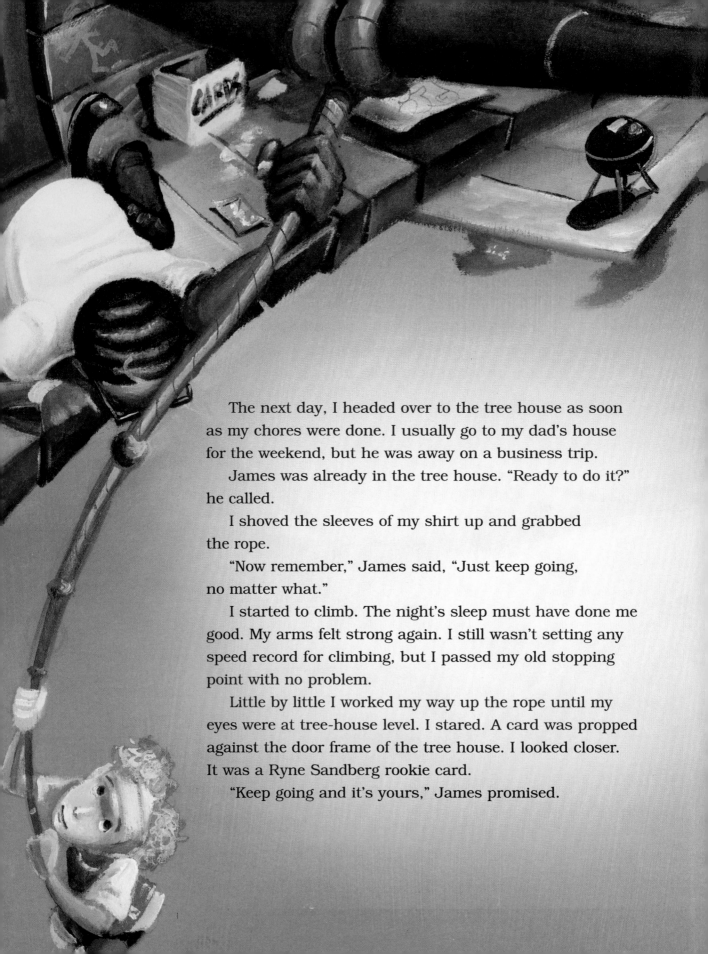

The next day, I headed over to the tree house as soon as my chores were done. I usually go to my dad's house for the weekend, but he was away on a business trip.

James was already in the tree house. "Ready to do it?" he called.

I shoved the sleeves of my shirt up and grabbed the rope.

"Now remember," James said, "Just keep going, no matter what."

I started to climb. The night's sleep must have done me good. My arms felt strong again. I still wasn't setting any speed record for climbing, but I passed my old stopping point with no problem.

Little by little I worked my way up the rope until my eyes were at tree-house level. I stared. A card was propped against the door frame of the tree house. I looked closer. It was a Ryne Sandberg rookie card.

"Keep going and it's yours," James promised.

"Now you tell me," I grunted. "I shouldn't have stopped to look at it."

My arms were getting shaky, and my feet slipped. I was much too high to drop to the ground.

"C'mon. Just a few more feet," James coaxed.

I took a deep breath and strained to pull myself up. Slowly, I climbed high enough to put my foot inside the doorway. I swung myself over and landed on the floor.

"Congratulations!" proclaimed James. He handed me the baseball card.

"Thanks." I grinned. I couldn't believe that I'd done it.

"There's only one thing I forgot to tell you," said James.

"What?" I asked.

"Climbing down is a lot harder than climbing up."

I groaned.

We stayed up in the tree house for a long time that morning, looking at James's stuff. He had been reading *Hatchet* up there and was already halfway through it.

He kept a metal fishing tackle box in the tree house all of the time. In it were an old battery-operated radio, gum, hard candy, a flashlight, a small notebook, and a pencil.

We talked a lot, too. I told James about my old house and yard, and about my mom and dad getting a divorce.

He told me about his best friend who had moved away at the beginning of summer. I was secretly glad that his friend had moved. If he hadn't, James wouldn't have been in the market for a new best friend.

Climbing down wasn't as bad as James had made it out to be. I just worked my way down slowly. James told me that he and his family were going away the next day, but that I should practice as much as I wanted.

On Sunday, I climbed the rope a dozen times or so. On my last climb of the day, I left a message for James in his tackle box notebook.

It said, "See you in gym class from the top of the rope!"

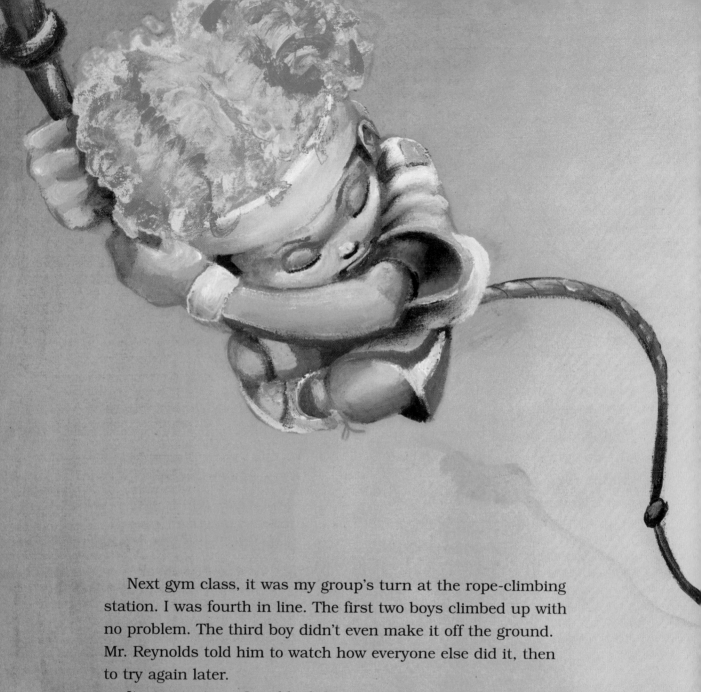

Next gym class, it was my group's turn at the rope-climbing station. I was fourth in line. The first two boys climbed up with no problem. The third boy didn't even make it off the ground. Mr. Reynolds told him to watch how everyone else did it, then to try again later.

It was my turn. I grabbed the rope and slowly started to climb. My hands were tender from practicing all weekend. My gym shorts were more slippery than the jeans that I had been wearing.

About halfway up, I almost stopped to rest. My hands were throbbing and my arms were starting to get that old shaky feeling. I didn't think I could go on.

Just then, I spotted James watching me from the sit-up station. He grinned and gave me a thumbs-up sign. I kept going.

Before I knew it, I had reached the top. I looked around for a few seconds. I was even higher than the basketball hoops. I had never paid much attention to the outline of the basketball court which was painted on the floor. From up above, its colorful boundaries stood out clearly.

Slowly I made my way back down. I knew that if I stopped to rest, my arms would give out. When I reached the bottom, Mr. Reynolds said, "Good job, Richard."

I didn't even know that he knew my name. He made a check mark on a list.

I looked up at the top of the rope. Thanks to James, I had seen the world from a place I'd never been before. I guess that's one of the things that friends do best.

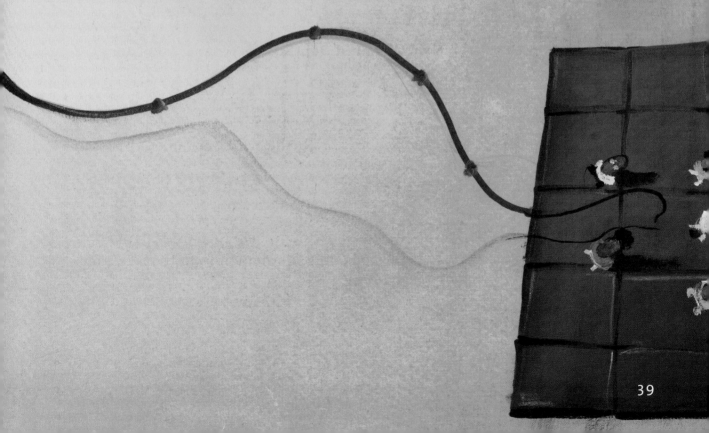

Think Critically

1 What is Richard's problem in "Rope Burn," and how does James help him solve it? PLOT: CONFLICT AND RESOLUTION

2 What reward is waiting for Richard when he climbs the rope into the tree house for the first time? NOTE DETAILS

3 How has Richard changed from the beginning of the story? CHARACTER ANALYSIS

4 What do you think would be the hardest thing about being a new student at school? EXPRESS PERSONAL OPINIONS

5 **WRITE** Why does James decide to help Richard learn to climb a rope? Use details and information from the selection to support your answer. SHORT RESPONSE

About the Author
Jan Siebold

Jan Siebold says that she comes from "a family of readers." When she was a child, her favorite gift was a new book. She says, "Books can show us what is possible in the world."

Besides being a writer of children's books, Jan Siebold has been an elementary school librarian for more than 25 years. She lives in East Aurora, New York, where she enjoys hiking, biking, and watching movies.

About the Illustrator
Frank Morrison

Growing up in New Jersey, Frank Morrison had a passion for painting and dance. He liked the energy of his neighborhood with its disc jockeys and graffiti art. In fact, as a teenager, he was a professional break dancer. Today, he is a successful painter and illustrator with his own studio and gallery. Frank Morrison lives in Georgia with his wife and their four children.

 www.harcourtschool.com/storytown

Tree Houses for Everyone

by Tiffany Sommers

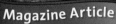

Magazine Article

Tree Houses

Burlington, Vermont

Watertown, Wisconsin

Lake Travis, Texas

Forever Young Treehouses cofounder Bill Allen shows Jennifer and Kyle his work.

for Everyone

by Tiffany Sommers

A Vermont group builds kids' dream houses.

Tree houses are great places to play with friends or even just to sit and dream. But for some kids, tree houses are only that— a dream. Many kids have never been in a tree house, because they have disabilities that prevent them from climbing. Bill Allen and Phil Trabulsy decided to make these kids' dreams come true. In 1998, Allen and Trabulsy started Forever Young Treehouses, a nonprofit group that creates tree houses that everyone can enjoy.

The Vermont-based organization designs tree houses that kids with disabilities can easily explore. Long wheelchair ramps let kids get into the house without having to climb a single branch.

Chris, 11, and Kristen, 17, had a chance to visit a tree house for the first time last week. "It was so cool," Chris told us. "It was amazing how big it was and how I could get around so easily."

Kristen agrees. "It was really great having a tree house that I could get into without any help," she says.

Forever Young Treehouses gets neighborhoods involved in building the houses. Much of the material is donated by local businesses. Volunteers help with the construction. Allen believes that the projects help to create communities. "It is a way to form friendships between kids with disabilities and kids without," he says.

So far, Allen's organization has built eight tree houses in the United States. Their goal is to build "one in every state by 2008." In September, 2004, a new tree house in Burlington, Vermont, welcomed visitors. Peter Clavelle, the city's mayor, is thrilled with the new addition to Burlington. "Many people face barriers," he says. "But this tree house gets rid of some of those barriers. This is a house where the doors are open for everyone."

Ashford, Connecticut

Connections

Comparing Texts

1. James helps Richard learn a new skill. When did a friend help you learn a new skill? Tell about it.

2. Compare the way Richard and James use the tree house with the way the children in "Tree Houses for Everyone" use the tree houses.

3. Richard's actions prove the truth of the statement "Practice makes perfect." To what other challenge could you apply this statement?

Vocabulary Review

Word Webs

Work with a partner. Choose two Vocabulary Words. Create a web for each word. In the outer circles, write words and phrases that are related to the Vocabulary Word. Explain how each word or phrase is related to the Vocabulary Word.

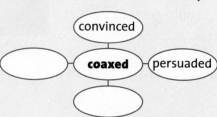

humiliation

expectations

fringes

hesitating

sincere

coaxed

Partner Reading

With a partner, choose three or four paragraphs from "Rope Burn." Read the paragraphs aloud as your partner follows along to check your accuracy. Ask your partner to tell you if you misread any words. Then trade roles. Reread the paragraphs until both of you can read them with accuracy.

Writing

Write a Note

Imagine that a new student is afraid of the rope-climbing test. Write a note from Richard to the new student that addresses the conflict and suggests an action that will lead to a resolution.

```
    Conflict
       ↓
    Actions
       ↓
   Resolution
```

My Writing Checklist

Writing Trait → Voice

✔ I used a voice that was appropriate for the character.

✔ I used a graphic organizer to identify the problem and plan the solution.

✔ I used correct spelling and punctuation.

Reading-Writing Connection

Analyze Writer's Craft: Narrative

A narrative is a story. It includes **characters**, a **setting**, and a series of **events** that make up the **plot**. When you write narratives, you can use the work of authors, such as Jan Siebold, as writing models. In the paragraph below from "Rope Burn," the main character is also the narrator of the story. Notice how the author reveals the narrator's personality through his **voice**.

Writing Trait

VOICE
Phrases, such as *blend in like a chameleon* and *the standard uniform*, make the narrator, Richard, sound creative and smart.

Writing Trait

VOICE
Words such as *survive* and *dead* **exaggerate** the danger of being a new student. They help reveal Richard's nervous personality.

I figured that the best way to survive was to blend in like a chameleon. If you're new, the minute you stand out or call attention to yourself, you're dead. That first week of school, I was careful to wear the standard uniform of most kids my age: jeans, a T-shirt, and sneakers. I have shaggy blond hair and brown eyes. I guess I'm pretty average-looking.

Personal Narrative

In a **personal narrative**, a writer tells about an experience in his or her life. The writer describes his or her feelings before, during, and after the experience and tells why it was important or memorable. As you read this personal narrative by a student named June, notice the humor and honesty in the writer's **voice**.

In the first paragraph, June describes a **conflict**: she wants to be athletic, but she is uncoordinated.

Writing Trait

VOICE
June reveals a funny, honest **personality** when she admits, *"Uncoordinated" is my middle name.*

Learning to Fall
by June M.

My two best friends were excited about learning to snowboard. "I'm in!" I said, not wanting to be left out. When we were actually in the snow at the top of a hill, with both feet strapped to a snowboard, I was secretly shaking. I've always wanted to be athletic, but "Uncoordinated" is my middle name.

"I guarantee you will fall!" yelled Mark, our instructor. "So you have to know how to fall the right way." This news did not make me feel any better. Mark held his arms up in front of his chest, fists together, elbows bent. He said something about never sticking your hands and arms out straight. The words "you might break your wrist" sent me into a cold sweat. "When you fall," Mark continued, "roll through your knees, up to your side, and onto your shoulder."

I tried to smile, but I felt sick to my stomach. My knees wobbled badly. With each passing minute, snowboarding sounded less and less like fun.

Mark swooped down below us and called us down the slope one by one. First, we had to point one end of the board downhill. Next, we had to slide and turn along one edge to stop. "Go!" Mark yelled when it was my turn. Then I really started shaking. I was frozen to the spot like an icicle. I was shaking so badly that the board began to move on its own. I looked helplessly at Mark as I picked up speed. "Tu-u-u-urn!" he yelled.

"Aaaaaaa!" I gargled. I felt my balance giving way, and then I was face down on the snow. For some reason, I started giggling.

"Good fall!" said Mark. He pointed out that I had first touched down with my knees and then rolled onto my side and shoulder. "Textbook example!" he said. At least I had done something right.

I had a lot more practice falling that day. I also learned to slide and turn. I learned that I am much more coordinated than I'd thought. For the first time, I felt like an athlete.

June uses words such as *first*, *next*, and *then* to help show the **order of events**.

In the end, June's conflict is **resolved.** She feels more athletic and more coordinated.

Now look at what June did to prepare to write her personal narrative.

Brainstorm Ideas

June used a web to help her choose an experience to write about. She decided to write about her first snowboarding lesson.

Organize Ideas

June used a graphic organizer to plan her personal narrative. First, she described the conflict she felt before her first snowboarding lesson. Then she listed the events that led to a resolution of her conflict. Finally, she described the resolution of the conflict.

Conflict
I wanted to be athletic, but I was uncoordinated.

↓

Plot Events
• I took a snowboarding lesson.
• I learned to fall.
• I learned to slide and turn.

↓

Resolution
I felt more athletic and coordinated.

Big 💡 Idea

In autobiographies, authors write stories about themselves that contain conflicts and resolutions.

Enduring ❗ Understanding

The time and place of a story can affect the conflict and resolution of the plot.

Essential ❓ Question

What influences the conflict of the story?

Spelling Words

Words with Long Vowels and Vowel Digraphs

needle	eager
speech	shadow
reason	saying
crease	mild
thief	coach
fade	smoke
obtain	twice
faint	human
steep	teenage
rayon	niece

Challenge

kneeling	amusement
retrieve	disappear
emerge	

Fluency

Accuracy

Comprehension

 Plot: Conflict and Resolution

 Use Story Structure

Robust Vocabulary

maven
mortified
reigned
conceited
designated
smirk
exhilarated

Writing

- Autobiographical Composition
- Voice

Lesson 2

Genre: Autobiography

Line Drive

by Tanya West Dean   illustrated by Wilson McLean

Ninth Inning

Genre: Poetry

Focus Skill

Plot: Conflict and Resolution

You know that in most stories, the **plot** includes a **conflict,** or problem, and actions, or events, that lead to a **resolution**. Authors usually introduce the conflict at the beginning of the story and conclude the story with the resolution. The actions or events in between are used to resolve the conflict in the plot.

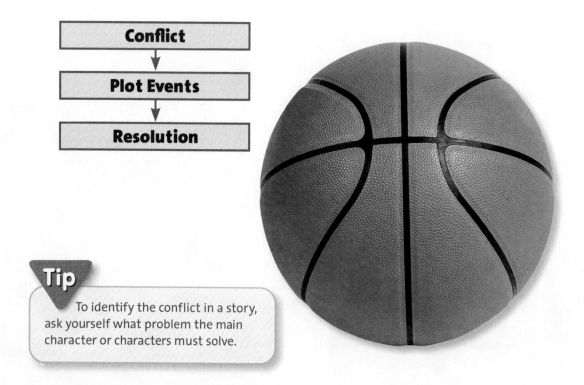

| Conflict |
| Plot Events |
| Resolution |

Tip

To identify the conflict in a story, ask yourself what problem the main character or characters must solve.

Read the paragraph below. Then look at the graphic organizer. It shows the conflict and actions that leads to the resolution.

Tim wanted to play basketball with his older brothers, but they insisted that he was still too small. Tim got them to agree to a deal—if he could make five free throws in a row, they would let him play. When Tim's first shot went in, his brothers called it luck. When the fifth shot went in, his oldest brother smiled and said, "You're on my team. Let's play."

Conflict
Tim's brothers won't let him play basketball.

↓

Plot Events
- Tim makes a deal with his brothers.
- Tim makes five free throws in a row.

↓

Resolution
Tim's brothers let him play.

Try This!

Look back at the paragraph. How might the outcome have been different if Tim hadn't made all five free throws?

www.harcourtschool.com/storytown

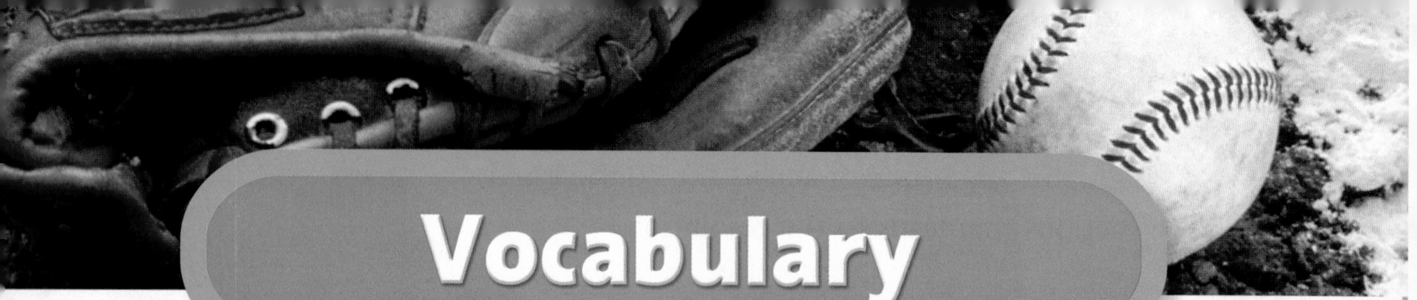

Vocabulary

Build Robust Vocabulary

- maven
- reigned
- smirk
- conceited
- mortified
- designated
- exhilarated

Surf's Up in Fish Town

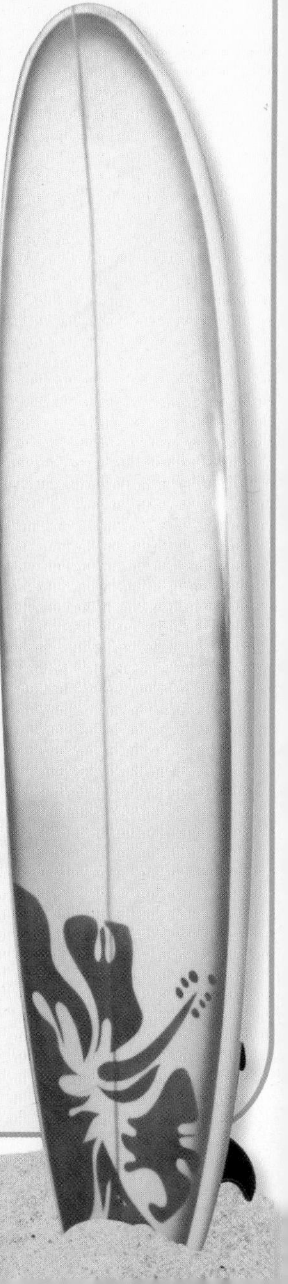

This past week, Fish Town held its annual all-woman surf championship. In a surprising upset, Andi Gold was crowned Women's Surf Champion. Many had believed local surfing **maven** Cat Brown would win, since she had **reigned** for the past two years. Others were not convinced Cat Brown was a sure thing.

"There's no way Andi's going to win," one observer said with a **smirk**.

"I disagree," another observer said. "I think Andi's the one to watch. She's a strong competitor, but she's not at all **conceited** about her skill."

In the final round of the contest, only Andi Gold and Cat Brown remained. They both dropped in on the same wave. Andi Gold crouched low and balanced on her board. Cat Brown tried to cut sharply into the wave, but she tumbled off her board into the surf.

"That wasn't even a big wave. It should have been easy for me. I'm **mortified**," Cat Brown said.

In the press area **designated** for the winner, Andi Gold told reporters, "That was the best ride. I feel **exhilarated**!"

 www.harcourtschool.com/storytown

Word Champion

Your challenge this week is to use Vocabulary Words outside of your classroom. Think of questions you can ask family members and friends using as many of the Vocabulary Words as possible. For example, you could ask, *When was a time that you felt exhilarated by something you did?* Write your question and their answers in your vocabulary journal. Share your writing with your classmates.

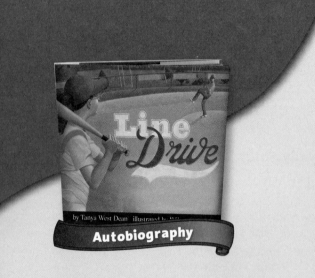

by Tanya West Dean illustrated by...

Autobiography

Genre Study

An autobiography is a person's account of his or her own life. As you read, look for

- the first-person point of view.

- details about important events in the author's life.

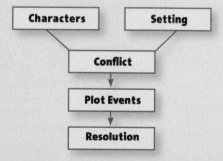

Characters → Setting → Conflict → Plot Events → Resolution

Comprehension Strategy

Use story structure to identify and remember the story's conflict and resolution.

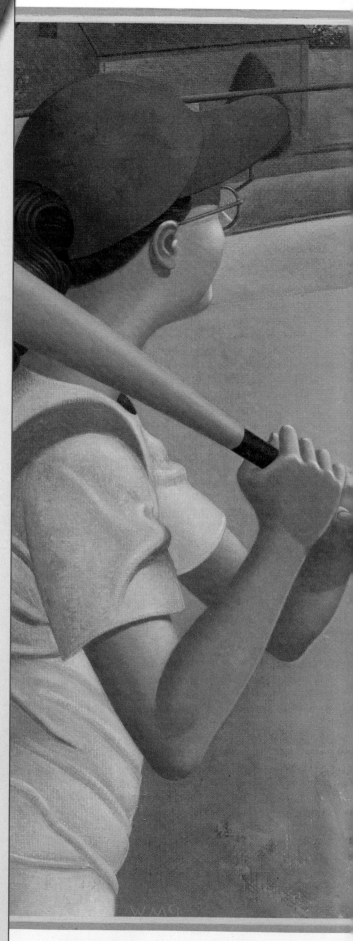

Line Drive

by Tanya West Dean
illustrated by Wilson McLean

Tanya West Dean loved to play baseball. In the 1960s, though, girls were not allowed to play on boys' teams, and girls often had no teams of their own. Tanya's only way to get close to a baseball game was to volunteer to keep score. From her spot on the bench, she waited patiently for the chance to prove that she could play the game just as well as any boy could.

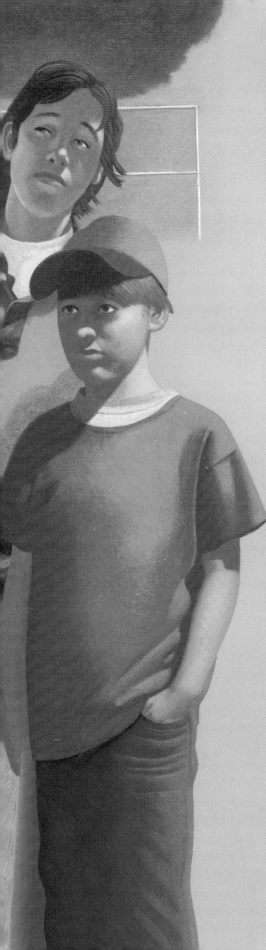

Growing up the oldest sister of three brothers doesn't always make you a tomboy, but it helps. And having a mom who would rather punt a football than sew a quilt sets the stage for some great sports memories, too. Obviously, no one ever told me that girls couldn't play baseball or ride a boy's bike or wrestle Indian-style. I could smack a grimy hardball across the fence with the best of the neighborhood boys—and I was just a skinny, short girl with glasses. Mom taught us—her sons and daughters—how to do all those things. A former baton twirler and field hockey maven, my mom was the next best thing to a real coach.

In fact, Mom usually showed up early with my brothers for Little League and helped the head coach "warm up the boys" by hitting line drives, grounders, and high fly balls. My brothers seemed caught between being really proud of Mom and being completely mortified that this five-foot-short lady could hammer a line drive to third while faking out the first baseman. I guess she figured she should do everything she could to be both a mom and dad to us kids. Actually, most dads couldn't hit and throw as well as she could. Or yell as loudly from the bleachers. But that's another story.

I think my first baseball glove must have been a cast-off from my one-year-younger brother, Bobby. It didn't matter. I was following in my mother's cleats. Bobby and I played pass, practiced pitching and catching, and teased our littler brother, Ricky, with games of keep-away. As soon as Ricky started catching more than missing, he joined us, too. That was when real baseball happened. One pitcher, one catcher, one batter. It was the best. We took turns playing each spot until it grew too dark to see the old, brown baseball.

My brothers didn't mind that I was a girl. Actually, I'm not even sure they noticed—until we moved across the street from Mark. Mark ran the dead-end neighborhood we had just joined. He was the loudest, mouthiest eleven-year-old I'd ever seen. His idea of playing catch with his dog was to throw the ball into the biggest bush he could find and then laugh and laugh when Sarge couldn't get past the brambles to retrieve it. Did I mention Mark was an only child? He was not used to sharing—especially the spotlight.

We had lived in our duplex farmhouse only a few weeks before Little League started. In those days, girls weren't allowed to play on the boys' teams. And there weren't any girls' teams. None. Zero. Nada. The only way I could sit on the bench with the guys was as the scorekeeper. So I learned all about lineups and substitutions and "the rules" of playing. The only rule I could never understand was unspoken: "No girls on the team." Mom could warm up the team, but I had to sit on the sidelines holding a pencil instead of a baseball.

Bobby and Ricky were close enough in age—nine and ten—to be on the same team. Tall, lanky Bobby reigned in the outfield or on first base. Short, quick Ricky started out at shortstop, but found his real place squatting behind the batter as the world's smallest catcher. And the pitcher Ricky had to catch for was usually Mark.

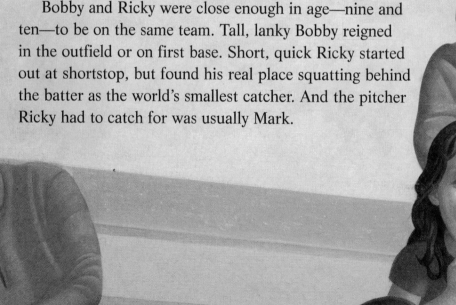

To say Mark was conceited about his pitching skills is like saying Godzilla was a big lizard. After striking out a batter, Mark would take off his ball cap, run his fingers through his curly black hair, and flash a wide smile at the giggling girls on the bleachers.

Bobby and Ricky found a way to get along with Mark. They just reminded him how good he was as often as possible. Thing is, he *was* good. No one could pitch as fast or as straight as Mark. He was all-star material, all right. And he made sure everyone knew it. I didn't like the sneer that so often slid across his face from one ear to the other. But I loved to watch him pitch. As I marked down the strikeouts in the team's scorebook, I knew this guy had something special. The coach loved him, the fans loved him, and he loved himself. And—I had to admit it—I was impressed with his fastball.

I felt my palms sweat when he'd sometimes have to sit beside me on the bench, waiting for his turn at bat. I squeaked every time I said, "Mark, you're on deck!" And I watched as he stood in the circle, practicing his swing and smiling at the crowd—but never at me. Who was I, anyway? Just the skinny girl with glasses who kept score.

Sometimes my brothers still played baseball with me in our backyard. But if Mark was home, they took off for his yard and left me in the dust. You'd think there was another girl in the neighborhood for me to play with, but there wasn't. If I was going to hang out with anybody, it was going to have to be with Bobby, Ricky, and Mark. And if Mark was ever going to notice me, it would have to be on his terms—playing baseball.

"Let me come with you," I begged one afternoon when my brothers were getting ready for a neighborhood game in Mark's yard. "I can play as well as you can. Just let me come and play outfield."

"I don't know," said Bobby. "Mark wouldn't like it. You're a girl. He doesn't have a sister or anything. You oughta stay home."

"Let me just try," I begged. "If he doesn't want me to play, I'll go home. I promise."

Bobby looked at Ricky, who just shrugged and tossed a short pop-up to catch.

"All right. But if he gets mad, you have to go home. Okay?"

"Okay," I agreed. I was happier than a mouse in a corncrib. I grabbed my old glove and followed the boys down the long gravel lane toward Mark's house, grinning so big that my cheeks pushed my glasses off my nose.

I stood in Mark's side yard, the designated baseball area, where the bases were brown spots of naked dirt. A plank of wood was half-buried in the middle—the pitcher's mound, Mark's territory. I stood on it for a second, balancing myself and looking straight ahead at the home-plate patch. I heard the guys emerge from the porch, Mark laughing at something Ricky had said. When I looked over, I could tell they hadn't mentioned anything about me coming over to play. Mark stared at me standing there on his pitcher's plank and stopped.

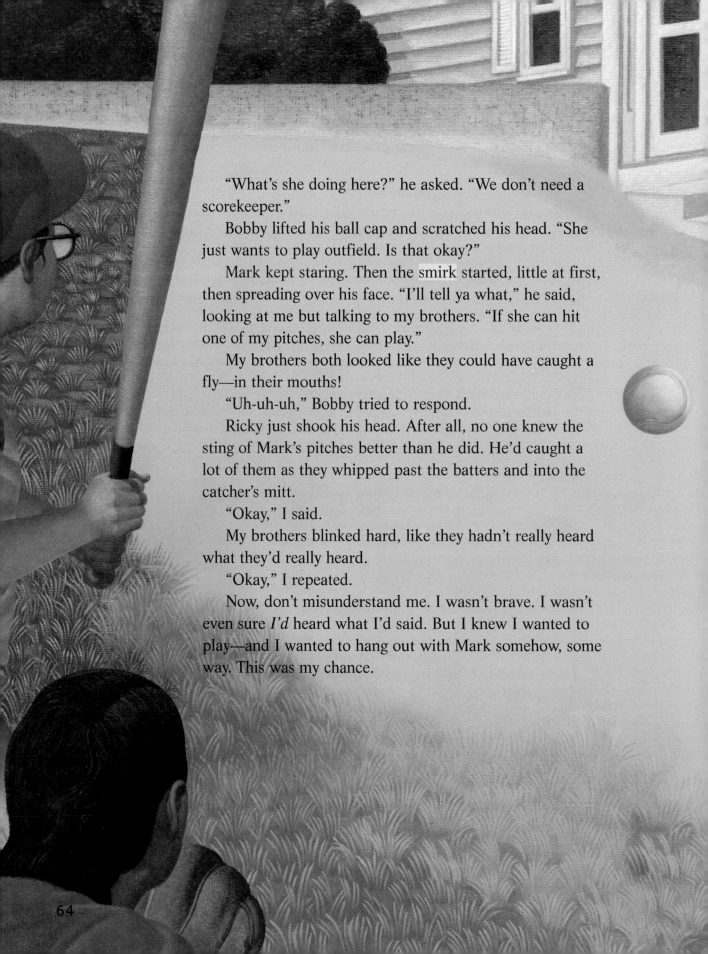

"What's she doing here?" he asked. "We don't need a scorekeeper."

Bobby lifted his ball cap and scratched his head. "She just wants to play outfield. Is that okay?"

Mark kept staring. Then the smirk started, little at first, then spreading over his face. "I'll tell ya what," he said, looking at me but talking to my brothers. "If she can hit one of my pitches, she can play."

My brothers both looked like they could have caught a fly—in their mouths!

"Uh-uh-uh," Bobby tried to respond.

Ricky just shook his head. After all, no one knew the sting of Mark's pitches better than he did. He'd caught a lot of them as they whipped past the batters and into the catcher's mitt.

"Okay," I said.

My brothers blinked hard, like they hadn't really heard what they'd really heard.

"Okay," I repeated.

Now, don't misunderstand me. I wasn't brave. I wasn't even sure *I'd* heard what I'd said. But I knew I wanted to play—and I wanted to hang out with Mark somehow, some way. This was my chance.

Bobby took first base, Ricky headed behind me to catch, and Mark claimed the throne—the pitcher's mound. I picked up the wooden bat that had Mark's name chiseled in the handle. It was heavy, but I wrapped my hands around it pretty well. My heart started to beat all the way into my ears. As I took a couple of practice swings, I realized that I was all lined up to be a dead girl. In less than a second, I could be hit by a baseball traveling the speed of a car on the interstate. And all the guys would say was: "She said she wanted to play."

Mark turned sideways and started his windup. I could sense Ricky's little body squatting lower as Mark got ready to launch the pitch.

Zing!

Snap!

Right into Ricky's mitt. I never even saw it.

"Strike one!" Mark called. A grin seemed to spread all over his head. I could tell he was thinking that it would take only two more pitches to finish me off.

I pounded the ground with the top of the bat and took another swing.

Just swing as soon as you see him let go, I told myself. This wasn't going to be about skill. This was going to be about luck— good or bad.

Mark caught the ball Ricky tossed back to him. He took his place back on the plank and turned sideways, staring right at me this time. I watched every little move. The settling of his arms down as he held the ball in his right hand and hid it inside the glove on his left. Then the knee, slowly lifting upward until it nearly touched his elbow. He leaned forward as his foot went down, and I watched as his right arm arched over his head, the ball barely peeking out from his fist. Then he let go . . .

And I swung as hard as I could.

Crack! The wood vibrated in my hands and I dropped the bat.

"O-o-o-o-f," Mark seemed to be sucking in all the air in the neighborhood. His arms dropped to his sides and the ball dribbled down his front and fell flat in front of him. I'd hit a line drive—right into Mark's gut.

He curled up on the ground, moaning and gasping for air. My brothers raced over to their star pitcher, but were afraid to get too close.

"You okay, man?" Ricky asked.

Mark moaned. I thought I saw a tear in the corner of his eye. Probably not.

"Hey, I'm really sorry," I said. But I wasn't. I was exhilarated! I was victorious! And I was in big trouble.

"I think you'd better go home," Bobby told me. I don't know if he was mad at me or scared for me.

Mark caught part of his breath just then. "Nah, . . . she doesn't have to," he half-whispered. "A deal's a deal." He looked up at me and I saw a real smile. "At least you don't hit like a girl," he said.

"Sure I do," I answered. "I hit just like my mom."

And nobody could argue with that.

Think Critically

1 According to the author, what options for playing team sports did girls in her area have when she was growing up? NOTE DETAILS

2 What is the main conflict in this story? How is it resolved? PLOT: CONFLICT AND RESOLUTION

3 Does the author believe that girls deserve to have as many opportunities as boys for participating in sports? What makes you think that? AUTHOR'S VIEWPOINT

4 The author has to prove herself to be allowed to play with the boys. Think about a time when you had to show that you were good at something. What did you have to do and why?

MAKE CONNECTIONS

5 **WRITE** How does the author feel about her mother's athletic abilities? Use information and details from the story to support your answer. SHORT RESPONSE

ABOUT THE AUTHOR
Tanya West Dean

In junior high school, Tanya West Dean discovered that volleyball was her best sport. She played volleyball throughout high school and college. After college, she coached girls' sports. During that time, girls had fewer opportunities to play sports than boys did. Girls sometimes had to wear the boys' old uniforms and leave the gym whenever the boys wanted to practice. These experiences helped inspire Tanya West Dean to write "Line Drive."

ABOUT THE ILLUSTRATOR
Wilson McLean

Wilson McLean was born in Scotland in 1937. When he was 15 years old, he got his first job as a professional illustrator. He worked at a silk-screen shop in London, England. Now Wilson McLean's work is known all over the world. He has even created the art for four postage stamps.

Ninth Inning

Poetry

Ninth

by Anna Levine

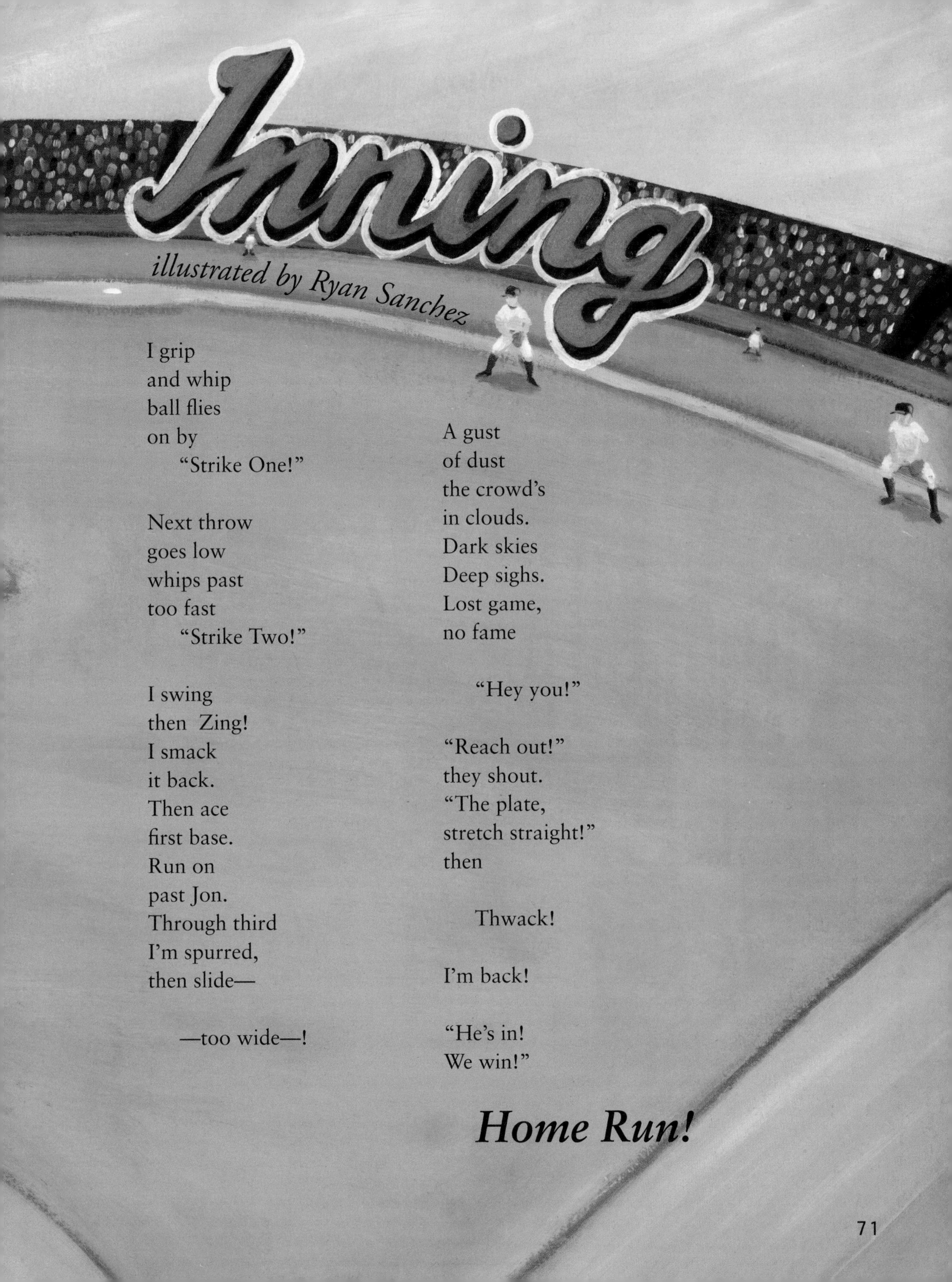

Inning

illustrated by Ryan Sanchez

I grip
and whip
ball flies
on by
    "Strike One!"

Next throw
goes low
whips past
too fast
    "Strike Two!"

I swing
then Zing!
I smack
it back.
Then ace
first base.
Run on
past Jon.
Through third
I'm spurred,
then slide—

    —too wide—!

A gust
of dust
the crowd's
in clouds.
Dark skies
Deep sighs.
Lost game,
no fame

    "Hey you!"

"Reach out!"
they shout.
"The plate,
stretch straight!"
then

    Thwack!

I'm back!

"He's in!
We win!"

Home Run!

Connections

Comparing Texts

1. Tanya West proved to Mark that she could play baseball. Describe a time when you convinced someone that you could do something.

2. Compare "Line Drive" with "Ninth Inning." How are the texts alike and different?

3. Tanya West wasn't able to join sports teams because there were none for girls in her area. Do you think she would face the same problem today? Explain.

Vocabulary Review

The puzzle maven reigned at the state finals.

Word Pairs

Work with a partner. Write the Vocabulary Words on index cards. Place the cards face down. Take turns flipping over two cards and writing a sentence using both words. Read aloud the sentence to your partner. You must use both words correctly to keep the cards. The player with more cards wins.

maven

mortified

reigned

conceited

designated

smirk

exhilarated

Fluency Practice

Partner Reading

Work with a partner. Take turns reading aloud three to five paragraphs of "Line Drive" and giving each other feedback. Continue rereading the paragraphs until you can both read them with accuracy.

Writing

Write a List of Tips

The author had a plan for making herself a part of the action on the baseball field. Write a set of tips for someone who wants to do the same thing. Use a web to brainstorm ideas.

Tips for Getting in the Game

Find a way to get close to the action.

Be patient.

My Writing Checklist

Writing Trait ➤ Voice

✔ I used a web to brainstorm ideas.

✔ My tips are focused and related to the topic.

✔ I used my personal voice to connect to the reader.

Big Idea

The characters in historical fiction depict feelings of real people.

Enduring ! Understanding

Authors identify a character's motives through the character's traits and actions.

Essential ? Question

How do authors reveal a character's motives and traits?

Spelling Words

Words with Variant Vowels and Diphthongs

counter	royalty
fraud	powder
oyster	annoying
appoint	cashew
drawn	scoop
awning	bamboo
laundry	browse
feud	ointment
shawl	rooster
jewel	rescue

Challenge

coiled	turquoise
authentic	cowered
shrewd	

Fluency

Reading Rate

Comprehension

 Character's Motives

 Monitor Comprehension: Reread

Robust Vocabulary

pried
desperately
sneered
indignantly
urgently
grudgingly

Writing

- Autobiographical Narrative
- Word Choice

Lesson 3

Chang and the Bamboo Flute

EVREN OZAN, MUSICIAN

Focus Skill

Character's Motives

A **character's motives** are the reasons the character acts as he or she does. Sometimes an author tells you what a character's motives are. Other times you must use clues in the text and your own knowledge to figure out the character's motives.

A character's motives are revealed through
- traits
- thoughts
- words
- actions

Understanding a character's motives can help you better understand why the events in a story happen.

Character	
Character's Traits, Thoughts, Words, Actions	**Character's Motives**

Tip

To figure out a character's motives, ask yourself, *What is this character's goal? How might he or she reach that goal?*

Read the paragraph below. Then look at
the graphic organizer. It shows how Doris's
motives are revealed by her traits and by what
she thinks and does.

Doris looked longingly at the guitar in
the window of the music shop. Her father's
guitar had been ruined in a fire. Dad seemed
sad without it. Doris missed the sound of Dad
softly strumming the guitar in the evenings.
"I wonder if I can work in exchange for a
guitar," she thought. Doris entered the shop
and shyly asked to speak with the owner.

Character: Doris	
Character's Traits, Thoughts, Words, Actions	**Character's Motives**
Trait: shy Thought: wonders if she can work in exchange for a guitar Action: asks to speak with the shop owner	Doris wants to make her dad happy by getting him a new guitar.

Try This!

Reread the paragraph. What is another motive Doris may
have for getting her father a new guitar?

GO online www.harcourtschool.com/storytown

Vocabulary

Build Robust Vocabulary

- desperately
- sneered
- urgently
- indignantly
- pried
- grudgingly

Monkey Business

It was the night of Hoover School's talent show, and things were not going well for Vivian Lee. She was dressed as a clown and trying **desperately** to make people laugh. She flopped around in her big shoes and honked her round, red nose, but no one laughed.

"This clown isn't funny at all," someone **sneered**.

Neil Cooper ran onstage. "Has anyone seen Rocco?" he asked **urgently**. "Rocco's a monkey. I need him for our talent trick."

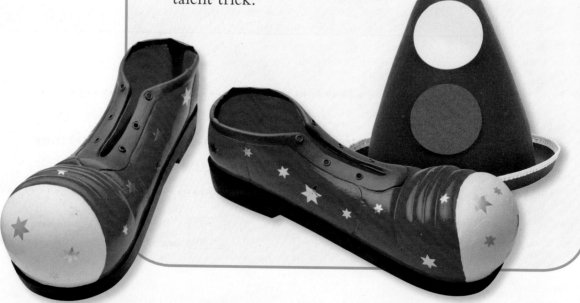

Just then, a shriek came from the audience. "Get this thing off me!" Sandy Paulsen shouted **indignantly**. Neil ran over. Rocco was holding on tightly to Sandy's long hair. Finally, Neil **pried** Rocco's paws off of Sandy's hair.

Rocco scrambled up Neil's arm all the way up to his head, and the audience roared with laughter.

"I guess monkeys are funnier than clowns," Vivian said **grudgingly**. Then Rocco tapped on Neil's head as if it were a drum, and even Vivian had to laugh.

 www.harcourtschool.com/storytown

Word Scribe

This week your task is to use Vocabulary Words in your writing. In your vocabulary journal, write sentences to show the meanings of the words. For example, you could write about something you grudgingly agreed to do, or about a time you pried open a stuck door or window. Use as many of the Vocabulary Words as you can. Share your writing with your classmates.

Chang and the Bamboo Flute

Historical Fiction

Genre Study

Historical fiction is about people, places, and events from the past. As you read, look for

- characters who have feelings that real people have.

- details that help the reader picture the setting.

Character	Character's Traits	Character's Motives

Comprehension Strategy

Monitor comprehension by stopping to **reread** text you did not understand.

Chang and the Bamboo Flute

by Elizabeth Starr Hill
illustrated by Nancy Lane

After a storm damages their houseboat, Chang's family finds shelter in a barn that belongs to the family of Mei Mei, Chang's good friend. Chang was born mute, but the music he plays on his flute is as beautiful as any voice. He worries about what has happened to his home and when he'll be able to play his flute in private again.

The next day the rain stopped, but the floodwaters were still high. Mei Mei and her family urged Chang and his parents to walk up to their house for a visit. "Won't you come and play your flute for us?" Mei Mei's father urged Chang.

Chang shook his head. His music was private and important to him, something to share only with his family and close friends.

For the next two days, Chang and his parents stayed in the barn. Mei Mei and her family continued to supply them with meals. They were grateful, but they longed to be home.

Chang was sick of the smell of hay. He could hardly wait to sit out on deck in the marshy air, while his mother cooked supper. He wanted to see the stars again, and to play night music without bothering buffaloes. He was homesick.

At last the river lowered and calmed. The sun sliced through the clouds and glittered on the water.

Chang's father said, "It's safe to go back now."

Both of Chang's parents thanked Mei Mei and her family for their kindness. Then they all squished through the muddy earth back to the wharf.

Smiles spread across their faces as they looked at the houseboat. The damage to the cabin hardly showed from this side. You could almost pretend nothing had happened.

His father said, "I'll go on board first and make sure it's safe." After a moment he called, "It's very damp in here, but steady enough."

Chang and his mother followed. Chang saw at once that the cabin was wrecked. There was a gaping hole in one side. Some of their shelves were gone. Water had soaked their bedding and clothes.

His mother sagged against a wall. Her face was pale and strained. "How can we ever fix this?" Her voice shook.

His father answered slowly, "I don't know."

Chang and his parents worked all day. They pried off a loose board and nailed it across the bottom of the hole in the cabin, so the water could not come in. They rinsed wet clothes and bedding and stretched them to dry in the hot sun. They mopped the floor and dried out the cabinet where their small stock of food was stored. They coiled up ropes and folded nets.

As the day went on, Chang's father spoke more hopefully. Soon he would be catching and selling fish again. Little by little, they would earn enough to buy lumber and other supplies to repair the cabin. It might take a long time, but eventually they would make the houseboat as snug and tight as ever.

Chang felt better when he heard this. Maybe things weren't so bad after all.

In the late afternoon, Mei Mei came over, carrying dry charcoal and matches, and a basket of fresh vegetables. "For your first supper at home."

Chang's mother took the basket. Her tired face brightened. "We'll have a grand meal! Thank you, Mei Mei. Please stay and eat with us."

The girl agreed. She and Chang sat out on the deck, swinging their legs. The sun was sinking behind the highest peak of the mountains. Chang's father had let the cormorants free in the river to fish for themselves. The birds splashed in the calm water, sending out showers of golden light.

"Let's go to the market tomorrow," Mei Mei suggested. "It'll probably be a nice day."

Chang nodded, almost contented now. In the river the birds played one of their games, tossing a stick. Mei Mei laughed, her laugh ringing like a bell.

Chang's mother cut up the vegetables and started charcoal burning in the brazier. Then she went inside, but in a minute she burst out of the cabin, eyes brimming with tears. "My wok!" she cried. "My wok is gone!"

"Ah, no!" her husband exclaimed. "We must find it!"

He and Chang and Mei Mei crowded into the cabin. The wok had been kept on a low shelf in an alcove. Somehow they still expected to see it there, but now the alcove was empty.

They looked everywhere. It was truly gone.

Stunned, the family realized that when the water swirled in and took out the shelves, it must have carried the utensil away.

Mei Mei thought they should search the cabin one more time. They did, but it was no use. "I'm so sorry," she said miserably. "You know what they say—in a flood, a wicked river spirit always steals something."

But why, Chang wondered, did it have to be the wok? Gladly he would have given up his checkers game instead, or even his kite with the dragon painted on it. He knew how much the wok meant to his mother.

She covered her face with her hands. "We'll never have the money to buy another." She began to cry.

Chang's father put his arms around her. "Boil up the vegetables in your iron pot," he suggested gently. "Supper will still be good."

She got out the old pot and made soup with the vegetables. But none of them felt like eating now. They ate a little, then stopped. Mei Mei went home.

In the night, Chang's mother cried and cried. As he listened, a sharp sorrow stabbed Chang. If only he had money . . . if only he were rich . . . .

Usually Chang did not think much about being poor. But now it struck him that so many things were out of his reach.

Once the village storyteller Bo Won had told a story about a poor boy who found treasure in a milk jug, but Chang had never known this to happen in real life.

The next morning Mei Mei came over early. Chang tucked his flute under his arm. He and Mei Mei walked the path to the market. Many other people were out today, smiling and enjoying the sunshine for the first time in days. The end of the flood had brought a holiday feeling to the village.

A tangle of thoughts stirred in Chang's mind. There was one way he might be able to do something for his mother. There was one hard, painful way.

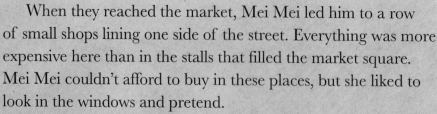

When they reached the market, Mei Mei led him to a row of small shops lining one side of the street. Everything was more expensive here than in the stalls that filled the market square. Mei Mei couldn't afford to buy in these places, but she liked to look in the windows and pretend.

"Maybe I'll get some of those silk flowers," she said with a giggle. "They're much prettier than cheap paper ones."

The next shop had fancy bowls and cups in the window. "Or the rice bowl shaped like a turtle," Mei Mei said.

The last window was full of cooking utensils, including woks. One of these caught Chang's attention. It was even handsomer than his mother's had been. It was bigger, and the handle was made of polished wood. And a lid came with it. His mother's had not had a lid.

Chang wanted this wok desperately, but the price on it made him feel poorer than ever. He moved on. At one of the stalls, Mei Mei bought a small almond cake for each of them.

They were near Zhao the trader's booth. Chang looked over the merchandise. The thoughts that had been stirring in his head grew clearer. He knew Zhao usually had some old pots and pans. Sure enough, amid all the rest of the junk, there was a cheap wok—not fine, not well made, not large. But a wok, at least.

He nudged Mei Mei nearer Zhao's booth.

"I don't want to see that awful man again," Mei Mei whispered. "We don't even have anything to trade."

Chang ignored this. He stepped over to the booth. Hard as it was, he *did* have something to trade. He touched Zhao's sleeve and pointed to the wok. Then he held up his flute.

The trader looked at Chang's offering and sneered. "Who would want that? It's nothing but a little bamboo stick!"

"It's not!" Mei Mei said hotly. "It's a flute! And all he wants for it is that old wok!"

"Never!" Zhao said indignantly. "I might give you a box of pencils for it, but nothing more."

Chang shook his head.

"It has to be the wok," Mei Mei repeated stubbornly.

"Well, it won't be!" Zhao retorted.

The argument went back and forth between them, louder and louder. People gathered.

Then a kindly voice asked, "Is that you, Mei Mei?"

Chang and Mei Mei turned to see Bo Won in the crowd. The blind old storyteller hobbled slowly toward them.

Mei Mei answered, "Yes, it's me." Quickly she explained about the loss of the wok and the trade Chang wanted to make.

"I've made you a fair offer," Zhao said. "Pencils for a stick." He laughed heartily.

Some in the crowd laughed, too, but others looked at the flute curiously.

"I'd like to hear a tune," a man called out.

Chang hesitated, embarrassed. Never in his life had he played for strangers. To them his music might be a poor thing, laughable, like his voice.

"Go on, boy. Play," Bo Won suggested quietly.

There was a silence. Chang stood frozen. The group around him was quite large now.

"*Play,*" Bo Won said again, more urgently.

Chang realized that this might be his last chance ever to make music.

Suddenly he didn't mind the crowd. Let them think whatever they liked.

He began to play. At first the notes were shaky, but then they steadied. The melody grew firmer, full of the sounds of his world. They were sounds that belonged to all these people, too. The murmur of the river that gave them a good life, and the drumming of long rains that could take it away again. Breezes in a bamboo grove. The springtime peeping of frogs.

The crowd listened attentively.

Chang went on. He played the ancient chants the fishermen sang as they poled their rafts in the evening.

Some people nodded, recognizing the tunes. They were pleased.

Bo Won untied a kerchief and took out a coin. He threw it at Chang's feet.

Chang was surprised by this. For a moment he didn't know what to make of it. Then he realized it was how people paid the old man to tell his stories.

A few people in the crowd noticed. Now that Bo Won had given them the idea, they, too, stepped forward to throw coins.

"The boy plays well," someone said, and more coins were thrown.

When Chang finally stopped playing, there was a pile of money around his feet.

Zhao cleared his throat. "Well, maybe somebody would like to have the flute, after all," he said grudgingly. "Who can offer me a good trade for it?"

Several people spoke up. But Bo Won advised, "Count your money first, Chang."

Chang scooped up the coins and counted them. He was amazed at how much there was. He remembered the wok in the shop, and saw that he had enough money to buy it.

He had found his treasure, not in a milk jug but inside himself, here in the market square.

He looked at Mei Mei, his face beaming with happiness, and tugged at her arm. They ran to the store. Chang pointed out the wok to the shopkeeper and poured his money on the table.

The shopkeeper counted it carefully, then gave Chang a few coins back. He put the wok in a box. "Would you like to have it wrapped as a gift?" he asked.

Wrapped as a gift! So this was how it felt to be rich! Chang nodded in delight.

The shopkeeper got a fine sheet of paper printed with butterflies.

It pays to shop in a good place, Chang thought.

Outside, the noodle man was calling, "Wontons and rice sticks, noodle nests and bean threads . . ."

Chang still had a little money left to spend, and his mother would need something to cook in her new wok. Fried bean threads! Chang could almost taste them already.

Think Critically

1 Name three effects the flood has on Chang and his family.
CAUSE AND EFFECT

2 What is Chang's motive for wanting to replace his mother's wok?
CHARACTER'S MOTIVES

3 How does Bo Won help Chang? Use details from the selection to support your answer. SYNTHESIZE

4 The wok is very important to Chang's mother. What is something that is very important to you? Why is it important? MAKE CONNECTIONS

5 **WRITE** How do Chang's feelings about sharing his music change during the story? Use story details to explain your answer. EXTENDED RESPONSE

About the Author
Elizabeth Starr Hill

Elizabeth Starr Hill published her first story when she was 13 years old. Since then, she has written many books for young readers. Elizabeth Starr Hill likes to write about realistic characters who grow and change as they learn about themselves through interactions with nature. She loves to spend time watching nature at her home in Winter Park, Florida.

About the Illustrator
Nancy Lane

Nancy Lane has been drawing pictures since before she could read. She enjoyed the art in her books so much that she decided to become an illustrator. She especially likes drawing people and animals as they enjoy nature. Nancy Lane enjoys walking in the woods at her home in Canandaigua, New York. While she worked on the paintings for this story, she listened to bamboo flute music for inspiration.

GO online www.harcourtschool.com/storytown

EVREN OZAN, MUSICIAN

Interview

EVREN OZAN₇

Time For Kids (TFK) reporter Harsha Viswanathan talked to award-winning Native American musician Evren Ozan. He plays the Native flute, which is a wood instrument. Harsha sat down with Evren when he was ten years old at his home in California. Here's her report:

Although artists in the music circle tend to describe Evren as the "Native American Flute Prodigy," "An Old Soul Returned to the People," and the "Future of Native American Music," I found him to be an exceptional ten-year-old who is smart, talented, creative, resourceful, inspiring, and on the whole, awesome.

MUSICIAN

by Harsha Viswanathan

TFK: *I heard that you got your first flute in the Grand Canyon. Can you elaborate on that experience?*

Evren: I went to a gift shop with my mom. I saw a flute that I liked and I picked it up. I started playing soon after that.

TFK: *I read that besides skateboarding and spending time with your dogs and duck, you also enjoy tree house building. What attracted you to this hobby? How did you go about building one in your front yard?*

Evren: My friends and I were bored one day, so we decided to ask my mom if we could build a tree house. We even tried to set up a business building tree houses, only the neighbors thought it was too dangerous, so we had to stop.

Once, my friends and I built a huge tree house and installed cool things in it like a shower. We used a hose with a special attachment in order to spurt the water out. My friends and I pretty much built the tree house by ourselves. Soon after we built our house, we ordered a pizza and we hoisted it up to the tree house like a house-warming party.

TFK: *What is your favorite song to play on the flute?*

Evren: Well, mostly when I play the flute, I improvise. I don't really have a lot of songs in my head. I do have ideas in my head and they are all different. I usually compose my songs on the spur of the moment, not knowing how they will sound till I hear myself playing them.

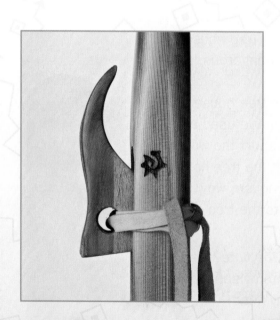

Some of Evren's Native flutes.

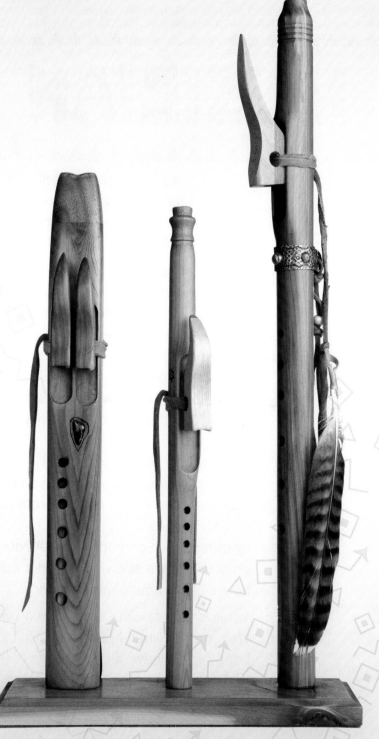

TFK: *How do you get the inspiration for your songs?*

Evren: If I am practicing the flute and I make a mistake, it might sound good. It usually sounds different, but in a good way. I work with that note and try to develop it into a song. I don't usually write out the songs. I keep them in my head.

TFK: *What is your life's ambition?*

Evren: I would like to make a couple more CDs. I want to be a professional flute player, both silver flute and Native.

TFK: *How did you get involved in making a CD?*

Evren: My teacher, Guillermo Martinez, makes wooden flutes. Once when we were on a trip to New Hampshire, we went to a flute shop to sell his flutes. As I was playing the flute to show the shopkeepers how it sounded, one of the shopkeepers asked me if I would like to make a recording of my song in his recording studio for free. I immediately thought, "That's pretty good." So, we recorded that CD, and we made another one after that.

TFK: *What happens when you go to the recording studio to make a CD?*

Evren: Sometimes when I go to the studio to record a CD, I make up my tunes right there and then. We compose the music just before we tape it.

TFK: *Do you ever get stage fright when you perform?*

Evren: I only get stage fright when there's a big audience. I only get nervous when I play a song which I learned. I sometimes make up my songs while I'm on the stage itself!

TFK: *Do you like being famous? How does it feel to be famous?*

Evren: I don't think that I'm famous. I just play the flute and have fun.

Connections

Comparing Texts

1. How would you feel about showing your talent? Would you feel as Chang does at the end of the story? Explain.

2. Compare the ways Chang and Evren Ozan feel about music.

3. Chang's family replaced something that was important with something even more valuable. Has this happened to you? Explain.

Vocabulary Review

Word Sort

Work in a group. Sort the Vocabulary Words into categories. Compare your sorted words with the group, explaining your choices. Then choose at least one Vocabulary Word from each category. Write a sentence for each word.

pried

desperately

sneered

indignantly

urgently

grudgingly

Verbs	Adverbs

Fluency Practice

Repeated Reading

Work with a partner. Choose three paragraphs from "Chang and the Bamboo Flute." Read the paragraphs aloud while your partner times you with a stopwatch. Then switch roles. Continue reading the paragraphs and timing each other. Note the improvement you make in your reading rate.

Writing

Extend the Ending

In "Chang and the Bamboo Flute," Chang buys a new wok for his mother. Write a new ending that tells how you think Chang's mother will react when she sees the new wok.

Chang's Mother's Reaction
Thoughts:
Words:
Actions:

My Writing Checklist

Writing Trait → Word Choice

✔ I used a graphic organizer to plan my writing.

✔ I chose specific words to describe a character's feelings.

✔ My ending gives the story a sense of completeness.

Big 💡 Idea

In a biography, the author writes a true story about a character and his or her motives.

Enduring ❗ Understanding

Readers get clues about a character's motivations that are revealed through thoughts, words, and actions.

Essential ❓ Question

How do readers use the character's thoughts, words, and actions to understand a character's motives?

Spelling Words

Words with Inflections -ed, -ing

talked	buying
hurried	dried
smiling	picnicking
dropped	scared
clapping	driving
stepped	obeyed
worried	playing
worrying	tried
changing	carried
stayed	hurrying

Challenge

applied	rumored
occurred	referred
conquered	

Fluency

Reading Rate

Comprehension

 Character's Motives

 Monitor Comprehension: Reread

Robust Vocabulary

- relented
- faze
- eccentric
- infuriated
- disheartened
- impassable
- crusaded

Writing

- Newspaper Story
- Word Choice

Lesson 4

Genre: Biography

Genre: Biography

THE DARING
NELLIE BLY
America's Star Reporter

BONNIE CHRISTENSEN

Nellie Bly's Book:
Around the World
in Seventy-two Days
by Nellie Bly

Genre: Personal Narrative

Focus Skill

Character's Motives

You have learned that a **character's motives** are the reasons the character acts as he or she does. In fiction stories, a character's traits, thoughts, words, and actions are clues to the character's motives. You can also use these clues to understand the motives of real people described in nonfiction texts.

Character	
Character's Traits, Thoughts, Words, Actions	**Character's Motives**

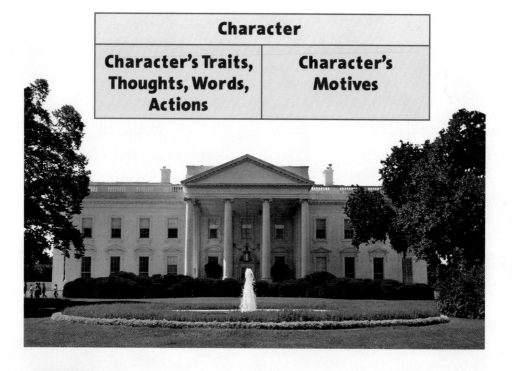

Tip

A character's motives are often related to the character's traits. For example, a kind person may be motivated by a desire to help others.

104

Read the paragraph below. Then look at the graphic organizer. It shows how the Dolley Madison's traits and actions are clues to understanding her motives.

Dolley Madison was the fourth First Lady of the United States. She made everyone who visited the White House feel welcome—from foreign leaders to poor farmers. She understood that the White House was an important symbol for the young nation. When the British attacked the capital during the War of 1812, Dolley Madison refused to leave the White House until important documents and special portraits were safe.

Character: Dolley Madison	
Character's Traits, Thoughts, Words, Actions	**Character's Motives**
Traits: hospitality, courage Action: She refused to leave the White House until important papers and special portraits were safe.	Dolley Madison wanted to keep the White House documents and portraits safe because they were important symbols for the nation.

Try This!

Look back at the paragraph. What do you think was Dolley Madison's motive for welcoming all kinds of people to the White House?

 www.harcourtschool.com/storytown

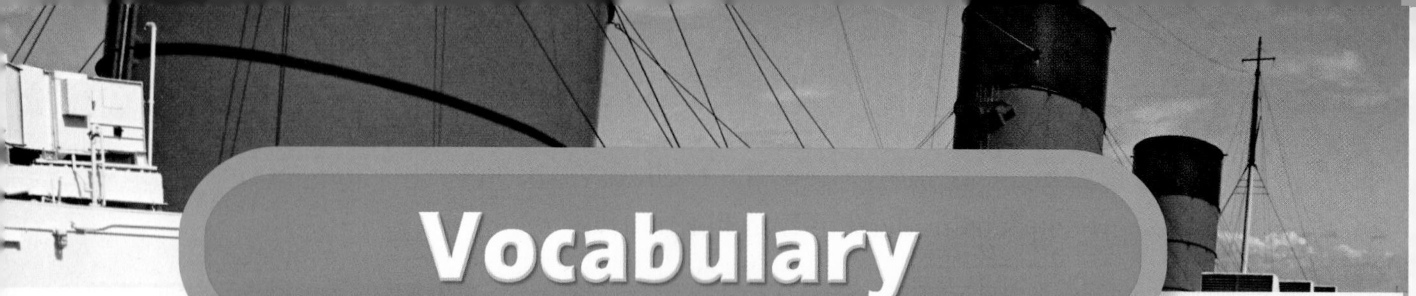

Vocabulary

Build Robust Vocabulary

- eccentric
- crusaded
- impassable
- infuriated
- relented
- disheartened
- faze

Local Hero Rescued

A Late-Night Call

On a cold January night, firefighters received a call from Annie Bell. Some people in Alderville think of Bell as an **eccentric** woman who lives alone on Pine Mountain. However, most people know her as a local hero. For 65 years, Bell has tirelessly **crusaded** for people who are less fortunate.

Stranded on Pine Mountain

Annie Bell needed to get to a doctor, but the road was **impassable**. High winds had knocked down a tree, and it lay across the road. "I was **infuriated** when I saw my way blocked. I didn't want to have to call for help," Bell said later. "But when I saw the fallen tree, I **relented**."

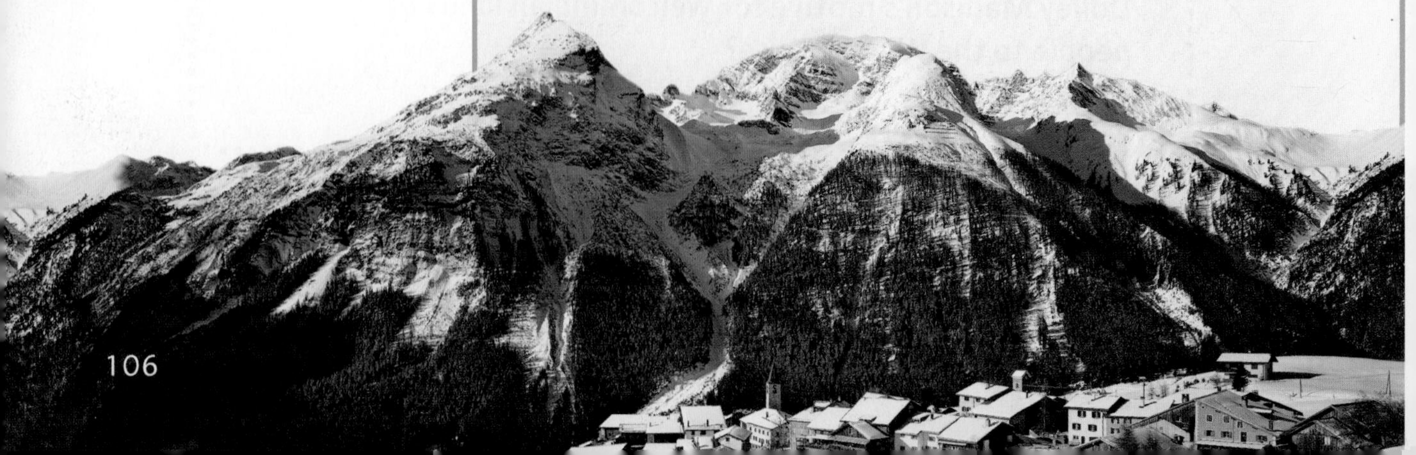

Fast Action

The fire chief and his crew sped toward Pine Mountain. At first, the crew was **disheartened** by the size of the fallen tree. "Don't let this **faze** you!" the chief said. They worked to remove the tree and then went on to Bell's house. From there, they were able to take Bell to the hospital for treatment.

On that cold winter night, it was Annie Bell who needed help.

 www.harcourtschool.com/storytown

Word Detective

 This week, search for the Vocabulary Words around you. Be alert for them as you watch television, read books, and listen to stories read aloud. In your vocabulary journal, write the words you find and list where you found each one.

Biography

Genre Study

A biography is a written account of a person's life, told by someone else. As you read, look for

- events presented in time order.

- information that shows why the person's life is important.

Character	Character's Traits	Character's Motives

Comprehension Strategy

Monitor comprehension by stopping to **reread** text you did not understand.

THE DARING
NELLIE BLY

America's Star Reporter

written and illustrated by Bonnie Christensen

ELIZABETH COCHRANE, who wrote under the name Nellie Bly, arrived in New York City in 1887 determined to get a job as a newspaper reporter. After six months of failure, she took a big risk by reporting on the unfair practices affecting the lives of ordinary women. Her news stories became a sensation, and Nellie Bly became a newspaper star.

Soon Nellie Bly was the *World*'s star stunt reporter, responsible for coming up with her own great story ideas.

One sleepless night she had an extraordinary idea. She would break the fictional record of Phileas Fogg, who went around the world in eighty days in Jules Verne's popular novel.

In the late 1800s it took many months to travel around the world. Boats were late, trains were slow, and connections were often missed. But Nellie checked the timetables and was convinced she could beat Fogg's record. Her editor was doubtful. A woman could not travel without a chaperone, he argued, and transferring her dozens of trunks would cause missed connections.

But Nellie was determined—she didn't need a chaperone and could travel with only one piece of hand luggage. Besides, if the *World* wouldn't send her, she'd simply find another newspaper that would. Finally her editor relented. The question was: Could she start her journey in two days?

The short notice didn't faze Nellie a bit. She visited a dressmaker and ordered a dress that would stand constant wear for three months. Then she bought a long, loose coat and one handbag, 16" x 7", into which she would squeeze all her essentials.

For Nellie Bly the clock began ticking at 9:40 A.M., November 14, 1889, when her ship, the *Augusta Victoria*, steamed away from its pier in **HOBOKEN, NEW JERSEY.** She had been warned of intense heat, bitter cold, terrible storms, shipwrecks, and fevers, but her greatest fear was failure. She said she'd rather return dead than "alive and behind time." Along the route she would cable stories back to the *World*, sharing with her readers rare glimpses into life on the other side of the globe.

No sooner had the *Augusta Victoria* left harbor than Bly was confronted with her first challenge—overcoming seasickness.

"And *she's* going around the world!" one man sneered. But Nellie's motto was "Energy rightly applied and directed will accomplish anything." By the time she arrived in Southampton, England, she had conquered her seasickness and was in good spirits.

From **SOUTHAMPTON** Nellie made a quick side trip to **AMIENS, FRANCE,** to meet Jules Verne. Together they charted her journey on the map Verne had used to outline Phileas Fogg's route. Then, worried about missing her train to **BRINDISI, ITALY,** Nellie departed.

Atlantic Ocean

Southampton

ENGLAND

FRANCE

Amiens

Hoboken, New Jersey

UNITED STATES

The trip through France and Italy was dark, cold, and foggy. When the train arrived at Brindisi two hours late, Nellie feared her ship, the *Victoria*, had sailed without her. Luckily, it was still in port, so on she traveled without delay. On through the **SUEZ CANAL** to **ADEN, YEMEN.** A shipboard friend told Nellie it was rumored she was "an eccentric American heiress, traveling about with a hairbrush and a bankbook."

Nellie reached **COLOMBO, CEYLON** (now Sri Lanka), two days ahead of schedule; then her luck ran out. Her next ship, the *Oriental*, was delayed five days. Any more delays between Colombo and Hong Kong would mean losing her race. Nellie lost patience when an elderly gentleman suggested that Colombo was a pleasant place to stay. "It may be," she exclaimed, "if staying there does not mean more than life to one!"

Brindisi

ITALY

Suez Canal

Aden

Colombo

CEYLON

113

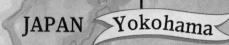

JAPAN ~Yokohama~

~Hong Kong~

~Singapore~

Nellie was infuriated by another daylong delay in
SINGAPORE, which she feared would seal her doom.
That night she endured agonies of "suspense and
impatience." The next day she toured the city, though,
and bought a monkey, whom she named McGinty.

When her ship finally sailed, it was wracked by raging
monsoons, which at one point filled Nellie's cabin with water.
Against all odds, they arrived two days early in **HONG
KONG.** Nellie was thrilled. It was the thirty-ninth day of
her journey and she'd traveled halfway around the world.

Then, at the steamship company, a man informed Nellie
that she had a competitor. Reporter Elizabeth Bisland had
been sent by a magazine to beat Nellie's time, and it looked
like she would succeed. Nellie was further disheartened to
learn that her own ship, the *Oceanic*, would be delayed five
days before sailing to Japan.

Pacific Ocean

San Francisco

UNITED STATES

Jersey City, New Jersey

On January 7 the *Oceanic* began the Pacific crossing from **YOKOHAMA, JAPAN,** to San Francisco. Nellie had an ocean and a continent to cross—8,000 miles—and only twenty-five days in which to do it. Everyone on board knew Nellie's story, and everyone was rooting for her. The ship's chief engineer had emblazoned across the engines, "For Nellie Bly, we'll win or die."

Thirteen days later **SAN FRANCISCO** was in sight, but there was more troubling news. The worst snowstorm in ten years had hit the Northwest. The planned train route was impassable. The *World* decided to hire a special train to take a southerly route cross-country. All along the way Nellie was greeted by crowds of well-wishers, bands, and fireworks. Telegrams, flowers, fruit, and candy poured in.

On January 25, 1890—seventy-two days, six hours, and eleven minutes after the start of her journey—Nellie Bly set foot in the Jersey City train station. A huge, cheering throng greeted her. Cannons roared. "The American girl will no longer be misunderstood," declared the mayor. "She will be recognized as pushing and determined, independent, able to take care of herself wherever she may go." Nellie Bly had won much more than her race against the clock.

Nellie's exploit increased the *World*'s circulation by 24,000. The newspaper described her as "the best known and most widely talked of young woman on earth today." It wasn't an exaggeration. Her picture appeared on games, toys, soaps, and medicines. A racehorse, hotel, and train were named after her. The name Nellie Bly was heard and recognized everywhere.

Throughout her life Nellie Bly continued to campaign for the rights of women and the working class. In 1895 she married Robert Seaman, a wealthy industrialist, and when he died, she successfully ran his huge manufacturing company as a model of social welfare. She invented the first steel barrel and held patents for twenty-five other inventions.

During World War I, Nellie Bly, at fifty, was the first woman journalist to report from the Eastern Front. After the war she returned to New York City, where she wrote a column for the *New York Journal* and crusaded tirelessly to find permanent homes for orphans.

Although she was in and out of the hospital from exhaustion, Nellie Bly continued her work, writing that each individual has a moral responsibility to "the whole wide world of mankind: good, bad and indifferent."

When Nellie Bly died on January 27, 1922, her friend and editor Arthur Brisbane dedicated an entire column to her. "She was the best reporter in America," he wrote. ". . . She takes with her from this earth all that she cared for, an honorable name, the respect and affection of her fellow workers, the memory of good fights well fought and of many good deeds never to be forgotten by those who had no friend but Nellie Bly."

Think Critically

1. What was the first challenge Nellie Bly faced when she started her journey around the world? SEQUENCE

2. Why did Nellie Bly want to break a record that had been set by a fictional character? CHARACTER'S MOTIVES

3. If you were a journalist, what kind of stories would you want to cover? IDENTIFY WITH CHARACTERS

4. How does the author show Nellie Bly's determination to meet her goal? Find three examples of Nellie Bly's determination in the selection. AUTHOR'S CRAFT/LANGUAGE USE

5. WRITE How did Nellie Bly's fans from around the world support her during her journey? Use details and information from the selection to support your answer. SHORT RESPONSE

Bonnie Christensen

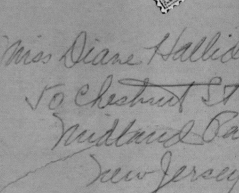

When Bonnie Christensen was growing up, her family moved a lot. She attended nine different schools. Her third-grade art teacher inspired her to develop her artistic skills. Bonnie Christensen practiced by drawing each of her new homes. Today, she is the author and illustrator of four books for children and has illustrated several others. Bonnie Christensen lives in Vermont with her daughter. Each summer, they travel to Venice, Italy, where they draw scenes of the city. On the cover art of each book she illustrates, Bonnie Christensen finds a way to include her daughter's name.

www.harcourtschool.com/storytown

Social Studies

Nellie Bly's Book: Around the World in Seventy-two Days by Nellie Bly

Personal Narrative

Nellie Bly's Book

Around the World in Seventy-two Days

by Nellie Bly

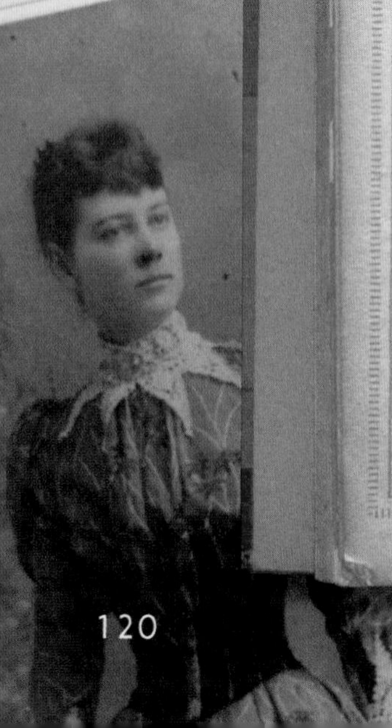

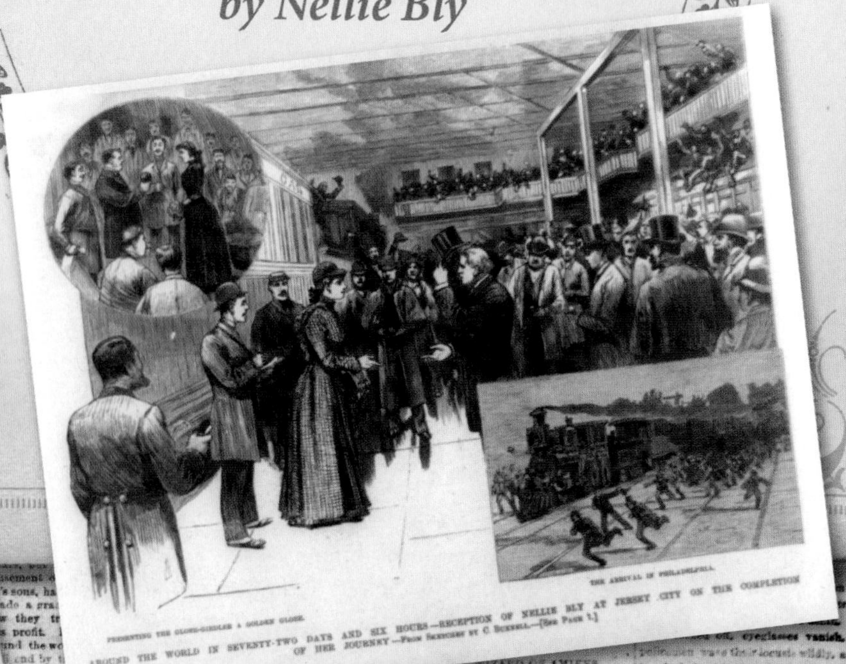

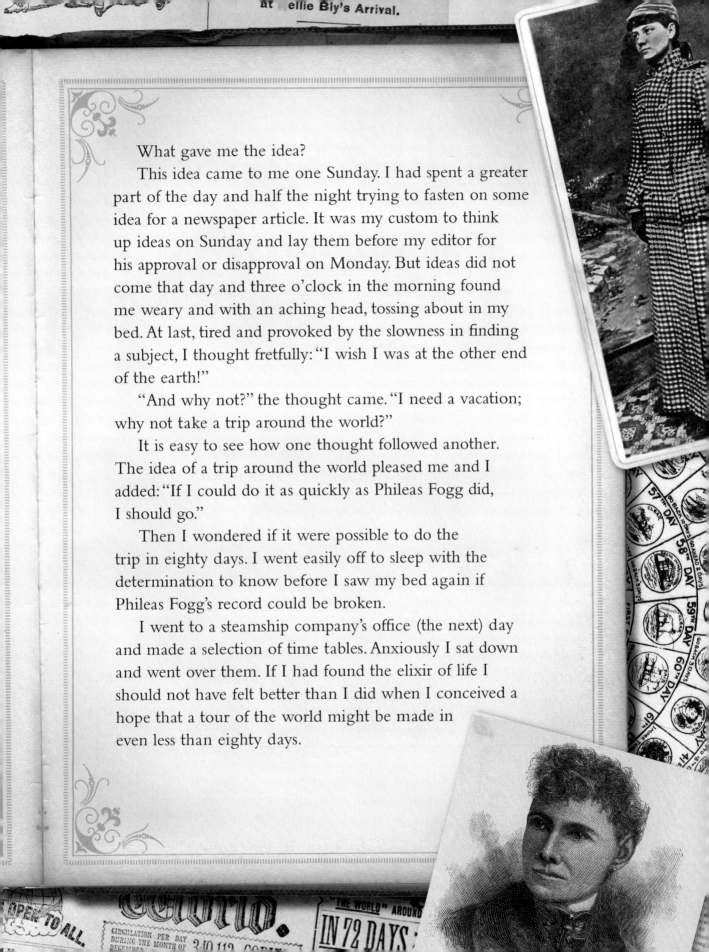

What gave me the idea?

This idea came to me one Sunday. I had spent a greater part of the day and half the night trying to fasten on some idea for a newspaper article. It was my custom to think up ideas on Sunday and lay them before my editor for his approval or disapproval on Monday. But ideas did not come that day and three o'clock in the morning found me weary and with an aching head, tossing about in my bed. At last, tired and provoked by the slowness in finding a subject, I thought fretfully: "I wish I was at the other end of the earth!"

"And why not?" the thought came. "I need a vacation; why not take a trip around the world?"

It is easy to see how one thought followed another. The idea of a trip around the world pleased me and I added: "If I could do it as quickly as Phileas Fogg did, I should go."

Then I wondered if it were possible to do the trip in eighty days. I went easily off to sleep with the determination to know before I saw my bed again if Phileas Fogg's record could be broken.

I went to a steamship company's office (the next) day and made a selection of time tables. Anxiously I sat down and went over them. If I had found the elixir of life I should not have felt better than I did when I conceived a hope that a tour of the world might be made in even less than eighty days.

Connections

Comparing Texts

1. People thought Nellie Bly's goal was impossible to reach. What goals do you have that others might find impossible?

2. Compare Nellie Bly's words about herself to her story told by a different author.

3. Nellie Bly's motto was "Energy rightly applied and directed will accomplish anything." Describe a situation to which this motto would apply.

Vocabulary Review

Rate a Situation

With a partner, read aloud each sentence below. Point to a spot on the line to show how happy you would be in each situation. Explain your choices.

Least Happy ———————————————— Most Happy

- Your best friend was **infuriated** with you.
- Your **eccentric** relative gave you a present.
- You **crusaded** for healthier school food.
- Rain made the roads to school **impassable**.

eccentric

infuriated

disheartened

impassable

relented

faze

crusaded

Fluency Practice

Timed Reading

Work with a partner to improve your reading rate. Choose three paragraphs from "The Daring Nellie Bly" to read aloud while your partner times your reading with a stopwatch. Reread the paragraphs three times, focusing on improving your reading rate each time. Then switch roles.

Writing

Write a Travel Diary Entry

Nellie Bly kept a travel diary of her journey. Imagine you are a first-time visitor to your town or city. Write a diary entry for a day you might spend there.

My Writing Checklist

Writing Trait — Word Choice

✔ I used a graphic organizer to plan my writing.

✔ I chose vivid words to describe the location.

✔ I used information from personal experience in my writing.

What?	
Where?	
When?	
Why?	
How?	

123

Big Idea

In a dramatic presentation, the conflict and resolution are based on the characters' motivations.

Enduring ! Understanding

In a drama, the story follows the main character through the challenges faced and the need to find solutions to the challenges.

Essential ? Question

How does the challenge of the main character define the development of the drama?

Spelling Words

Review

stretch	drawn
cactus	feud
measure	jewel
reason	fraud
coach	royalty
kneeling	hurried
twice	scared
rayon	changing
appoint	buying
scoop	obeyed

Fluency

Review Accuracy, Reading Rate

Robust Vocabulary

genial
prognostication
stricken
dramatically
restrain
protest
feverishly
overcome
flop
spectacular

Comprehension

Review

 Plot: Conflict and Resolution, Character's Motives

 Use Story Structure, Monitor Comprehension: Reread

Writing

- *Review* Voice, Word Choice
- Revise and Publish

Lesson 5
Theme Review and Vocabulary Builder

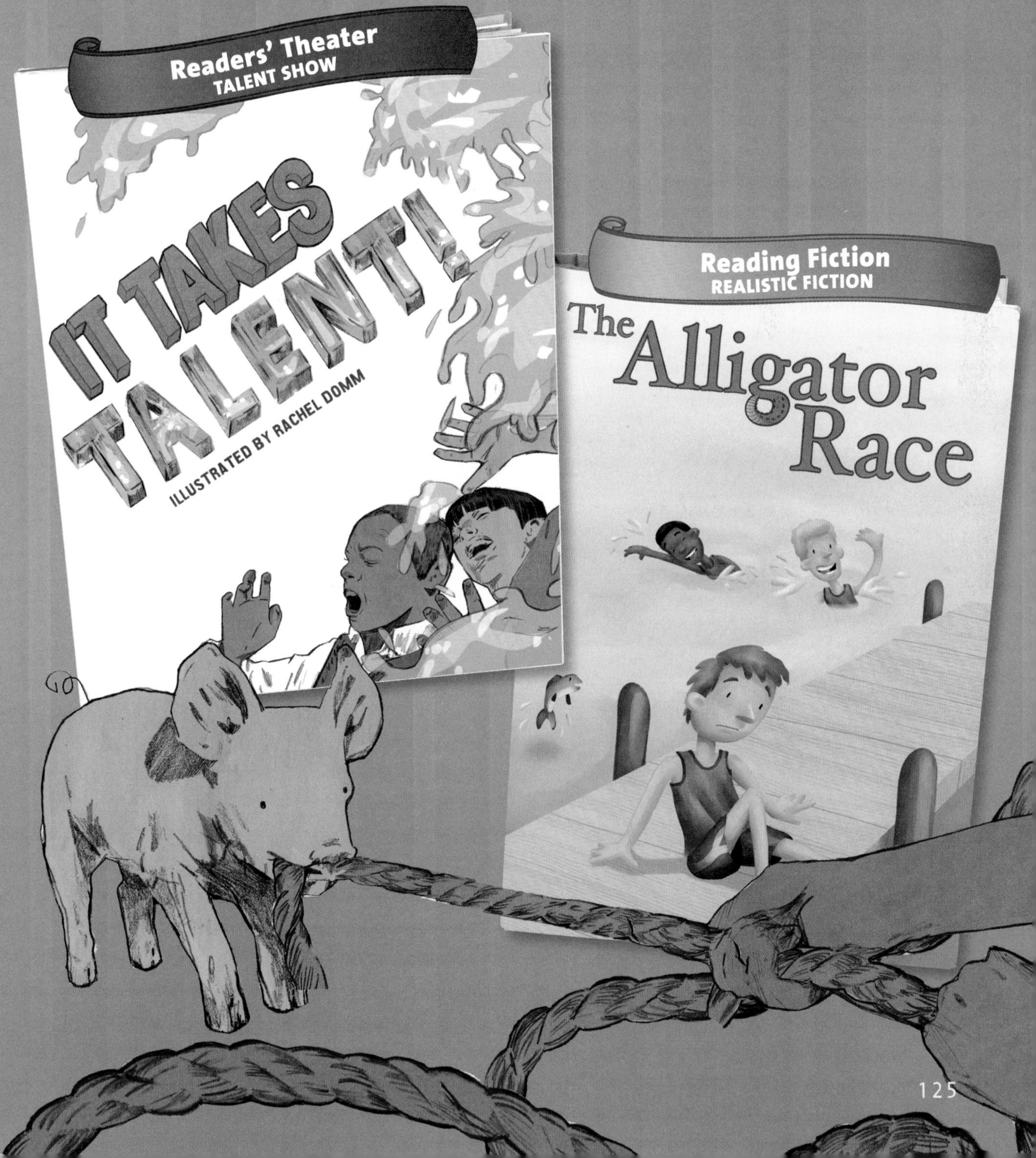

Readers' Theater
TALENT SHOW
IT TAKES TALENT!
ILLUSTRATED BY RACHEL DOMM
Reading Fiction
REALISTIC FICTION
The Alligator Race

READERS' THEATER

genial

prognostication

stricken

dramatically

restrain

protest

feverishly

overcome

flop

spectacular

Reading for Fluency

When reading a script aloud,

- Read with accuracy.

- Your reading rate should help your listeners understand your lines.

IT TAKES TALENT!

illustrated by Rachel Domm

Characters

Narrator	Deon	Michelle
Andres	Mr. Herbert	Rob
Tara	Chorus	

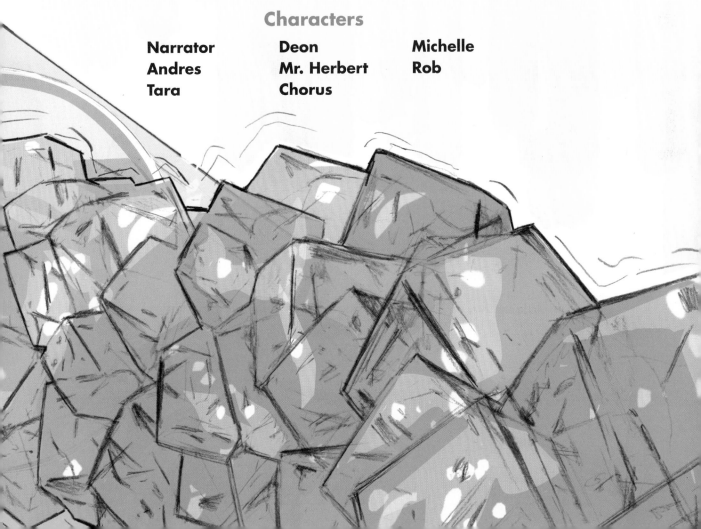

Narrator: It's lunchtime, and Deon, Andres, and Tara are eating lunch together.

Andres: Aren't you going to eat your gelatin?

Tara: You don't want to miss out. The cafeteria serves Galaxy Goo only once a month.

Deon: No thanks. Neon-green jiggly stuff isn't my idea of dessert.

Andres: I'll take it. I'll use it to make my tallest gelatin tower yet.

Narrator: Andres adds Deon's gelatin on top of his own. Mr. Herbert, their teacher, strolls by.

Mr. Herbert: Ah! Here are my genial students.

Tara: Hi, Mr. Herbert. What's going on? You look especially cheerful.

Fluency Tip

Read your lines several times to improve your accuracy. Be sure you know how to say all the words in each line.

Mr. Herbert: I am. I have great news!

Chorus: What's that, Mr. Herbert?

Mr. Herbert: The annual student talent show will happen next month!

Chorus: We're going to have a talent show!

Mr. Herbert: I know everyone at this school has amazing abilities. With all that talent, my expectations for the show are sky-high!

Andres: I'll build the tallest gelatin tower the world has ever seen.

Tara: Maybe Michelle will dance while I play a song on the piano.

Mr. Herbert: What about you, Deon?

Deon: Umm, errr, uhhhh . . . my talent is prognostication.

Andres: Prognosti-what?

Deon: Prognostication—predicting the future.

Tara: Oh yeah? Make a prediction for us now.

Deon: I predict that I will be stricken with a terrible cold on the day of the talent show. In fact, I'm sure I'll be forced to stay home in bed.

Chorus: Ha, ha, ha! That's a good one!

Andres: You have to be in the talent show.

Tara: Yeah! We know you're multi-talented.

Narrator: Deon grabs the empty carton on his tray and dramatically turns it over.

Deon: I'm like this empty milk carton—not one drop of talent. Performing in the talent show would be total humiliation.

Mr. Herbert: I don't believe it, Deon. But if you want to be in the show without performing, there is something you can do.

Deon: What's that?

Mr. Herbert: I need a volunteer for the master of ceremonies. As the emcee, you would introduce each performer.

Deon: I wouldn't have to perform?

Mr. Herbert: No.

Deon: All right. I can do that.

Mr. Herbert: I'm glad you relented, Deon. I have a hunch that this is going to work out beautifully.

Narrator: It's the day of the talent show. The performers are backstage at the school's auditorium.

Chorus: We can't wait for the show to begin!

Mr. Herbert: Emcee, are you ready to introduce the first act?

Narrator: Deon nods nervously and walks onstage. The red velvet curtain rises. Deon stares into the crowded auditorium.

Deon: Hi, I'm Deon, your emcee. Welcome to the Twelfth Annual Stu—

Narrator: Deon's words are interrupted as the curtain suddenly falls down, covering him. He untangles himself and runs backstage.

Deon: Who lowered the curtain?

Michelle: It was Grumpy, Rob's pig. He's munching on the curtain's cord!

Mr. Herbert: Rob, restrain your pig!

Rob: Sorry, Mr. Herbert. Grumpy likes the spotlight.

Mr. Herbert: Deon, you need to get back onstage! The show must go on, no matter what.

Narrator: Deon grabs one end of the curtain cord and runs back onstage. Grumpy follows Deon and tries to pull the cord from him.

Chorus: It's a tug-of-war!

Rob: Grumpy, no! Bad pig! Our tug-of-war trick happens later in the show.

Deon: Let go, Grumpy! *I'm* this show's emcee, not you!

Narrator: Mr. Herbert, Tara, Rob, and Michelle rush onstage and grab the pig. Grumpy squeals in protest but finally lets go of the cord. He runs backstage and everyone follows him, leaving Deon alone onstage.

Deon: Sorry, folks! As you can see, Grumpy likes to . . . *hog* the spotlight.

Narrator: The audience laughs. From offstage, Mr. Herbert gives Deon a thumbs-up.

Deon: Let's welcome our first performer, Andres. He's a talented architect, and his favorite building material is our own cafeteria's special gelatin— Galaxy Goo.

Andres: Prepare to be amazed, ladies and gentlemen. I will now construct the world's tallest gelatin tower. Don't try this at home, kids!

Narrator: Andres builds feverishly.

Deon: Is the bottom of your tower supposed to ooze like that?

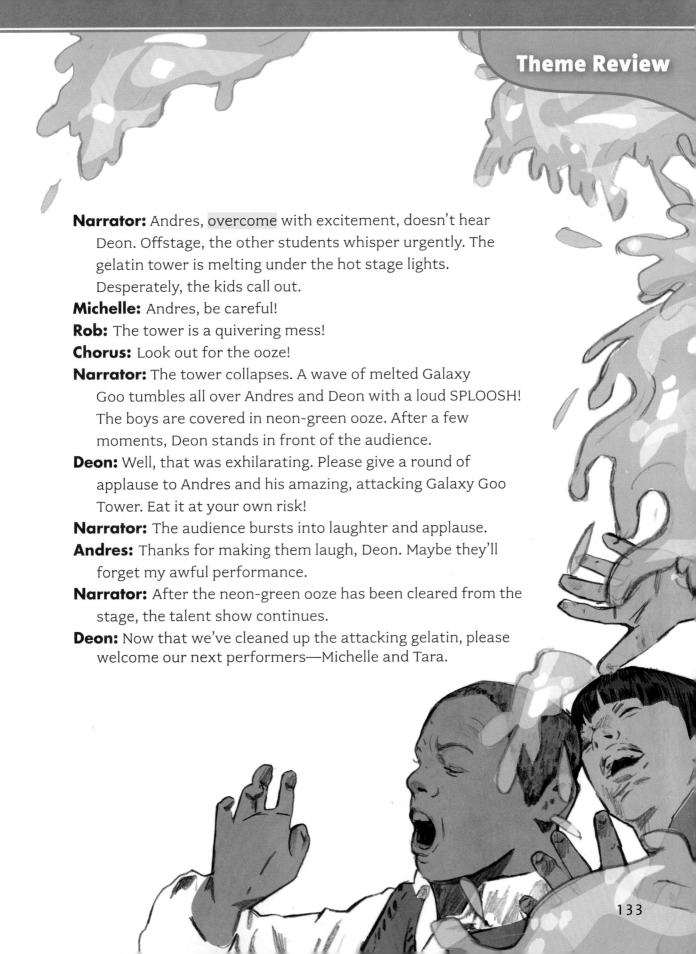

Narrator: Andres, overcome with excitement, doesn't hear Deon. Offstage, the other students whisper urgently. The gelatin tower is melting under the hot stage lights. Desperately, the kids call out.

Michelle: Andres, be careful!

Rob: The tower is a quivering mess!

Chorus: Look out for the ooze!

Narrator: The tower collapses. A wave of melted Galaxy Goo tumbles all over Andres and Deon with a loud SPLOOSH! The boys are covered in neon-green ooze. After a few moments, Deon stands in front of the audience.

Deon: Well, that was exhilarating. Please give a round of applause to Andres and his amazing, attacking Galaxy Goo Tower. Eat it at your own risk!

Narrator: The audience bursts into laughter and applause.

Andres: Thanks for making them laugh, Deon. Maybe they'll forget my awful performance.

Narrator: After the neon-green ooze has been cleared from the stage, the talent show continues.

Deon: Now that we've cleaned up the attacking gelatin, please welcome our next performers—Michelle and Tara.

Narrator: Michelle and Tara are hesitating in the wings.

Michelle: Why are we doing this? What if I don't remember all of the moves? I'll be mortified!

Tara: Don't worry. We'll be great. I hope.

Mr. Herbert: No time for second thoughts. The show must go on!

Deon: And now, Michelle will dance while Tara plays the piano!

Narrator: Grudgingly, Tara walks onstage and sits on the bench in front of the piano. She begins to play. Michelle twirls onto the stage. Halfway across the stage, she slips in a leftover puddle of melted gelatin. Deon rushes forward.

Deon: Are you okay? Here, let me clean up that puddle.

Narrator: Deon grabs a mop from offstage and runs back onstage. He mops up the mess while waltzing to the music with the mop. Michelle and Tara complete their performance.

Michelle: Deon, you are a lifesaver!

Tara: Yes, you make a great emcee.

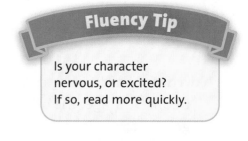

Fluency Tip

Is your character nervous, or excited? If so, read more quickly.

Mr. Herbert: Okay, everyone! Time for the curtain call.

Chorus: Where's Deon?

Michelle: We can't take our bow without him.

Tara: If it hadn't been for Deon, our performance would have been a flop.

Andres: When my tower collapsed, he wasn't fazed at all.

Rob: Deon is a spectacular emcee.

Chorus: Get out here, Deon!

Narrator: Deon walks onstage. As he appears, the students in the audience jump to their feet and cheer.

Tara: They love you.

Deon: Me? What did I do? I was only the emcee.

Andres: You were the best part of the whole show. You reigned supreme!

Chorus: You made us laugh.

Rob: The talent show wouldn't have been as good without you.

Michelle: You've got a real gift for comedy.

Deon: Maybe you're right. After tonight's success, I think we should take the school talent show to Broadway.

Mr. Herbert: Now *that* sounds like a hit!

COMPREHENSION STRATEGIES
Review

Reading Fiction

Bridge to Reading for Meaning Realistic fiction tells about characters and events that could happen in real life. The notes on page 137 point out text features of realistic fiction, including characters, plot conflict, and dialogue. How can you use these features to help you better understand the story?

Review the Focus Strategies

If you do not understand what you are reading, use the strategies you learned about in this theme.

 Use Story Structure
As you read, think about the characters, setting, and plot events of the story. Identify the problem the main character needs to solve and how it is resolved.

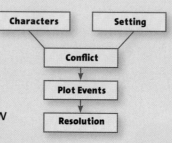

 Monitor Comprehension: Reread
Monitor your comprehension as you read. If you don't understand something, reread it for clarification.

As you read "The Alligator Race" on pages 138–141, think about where and how to use the strategies.

CHARACTERS
In realistic fiction, the characters have the same feelings that people in real life do.

The Alligator Race

by Karen Dowicz Haas
illustrated by Barry Gott

What was I doing here? And in a tournament, of all things! The Allie Pond Challenge was an annual water-sport competition for kids from all over town. My blooper had just cost us the Ring-Diving Contest.

"Don't feel bad, Steve," Brian said to me.

"Yeah, Steve," Tyrone said. "I didn't find any rings either."

"Of course," Brian added, "it might have helped if you'd been in the water. But maybe searching the dock was smarter. The light is better over there."

No matter what Brian and Tyrone said, I was the reason we were losing. I didn't mind so much for myself, but I hated taking my friends down with me. Before, at least the score had been close. Now our team was dead last.

"Why didn't you guys dump me when you still had a chance?" I said.

"We couldn't do that to you," Tyrone said.

"Yeah," Brian added. "We tried. They wouldn't let us." He looked at me. "Just kidding!"

"Lighten up!" Tyrone nudged my shoulder. "It's supposed to be fun." Some fun.

I had moved to this town from the city and fallen into life pretty well, except for times like this. All the Allie Pond kids could swim like fish, and they loved to compete. I'd never been a great swimmer.

To make things worse, it required bravery for me even to enter the water of a lake this big, with real live fish and a mucky bottom. I always held my breath whenever I stuck my toes in.

Maybe that's why we had also lost the easiest challenge, the Ping-Pong Derby. Because I had to stand with my feet in the gooey lake bottom. I couldn't relax long enough to blow the silly ball to my teammate.

Next to my two expert friends, I felt like that green goopy stuff in the water. Unwanted, and not particularly useful.

Captain Dale tallied scores on a blackboard, then bellowed into his bullhorn, "Final race is worth twenty-five points. It decides the winner."

PLOT CONFLICT
The plot conflict is a problem the main character faces.

DIALOGUE
Dialogue gives you clues about what the characters are like.

Apply the Strategies Read this story about a boy who succeeds at something with help from his friends. As you read, use different comprehension strategies, such as rereading, to help you understand.

The Alligator Race

by Karen Dowicz Haas
illustrated by Barry Gott

What was I doing here? And in a tournament, of all things! The Allie Pond Challenge was an annual water-sport competition for kids from all over town. My blooper had just cost us the Ring-Diving Contest.

"Don't feel bad, Steve," Brian said to me.

"Yeah, Steve," Tyrone said. "I didn't find any rings either."

"Of course," Brian added, "it might have helped if you'd been in the water. But maybe searching the dock was smarter. The light is better over there."

Stop and Think

As you read, look for the way the characters' behavior affects the plot events. USE STORY STRUCTURE

No matter what Brian and Tyrone said, I was the reason we were losing. I didn't mind so much for myself, but I hated taking my friends down with me. Before, at least the score had been close. Now our team was dead last.

"Why didn't you guys dump me when you still had a chance?" I said.

"We couldn't do that to you," Tyrone said.

"Yeah," Brian added. "We tried. They wouldn't let us." He looked at me. "Just kidding!"

"Lighten up!" Tyrone nudged my shoulder. "It's supposed to be fun."

Some fun.

I had moved to this town from the city and fallen into life pretty well, except for times like this. All the Allie Pond kids could swim like fish, and they loved to compete. I'd never been a great swimmer.

To make things worse, it required bravery for me even to enter the water of a lake this big, with real live fish and a mucky bottom. I always held my breath whenever I stuck my toes in.

Maybe that's why we had also lost the easiest challenge, the Ping-Pong Derby. Because I had to stand with my feet in the gooey lake bottom. I couldn't relax long enough to blow the silly ball to my teammate.

Next to my two expert friends, I felt like that green goopy stuff in the water. Unwanted, and not particularly useful.

Captain Dale tallied scores on a blackboard, then bellowed into his bullhorn, "Final race is worth twenty-five points. It decides the winner."

Someone shouted, "Which race is it?"

Captain Dale checked his clipboard. "The Alligator Race!"

"What's that?" I asked Brian. "There aren't any alligators in this lake." Fear shot through me. I looked around. Come to think of it, I had heard about alligators in city sewers. Anything was possible. "Are there?"

"Don't worry—too much," Brian said. "They'll just nip your freckles. After all, why do you think they call it Allie Pond?"

After a long minute, I realized that he was joking. "Very funny," I said.

"Don't mind him," Tyrone said. "Here's the deal. Three kids are on their backs, right? They're hanging on to each other. First team across the finish line wins."

"Why do they call it the Alligator Race?"

Tyrone explained, "The first guy uses his arms. Second guy holds his legs. The third guy holds the second guy's legs but kicks his own legs. All together it looks like a giant alligator racing in the water."

"Remind me," I said. "How is this supposed to be fun?"

They rolled their eyes.

I sighed. I wanted to quit. "Look, guys," I said. "I have to tell you something."

"We know," Brian said.

"It's OK," Tyrone added.

"What do you know?" I said. "I haven't confessed anything yet."

"You can't swim, right?" Brian asked.

"It's pretty obvious," Tyrone said. "Not that there's anything wrong with that."

"That's not what I was going to say!" I said.

They looked at me patiently.

I decided to level with them. "I can swim—a little. In a pool. Not too well, but good enough. I'm just so nervous here. All I'm doing is holding my breath and hoping fish aren't—"

Brian shook my shoulders and started to dance. "We're gonna win!"

Tyrone laughed. "Steve! You're going to win the whole competition for us! All you have to do is hold on."

"Yeah, we'll do the rest," said Brian.

I looked around. There were four lifeguards and the water was only up to my chest. I could do this.

Stop and Think

If you don't understand how Tyrone and Brian think Steve will help them win the race, reread page 140. MONITOR COMPREHENSION: REREAD

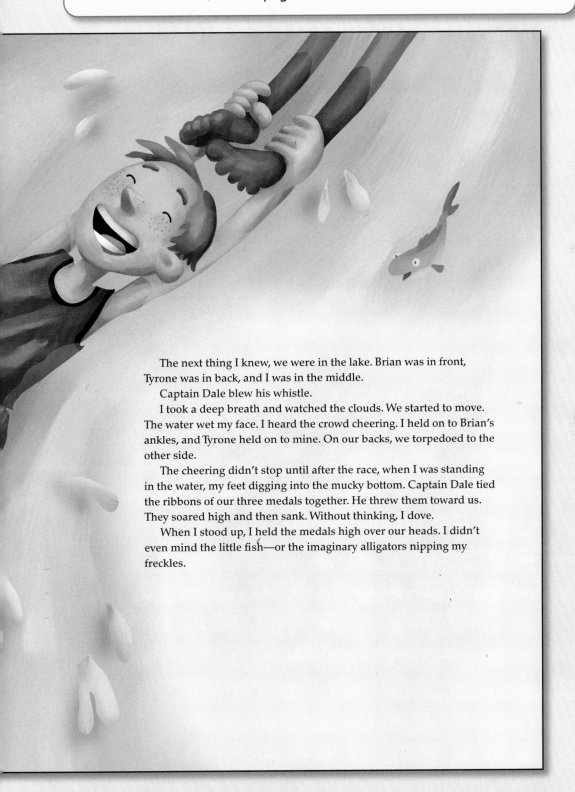

The next thing I knew, we were in the lake. Brian was in front, Tyrone was in back, and I was in the middle.

Captain Dale blew his whistle.

I took a deep breath and watched the clouds. We started to move. The water wet my face. I heard the crowd cheering. I held on to Brian's ankles, and Tyrone held on to mine. On our backs, we torpedoed to the other side.

The cheering didn't stop until after the race, when I was standing in the water, my feet digging into the mucky bottom. Captain Dale tied the ribbons of our three medals together. He threw them toward us. They soared high and then sank. Without thinking, I dove.

When I stood up, I held the medals high over our heads. I didn't even mind the little fish—or the imaginary alligators nipping my freckles.

READING-WRITING
CONNECTION

Theme 2 Common Goals

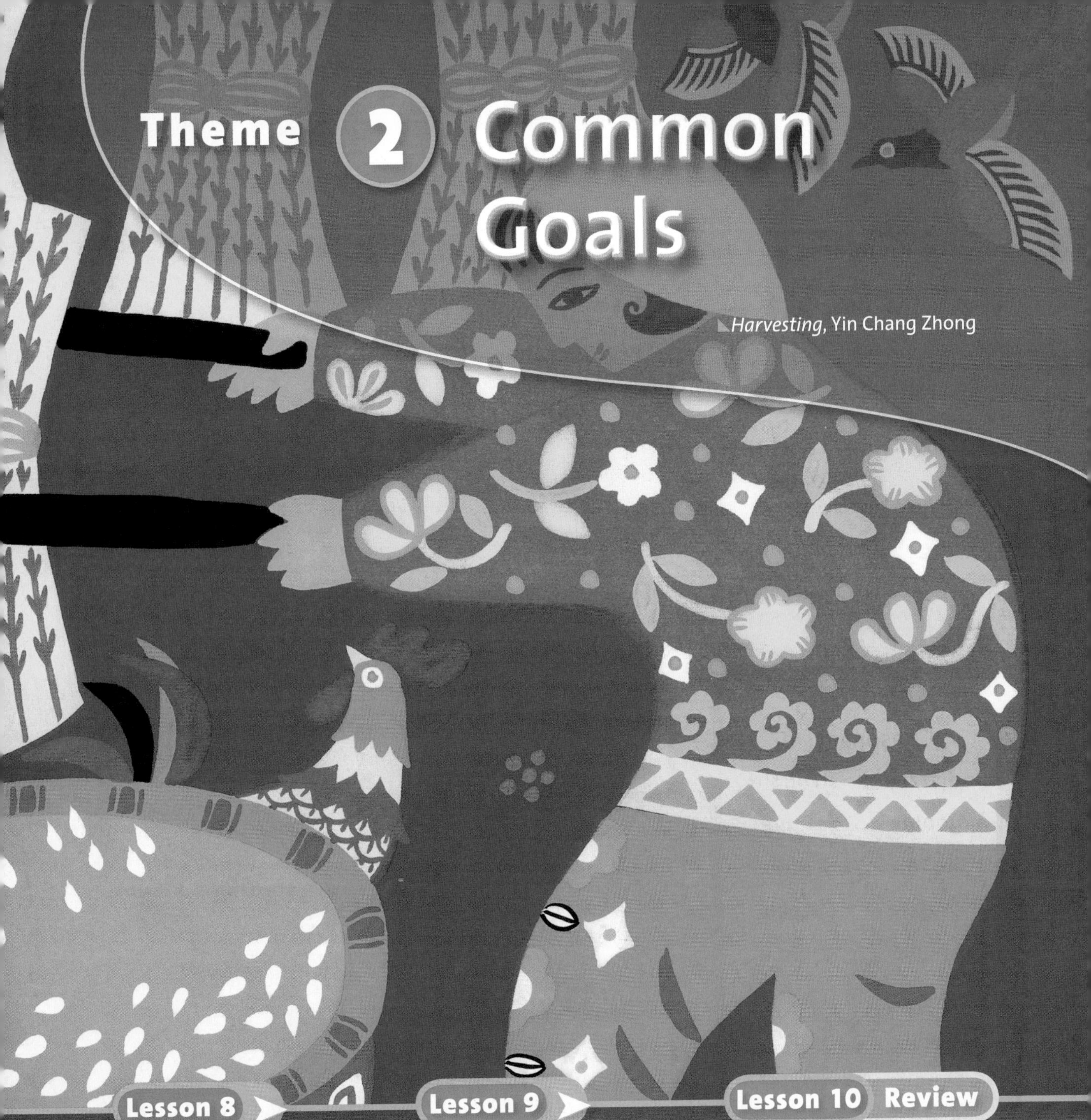

Harvesting, Yin Chang Zhong

Lesson 8	Lesson 9	Lesson 10 Review
When Washington Crossed the Delaware In 1776	**Leonardo's Horse** Bellerophon and Pegasus: A Greek Myth	**The Secret Ingredient** **Ants**
Use Graphic Organizers	Use Graphic Organizers	Review Skills and Strategies
Text Structure: Sequence	Text Structure: Sequence	

Lesson 6 GPS Focus Wall

GEORGIA

Big Idea

All stories have a theme that is often a lesson or message about life.

Enduring Understanding

A character's qualities, motives, and actions help reveal a story's theme.

Essential Question

How does a character's actions relate to the theme of a story?

Spelling Words

Words with Consonant *-le*

drizzle	struggle
gobble	wiggle
meddle	spindle
shuffle	speckle
bundle	griddle
pickle	ripple
hobble	article
topple	triple
hurtle	jingle
vehicle	bugle

Challenge

grumble	nimble
stumble	supple
rectangle	

Fluency

Expression

Comprehension

Focus Skill: Theme

Focus Strategy: Ask Questions

Robust Vocabulary

- wistful
- grateful
- grim
- raspy
- swarmed
- revelers
- irresistible

Writing

- Personal Response Paragraph
- Ideas

Lesson 6

Genre: Realistic Fiction

Salsa
Stories

Lulu Delacre

Tejano
CONJUNTO
FESTIVAL

by Kathleen D. Lindsey

Genre: Photo Essay

Focus Skill

 **Theme**

All stories have a **theme**, or message, that runs through them. A story's theme is not usually stated directly. The reader may determine the theme of a story by looking at the characters' qualities and motives and the way in which they respond to plot conflicts. Readers should look for the message about life that the author wants to give them.

Character's Qualities	Character's Motives	Character's Actions

Theme

> **Tip**
>
> Look for the conflicts in the story. The characters' reactions to problems may provide clues to the theme.

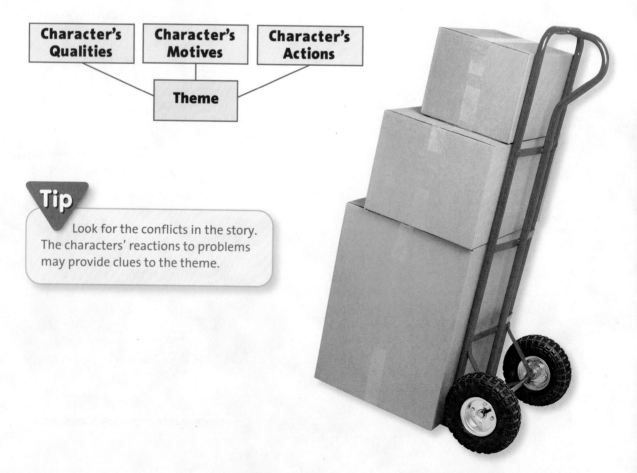

Read the paragraph below. Then look at the graphic organizer. Note the ways in which Carolina's personality, motives, and actions contribute to the theme of the paragraph.

Carolina had never left San Juan, Puerto Rico, and now her family was packing up to move to the United States. Her parents assured Carolina that before long, she would feel right at home in Denver, Colorado. Carolina didn't see how. Denver would be nothing like San Juan. There was no ocean nearby, and it snowed there. It never snowed in San Juan. Instead of starting to pack her things, Carolina went out for a walk.

Character's Qualities	**Character's Motives**	**Character's Actions**
worried, sad	does not want to accept her new home, Colorado	Carolina goes for a walk instead of packing her things.

Theme
Moving to a new place can be scary.

Try This!

Look back at the paragraph. How would the theme be different if Carolina were excited about the move to Denver?

 www.harcourtschool.com/storytown

Vocabulary

Build Robust Vocabulary

wistful

grateful

irresistible

revelers

grim

raspy

swarmed

The Birthday Piñata

When Maria arrived at her friend Arturo's birthday party, she noticed a colorful piñata hanging outside. "I wonder if I can stay long enough to help break it," she told Arturo with a **wistful** sigh. "My mom is picking me up early."

"I'll ask Dad if we can do it now," said Arturo.

"Oh, thank you!" Maria was **grateful** that her friend wasn't going to let her miss the fun. She imagined the inside of the piñata, stuffed full of **irresistible** treats.

Arturo went to talk to his dad, and soon Maria heard Arturo's father calling the birthday **revelers** into the dining room.

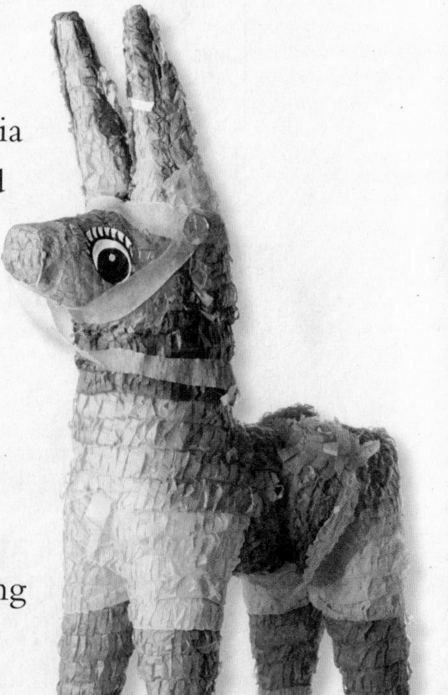

Juliana was the first to take a turn. She put on a blindfold and grasped the broom. With a **grim** and determined look on her face, Juliana swung. Whap! The broom hit the piñata squarely.

Now it was Maria's turn. The broom scraped the side of the piñata, making a **raspy** sound. No luck for her!

Finally, after everyone had swung several times, the piñata spilled its contents. Cheering, the children **swarmed** toward the treats that lay scattered on the floor.

GO online www.harcourtschool.com/storytown

Word Scribe

This week, your task is to use the Vocabulary Words in your writing. In your vocabulary journal, write sentences to show the meanings of the words. For example, you could write about something that was irresistible or about a time when you felt grateful for a friend's help. Use as many of the Vocabulary Words in your writing as you can. Share your writing with your classmates.

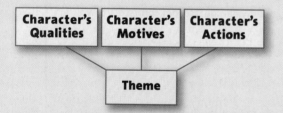

Realistic Fiction

Genre Study

Realistic fiction has characters and events that are like people and events in real life. As you read, look for

- a setting that could be a real place.

- challenges and problems that might happen in real life.

Character's Qualities	Character's Motives	Character's Actions

Theme

Comprehension Strategy

Ask questions about the author's message in the text.

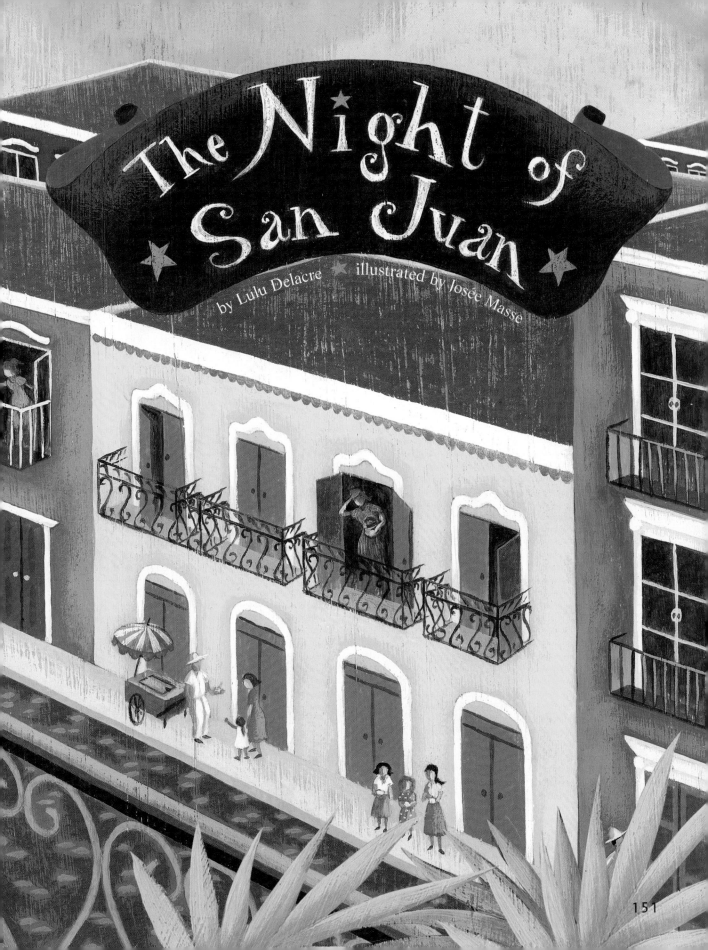

The Night of San Juan

by Lulu Delacre ★ illustrated by Josée Massé

152

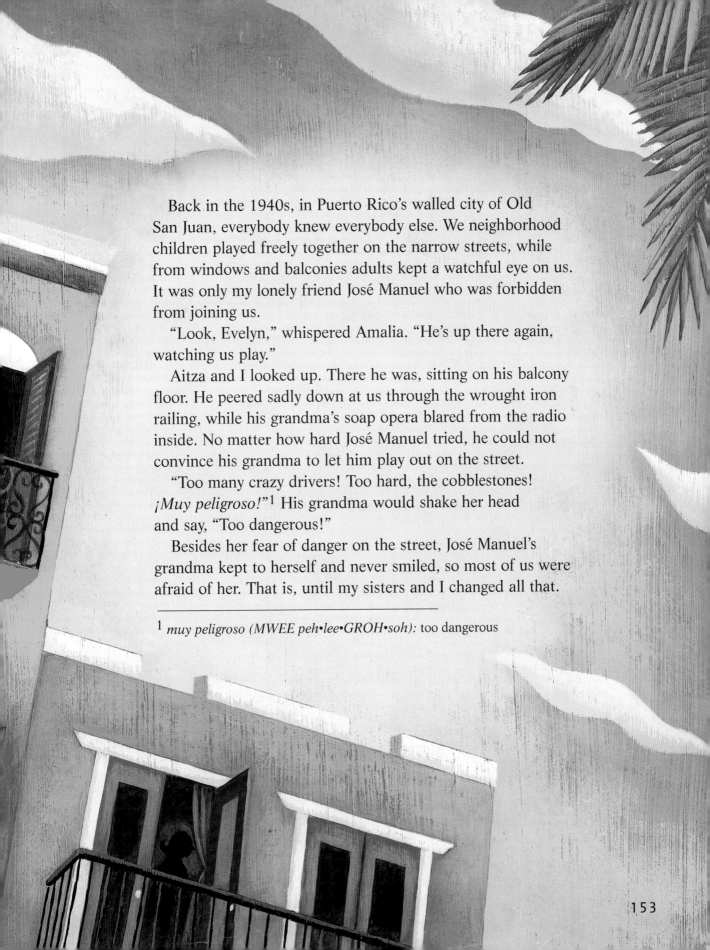

Back in the 1940s, in Puerto Rico's walled city of Old San Juan, everybody knew everybody else. We neighborhood children played freely together on the narrow streets, while from windows and balconies adults kept a watchful eye on us. It was only my lonely friend José Manuel who was forbidden from joining us.

"Look, Evelyn," whispered Amalia. "He's up there again, watching us play."

Aitza and I looked up. There he was, sitting on his balcony floor. He peered sadly down at us through the wrought iron railing, while his grandma's soap opera blared from the radio inside. No matter how hard José Manuel tried, he could not convince his grandma to let him play out on the street.

"Too many crazy drivers! Too hard, the cobblestones! *¡Muy peligroso!*"[1] His grandma would shake her head and say, "Too dangerous!"

Besides her fear of danger on the street, José Manuel's grandma kept to herself and never smiled, so most of us were afraid of her. That is, until my sisters and I changed all that.

---

1 *muy peligroso (MWEE peh•lee•GROH•soh):* too dangerous

153

"One day," Amalia suddenly announced, "I'm going to ask his grandma to let him come down and play." If anyone would have the courage to do that, it was my little sister Amalia. Even though she was only seven, she was also the most daring of the three of us.

We never knew what she would do next. In fact, at that very moment I could see a mischievous grin spreading across her freckled face as two elegant women turned the corner of Calle Sol. Once they strolled down the street in front of us, Amalia swiftly snuck up behind them and flipped their skirts up to expose their lace-trimmed slips.

"*¡Sinvergüenza!*"[2] the women cried out. "Little rascal!"

We could hardly hold our laughter in. We all looked up to make sure none of the neighbors had seen her. If anyone had, we would surely have been scolded as soon as we got home. News traveled fast in our neighborhood.

Luckily, only José Manuel was watching us with amusement in his wistful eyes. Grateful for an audience, Amalia smiled at him, curtsied, and ran down the street toward the old cathedral with us chasing after her. I couldn't help but feel sorry for my friend as we left him behind.

There was hardly any sea breeze that day, and running in the humidity made us quite hot.

"Let's get some coconut sherbet," said Amalia, peeling her damp red curls away from her sweaty neck.

"*¡Sí, sí!*"[3] we agreed, and we chattered excitedly about our plans for that night all the way to the ice cream vendor's wooden cart by the harbor.

---

[2] *sinvergüenza (sin•vair•GWEHN•zah):* little rascal
[3] *sí (SEE):* yes

It was June twenty-third, and that night was the Night of
San Juan. For this holiday, the tradition was to go to the beach,
and at exactly midnight, everyone would walk backward into
the sea. People say that doing this three times on the Night of
San Juan brings good luck. I thought of my friend José Manuel.
Perhaps if he did this with us, his luck would change, and his
grandma would allow him to play with us outside on the street.

I thought about this as we bought our coconut sherbet and
then ate it perched on the knobby roots of the ancient tree
above the port. Excitement stirred in me while the distant
ships disappeared over the horizon.

"How can we get José Manuel to go to the beach tonight?"
I asked my sisters.

"Evelyn, you know very well his grandma will never
let him go," Aitza said. "You know what she will say—"

"*¡Muy peligroso!*" Aitza and Amalia teased at once.
"Too dangerous!"

It was getting close to dinnertime, and we knew we had to be home soon if we wanted our parents to take us to the beach that night. So we took the shortcut back across the main square. In the plaza, groups of men played dominoes while the women sat by the fountain and gossiped. Back on the street we heard the vegetable vendor chanting:

"*¡Vendo yuca, plátanos, tomates!*"[4]

He came around every evening to sell his fresh cassava, plantains, tomatoes, and other fruits and vegetables.

Leaning from her balcony, a big woman lowered a basket that was tied by a cord to the rail. In it was the money that the vendor replaced with two green plantains. As we approached our street I saw José Manuel and his grandma out on the second floor. She gave José Manuel money and went back inside. He was about to lower his basket when I had an idea. Maybe there was a way we could ask him to join us.

"What if we send José Manuel a note in his grandma's basket inviting him to go to the beach with us tonight?" I offered.

"It will never work," Aitza said. "His grandma will not like it. We could get into trouble."

"Then we could ask her personally," I said.

"But what excuse could we use to go up there?" said Aitza. "Nobody ever shows up uninvited at José Manuel's house."

"Wait! I know what we can do," Amalia said, jumping up and down. "We'll tell him to drop something. Then we'll go up to return it."

---

4 *vendo yuca, plátanos, tomates (VEN•doh YOO•kah PLAH•tah•nohs toh•MAH•tehs):* I sell cassava, plantains, tomatoes

Even though Aitza was very reluctant, we convinced her to try our plan. We wrote the note and asked the vegetable vendor to please place it in José Manuel's basket next to the vegetables. We impatiently waited on the corner as we watched. When he opened the note, he looked puzzled. He took the tomatoes he had purchased in to his grandmother. Soon he returned with his little red ball. He had just sat down to play when suddenly the ball fell from the balcony. It bounced several times, rolled down the hill, and bumped into a wall. Amalia flew after it. "I got it!" she called triumphantly, offering me her find.

With José Manuel's ball in my hand we climbed up the worn stairs of his pink apartment house. And while Aitza and I stood nervously outside his apartment trying to catch our breath, Amalia knocked loudly on the wooden door. With a squeaking sound it slowly opened, and there stood José Manuel's grandma wearing a frown as grim as her black widow's dress.

"¿Sí?" she said. "How can I help you?"

Aitza and I looked at each other. She looked as afraid as I felt.
But without hesitation, Amalia took the little ball from my hand and
proudly showed it to José Manuel's grandma. I wanted to run, but a
glimpse of José Manuel's hopeful expression made me stay.

"This belongs to José Manuel," Amalia declared. "We came to
return it." Amalia took a deep breath, then took a step forward.
"We also wanted to know if he could come to the beach tonight with
our family."

Aitza and I meekly stood behind Amalia.

"The beach?" José Manuel's grandma asked, surprised, as she
took the little ball from Amalia's palm.

"Y-y-yes," I stuttered. "Tonight is the Night of San Juan, and our
parents take us to the beach every year."

José Manuel's grandma scowled at us. How silly to think she
would ever let him go. I suddenly felt embarrassed and turned to
leave, pulling both sisters with me by their arms.

"Wait," we heard her raspy voice behind us. "Come inside for a
surullito de maíz."[5]

It was then that I smelled the aroma of the corn fritters that was
escaping from the kitchen. José Manuel's grandma was making
surullitos for dinner.

"Oh, yes!" Amalia followed her in without a thought. And before
we knew it, we were all seated in the living room rocking chairs
next to José Manuel, eating the most delicious corn fritters that we
dipped in garlicky sauce. Somehow, sitting there with José Manuel,
his grandma seemed less scary. After we finished, José Manuel's
grandma thanked us for our invitation and said she would let
us know.

José Manuel smiled.

---

[5] *surullito de maíz (soo•roo•LYEE•toh day mah•YEES):* a cornmeal-and-cheese dish

159

When we got home we found Mami waiting with her hands on her hips. She had just hung up the phone with José Manuel's grandma. She had reason to be upset. Not only were we late for supper, but in our excitement we had forgotten to ask for permission before inviting José Manuel to the beach. We all looked down, not knowing what to do or say.

"It wasn't my fault. It was Evelyn and Amalia's idea," volunteered Aitza, the coward.

"*Bendito*,[6] Mami," I said. "Don't punish us, we forgot."

"Forgot?" Mami asked.

"*Sí*, Mami," we all said at once. "We are sorry."

"Actually it was very nice of you girls to invite him," said Mami. "But please remember to ask me first next time."

---

[6] *bendito (ben•DEE•toh):* I'm sorry

Late that night the whole family went to the beach as was our tradition on the Night of San Juan. But this time was special, for we had José Manuel with us.

The full moon shone against the velvet sky. The tide was high, and the beach swarmed with young revelers who, like us, had waited all year for this night's irresistible dip in the dark ocean. The moment we reached the water we all turned around, held hands, and jumped backward into the rushing waves. Amalia stumbled forward, Aitza joyfully splashed back, and so did I as I let go of my sister's hand. But my other hand remained tightly clasped to José Manuel's. When my friend and I took our third plunge into the sea, I wished good luck would come to him, and that from then on, his grandma would allow him to play with us out on the street. And as a wave lifted us high in the water, I suddenly knew this wish would come true.

Think Critically

1. What theme about friendship do the character's actions suggest? THEME

2. The characters in "The Night of San Juan" look forward to this special event all year. To what yearly celebration or event do you especially look forward? MAKE CONNECTIONS

3. Explain how the adults in San Juan keep a careful watch over the children, despite the freedom the children enjoy. SYNTHESIZE

4. How do you think José Manuel's life will change after the Night of San Juan? MAKE PREDICTIONS

5. **WRITE** Why do you think José Manuel's grandma seems less scary when the girls sit down with her to eat corn fritters? Use details from the story to support your response. SHORT RESPONSE

ACEITE VEGETAL

ABOUT THE AUTHOR
Lulu Delacre

Lulu Delacre was born in Río Piedras, Puerto Rico. She grew up hunting lizards and climbing tamarind trees. When she was young, she drew scenes from her homeland and wrote stories about her cultural heritage. Now Lulu Delacre is fulfilling her dream of writing books about the traditions and folklore of Latin America.

ABOUT THE ILLUSTRATOR
Josée Masse

www.harcourtschool.com/storytown

Josée Masse lives and works near Montreal, Canada, and has been drawing as long as she can remember. Josée Masse says that she feels complete freedom to use her imagination when she illustrates a children's book. She advises readers to "let yourself be transported by the illustrations, because they have as much power as the words."

Photo Essay

Tejano CONJUNTO FESTIVAL

by Kathleen D. Lindsey

May is a special time in San Antonio, Texas. It's when musicians and fans gather for the Tejano Conjunto festival. This festival celebrates conjunto (kohn•HOON•toh), a unique sound that began in Texas.

Texans with Mexican heritage call themselves *tejanos* (teh•HAH•nohs). In the late 1800s, tejanos developed a new style of music. They combined the sounds of the Mexican 12-string bass guitar with the sounds of the accordion. The new sound was *conjunto*. Conjunto means *ensemble*. Today, musicians still use the accordion and the Mexican guitar. They also add drums, saxophones, keyboards, and other instruments to make the sound unique to them.

German settlers brought the button accordion with them to Texas.

▲ Dancing is a big part of the celebration. Like the music, the dances are a mix of styles. Mexican Americans combined European waltzes and polkas with their own dances to create new ones.

▲ At first, conjunto bands used only two instruments, the Mexican 12-string guitar for rhythm and the accordion for melody.

To appeal to larger audiences, conjunto bands started using microphones and adding new instruments, such as drums, electric basses, or saxophones.

Connections

Comparing Texts

1. In "The Night of San Juan," the sisters make a plan. Describe a time when you made a plan to achieve a goal.

2. What common characteristics of culture are expressed in both "The Night of San Juan" and the "Tejano Conjunto Festival"?

3. Evelyn and her sisters change their opinion of José Manuel's grandmother. When have you changed your opinion of someone?

Vocabulary Review

Rate a Situation

With a partner, read aloud each sentence below. Point to a spot on the line to show how happy you would feel in each situation. Explain your choices.

Least Happy ————————————— Most Happy

- You woke up with a **raspy** voice.
- A group of **revelers** made a lot of noise.
- Bees **swarmed** near your favorite lunch spot.
- Your mom cooked a meal you found **irresistible**.

wistful

grateful

grim

raspy

swarmed

revelers

irresistible

Fluency Practice

Partner Reading

Work with a partner to reread aloud a portion of dialogue from "The Night of San Juan." For example, you may read several lines of dialogue on page 156. Ask your partner for feedback on how well you read with expression. Then switch roles.

Writing

Write a Short Story

Imagine the experience of a first-time visitor to the beach on the Night of San Juan. Write a short story about this character's experience.

My Writing Checklist

Writing Trait ▸ Ideas

✓ My writing is focused on one character's feelings and actions.

✓ I used a graphic organizer to help me develop my character.

✓ My story has a beginning, middle, and end.

Character's Qualities	Character's Motives	Character's Actions

Reading-Writing Connection

Analyze a Narrative: Response to Literature

A **response to literature** explains what you think about a story you have read. Before you write a response to literature, ask yourself questions about the characters and events in the story. **Form opinions** about the story and think about how it **connects to your life.**

Read the passage below from "Chang and the Bamboo Flute." Think about the questions in the boxes.

FORM OPINIONS
What is your opinion about Mei Mei's behavior? What kind of friend is Mei Mei?

CONNECT TO YOUR LIFE Did a friend ever help you get what you wanted? How did you feel about that friend?

The trader looked at Chang's offering and sneered. "Who would want that? It's nothing but a little bamboo stick!"

"It's not!" Mei Mei said hotly. "It's a flute! And all he wants for it is that old wok!"

"Never!" Zhao said indignantly. "I might give you a box of pencils for it, but nothing more."

Chang shook his head.

"It has to be the wok," Mei Mei repeated stubbornly.

Response to Literature

A student named Justin wrote this response to "Chang and the Bamboo Flute." As you read it, look for Justin's summary of the story, his opinions about it, and how he connects it to his own life. Note how he makes his **ideas clear**.

Student Writing Model

My Response to "Chang and the Bamboo Flute"
by Justin B.

Writing Trait

IDEAS
Justin begins by telling what the main character learns. Then he writes a brief summary of the story. He describes the **setting**, the **main character**, and the **plot events**.

In the second paragraph, Justin gives his **opinion** about the characters and events in the story. He also **connects** the story to experiences in his life.

In "Chang and the Bamboo Flute," a boy learns that family is more important than possessions. Chang lives with his parents on a houseboat. When a storm damages their boat, Chang's mother loses her wok, the family cooking pot, and is very upset. Chang offers to trade his precious flute to help his mother. Instead of trading his flute, he plays it to earn enough money to buy a wok.

I think Chang's friend, Mei Mei, is a very good friend to Chang. She goes with him to the market to keep his mind off the missing wok. Mei Mei also helps Chang bargain with a mean merchant. She reminds me of my best friend, Carlos, who helped me when I first moved here. I didn't know anyone, but Carlos introduced me to all of his friends.

169

Chang's father is my favorite character. He is brave, and he works hard to repair the boat. He comforts Chang's mother when she cries about her lost wok. "Supper will still be good," he says. I also liked the storyteller, Bo Won. He shows up at the right time and persuades Chang to play for the crowd at the market. Soon the crowd is throwing money to Chang for his flute-playing.

This story shows how a strong family survives after a big loss. Chang learns that he has a unique gift that is of value. By using his gift, Chang is able to help his family.

Now look at how Justin prepared his response to literature.

Summarize

First, he used a story map to help him write a **summary** of the **plot events.**

Characters	Setting
Chang, Mei Mei, Chang's family, Bo Won	a village near a river in China

Plot Events
- Chang's mother loses her wok in a storm.
- Chang tries to trade his flute for a wok at the market.
- Bo Won convinces Chang to play the flute and Chang receives money for playing it.

Form Opinions and Make Connections

As Justin read the story, he formed opinions about the characters and events. He used note cards to write characters' exact words to support his opinions. He made notes about how the story connected to his life and what the main character learned.

What is my opinion of the characters and events?
Chang's father is kind. "Supper will still be good."
How does this story connect to my life?
I have a friend as kind as Mei Mei.
What did the main character learn?
Family is important; that he has a unique gift he can use to help his family.

Organize Information

Then Justin made a list to organize his ideas. This list shows what Justin planned to include in each paragraph.

1. Summarize plot events.
2. State my opinions, connect to my life.
3. Describe my favorite character.
4. Tell what the main character learned.

Big 💡 Idea

Details about characters help develop the themes of historical fiction.

Enduring ❗ Understanding

Readers can learn about the theme by paying close attention to what the characters say and do.

Essential ❓ Question

How do readers use details about the characters to identify a story's theme?

Spelling Words

Words with VCCV: Same Medial Consonants

suppose	collect
hurricane	slippery
ballad	common
bellow	arrange
success	suffer
appeal	follow
announcer	kennel
tissue	squirrel
excellent	message
terrific	summary

Challenge

marriage	comma
official	rugged
motto	

Fluency

Expression

Comprehension

Theme

Ask Questions

Robust Vocabulary

- fret
- assured
- nudged
- outlandish
- ruckus
- proclaimed

Writing

- Journal Entry
- Ideas

Lesson 7

Genre: Historical Fiction

By the Newbery Honor author of Dragonwings and Dragon's Gate

When the Circus Came to Town

LAURENCE YEP

Genre: Historical Fiction

POETRY beat

Genre: Poetry

Focus Skill

 **Theme**

You have learned that the **theme** is the meaning or message of a story. The story's setting, as well as the characters' qualities and actions, all contribute to the theme. In fables and some folktales, authors state the theme directly, as a moral. In most stories, you can figure out the theme by asking yourself what the main character learns by the end of the story.

Character's Qualities	Character's Motives	Character's Actions

Theme

Tip
Put together story details about characters, setting, and plot to determine the theme.

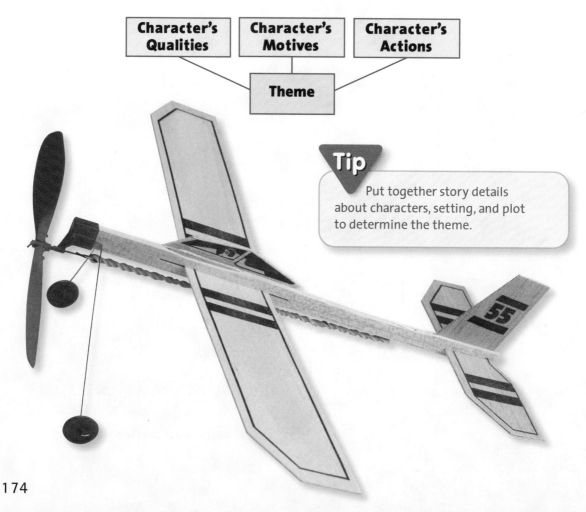

Read the paragraph below. Then look at the graphic organizer. It shows how the main character's qualities, his actions, and the setting contribute to the theme of the story.

Alex looked at the new kid, Tony. He had been in the class for a week, but he still had no friends. Alex had been a new student last year, but he had made friends right away. He wasn't afraid to walk up to someone he didn't know and just start talking. He decided to do that now and sat next to Tony at the lunch table. During lunch, the boys discovered that they both enjoyed building model airplanes. They made a plan to build a new one together.

Character's Qualities	**Character's Motives**	**Character's Actions**
Alex is outgoing and makes friends easily.	Alex feels bad that Tony has no friends yet.	Alex sits next to Tony and talks to him.

Theme
Someone has to take the first step to make a new friend.

Try This!

Look at the paragraph. How does Alex's action contribute to the theme of the story?

GO online www.harcourtschool.com/storytown

Vocabulary

Build Robust Vocabulary

- fret
- proclaimed
- assured
- outlandish
- nudged
- ruckus

The Biggest Show

Aunt Lily would be here any minute. The four of us were feeling restless and impatient, but we were trying hard not to **fret**. Aunt Lily's annual visit always sparked excitement. What surprise would she have for us this year? One year, she brought costumes and we put on a play. Another time, she took us on a ferryboat ride.

All of a sudden, the door flew open, and Aunt Lily burst into the house. "Everyone, get your coats—we're going to see a show!" she **proclaimed**. We rushed for our coats and piled into her van.

"What kind of show is it?" Jim asked.

"You'll find out soon enough," Aunt Lily **assured** us.

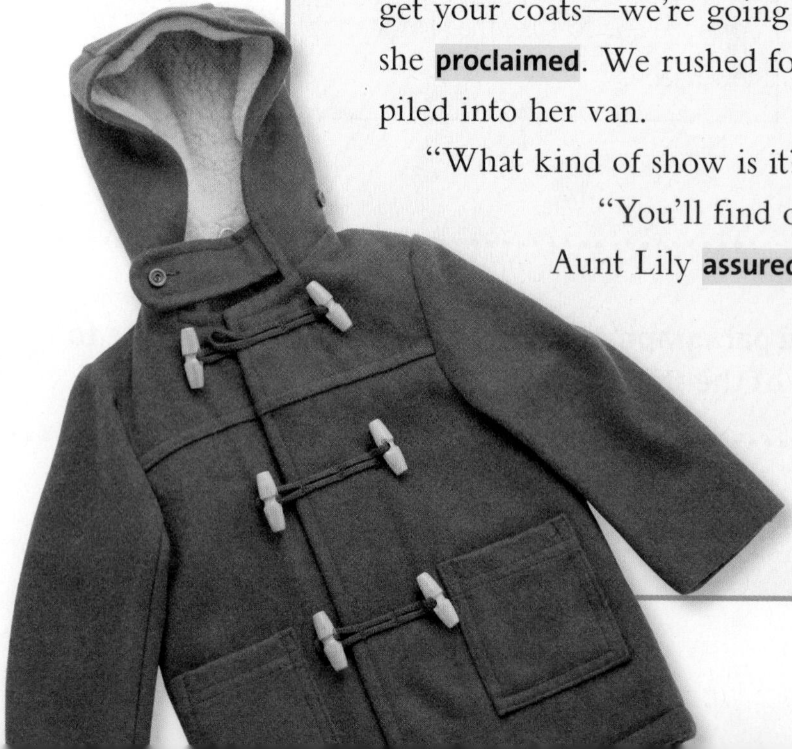

Eventually, we arrived at a parking lot and jumped out of the van. The first clue to the surprise was a horse in an **outlandish** costume being led into a red tent. I **nudged** my brother Tim. "It's a circus!" I whispered.

"I bet you're right!" he replied.

Aunt Lily led us past the ticket-taker. The crowd inside the tent was making quite a **ruckus**! Stepping inside, we saw clowns, acrobats, and a towering trapeze. We knew we were in for a great time once again!

 www.harcourtschool.com/storytown

Word Detective

This week, search for the Vocabulary Words around you. Pay attention as you watch television, read books, and listen to conversations. Write the words you find in your vocabulary journal. Be sure to tell where you found each word.

Historical Fiction

Genre Study

Historical fiction is about people, places, and events from the past. As you read, look for

- characters who have feelings that real people have.

- a main character who overcomes a challenge.

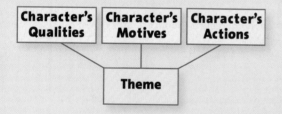

Comprehension Strategy

Ask questions about the author's message in the text.

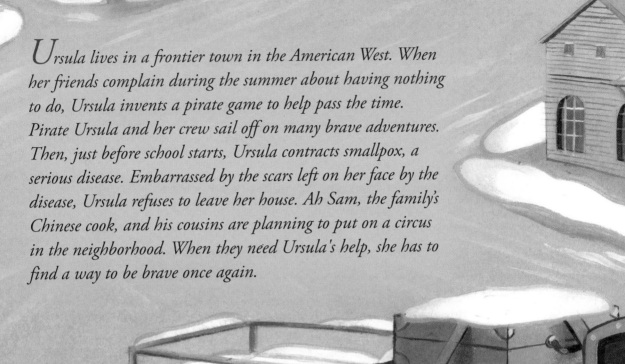

Ursula lives in a frontier town in the American West. When her friends complain during the summer about having nothing to do, Ursula invents a pirate game to help pass the time. Pirate Ursula and her crew sail off on many brave adventures. Then, just before school starts, Ursula contracts smallpox, a serious disease. Embarrassed by the scars left on her face by the disease, Ursula refuses to leave her house. Ah Sam, the family's Chinese cook, and his cousins are planning to put on a circus in the neighborhood. When they need Ursula's help, she has to find a way to be brave once again.

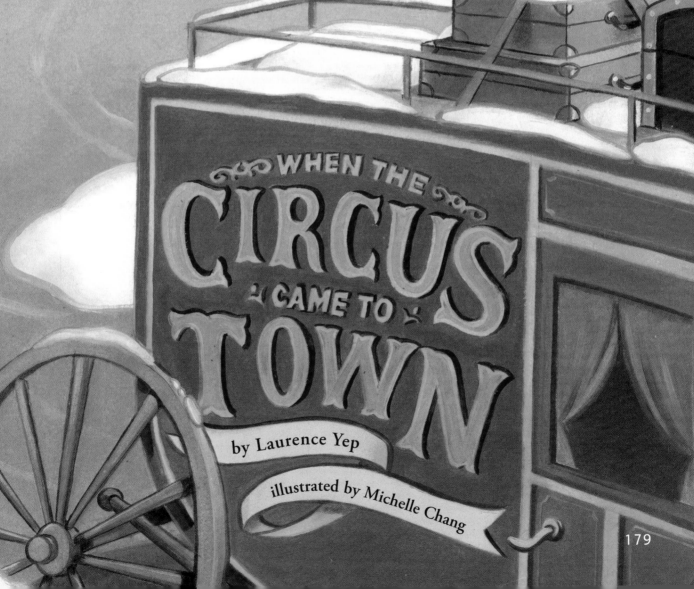

WHEN THE CIRCUS CAME TO TOWN

by Laurence Yep

illustrated by Michelle Chang

179

The night before the circus, I hardly slept. I hadn't been so excited since Pirate Ursula had been born.

I woke up before sunrise. So I heard the noise in the street. When I peeked out, I saw John from the Circle-T ranch. His family rode on a buckboard while all the cowboys trotted behind them. Word must have spread out there somehow.

As he passed my window, John gave the secret pirate sign for hello.

Shortly afterward tall Tom came in on snowshoes. He must have walked all night down from his hills.

Then I heard a loud *shoosh-shoosh* sound. It was the miners on skis they had made themselves. Even they had quit work and left their coal mine. Harry rode on his father's shoulders. He gave me the secret greeting too.

The whole pirate crew arrived for the circus. In fact, the whole town shut down. Mr. Schultz, Peter's father, came out of his barber shop with a shovel. As he started to clear the snow off the street, Pa got his shovel and joined him. Soon there were a dozen people working. Snow fountained up on either side like a tail of white plumes.

When that was done, people piled up logs and old lumber and crates. Soon flames roared upward. Everyone gathered around the bonfire to keep warm.

Then I heard the front door slam. "Everything's ready," Pa announced excitedly. His lower lip was all swollen, though.

"What happened to your mouth?" asked Ma.

"Oh, that old shovel handle reared up and hit me in the face," Pa said.

I put my scarf around my face and went out into the dining room. Ma was waiting to see Ah Sam and his three cousins off.

Ah Sam came out from behind the blankets in his regular Christmas clothes. However, his cousins wore satin costumes of red and blue with designs in gold thread. I felt like parrots had landed in my home.

"Don't forget. You're supposed to do it in front of my window," I reminded him anxiously.

Ah Sam didn't look happy. "We've tried and tried our routines without music. But they don't work. My cousins count on songs to get the right rhythm."

"Just try your best," I told his cousins. "No one will know the difference."

Ah Bing lifted his head proudly. "But we will know. We cannot do."

"Won't you play your harmonica for us, Ursula?" asked Ah Sam.

My stomach did flip-flops again. "Pa could."

Pa touched his swollen lip. "Not with this."

My worst nightmare was rearing up to bite me. "I don't go outside," I insisted. "I'm going to watch from the window."

Ah Sam suddenly spread his arms. "I got an idea. What if we sneak you out when no one's looking? You can stand behind the crowd."

I shook my head. "Nope."

Ah Sam sighed. "Then we'll just have to call off the circus."

"Oh, dear," said Mama. "Everybody will be so disappointed."

"They'll just have to understand." Pa shrugged.

"I don't go outside," I snapped.

But then I thought of all the people outside. I thought of Peter and Susie and all my old pirate crew. I thought of the cowboys from their ranch and Tom from his hill far away and the miners from their mountain. I could just imagine their sad faces. Pa looked the most disappointed of all.

That almost broke my heart. "Are you sure everybody will be watching the circus?"

"I promise," said Ah Sam.

"All right," I mumbled, "but if any head turns toward me, I scoot right back inside."

"Thank you," said Ah Bing.

Ma commenced to fret then about our guests' thin costumes. "Aren't you going to be cold outside?"

"We move around. Keep warm," Ah Bing assured her. "Now that Ursula help us."

I wish I could have been as sure as he was about me. "I don't know how much help I'll be."

"You'll do just fine," Ah Sam whispered.

He didn't have a crystal ball, though. And if I'd had one right then, I would have read doom, gloom and the End of the World for sure.

In my bedroom my fingers were trembling so much, I had a hard time putting on my coat and boots. I wrapped the scarf around my face real careful again.

When I went back into the dining room, Ma was already dressed for outside.

Nervously I asked Ah Sam, "What should I play?"

He checked with his cousins and then told me, "Anything fast and lively."

While Ah Sam's cousins marched outside, I was feeling so scared that my tummy did flip-flops like an acrobat. Then everyone started to clap. It sounded like a thunderstorm had fallen onto my street. And I felt like my stomach was putting on a whole circus of its own.

While they were bowing, Mama poked me and whispered, "I think it's okay."

I nudged her back. "You go first, and make sure."

She stepped outside and then nodded. "No one's looking."

The cold air hit my face. It stole my breath. The sweet, fresh air smelled good, though. I hadn't been outside in a long time. Overhead, the big sky stretched like a gray, pebbly road.

Quiet as a mouse, I tiptoed behind the crowd. Ah Sam took his place at the side. When he raised his hand, I glanced around. No one was watching me.

I took a deep breath and pulled down my scarf. Putting the harmonica to my lips, I started to play "Tramp! Tramp! Tramp! The Boys Are Marching."

With a hop and a skip Ah Sam's cousins began to bounce around like human balls.

"They look like they're made of rubber," Susie said out loud in wonder.

They twisted their bodies into hoops and rolled around the street. Lung even slipped right through Ah Bing's circle.

In the meantime Ah Sam brought out a whole bunch of small benches. I didn't pay them much mind because they looked so ordinary. I figured they were for the audience, who were all standing.

While Lung disappeared inside the station, Ah Sam swung the benches in front of the crowd.

Before anyone could sit on any of them, though, Ah Bing lay down on his back on one of them. Then he stuck his feet in the air like a dead beetle.

As Ah Sam handed her the benches, Ah Loo began to build a pyramid of benches on top of Ah Bing's feet and climb up it. Higher and higher went the pyramid. Higher and higher went Ah Loo. Finally she was as high as the tallest building. Everyone had to lean far back to look up at her as she twirled and spun, graceful as a spider on a thread.

To me, getting down seemed trickier than going up. However, Ah Loo neatly took apart the pyramid as she climbed down.

While Mama and Papa caught their breath, Ah Sam quickly turned the benches into ramps and tables. Then Lung rolled out of our station on a unicycle, cycling up and down, quick and nimble as a flea. He did better on one wheel than I could have done running on two legs. And it was all on ordinary benches.

Everybody craned their heads to look when Ah Sam came out of the station with a basket of small balls and a sword as long as my arm.

"Aw, I bet that sword isn't sharp," called Peter from the front row.

"Go ahead and touch one," Ah Sam said, "but be careful."

Naturally Peter put his finger against the tip. "Ow." He snatched his finger back. When Ah Sam had tied up his finger in a clean rag, he warned everyone, "Now, my cousin knows what she's doing. Don't any of you children try this." He looked right at Peter.

Ah Loo commenced to swallow some balls, spitting them out and catching them again like she was a fountain. Then she took the sword and held it over her head with the point aimed at her mouth. I didn't think she'd get more than the tip inside. I got so excited that I forgot to breathe.

Hurriedly Ah Sam waved his arm at me. Some orchestra I was! I began blowing "Sweet Betsy from Pike" on my harmonica.

Slowly, inch by inch, Ah Loo lowered that sword into her mouth. I thought she'd cut up her insides something awful, but she slid the sword back out with a smile.

As everyone clapped, Ah Sam lit a couple of torches from the bonfire. Then he presented them to her like a bouquet. And pretty as you please, she commenced to dine on them daintily. You would have thought she was having her daily snack. And for her main course, Ah Loo ate fire and spat it out from her mouth.

As she skipped into the station, we heard enough clanging and clatter to wake the dead. I thought a locomotive was chugging through it.

It was Ah Bing. He waddled out in an apron with his arms full of pots and pans.

Cheerfully he went right up to Susie. Putting a hand behind her ear, he plucked out an egg. He held it up to everyone as we started to laugh. Quickly he scampered around the audience, gathering eggs from people. The biggest one came from the beard of Mr. Schultz, Peter's father. Mr. Schultz laughed the loudest of anyone. Ah Bing might not be dressed up like a regular clown, but he was just as funny.

However, when Ah Bing cooked the eggs, his meal turned out all wrong. As things got worse and worse, people laughed harder and harder. I got a little scared when a pot caught on fire. But when Ah Bing raised the lid, the flames had changed into bright red and yellow flowers.

By now I had played every tune I knew, and I knew lots of them. So I started over with "Battle Hymn of the Republic."

Ah Sam took off his winter clothes. Underneath, he was decked out in an outfit just like his cousins. It was such an outlandish outfit that my jaw dropped open and I stopped playing.

"Why are you in that getup?" Susie cried out.

Ah Sam gave a little bow. Then he announced, "In China I was in a circus too. But then I retired and came to America. I went to work as a cook. However, today, for you, I will do my act."

I blinked. I saw Ah Sam's face on top of a parrot costume. He had changed from a cook and my friend to a juggler. Maybe there was magic after all—circus magic.

From his bag Ah Sam hauled out all his big Chinese kitchen knives and some cups and balls, just as a wind roared into town. It drove the snow from outside town through the street. It crawled and twisted down the street like snakes twenty feet high.

Ah Sam waited with his juggling gear in his hands.

"That's your cue," Ma whispered to me.

Here I was sleeping on the job again. Embarrassed, I put the harmonica to my mouth and began to play.

Ah Sam started to juggle the cups and balls. They circled over his head, always landing in his hands. As they went up and down, they formed pretty patterns in the air.

However, when Ah Sam tried to add the knives into the air, they stayed in his hands. The balls bounced on the ground, and the cups cracked.

Ah Sam lowered the knives. "I'm sorry. The metal handles are stuck to my palms."

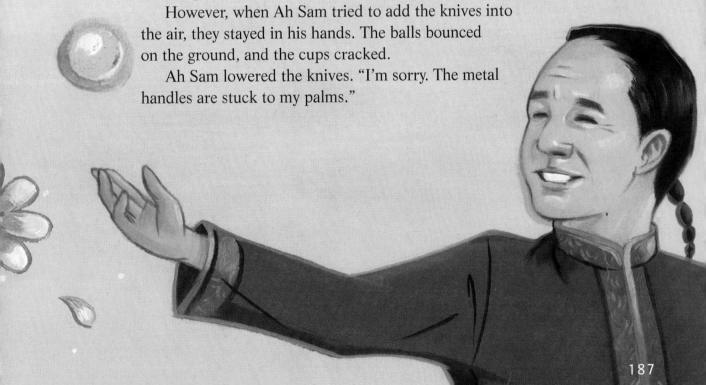

Mr. Schultz shot to his feet. He spoke with a thick accent because he had just come to America, but he could talk loud. "Let him get closer to the fire," he said.

The whole crowd shuffled around so the bonfire was between them and Ah Sam.

I'd retreated farther back. As Ah Sam warmed himself by the fire, I reckoned I'd entertain the audience with more music. In his honor, I figured I'd play his favorite tune, "Sweet and Low."

However, the moment the harmonica touched my lips, the cold metal stuck. It was freezing this far away from the bonfire. I tried to dart for the station. Too late.

Mr. Schultz came over with a big grin. "We got to have music too."

My harmonica was stuck to my lips, and I kept my hands on it. Between it and my mittens, my face was still covered.

I tried to tell Mr. Schultz to go away, but the harmonica got in the way of talking. All I could do was mumble into the harmonica.

"Wait," Ma said to Mr. Schultz as he wrapped his bearlike arms around me.

However, he had already hoisted me into the air. "Here comes the band," he announced as he carried me over in front of the crowd by the fire.

I wanted to run into the house, but Ah Sam whispered, "Ursula, we need you."

I tried to curl up into a little ball as I muttered from around my harmonica, "I can't."

Ah Sam turned to the audience. "Don't we need our band?" he asked them.

They clapped real loud. At first I didn't know what for. My eyes darted around.

"Huzzah!" shouted Susie, and gave me the secret pirate sign for welcome.

It took awhile for it to sink in: All the applause and smiling faces were for me. And they kept it up until I felt my harmonica get loose between my lips.

In all the ruckus, I hadn't noticed my scarf was untied; but then it slid right off my shoulders. I didn't bother to pick it up, though.

To my crew I gave the secret pirate sign for "No quarter." Pirate Ursula was back. And whether she was ramming Deadly Dan the Viceroy or playing the harmonica, Pirate Ursula did everything at full speed and without mercy.

"I'm ready anytime you are, Ursula," Ah Sam said.

I began to play sea chanteys, since Pirate Ursula had returned. At the same time, Ah Sam started to juggle the balls. When he added the knives, they flashed in the sunlight.

Ah Sam was fearless as he snatched knives from the air and tossed them back up again.

"Does anyone in the audience have anything they want to add to my collection?" Ah Sam invited.

Tom threw in his big hat, and it began to dance with everything else. A huge turnip joined it. I wondered who had been carrying that thing around.

Mr. Schultz jerked off a boot, and soon that was bobbing merrily up and down too.

"Who'd have thought my boot was so talented?" Mr. Schultz hooted in delight as he wrapped his scarf around his stockinged foot.

And I saw that Ah Sam was right. It didn't matter how big or small a circus was. The magic came from inside. And it could touch even ordinary things like boots and turnips and hats and make them dance in the air like they were alive.

When Ah Sam signaled me to stop, he told the audience, "What is a circus without at least one animal? So now, especially for Ursula, we have a Chinese lion."

And from our station Lung rolled out a ball big as him. Prancing behind him was the Chinese lion. It looked more like a big shaggy dog with long fur, but it had lots of teeth.

When Lung had stepped out of the way, the lion hopped on top of the ball. Then it rolled all around and did tricks. It even scratched itself and tried to bite fleas like a real lion. In the meantime Lung and Ah Sam had been setting up rows of poles. For its finale the lion leaped from one tall pole to another. When the lion hopped down from the ball, Ah Loo and Ah Bing got out of the costume.

They were sure talented folk. I never would have guessed it was two people doing the jumps together.

"And now for our final trick," Ah Sam said. "It is something all new. No one has ever seen it before," he proclaimed, and his cousins started to twist themselves into all kinds of shapes. They didn't seem to have a bone in their bodies.

Ah Sam whispered to me, "This is their new trick." And they began to turn into letters. Ah Bing became a "T" and Ah Loo became an "H" and somehow Lung became an "A."

Slowly they spelled out, "Thank You, Ursula."

The applause sounded like a dozen thunderstorms now. I felt my face burning a bright red.

Ah Sam nudged me. "In China performers thank the audience, too," he said. So he and I and his cousins faced the audience and began to clap.

"Did you plan this all the time?" I whispered back.

"It just happened," Ah Sam insisted innocently. "Blame it on the magic—circus magic."

And I left it at that. Because sometimes the magic changes you on the outside and turns a cook into a juggler.

And sometimes it changes you on the inside and turns a monster back into a person.

Think Critically

1. What is the theme of "When the Circus Came to Town"? THEME

2. Why does Ursula say that she feels "like parrots had landed" in her home when she sees Ah Sam's cousins? FIGURATIVE LANGUAGE

3. How do Ah Sam and his cousins turn ordinary objects into "magic"? MAKE INFERENCES

4. Ah Sam helps Ursula become part of the community again. When have you helped someone overcome a challenge? MAKE CONNECTIONS

5. **WRITE** What emotional change does Ursula go through in the story? Use information from the story to support your answer. EXTENDED RESPONSE

About the Author
Laurence Yep

Laurence Yep was born in San Francisco, California, in 1948. When he was eighteen, he published his first story, getting paid only one penny per word. He has always been interested in writing about people who are treated as if they are outsiders and strangers. He also likes to include the characters' use of imagination as themes in his stories. Laurence Yep teaches and writes in San Francisco.

About the Illustrator
Michelle Chang

Michelle Chang was born in Korea but grew up in New York City. She has studied art since childhood. As an adult, she has worked as an interior designer and an illustrator. Her artwork has appeared in many magazines as well as in children's books. People describe her artwork as "rich," "dreamy," and filled with "a spirit of warmth."

www.harcourtschool.com/storytown

Poetry

POETRY beat

illustrated by Aaron Meshon

Limerick

There was a Young Lady whose chin
resembled the point of a pin;
So she had it made sharp, and purchased a harp,
And played several tunes with her chin.

—*Edward Lear*

194

Take a Bow!

Sensing my mood
of solitude
he rests

waiting for a sign
or the right time
to suggest

a deep bluesy beat
or a giddy Bach suite
unless

we choose to rock and roll
and lose control.
Oh yes,

You are the best!
My favorite fellow
my honey-yellow
cello

—*Anna Levine*

Summer Hummers

Bees, you work so hard,
but your buzz makes me sleepy.
Backyard lullaby.
—*Linda Sue Park*

Connections

Comparing Texts

1. In "When the Circus Came to Town," the acrobats transform themselves into unusual characters. Into what kind of character might you transform yourself?

2. Compare the poet's feelings in "Take a Bow!" to Ursula's feelings about the circus. What theme do these selections both suggest?

3. The characters you read about had extraordinary talent. Describe someone whom you think has an extraordinary talent.

Vocabulary Review

Word Sort

Work in a group. Sort the Vocabulary Words into categories. Discuss your sorted words with your group, explaining your choices. Then choose at least one Vocabulary Word from each category. Write a sentence for each word.

Nouns	Verbs	Adjectives

fret

assured

nudged

outlandish

ruckus

proclaimed

Fluency Practice

Repeated Reading

Read aloud page 182 of "When the Circus Came to Town," thinking about how you would speak if you were as nervous as Ursula. Then reread the page to a partner, and ask for feedback on your expression.

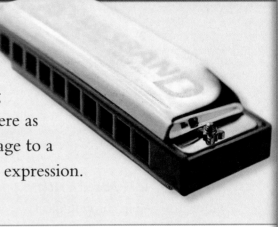

Writing

Write a Poem

Write a poem about music. Use one of the poems you read as a model. You might write about a particular musical instrument, as the author of "Take a Bow!" does.

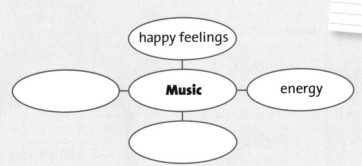

My Writing Checklist

Writing Trait ▶ Ideas

✔ My poem is focused on the theme of music.

✔ I used a graphic organizer to plan my writing.

✔ I chose an appropriate form for my poem.

Big 💡 Idea
Nonfiction texts are organized by text structures.

Enduring ❗ Understanding
Events arranged in chronological order are sequenced events.

Essential ❓ Question
How can readers identify the sequencing of events in narrative nonfiction?

Spelling Words

Words with VCCV: Different Medial Consonants

entire	wisdom
hospital	journey
public	condition
combine	whisper
golden	identify
chimney	establish
pretzel	furnace
survive	capture
absorb	marvelous
turmoil	nursery

Challenge

utensils	velvet
linger	cascade
victor	

Fluency

Phrasing

Comprehension

 Text Structure: Sequence

 Use Graphic Organizers

Robust Vocabulary

- crucial
- crisis
- maneuvered
- perseverance
- encountered
- persuading
- appealed
- destiny

Writing

- Biography
- Organization

198

Lesson 8

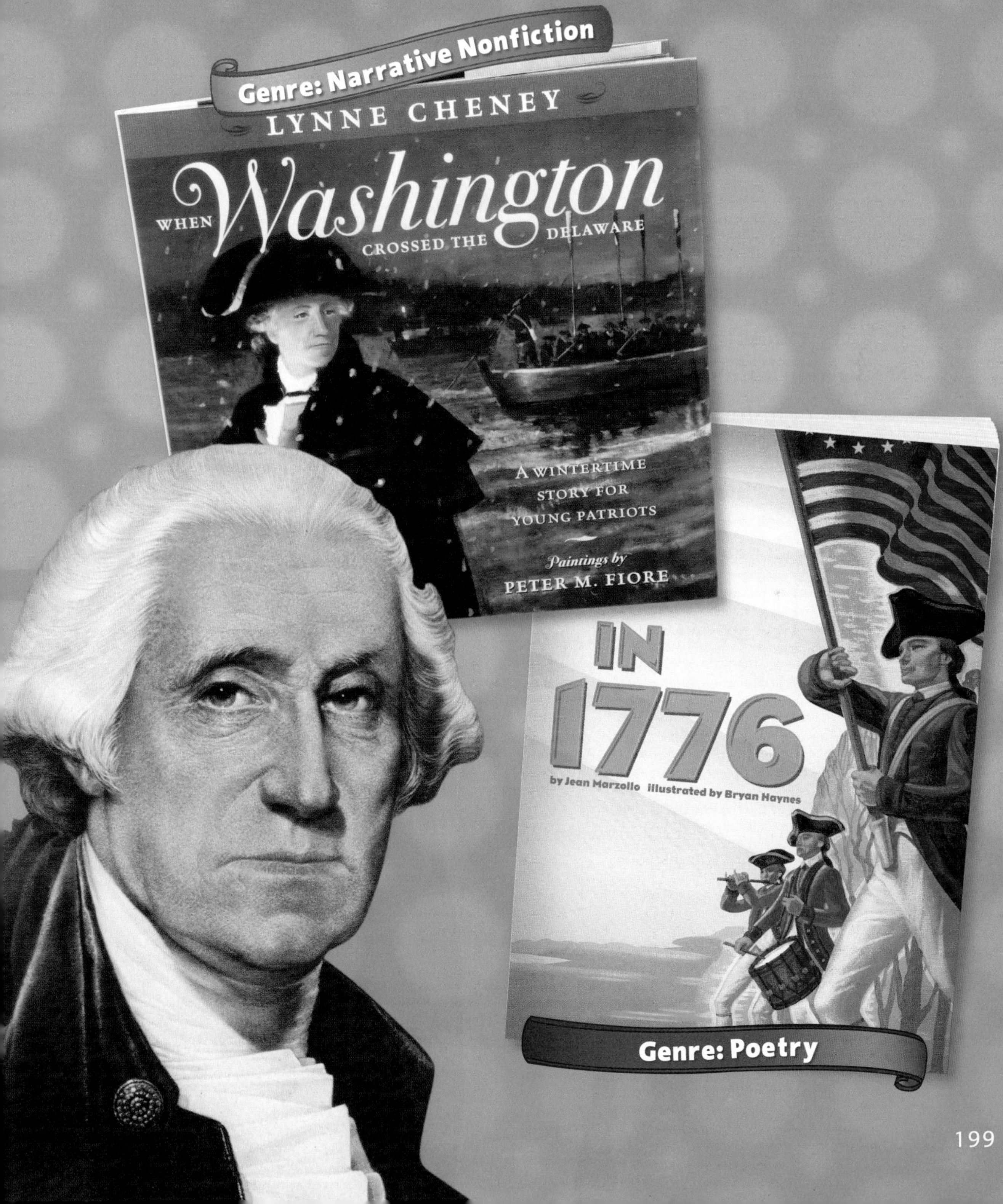
Genre: Narrative Nonfiction
LYNNE CHENEY
WHEN Washington CROSSED THE DELAWARE
A WINTERTIME STORY FOR YOUNG PATRIOTS
Paintings by
PETER M. FIORE
IN 1776
by Jean Marzollo illustrated by Bryan Haynes
Genre: Poetry

Text Structure: Sequence

Authors of nonfiction text organize their ideas in certain ways, called **text structures**. One kind of text structure is **sequence**. In texts with this structure, events may be arranged in chronological, or time, order. Authors of historical texts often use this text structure to present real events in the order in which they happened.

| First Event | → | Next Event | → | Next Event | → | Last Event |

Tip

As you read, look for dates and other points in time that tell you what happened first, next, and so on.

200

The events in the paragraph below are organized in chronological order. Read the paragraph. Then look at the graphic organizer. It shows the sequence of events in the paragraph.

George Washington was born in 1732. At the age of fifteen, he became a surveyor. This job paid well and helped Washington learn why some pieces of land were more valuable than others. As good land came up for sale, he bought what he could. By the time Washington was twenty, he owned more than 2,000 acres. During that same year, Washington joined the colonial troops.

First Event	**Next Event**	**Next Event**	**Last Event**
George Washington was born in 1732.	At the age of fifteen, he became a surveyor.	He bought good land that came up for sale.	By the age of twenty, he owned 2,000 acres of land.

Try This!

Look back at the paragraph. How old was George Washington when he joined the colonial troops? How do you know?

  www.harcourtschool.com/storytown

Vocabulary

Build Robust Vocabulary

persuading

crucial

maneuvered

encountered

crisis

appealed

perseverance

destiny

Bunker Hill

In 1775, fighting between British troops and American colonists began. In the battles of Concord and Lexington, about one hundred colonists lost their lives. Word of the fighting spread rapidly, **persuading** hundreds of colonists to gather outside Boston. They were ready to fight. Both the British and the Americans felt that occupying the hills outside Boston was **crucial.** The Americans took a position at Breed's Hill.

The Americans were poorly trained and had inferior weapons, but they had great spirit.

202

Soon, the British troops **maneuvered** into positions around the hill and attacked. The Americans **encountered** heavy fire but held their ground. In time, though, the colonists faced a **crisis**. They were running out of gunpowder. American leaders **appealed** to the soldiers to use their ammunition sparingly. The troops did as they were asked, but eventually ran out of ammunition. Despite their **perseverance**, the colonists lost the battle. However, they still felt that it was their **destiny** to win the war.

The fight for Breed's Hill became known as the Battle of Bunker Hill.

 www.harcourtschool.com/storytown

Word Champion

Your mission this week is to use the Vocabulary Words outside your classroom. Use as many of the words as you can when you talk with family members and friends. For example, you might tell a family member that it is crucial for you go to the library to complete a school assignment. Write in your vocabulary journal the sentences you used that contained the words.

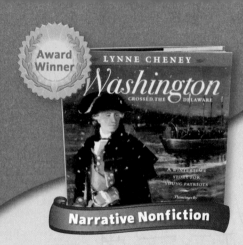

Award Winner

LYNNE CHENEY

Washington
CROSSED THE DELAWARE

A WINTERTIME STORY FOR YOUNG PATRIOTS

Paintings by

Narrative Nonfiction

Genre Study

Narrative nonfiction tells about people, events, or places that are real. As you read, look for

- events told in time order.

- factual information that tells a story.

First Event

↓

Next Event

↓

Next Event

↓

Last Event

Comprehension Strategy

Use graphic organizers like the one above to show the order of events in the text.

WHEN

Was

CROSSED THE

hington

DELAWARE

by Lynne Cheney

paintings by Peter M. Fiore

It was November 1776, a time of trouble for our young country. We were fighting for our independence from Britain, and the war was not going well. The British had defeated General George Washington and his men on Long Island, had driven them out of New York, and were pursuing them across New Jersey.

George Washington was discouraged. How could the Americans, who were mostly new to fighting, ever hope to defeat the well-trained redcoats?

"The rebels fly before us."

WILLIAM BAMFORD, CAPTAIN, BRITISH ARMY

The Americans retreated through cold and rain. Many had no jackets to keep them warm. Many had no shoes and marched with rags wrapped around their feet. Everyone was hungry.

In early December the Americans made it across the Delaware River into Pennsylvania. Under General Washington's orders they had taken every boat they could find with them, so they knew they were safe from the British for a while. But they were sick, exhausted, and cold.

Even when the struggle seemed hopeless, George Washington did not give up. On the other side of the river the British had stationed Hessians—German soldiers the British had hired to fight for them. The Hessians didn't have much respect for American soldiers. They didn't think the Americans would do anything bold or daring— and so George Washington decided on a bold and daring course.

He called a meeting of his generals and worked out a plan. On Christmas night American troops would cross the Delaware River in several different places. Before dawn on December 26 they would attack the Hessians at Trenton, New Jersey.

Washington warned his officers to keep the plan a secret. It could only succeed, he believed, if the Americans caught the Hessians by surprise.

206

Also crucial to success was the spirit of the American troops. Beaten down as they were, could they fight another battle?

A man named Thomas Paine had marched with the Americans as they retreated across New Jersey. Now he came up with words to encourage them. "These are the times that try men's souls," he wrote. "The summer soldier and the sunshine patriot will, in this crisis, shrink from the service of their country; but he that stands it *now*, deserves the love and thanks of man and woman."

In the camps along the Delaware, George Washington's men read Paine's words and drew strength from them for the battle ahead.

On Christmas night, 1776, General Washington led twenty-four hundred men, the main body of his army, to a crossing point about nine miles upstream from Trenton. There the soldiers crowded into the large black boats that would take them to the opposite shore.

The night was cold, and the men faced a difficult crossing. They had to break through ice to get the boats into the river. They had to fend off large chunks of floating ice once they were underway.

But Washington had seafarers with him that night who knew how to navigate treacherous waters. The sailors of Massachusetts's Marblehead Battalion maneuvered boat after boat across the icy river. As soon as they got one group of men to the New Jersey shore, they returned to pick up another.

Washington arrived on the New Jersey side of the Delaware in the early hours of the crossing. Wrapped in his cloak, he watched his cold, wet soldiers make their way onto land. Their spirits were good, but he was worried. The crossing was taking longer than he had planned.

Washington's army had eighteen cannon, and getting them across the river was especially hard. A gun with its carriage and ammunition could weigh two thousand pounds, and loading it on and off a slippery ferry was slow and dangerous work.

Downstream two of Washington's commanders also struggled to get men and guns across the river. In the end neither General James Ewing nor Colonel John Cadwalader could get through the ice on the Delaware. They had to give up on the idea of fighting at Trenton.

But at three o'clock in the morning George Washington's crossing succeeded. The last gun was onshore, and the general and his men prepared for the nine-mile march to Trenton.

"*Perseverance* accomplished what at first seemed impossible."

HENRY KNOX, COLONEL, CONTINENTAL ARMY

It was four o'clock in the morning before the army was ready to move out, hours later than Washington had planned. He had hoped to attack the Hessians while it was still dark, but now the sun would be up before the Americans reached Trenton. Would an attack in daylight still be a surprise?

But there was no turning back. Through cold and sleet the American troops moved along icy roads toward Trenton. Washington and his officers rode alongside the men, encouraging them onward.

"*Remember now what you are about to fight for.*"

GENERAL GEORGE WASHINGTON

211

When the Americans encountered the first Hessians, it was clear that the surprise had worked. The startled Hessians retreated. The Americans pressed forward with such determination that the Hessians had little time to organize a defense. When American artillery began to bombard them, the German soldiers had no choice but to abandon the streets of Trenton and withdraw to an orchard nearby.

Nineteen-year-old Captain Alexander Hamilton led one of the companies firing on the Hessians. He would later sign the U.S. Constitution and help insure that the states accepted it. He would become our country's first secretary of the treasury.

Another soldier fighting that day was eighteen-year-old Lieutenant James Monroe. When the Hessians managed to get two of their cannon into operation, Monroe was one of the officers who charged the guns. He was badly wounded, but he would live to become our nation's fifth president.

The Hessians tried an attack of their own. With drums beating they marched from the orchard toward the center of town. But the Americans were strong. In the fight that followed, the Hessian commander, Colonel Johann Rall, was mortally wounded and many of his men were killed.

The rest of the Hessians retreated, but the Americans soon had them surrounded. Two German regiments decided it was time to quit fighting, and they lowered their flags to the ground. Then the third—and last—regiment surrendered.

Two hours from the time it had started, the Battle of Trenton was over. With few losses of their own the Americans had captured nearly nine hundred Hessians. After many defeats they had won a great victory.

"This is a glorious day for our country."

GENERAL GEORGE WASHINGTON

Most of Washington's men had the right to go home at the end of the year, but Washington needed them to stay. Persuading them to keep fighting would be hard, he knew. He could see how tired they were as they transported their Hessian prisoners across the Delaware to Pennsylvania. He could see that they were cold. Many marched without shoes and left bloody footprints in the snow.

Once his men were back in New Jersey, Washington promised extra pay to those who would serve longer. And he appealed to their love for their country. This was an hour of destiny, he told one regiment, a time that would decide America's fate. If they wanted their country to be free, they had to keep fighting.

Drums rolled. A few of the men stepped forward, then more, and then more. Many of Washington's battle-tested soldiers resolved to stay at his side.

There were thousands of British and Hessian troops gathering at Princeton, New Jersey, a pretty college town northeast of Trenton. Certain that they would soon attack, Washington sent out a call for more forces. Veteran fighters joined him, as did many men who had never fought before.

Washington ordered most of his troops to line up along a ridge on the south side of Assunpink Creek. He also sent a force to the north side of the creek, where the British and Hessians were advancing. Washington ordered these men to slow the enemy down.

"I pressed against the shoulder of the General's horse and in contact with the boot of the General. The horse stood as firm as the rider."

JOHN HOWLAND, PRIVATE,
LIPPITT'S RHODE ISLAND REGIMENT

Near evening on January 2, 1777, the troops sent to delay the British had done all they could. They ran for a narrow bridge that would take them back across the Assunpink. As they crowded onto it, they saw General Washington at the far end. The enemy was right behind them, but the sight of their commander, firm and steady, gave them courage.

General Charles Cornwallis, the British commander, thought he had Washington trapped. He thought he could wait until morning to attack the Americans.

But Washington had other plans. He knew that Cornwallis had brought most of his forces with him. That meant there would be far fewer of the enemy in Princeton, and so Washington readied his army for a march that would take them around Cornwallis's troops and toward the college town.

He ordered some of his men to stay behind. They were to keep campfires burning and to make noises with their axes and shovels so that the British wouldn't realize what the Americans were doing.

About one o'clock in the morning on January 3, Washington and the main body of his army moved out. Cannon wheels were muffled with rags. Officers whispered orders. The Americans did everything they could to be quiet, and their plan worked. It was dawn before Cornwallis realized they were gone.

The morning was clear and cold as Washington and his men neared Princeton. In farmland outside the town a part of the American army encountered British troops. During the fight that followed, many of the Americans fell. The dazed survivors retreated.

Washington rushed to rally his troops, and astride a white horse he led them forward, taking them to within thirty yards of the British line. American muskets were pointed at the British. British arms were leveled at the Americans. Washington was in between. Once the two sides started firing, it seemed impossible that he would survive.

Muskets roared, but when the smoke cleared, General Washington was safe. His troops held steady, but the British line broke and fell back.

The Americans advanced. British officers tried to rally the redcoats, but soon they began to flee. When the American troops ran after them, Washington paused just long enough to give a few orders. Then, spurring his horse, he joined in the pursuit.

> ## *"Away, my dear colonel, and bring up the troops— the day is our own."*
>
> GENERAL GEORGE WASHINGTON TO
> COLONEL JOHN FITZGERALD

Within a few hours the battle was over. George Washington and his men had once again defeated the greatest military power in the world.

General Washington and his men had stood with their country in a time of crisis. When they were cold and hungry, they did not quit. When the conflict was hard, they fought on. And when they won, the victory was sweet. News of Trenton and Princeton spread across the land, lifting the spirits of patriots everywhere. Many a battle lay ahead, but now Americans could think of winning their war for independence. Now they could imagine that their great struggle would have a glorious end.

Think Critically

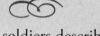

1 Two young American soldiers described in "When Washington Crossed the Delaware" later became important figures in United States history. Who were they, and what office did each hold?
NOTE DETAILS

2 After the Battle of Trenton, Washington's soldiers were tired, sick, and cold. They agreed to keep fighting, even though they did not have to do so. Why did they make this decision? DRAW CONCLUSIONS

3 How did the author organize the information in "When Washington Crossed the Delaware"? Is this text structure appropriate for the topic? Explain your answer. TEXT STRUCTURE: SEQUENCE

4 Why did the author include quotations from people who were present when George Washington and his troops crossed the Delaware? What effect do these first-person observations have on readers today? AUTHOR'S CRAFT

5 **WRITE** Do you think the Americans could have won the Revolutionary War without George Washington's leadership? Explain. Use details and information from the selection to support your answer. SHORT RESPONSE

About the Author
Lynne Cheney

Lynne Cheney has loved history for as long as she can remember. She feels that it is important for young people to study history and understand how the events of the past affect their lives. Lynne Cheney has written many articles and books for both children and adults. She is married to Dick Cheney, the 46th Vice President of the United States.

GO online www.harcourtschool.com/storytown

219

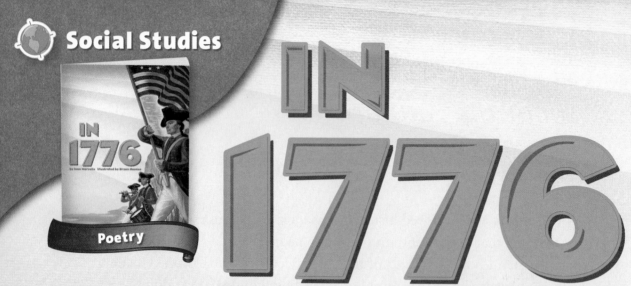

IN 1776

Poetry

by Jean Marzollo illustrated by Bryan Haynes

In seventeen hundred and seventy-five,
A long, long time ago,
Great Britain ruled America—
There was some trouble, though.

The colonists were angry
Because they had no say
When the British king gave orders
Three thousand miles away.

The king said, "Pay more taxes!"
Americans said, "No!"
Some even told the British,
"It's time for you to go."

The British marched from Boston;
The farmers didn't run;
In Lexington and Concord
The fighting was begun.

In seventeen hundred and seventy-six,
Excitement filled the air;
But what the colonists needed
Was a statement to declare.

So their leaders met in Philly,
In June and in July,
They picked some men to tell the king,
"We must be free—here's why!"

The committee talked and wrote for days;
At times it wasn't fun;
Then Thomas Jefferson penned the words,
And the Declaration was done.

*We hold these truths to be self-evident,
that all men are created equal, that they
are endowed by their Creator with certain
unalienable Rights, that among these are
Life, Liberty, and the pursuit of Happiness.*

The Declaration of Independence
Said everyone has the right
To life, liberty, and the pursuit of happiness;
For this, men said, we'll fight!

On the Fourth of July, in seventy-six,
After a long and heated morn,
The Declaration was approved,
And the U.S.A. was born.

Americans had their statement—
Ideals worth fighting for,
A country of their very own
With liberty at the core.

American forces continued to fight;
George Washington was the chief.
Through heat and cold, they won the war . . .

And felt a great relief.

No longer ruled by a bossy king
On a distant British throne,
Americans voted in eighty-nine
For a president of their own.

Can you guess who won the vote?
Can you guess who won the day?
The winner was George Washington—
Number One in the U.S.A.

The war was over long ago;
The U.S. and Britain are now good friends.
The Declaration still guides us all;
The struggle for liberty never ends.

Connections

Comparing Texts

1. How do the events in "When Washington Crossed the Delaware" connect to the rights you enjoy?

2. How are "When Washington Crossed the Delaware" and "In 1776" alike? How are they different?

3. Henry Fox, a colonel in the Continental Army, said, "Perseverance accomplished what at first seemed impossible." To what other event could you apply this quote?

Vocabulary Review

Word Pairs

Work with a partner. Write the Vocabulary Words on index cards. Place the cards face down. Take turns flipping over two cards and writing a sentence using both words. Read aloud the sentence to your partner. If you use the words correctly, you keep the cards. The player with more cards at the end wins.

> Jenn appealed to her sister, saying it was her destiny to have the top bunk.

crucial

crisis

maneuvered

perseverance

encountered

persuading

appealed

destiny

Fluency Practice

Partner Reading

With a partner, choose a paragraph from "When Washington Crossed the Delaware." Read it aloud as your partner follows along. Use the punctuation marks in the text to help your phrasing. Switch roles with your partner, and repeat the process. Give each other feedback about your phrasing.

Writing

Write a Narrative Paragraph

Write a paragraph describing how George Washington led his soldiers across the Delaware River on Christmas night, 1776. Tell about the challenges he and the troops overcame.

My Writing Checklist

Writing Trait ▶ Organization

✔ I used details to develop the topic.

✔ I used a graphic organizer to organize the events.

✔ I used information from the selection in my writing.

| First Event | → | Next Event | → | Next Event | → | Last Event |

Big Idea
Text structure assists in organizing nonfiction texts.

Enduring Understanding
The readers' understanding of nonfiction text is based on the identification of the text structure.

Essential Question
How do readers use a text structure of sequence of events?

Spelling Words

Words with VCCCV

congress	umbrella
English	merchandise
fortress	remembrance
expression	concrete
conclude	goggles
complain	portray
complex	technique
distrust	accomplish
contribute	function
explode	membrane

Challenge

orchestra	apprentice
upholster	appraise
embroidery	

Fluency

Phrasing

Comprehension

 Text Structure: Sequence

 Use Graphic Organizers

Robust Vocabulary

scholars
specialized
gesture
envisioned
proportion
resisted

Writing

- Summary
- Organization

Lesson 9

Genre: Narrative Nonfiction

LEONARDO'S HORSE

Jean Fritz ◆ Hudson Talbott

Bellerophon AND Pegasus
A GREEK MYTH

Genre: Myth

225

Text Structure: Sequence

Authors of nonfiction texts may organize information in a **sequence text structure**. In texts with this structure, the author tells events in chronological order, the order in which they happened. You can use a graphic organizer like this one to keep track of the sequence of events in a text.

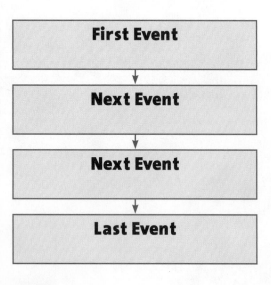

First Event
↓
Next Event
↓
Next Event
↓
Last Event

Tip

Knowing the order in which events happened can help you understand why they happened.

226

Read the paragraph below. Then look at the graphic organizer. It shows the chronological order of events telling how the Tower of Pisa began to lean.

In 1173, builders in Pisa, Italy, began construction of an eight-story marble bell tower. By the time the builders finished the first three stories, the ground under the tower had begun to sink and tilt. Workers kept on building, however, and by 1370, the tower was complete. The ground sank a little more with each passing year. Today, the Tower of Pisa still stands, but it leans 14 feet to one side.

First Event
In 1173, builders began the tower.

↓

Next Event
After the first three stories were built, the ground began to sink.

↓

Next Event
In 1370, the tower was complete.

↓

Last Event
The tower still stands, but it leans.

Try This!

Look back at the paragraph. What happened to the tower after it was completed? What words and phrases about points in time did the author use to help you understand what happened?

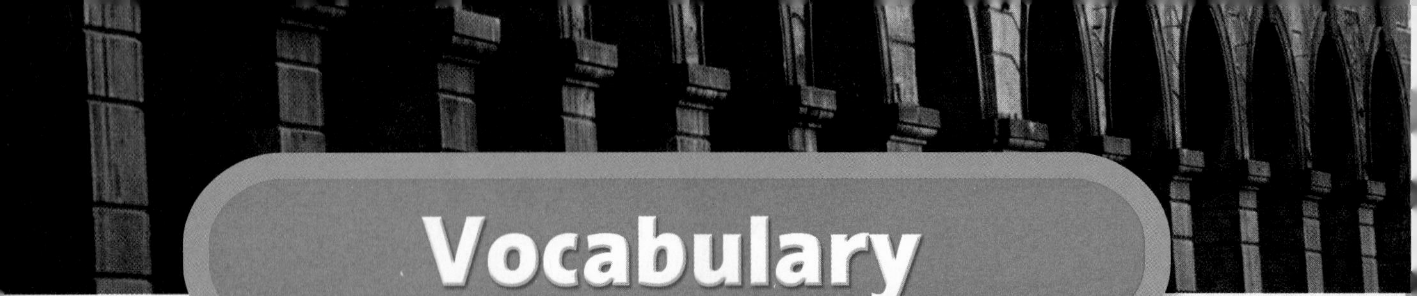

Vocabulary

Build Robust Vocabulary

- gesture
- specialized
- proportion
- envisioned
- resisted
- scholars

Leonardo da Vinci

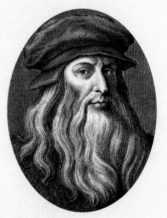

Leonardo da Vinci was born in Vinci, Italy, in 1452. He died in 1519.

It is a **gesture** of respect to Leonardo da Vinci's skill that so many people have **specialized** in studying his work.

Leonardo da Vinci left behind dozens of notebooks filled with drawings and notes. They show his interest in many things, including human anatomy. He studied the way the body is put together and what makes it move. This careful study helped him capture accurate human **proportion** in his paintings and drawings. The notebooks also contain sketches of his inventions. One was a kind of helicopter he **envisioned**.

In da Vinci's time, most artists used traditional paint techniques. Artworks made with these techniques **resisted** the effects of time and weather. However, da Vinci tried new techniques and paints. Sometimes his methods were not successful, and the paint flaked off years after it was applied. Fortunately, enough of his work remains so that people today can learn from and appreciate it.

Scholars have wondered for years just who the woman was in this painting known as *Mona Lisa*.

GO online www.harcourtschool.com/storytown

Word Scribe

This week, your task is to use the Vocabulary Words in your writing. For example, you could write about a new game or gadget you have envisioned. Write about as many Vocabulary Words as you can. Share your writing with your classmates.

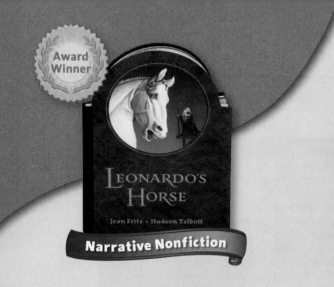

Award Winner

LEONARDO'S HORSE

Jean Fritz • Hudson Talbott

Narrative Nonfiction

Genre Study

Narrative nonfiction tells about people, events, or places that are real. As you read, look for

- factual information that tells a story.

- events told in time order.

First Event
↓
Next Event
↓
Next Event
↓
Final Event

Comprehension Strategy

Use graphic organizers like the one above to show the order of events in the text.

LEONARDO'S HORSE

by Jean Fritz   illustrated by Hudson Talbott

From the time he was a young boy in Italy, Leonardo da Vinci
asked questions about everything. Because of his curiosity, Leonardo
accomplished many things during his lifetime. He created some
of the most famous paintings in the world. He was also known
as a musician, an engineer, an architect, an astronomer, and a
philosopher. However, one important project remained unfinished at
the time of Leonardo's death—a larger-than-life sculpture of a horse.

231

Leonardo da Vinci

Charles Dent

Leonardo has been remembered for hundreds of years, especially for his paintings *Mona Lisa* and *The Last Supper*. But not for his horse. That story was almost forgotten until 1977, when it was told in a magazine. And the right man read it. His name was Charles Dent. And Charlie loved art—reading about it, making it, looking at it, collecting it. Leonardo would have liked Charlie. They were both dreamers with big dreams. Yet Leonardo may have been envious. Charlie did what Leonardo had always longed to do. He flew, soaring through the sky like a bird freed from its cage. Charlie was an airline pilot, and whenever he traveled, he looked for art to take home.

The more Charlie read about Leonardo and his horse, the more he cared about Leonardo. When he read that Leonardo died still grieving for his horse, Charlie couldn't stand it. Right then he had the biggest dream of his life.

"Let's give Leonardo his horse," he said. It would be a gift from the American people to the people of Italy.

But could he really give Leonardo his horse? Could anyone? Charlie went to see famous scholars who had specialized in the study of Leonardo. When he came home, Charlie was smiling; he could go ahead.

232

But where would he build his horse? He needed a special building, he decided—a round building shaped like a dome, tall enough for a horse. On top there would be windows to let in the light.

Charlie didn't know a thing about domes, but luckily he found a man who did. When at last the Dome was finished, Charlie hung the pictures he had collected on the walls and arranged other art objects around the room.

All that was needed was the horse.

Every day Charlie could see the horse more clearly. Wherever he went, he carried a small piece of wax or a piece of clay and made miniature models of the horse. But he needed to be around real horses. He borrowed two champion Morgan horses and studied them for months, running his hands over their bodies so he could feel where the muscles and bones were. He measured every inch of the horses just as Leonardo would have done.

Then, in 1988, he began the eight-foot model of the horse. Over the wooden skeleton, he applied one thousand pounds of clay. To hold the horse steady, a post ran through the belly of the horse to the ground. To fill the belly, the horse was stuffed with slats of wood and plastic foam. So now the Dome had a clay horse—his left foreleg raised and bent, his right rear leg off the ground. Free. The muscles in his hindquarters were tense, his ears pointed forward, his nostrils were beginning to flare.

By 1993 the eight-foot plaster model of the clay horse was completed and ready to be cast into a twenty-four-foot bronze horse.

For that it would have to be sent to a foundry where it could be enlarged; a twenty-four-foot clay model sculpted; then the twenty-four-foot bronze horse cast.

In 1994, however, the people at the Dome were less concerned about the horse than they were worried about Charlie. He became sick and no one knew what was the matter. Then he was told that he had Lou Gehrig's disease and it could not be cured. He would not be alive when the horse arrived in Milan. All Charlie said was what he always said: He had never been interested in taking credit for the horse; the gift of the horse was a gesture of friendship from the American people to the Italian people, a salute across the centuries to Leonardo.

On December 13, Charlie's family and friends gathered around his bedside and promised him that the horse would be finished.

On Christmas morning 1994, Charlie died.

On August 1, 1995, the horse was ready to go to the foundry. He was hoisted into a van, tied, padded, and driven off for his great adventure.

At the Tallix Foundry in Beacon, New York, his transformation began. He was enlarged and cut up into sixty separate pieces. They were laid against the wall of the foundry while the Dome people gathered to watch the pieces being put together. It was certainly a huge horse, but was it as grand as Charlie had envisioned?

The Dome friends walked quietly around the horse. They seemed uneasy.

The horse wasn't right.

Art experts were called in. They shook their heads. No, the horse wasn't right.

He looked awkward. Out of proportion. One of his rear legs appeared to be short. His eyes were not exactly parallel. He needed help.

Fortunately, a talented sculptor from New York City, Nina Akamu, agreed to try to fix him. But when she went to work on the twenty-four-foot horse, she found that the cementlike plaster that covered him resisted change. No matter how hard she tried, she couldn't fix him.

Everyone recognized that there was only one thing to do, but it took a while for anyone to say it out loud. Yet it had to be said. Nina would have to start from scratch and make another horse. For some, the idea of doing away with Charlie's horse was almost more than they could bear, yet they all knew that Charlie would want his horse to be as perfect as possible.

The horse would always be Charlie's dream, but as soon as Nina went to work, he had to become her horse, too. She had studied in Italy for eleven years. Her favorite Renaissance artist was Verrochio, Leonardo's teacher. It was lucky that she was there to carry on with Charlie's dream.

First Nina made an eight-foot clay horse. From it a second eight-foot horse was made of plaster. Using the plaster model as a guide, a twenty-four-foot horse was made in clay.

Everyone went to work to get the horse exactly right. Finally he was ready to be cast in bronze.

FROM CLAY • TO PLASTER • TO BRONZE

1 Thin metal pieces called shims were stuck in the clay to divide the horse into sections.

2 Liquid rubber was sprayed onto the horse to make the molds.

3 Each rubber-coated section was removed . . .

4 . . . then filled with plaster.

5 Each section hardened into a plaster mold.

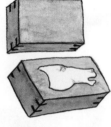

6 The top and bottom of a box were filled with a mixture of sand and cement. The mold was pressed firmly into the bottom, and the top closed, encasing the mold in the mixture.

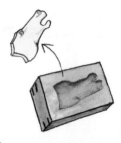

7 When the mixture hardened, the box was opened and the mold removed.

8 The box was closed again and molten bronze was poured through a hole in the top to fill the impression left by the plaster mold.

9 After the bronze cooled, the box was opened and out came a bronze piece in the exact shape of the plaster mold.

10 One by one the bronze pieces were welded together, and the horse began to take shape.

238

But how could such a large bronze sculpture stand on two legs? First they built a steel skeleton inside the body of the horse to support the sides, and then they inserted steel tubes in the two legs. The tubes were bolted to steel anchor plates below the hooves and embedded in concrete.

Finally, the horse was complete. Everyone stood back and looked up at him. They agreed that he was ready for his new home.

239

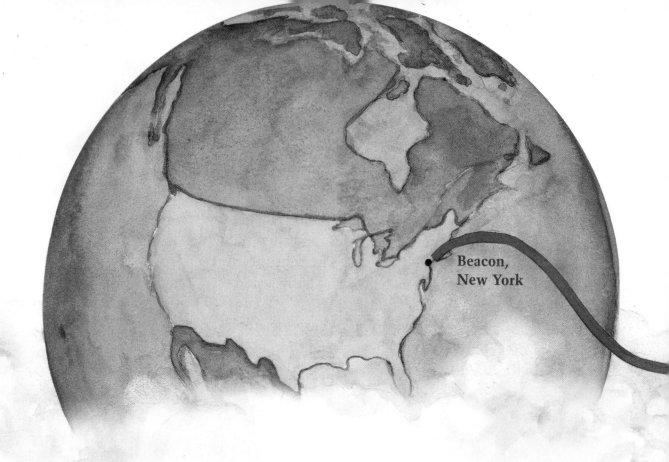

Beacon,
New York

If Leonardo had finished his horse, he would only have had to move it from the vineyard where he worked to the front of the duke's palace. Charlie's horse had to cross the ocean to Italy. But he was too big.

So he was cut up into separate pieces, crated, and flown to Milan, where the Tallix people and the Dome people waited to reassemble him. Workers would crawl through a trapdoor in the horse's belly to fasten the pieces together.

He would stand on a pedestal in a small park in front of Milan's famous racetrack, within whinnying distance of the racing stable.

On June 27, 1999, the horse took off.

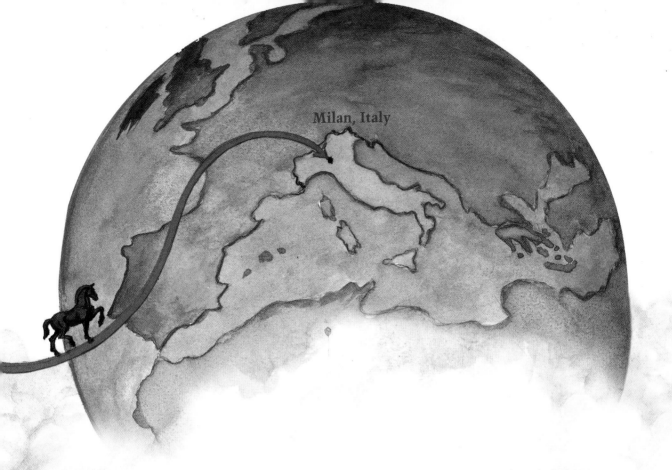

September 10, 1999, was the date set for the unveiling of the statue, exactly five hundred years to the day since the French invaded Milan and destroyed Leonardo's horse.

An enormous cloth was spread over the horse so he couldn't be seen. Two huge clusters of blue and white balloons were attached to either end of the cloth. On the pupil of one eye of the horse, Nina had written in tiny letters *Leonardo da Vinci*. On the other eye she had written *Charles Dent*. She had put her own name in the curly mane of the horse.

As a large crowd of Italians and Americans took their seats, the horse stayed in hiding. Speeches were made. The Italian national anthem was sung. Then the American national anthem.

Finally the strings anchoring the balloons were cut and the cloth rose into the sky.

Ahhhhhhh!

At last Leonardo's horse was home.

Think Critically

1 How does the organization of information in "Leonardo's Horse" help readers understand the text? TEXT STRUCTURE: SEQUENCE

2 Explain what happened after the sculpture was completed. SUMMARIZE

3 Would Leonardo have agreed with the decision to start over and design a horse that had the proper proportions? Explain. SPECULATE

4 If you wanted to design a huge sculpture for your school or community, what would you create, and where would you want the sculpture to stand? MAKE CONNECTIONS

5 **WRITE** Write a note from Nina Akamu to Charlie Dent explaining why the team decided to start over with a new design. Use details and information from the selection to support your explanation. SHORT RESPONSE

ABOUT THE AUTHOR
Jean Fritz

Jean Fritz was born in Hankow, China, in 1915. As a child, she kept a journal and read many books. As an adult, Jean Fritz became a children's book author, and she has now been writing for more than fifty years. When she works on a book about a historic event or person, she first spends a lot of time researching. During her research, she often travels to the places she writes about in her books. Jean Fritz was in Italy when Leonardo's horse was unveiled. She said, "It was one of my most exciting adventures."

 www.harcourtschool.com/storytown

ABOUT THE ILLUSTRATOR
Hudson Talbott

Hudson Talbott loves to travel. On one trip to Italy, he wanted to see Leonardo's horse, but he did not have a chance. When he returned home, he found a message on his answering machine asking him to work on a book about the horse! He happily agreed. Hudson Talbott grew up surrounded by horses in Kentucky. He has written and illustrated more than a dozen books for children.

Myth

Bellerophon
AND
Pegasus

A GREEK MYTH

illustrated by David Austin Clar

BELLEROPHON
(buh·LAIR·uh·fuhn)
A prince and great horse tamer

CHIMERA
(ky·MIR·uh)
A fire-breathing creature

ATHENA
The Greek goddess of wisdom

PEGASUS
A winged horse

Long ago, a young prince named Bellerophon traveled to Lycia (LISH·ee·uh), in Asia. When he arrived, he learned that a horrible monster, the Chimera, was destroying the kingdom.

"Save my land and my people," the king of Lycia pleaded.

Bellerophon agreed to help, but he did not know how. An old, wise man suggested the young hero spend the night in the temple of Athena.

In his dreams, Bellerophon was given a golden bridle by the goddess. "Use this to capture Pegasus. He can help you defeat the Chimera." When Bellerophon awoke, the bridle was in his hands.

Bellerophon found Pegasus drinking by a spring. Seeing the bridle, wild Pegasus became tame. The winged horse allowed Bellerophon to slip the bridle over his head and jump onto his back.

Pegasus galloped through the air until they found the Chimera, breathing fire across the land. The creature had the head of a lion, the body of a goat, and the tail of a dragon.

Pegasus flew as close as he dared. After a brutal fight, the monster lay dead. The people of Lycia were safe.

Bellerophon and Pegasus had many more adventures. Eventually, Pegasus flew on to Olympus alone, where he carried Zeus's thunderbolts.

Connections

Comparing Texts

1. The artists in "Leonardo's Horse" decided to start over when they saw that Charlie Dent's horse was out of proportion. When have you had to start over on a project, and why?

2. Compare the genre of "Leonardo's Horse" with the genre of "Bellerophon and Pegasus." What is the purpose of each kind of literature?

3. Charlie Dent wanted to give the horse to the people of Italy as a gift from the people of the United States. Why might one country want to give another country a gift?

Vocabulary Review

Word Webs

Create a word web for each Vocabulary Word. In the outer circles, write words and phrases related to the Vocabulary Word. Explain how the words in your webs are related.

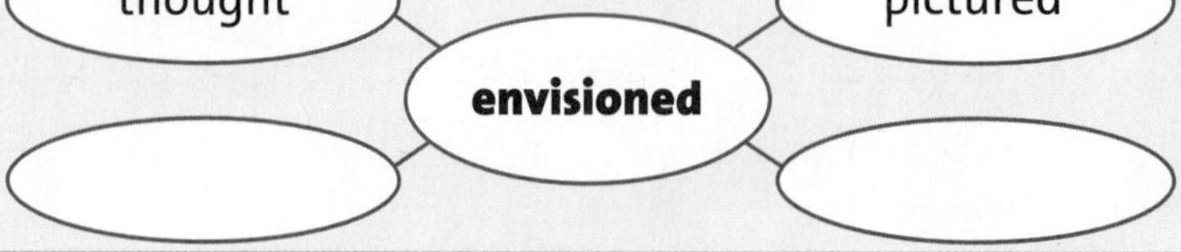

scholars

specialized

gesture

envisioned

proportion

resisted

thought — envisioned — pictured

Fluency Practice

Recorded Text

Listen to the first sentence of "Leonardo's Horse" on *Audiotext 2* and track the print. Note how the reader groups words together and listen for pauses. Then read the sentence aloud, matching the reader's phrasing. Continue sentence by sentence, until you have listened to and read aloud the first two paragraphs of the selection.

Writing

Write Instructions

Select one process described in "Leonardo's Horse," such as building the horse's structure. Write instructions that explain how to accomplish this process.

My Writing Checklist

Writing Trait ➤ Organization

✔ I used a graphic organizer to organize my steps.

✔ I made my instructions clear to readers.

✔ I used transition words, such as *first, next,* and *last.*

First Event	→	Next Event	→	Next Event	→	Last Event

Big 💡 Idea

A play's theme develops as the audience watches the characters react to new challenges.

Enduring ❗ Understanding

The audience gains meaning and experiences excitement through the characters' words and actions with the author's use of hyperbole, or exaggeration.

Essential ❓ Question

How does the audience identify the use of hyperbole?

Spelling Words

Review

bundle	message
vehicle	arrange
struggle	whisper
hurtle	terrific
triple	expression
hurricane	conclude
golden	merchandise
journey	technique
hospital	accomplish
excellent	orchestra

Fluency

Review Expression, Phrasing

Comprehension

Review
 Theme, Text Structure: Sequence

 Ask Questions, Use Graphic Organizers

Robust Vocabulary

- eminent
- charity
- modest
- disgruntled
- inadequate
- aghast
- dismayed
- amends
- absentminded
- concoction

Writing

- *Review* Ideas, Organization
- Revise and Publish

Lesson 10
Theme Review and Vocabulary Builder

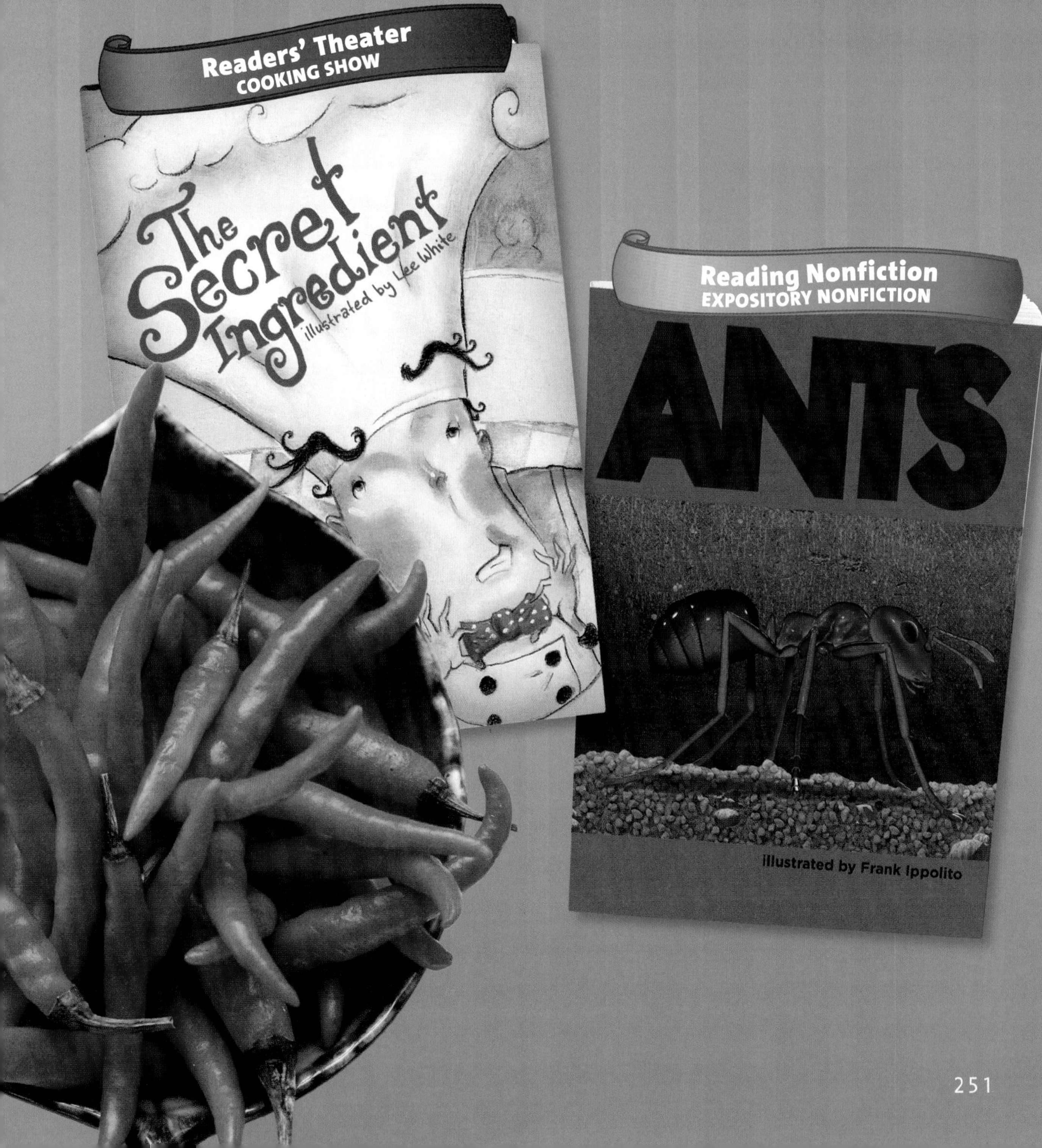

Readers' Theater
COOKING SHOW
The Secret Ingredient
illustrated by Lee White
Reading Nonfiction
EXPOSITORY NONFICTION
ANTS
illustrated by Frank Ippolito

eminent

charity

modest

disgruntled

inadequate

aghast

dismayed

amends

absentminded

concoction

Reading for Fluency

When reading a script aloud,

- Think about how the characters feel to help you read with expression.

- Pay attention to phrasing by pausing between groups of words that go together.

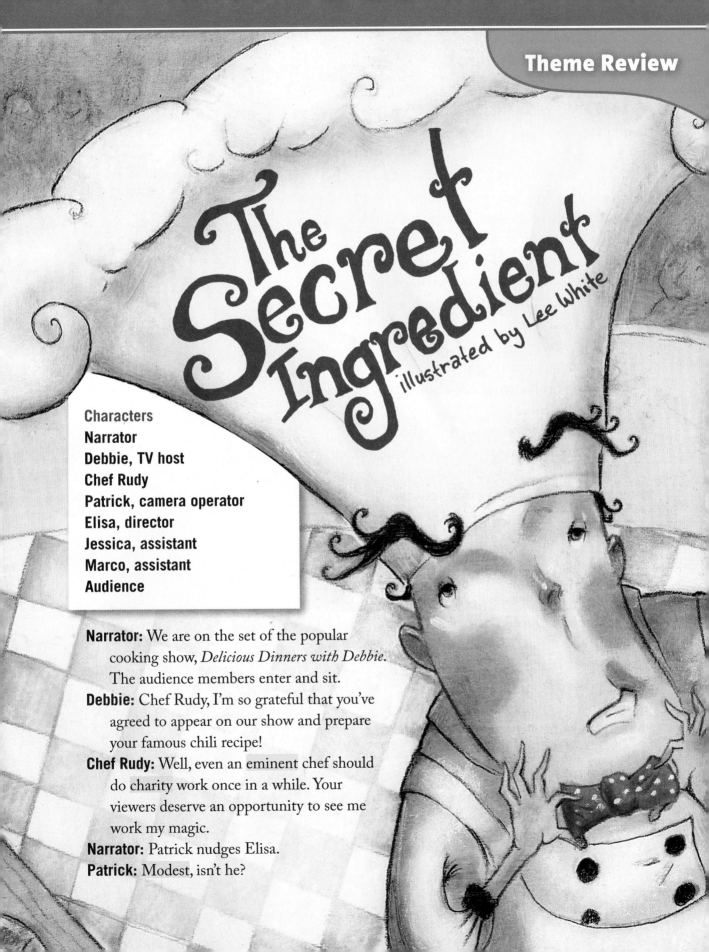

The Secret Ingredient

illustrated by Lee White

Characters
Narrator
Debbie, TV host
Chef Rudy
Patrick, camera operator
Elisa, director
Jessica, assistant
Marco, assistant
Audience

Narrator: We are on the set of the popular cooking show, *Delicious Dinners with Debbie.* The audience members enter and sit.

Debbie: Chef Rudy, I'm so grateful that you've agreed to appear on our show and prepare your famous chili recipe!

Chef Rudy: Well, even an eminent chef should do charity work once in a while. Your viewers deserve an opportunity to see me work my magic.

Narrator: Patrick nudges Elisa.

Patrick: Modest, isn't he?

Narrator: Chef Rudy gives the kitchen a disgruntled look.

Chef Rudy: Am I expected to prepare my masterpiece in these inadequate conditions?

Elisa: We brought in all of the equipment you asked for.

Debbie: We had an extra cleaning crew here last night, too.

Narrator: Chef Rudy runs a finger across the counter top and looks at his finger, frowning.

Debbie: Don't fret, Chef Rudy. The show is going to be great!

Chef Rudy: Of course the show will be great. I am Chef Rudy Lancaster, the Chief of Chili, the Prime Minister of Peppers, the Sultan of Spice!

Marco: Chef Rudy?

Chef Rudy: What's wrong? Shouldn't you two be chopping and measuring my ingredients so that everything is ready?

Jessica: Yes, except . . .

Marco: We can't find one of the ingredients.

Chef Rudy: All of my ingredients are crucial! Which one is missing?

Jessica: Your own special canned tomatoes.

Marco: We can't find them anywhere.

Narrator: Chef Rudy looks aghast.

Debbie: Don't be dismayed, Chef Rudy. We'll send someone to the store to buy canned tomatoes.

Chef Rudy: I can't use ordinary canned tomatoes. My zesty tomatoes are canned especially for me in Mexico. They're what make my chili irresistible!

Elisa: I have a friend who lives down the street. She grows tomatoes in her backyard. They're not from Mexico, but they're the best in town.

Patrick: It's worth a try, don't you think? What have you got to lose?

Chef Rudy: I suppose I have no choice, but my chili won't be the same.

Debbie: Meanwhile, Chef Rudy, why don't you work out the proportions for the fresh tomatoes?

Jessica and Marco are nervous. How can you use your voice to show this emotion?

Narrator: While Chef Rudy amends his recipe, Marco and Jessica whisper to each other.

Marco: This is my fault. I'm always so absentminded.

Jessica: No. I was in charge of bringing the ingredients. It's my fault.

Narrator: Elisa walks in holding a basket of tomatoes.

Elisa: Here's a basket of the sweetest, tangiest tomatoes on the planet.

Chef Rudy: And here is the revised recipe.

Debbie: The show will start soon. If we all work together, we can get the ingredients ready in time.

Elisa: I'll rinse and chop the tomatoes.

Patrick: I'll chop the garlic and onions.

Jessica: I'll take care of the chili peppers.

Marco: I'll measure the spices.

Elisa: Places, everyone. One minute to showtime!

Narrator: Chef Rudy and Debbie stand behind the table and look into the camera. Patrick moves behind the camera.

Elisa: We're live in 5, 4, 3, 2, 1.

Debbie: Welcome to *Delicious Dinners with Debbie*. I'm your host, Debbie DeVille.

Audience: Hello, Debbie!

Debbie: Today we have a very special guest on our show. All the way from El Paso, Texas, the internationally famous Chef Rudy Lancaster!

Audience: Hello, Chef Rudy!

Chef Rudy: Today, I'm going to make some out-of-this-world chili.

Audience: We can't wait!

Chef Rudy: The recipe takes one pound of ground beef, three cups of fresh, hand-chopped tomatoes, two chopped chili peppers with seeds removed, one chopped garlic clove, one chopped onion, spices, salt, and one secret ingredient.

Audience: Ooooh, a secret ingredient!

Narrator: Chef Rudy places a pan on the stove, puts the beef in it, and starts to cook.

Chef Rudy: Now, we add the onion and garlic. Debbie, would you help me?

Debbie: Sure thing.

Chef Rudy: Sauté the mixture until the onion softens. Then drain the mixture and transfer it to a large pot.

Fluency Tip

Read groups of words in chunks to make your phrasing sound natural.

Debbie: What's next?

Chef Rudy: Next, we mix in the hand-chopped tomatoes. Now we add the spices, and don't forget the chopped chili peppers. Finally, we add the secret ingredient . . .

Narrator: Smiling, Chef Rudy reaches into his pocket. His smile turns to a frown as he frantically searches all of his pockets.

Chef Rudy: I can't find it! Without the secret ingredient, my chili will be so . . . ordinary!

Debbie: We'll be back to *Delicious Dinners with Debbie* after these messages.

Narrator: Patrick turns off the camera. Debbie, Marco, and Jessica sneak tastes of the chili.

Marco and Jessica: It's . . . delicious!

Debbie: This is the best chili I've ever had!

Chef Rudy: Impossible! It can't be any good without my own special canned tomatoes and the secret ingredient.

Debbie: I assure you, there is no better chili than this.

Chef Rudy: Do you really think so?

Narrator: He tastes the chili and smacks his lips.

Chef Rudy: Hmmm . . . you may be right!

Elisa: Places, everyone. We're live in 5, 4, 3, 2, 1.

Debbie: Welcome back to *Delicious Dinners with Debbie.*

Chef Rudy: I have exciting news.

Audience: Did you find the secret ingredient?

Chef Rudy: No. As of today, I've changed my recipe!

Audience: What do you mean?

Chef Rudy: We had to improvise with the ingredients today. Much to my surprise, we've created a new chili that puts my old chili to shame!

Debbie: What made the difference?

Chef Rudy: It was the tomatoes. I never envisioned that fresh, homegrown tomatoes could be better than my own special canned tomatoes. They make my chili taste . . . fresher!

Debbie: It's time for another short commercial break. When we come back, we'll see how the audience likes Chef Rudy's newest concoction.

Audience: We can't wait!

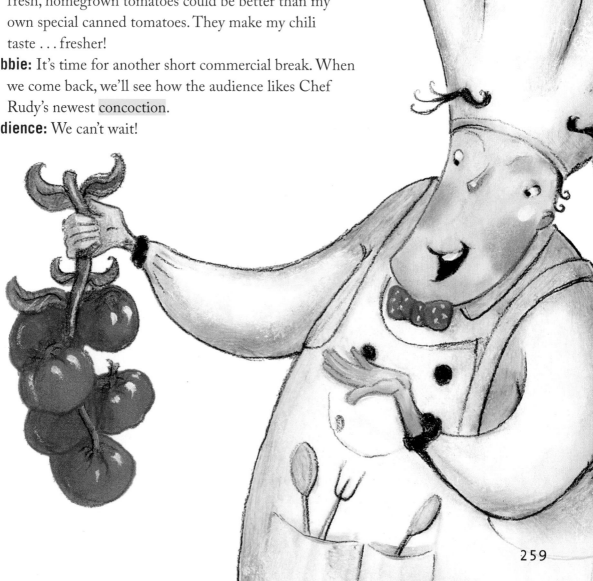

Narrator: Marco and Jessica pass out bowls of chili to the audience.

Debbie: We're back, and Chef Rudy's new, improved chili is ready for tasting.

Chef Rudy: Is the audience ready?

Audience: Yes!

Narrator: The audience eagerly tries the chili.

Audience: Wow! This chili is great!

Debbie: Is there anything you would change about Chef Rudy's recipe?

Audience: No! Not a thing! It's perfect!

Chef Rudy: Of course it's perfect. It's made with hand-chopped, homegrown tomatoes!

Audience: Hooray for the homegrown tomatoes!

Debbie: That's all the time we have for today. Thanks for watching *Delicious Dinners with Debbie*. Good night!

Narrator: Patrick turns off the camera. The audience leaves the studio. Patrick, Elisa, Marco, and Jessica join Debbie and Chef Rudy on the set. Everyone is smiling.

Fluency Tip

Use punctuation to adjust your phrasing. Words set off by commas often form a phrase and indicate where you should pause.

Elisa: Great show, everybody!

Chef Rudy: It certainly was. Thanks to all of you, we created a masterpiece! I want to thank everyone.

Marco, Jessica, Debbie, Elisa, and Patrick: You're welcome, Chef Rudy.

Chef Rudy: I also want to apologize for my earlier behavior. Sometimes I tend to act a bit self-important.

Patrick: We know you just want everything to be perfect.

Elisa: The situation looked grim for a while, but we did it.

Debbie: Little did we know that our solution to the crisis would make the chili better than ever!

Chef Rudy: Yes, my chili recipe is much better, thanks to the new secret ingredient—teamwork!

Jessica: Teamwork! Does that mean we can all call ourselves Chiefs of Chili?

Marco: Prime Ministers of Peppers?

Patrick: Sultans of Spice?

Chef Rudy: Well, let's not get too carried away!

COMPREHENSION STRATEGIES
Review

Reading Expository Nonfiction

Bridge to Reading for Information Expository nonfiction gives facts and information about a real-life subject. The notes on page 263 point out features of expository nonfiction, including subheads and illustration labels. These features provide information that can help you locate information.

Review the Focus Strategies

If you do not understand what you are reading, use the strategies you learned about in this theme.

 Ask Questions

Ask yourself questions before, during, and after you read. Think about the information the author is sharing. What is the text mostly about?

 Use Graphic Organizers

Use graphic organizers to keep track of important ideas. Fill in information about the text as you read.

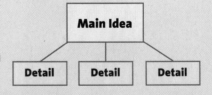

As you read "Ants" on pages 264–267, think about where and how to use comprehension strategies.

KEY
A key is a list of symbols, numbers, or abbreviations that provide information about a diagram.

ANTS

1. **ANTENNAE** The antennae are used for smelling, touching, feeling movement, and tasting.
2. **COMPOUND EYE** Ants see through compound eyes that are made up of tiny lenses.
3. **HEAD**
4. **THORAX**
5. **WAIST**
6. **ABDOMEN**
7. **GASTER** The gaster is the second half of the abdomen. The ant's stomach is located in the gaster.
8. **STINGER** Some ants have a stinger at the end of the gaster.
9. **SIX LEGS**
10. **MANDIBLES** Mandibles are used to dig, fight, and carry objects.

No matter where you live, you've probably come across a trail of marching ants. That's because ants are found in any type of climate as long as it is not extremely cold. There are almost 20,000 different species of ants. Some are as small as a grain of salt. Others are more than an inch long. However, no matter their size, ants are extremely strong. Some can lift up to 50 times their body weight.

KINDS OF ANTS
Different kinds of ants have different ways of life. Some ants, such as harvester ants, gather and store seeds and food in their nests. Fungus-growing ants carry plant pieces to their nest, where they grow and harvest fungus to eat. Another type of ant, the dairying ant, grows and protects a type of insect that produces honeydew, a sweet liquid ants drink.

SUBHEAD
Subheads are words or phrases that describe sections of text.

LABELS
Illustrations or diagrams may include labels to identify their parts. These numbers correspond to those in the key.

Apply the Strategies Read this text about ants and their community. As you read, use different comprehension strategies, such as asking questions, to help you understand the text.

ANTS

No matter where you live, you've probably come across a trail of marching ants. That's because ants are found in any type of climate as long as it is not extremely cold. There are almost 20,000 different species of ants. Some are as small as a grain of salt. Others are more than an inch long. However, no matter their size, ants are extremely strong. Some can lift up to 50 times their body weight.

KINDS OF ANTS

Different kinds of ants have different ways of life. Some ants, such as harvester ants, gather and store seeds and food in their nests. Fungus-growing ants carry plant pieces to their nests where they grow and harvest fungus to eat. Another type of ant, the dairying ant, grows and protects a type of insect that produces honeydew, a sweet liquid ants drink.

Stop and Think

As you read, ask questions such as *How strong are ants?*

ASK QUESTIONS

1. **ANTENNAE** The antennae are used for smelling, touching, feeling movement, and tasting.
2. **COMPOUND EYE** Ants see through compound eyes that are made up of tiny lenses.
3. **HEAD**
4. **THORAX**
5. **WAIST**
6. **ABDOMEN**
7. **GASTER** The gaster is the second half of the abdomen. The ant's stomach is located in the gaster.
8. **STINGER** Some ants have a stinger at the end of the gaster.
9. **SIX LEGS**
10. **MANDIBLES** Mandibles are used to dig, fight, and carry objects.

THE SOCIAL INSECT

Ants are social insects. This means that they live in organized communities called colonies. Most colonies consist of many worker ants and one or more queen ants. The worker ants build the nests.

NEST CHAMBERS

Most ants build their nests underground. Some of these nests are large—as big as a tennis court. Large nests are made up of different chambers.

IMPORTANCE OF ANTS

Ants have an important role in the world. They are a food source for many animals, such as birds, lizards, anteaters, monkeys, and frogs. Ants also eat small insects such as termites and keep their numbers from getting too big. Additionally, ants break up soil when they build their nests. This makes the soil better for growing plants. Ants are part of the balance of nature.

Stop and Think

How can you use this graphic organizer to help you understand the text? USE GRAPHIC ORGANIZERS

Main Idea

Detail Detail Detail

Nurseries
Worker ants care for larvae and pupae here.

Worker Resting Chambers
Most chambers are for adult worker ants.

Queen's Chamber
The queen ant has her own chamber. Here, the queen lays her eggs. Worker ants go to the chamber to feed the queen. They also collect her eggs and take them to the nurseries.

New Chamber
Ants are continuously building.

Storage Chambers
Ants that collect or grow their own food build food-storage chambers.

Winter Quarters
Deep underground, chambers are warmer than up by the topsoil. Ants live here when the weather turns cold.

267

Theme 3 Go with the Flow

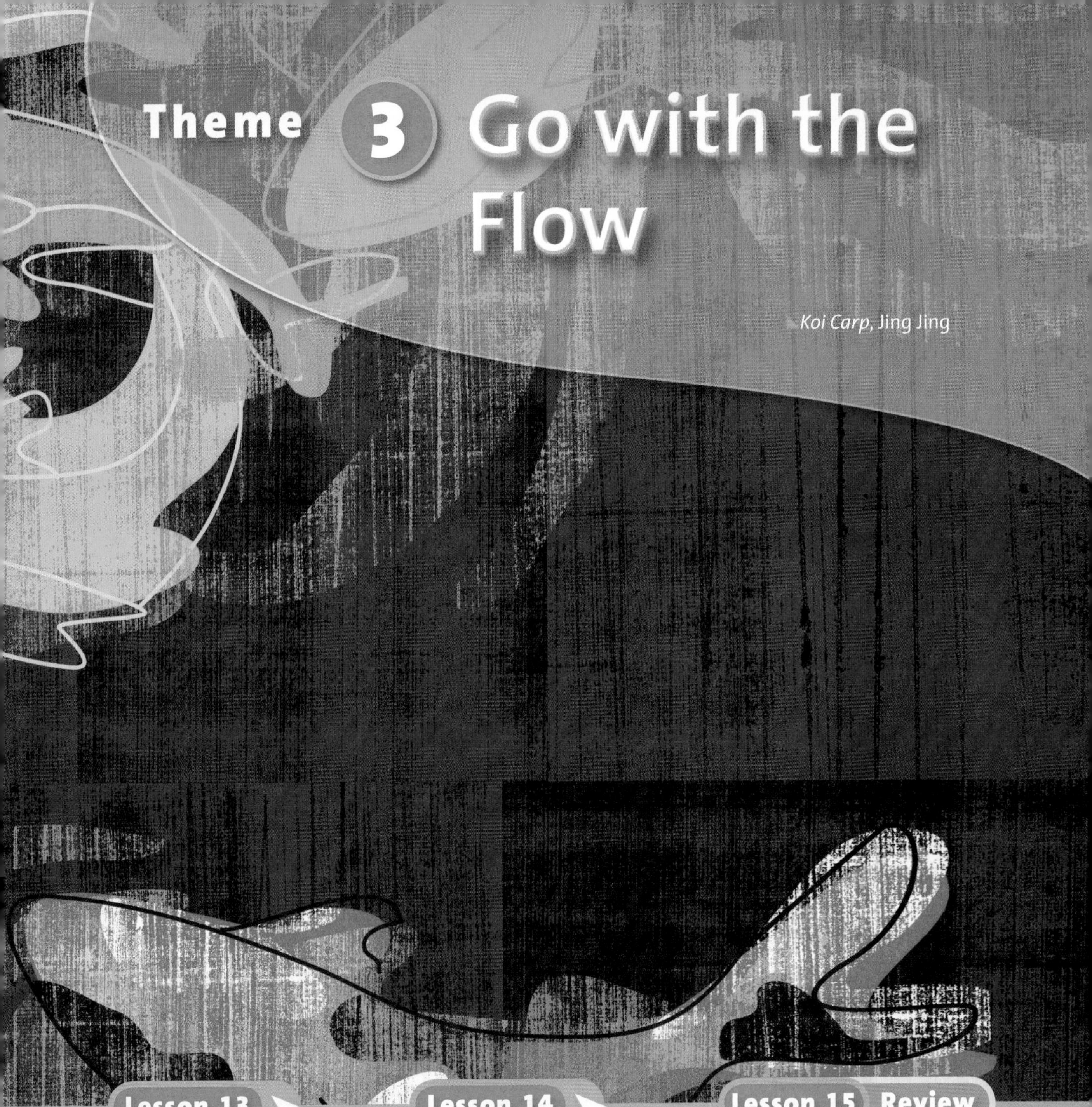

Koi Carp, Jing Jing

Lesson 13	Lesson 14	Lesson 15 Review
Stormalong Paul Bunyan Makes Progress	**A Drop of Water** Rain, Dance!; Steam; Ice Cycle	**How Prairie Became Ocean** **How Does Ocean Water Move?**
Use Graphic Organizers	Use Graphic Organizers	**Review** Skills and Strategies
Cause and Effect	Text Structure: Cause and Effect	

Big Idea

Comparisons and contrasts in texts show how things and people are alike or different.

Enduring ! Understanding
Readers can identify comparisons and contrasts through word clues.

Essential ? Question
How can readers identify comparisons and contrasts in text?

Spelling Words

Words with VCV

enemy	minute
balance	model
basis	protest
closet	ocean
decent	pretend
define	private
eleven	radar
fanatic	second
honest	slogan
humor	editor

Challenge

elaborate	dutiful
rotate	notice
coma	

Fluency

Intonation

Comprehension

 Compare and Contrast

 Monitor Comprehension: Self-Correct

Robust Vocabulary

- inflammable
- dignified
- rowdy
- seldom
- conducted
- shatter
- broached

Writing

- Descriptive Paragraph: Setting
- Sentence Fluency

Lesson 11

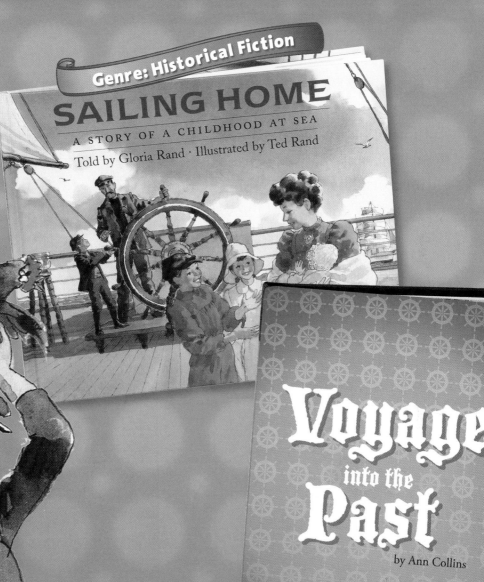

Genre: Historical Fiction

SAILING HOME

A STORY OF A CHILDHOOD AT SEA

Told by Gloria Rand · Illustrated by Ted Rand

Voyage into the Past

by Ann Collins

Genre: Expository Nonfiction

Focus Skill

Compare and Contrast

Authors of fiction texts may show the relationships between characters, settings, or plot events by pointing out how they are alike and how they are different. To **compare** is to tell how things are alike. To **contrast** is to tell how they are different. Words such as *and, both, too, like,* and *similarly* signal a comparison. The words *but, unlike, although, while,* and *nevertheless* signal a contrast.

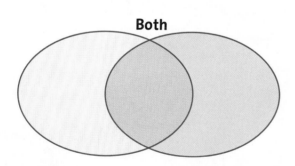

Both

Tip

A Venn diagram is a graphic organizer that may be used to compare and contrast two things.

Read the paragraph below. Then look at the graphic organizer. It compares and contrasts Maya and Bo, two characters in the paragraph. The graphic organizer shows that Maya loves to sit on the boat's deck, while Bo prefers to stay in the cabin. Both characters love to sail.

Each weekend, Maya and Bo go sailing with their dad. They look forward to the outing all week. Maya loves to sit on the deck of the boat and feel the wind and salt spray on her face. Unlike Maya, Bo enjoys staying in the cabin and playing his guitar. Maya and Bo usually take their pet dogs on the boat. The two dogs behave like their owners—Lulu enjoys the wind, while Frankie rests in the cabin.

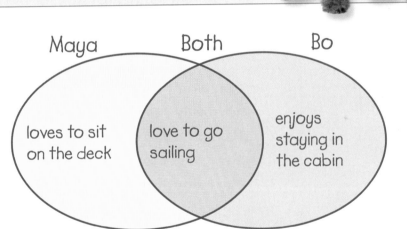

Maya	Both	Bo
loves to sit on the deck	love to go sailing	enjoys staying in the cabin

Try This!

Look back at the paragraph. What is another comparison the author has made? What clue word helped you identify it?

 www.harcourtschool.com/storytown

Vocabulary

Build Robust Vocabulary

- conducted
- rowdy
- dignified
- shatter
- inflammable
- seldom
- broached

Captain Cal's Sailing Tips

Sailing the open sea is not as easy as sailing in local waters. I've put together these tips to help new sailors have a safe and successful ocean sailing experience. It's like taking a class **conducted** by an expert sailor.

- On a long voyage, some sailors start to act **rowdy**. Such behavior causes problems. Remind everyone that **dignified** sailors always act properly. They do not **shatter** glasses or dishes for fun.

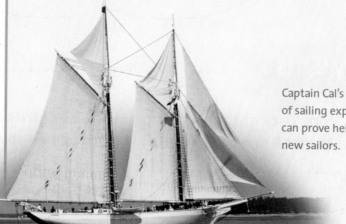

Captain Cal's years of sailing experience can prove helpful to new sailors.

- Be very careful with fire. Although there is water all around you, your ship is still **inflammable**.
- When sailing the seas, you **seldom** have an opportunity to eat fresh fruits and vegetables. Eat your fill of these foods whenever you have the chance.
- Storms create huge waves. Steer your ship's bow into each swell. A ship that has **broached** is likely to sink.
- Above all, keep your boat shipshape and your mind alert!

 GO online www.harcourtschool.com/storytown

Word Champion

Your challenge this week is to use the Vocabulary Words outside of your classroom. Keep a list of the words in a place at home where you can see it. Use as many of the words as you can when you speak to family members and friends. For example, you might ask friends to share a time when they behaved in a dignified manner. Write in your vocabulary journal the sentences you spoke that contained the words.

Historical Fiction

Genre Study

Historical fiction tells about people, events, or places that are real or could be real. As you read, look for

- a real time and place of the past.

- events that may have happened.

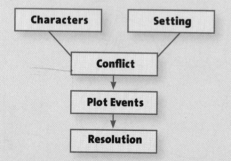

Comprehension Strategy

Monitor comprehension as you read. Stop and **self-correct** mistakes that change the meaning of the text.

SAILING HOME

A STORY OF A CHILDHOOD AT SEA

by Gloria Rand
illustrated by Ted Rand

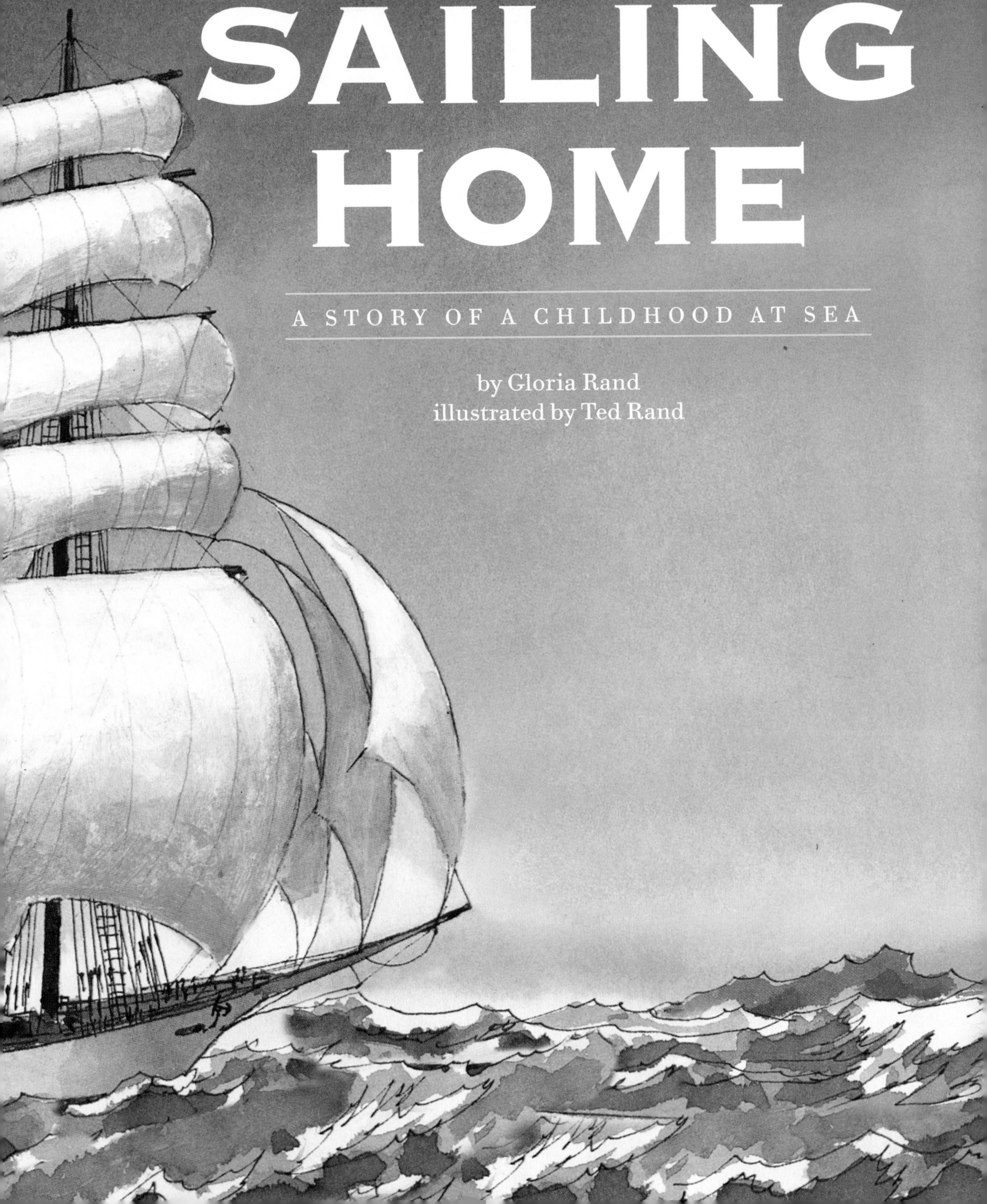

Ours was a wonderful childhood, a childhood spent at sea. My sister Dagmar, my brother, Albert, and I, Matilda, grew up aboard the *John Ena*, a four-masted sailing bark that carried cargo all over the world.

Our father was the ship's captain; the ship was our home. Only when the cargo was coal, which is highly inflammable, did we have to live ashore.

The *John Ena* had bedrooms, a bathroom, and a main room that was a combination living room with a pink marble fireplace and a dining room with a big round table. There was a kitchen called the galley, and a storage room full of everything we needed.

Unlike most homes, ours didn't stay put. At night, the ship kept moving, so every morning we woke up far away from where we'd gone to sleep.

It often seemed as if we lived on a farm, not a ship. Roosters crowed, hens clucked, and ducks quacked. Mother raised them all in neat pens below deck, so we'd have fresh meat and eggs to add to the ship's food supply. Dagmar and I collected the eggs.

We all took turns caring for our pets as we traveled around the world. There was Minnie the cat and a dog named Murphy. We had a mongoose, a monkey, a pig, and even a kangaroo.

The day the kangaroo accidentally jumped overboard we screamed for help. The crew quickly lowered a life boat and rescued it.

Our pet pig wasn't so lucky. She fell into a pot of hot tar the men were using to repair the ship's deck. Piggy died. We had a real funeral for her and a dignified burial at sea.

Instead of a backyard or a playground we had a great wooden deck where we played tag, hide-and-seek, and catch, always with beanbags, because balls bounced overboard. We swung on rope swings and, after our baby sister Ena was born, we took turns wheeling her around the deck in a baby buggy.

When the winds were blowing hard and the sea was full of big waves, we played inside. Our favorite game was sliding across the main room floor in cardboard boxes, crashing into one another as the ship rolled from side to side.

"Time to calm down," Mother would say softly when we got rowdy. "Let's read for a while."

Mother taught us how to read and count. She was a good teacher. Father was a good teacher, too.

"Name that planet," he'd say, pointing to a bright steady light in the dark night sky. Before long we could tell planets from stars, and even understood about celestial navigation. As a special treat Father gave us our own set of signaling flags, and we learned to send messages. From the stern of the ship we sent messages to Father at the bow, and he signaled messages back to us.

There were no radios then, and when we were out at sea we seldom saw another ship. If a ship did pass close enough for us to see each other clearly, Father, or one of the crew, exchanged greetings and information using signaling flags.

Real school began when Miss Shipman, a governess, came aboard as our teacher. Albert didn't like her at all. Dagmar said she looked mean, but I thought she was nice.

With Miss Shipman in charge, we went to school at the dining table six days a week, mornings and afternoons, with only an hour off for lunch and no recesses.

Miss Shipman was good at teaching us history, science, mathematics, and languages. But teaching us geography was impossible for her. We'd seen so much of the world, we knew more than she did. We'd tell her about our family picnics in Japan and all about palaces and cathedrals we had visited in Europe. Miss Shipman was impressed, but not with Albert.

Albert didn't like school. He played hooky a lot. He'd sneak off to mend sails with the ship's carpenter, or help the crew scrub down the deck with flat stones. Sometimes Albert crawled up and hid in a little cubbyhole by the masthead. Miss Shipman would tattle to Father, and Father would bring Albert back to school.

I liked to get away, too, and be alone up in the rigging, high above the deck. I liked to feel the wind, smell the salty air, and watch the rolling ocean for as far as I could see. But I never got to stay up there for long. As soon as one of the crew spotted me, I'd hear a loud shout, "Get down, Matilda, you little spider!"

The crew watched us all the time to make sure we didn't get into serious trouble. They watched us even when they were working, scrubbing sails, laying them out to dry, polishing brass cleats and handles, and mending ropes.

The carpenter made toys for us, the sailmaker taught us how to tie nautical knots, and the cook baked us special treats. We had the whole crew for friends.

Even though our life was different from other children's, we didn't miss out on anything. We had marshmallow roasts at the fireplace, taffy pulls in the galley, and footraces out on deck. Mother always brought along Christmas and birthday presents, and decorations for every holiday.

Only once, when I was ten, we almost didn't have Christmas. That year, as we crossed the China Sea, the weather turned wild. We had just started to put up red and green garlands and ropes of sparkling tinsel when Father rushed in.

"Here, grab this end, and tie up that chair," Father ordered as he unwound a big coil of heavy line.

We all knew what to do. Like experts we tied the piano and all the furniture to the railing that ran along the walls of the main room and to big hooks the carpenter was screwing into the floor. Mother put little things, lamps, knickknacks, and our candy dish into a heavy sea chest. Everything had to be tied up or put away, otherwise, when the ship pitched and rolled, there would have been stuff crashing and flying all over the place.

It wasn't long before we were in the middle of a terrible storm that stayed with us for days. The sky was black. There were huge bolts of lightning, and thunder roared so loud you could hardly think.

No matter how bad the storm became, Miss Shipman made us go to school. The seas got so rough it wasn't safe to sit at the dining table, so we all sat on the floor while Miss Shipman conducted class. We slid back and forth across the floor as the ship rode the waves. It was like riding a roller coaster.

After school we pressed our faces against the portholes and cheered as tons of water smashed against the glass. When Mother saw what we were doing she pulled us back.

"I don't want you to get hurt," she said. "Those waves could shatter the glass."

Two of the crew did get hurt when a gigantic wave swept them down the length of the ship. Father dashed out and pulled them to safety. Mother sewed up their bad cuts with ordinary needle and thread. One of the sailors cried.

The storm got worse and worse. Lifeboats were torn loose and smashed into pieces by gigantic waves, and the sails were ripped to shreds by screaming winds. But lucky for us we didn't get seasick. We never did. Father decided the safest place for all of us to be was on the floor of the ship's chart room. That's when we began to get scared. Father tried to get us to think about something else, like having a Christmas party.

"When we get through this storm," he promised, "we're going to have a grand holiday celebration. It will be the most wonderful party we've ever had. Let's start planning it now."

At that moment the ship rolled onto her side, and didn't roll back. We all clung together.

"Mary," he said as he kissed our mother, "the ship has broached, and I think we're about to sink."

"Yes, dear," said Mother, looking Father right in the eye and smiling the bravest smile you'd ever hope to see.

Neither of them showed any panic or fear, and that made us children feel brave, too. Father kissed each of us and told us we were great sailors.

It seemed our family stayed hugging together forever, then the *John Ena* quivered a strange quiver and slowly righted herself!

Gradually, the storm ended, and the sea became calm.

"Time to get our celebration ready," said Father. He had never sounded so happy.

With all of us helping, everything was soon put back where it belonged.

"Girls, hang all this ribbon and tinsel up everywhere. And Albert, you're in charge of decorating the wooden Christmas tree, the one the carpenter made for us." Mother was excited.

"Don't look, I'm about to bring out the presents. Your father has a surprise for you, too, don't you, dear?"

We all laughed because we knew what Father's surprise always was at Christmas. He became Santa.

That night we dressed up in our party clothes. The crew sang "My Bonnie Lies Over the Ocean." They sang the best they had ever sung. The cook filled the table with delicious treats, and we played the gramophone and clapped and cheered watching Father dance with Mother. They were such good dancers.

As promised, it was the best Christmas ever. We were safe, right where we loved to be. We were at home, home on the sea.

Think Critically

1 Compare and contrast Matilda's childhood with the childhood of a character in another book you have read.
COMPARE AND CONTRAST

2 What did Matilda's family do to prepare for the huge storm?
NOTE DETAILS

3 What do you think would be the most difficult part of living on a ship? PERSONAL RESPONSE

4 Explain why the Christmas celebration described in the story was so special. SYNTHESIZE

5 **WRITE** Matilda and her brother and sisters found many ways to have fun aboard the ship. Use information and details from the story to explain how
- their activities were **SIMILAR** to those of children who lived on land; and
- living on a ship led to **DIFFERENT** types of activities.

 EXTENDED RESPONSE

Gloria Rand

Gloria and Ted Rand have written and illustrated several books together. The Rands based "Sailing Home: A Story of a Childhood at Sea" on the real adventures of the Madsen family who lived aboard the *John Ena*. The captain's granddaughter told Gloria Rand the stories of her family, and Gloria Rand retold them in the book. She advises young writers to write about things that interest them and to research a subject if they don't know it well. Most importantly, she says, "Don't talk about writing—write."

Albert, Dagmar, and Matilda sitting on the ship's anchor

Baby Ena in a wicker carriage

 www.harcourtschool.com/storytown

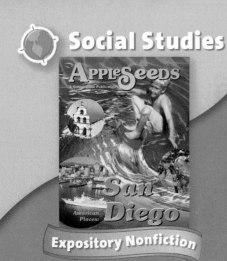

AppleSeeds

San Diego

American Places!

Expository Nonfiction

Voyage into the Past

by Ann Collins

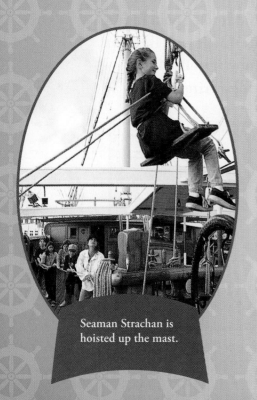

Seaman Strachan is hoisted up the mast.

"Men, that's a shoddy crew line!" shouts the first mate. "I want you shoulder to shoulder, heel to toe, like mackerels in a sardine can."

The "men" are boys and girls, ages 9 to 12. They stand at attention aboard the three-masted bark *Star of India* in San Diego Bay.

The port of San Diego has long welcomed sailors and ships. In the 1800s, many tall masts jutted into the sky. Today, the 136-year-old *Star of India* is part of the San Diego Maritime Museum. The sailing ship takes children on a one-night imaginary voyage into the past.

They follow the captain's orders by answering, "Aye, aye, sir!" The sailors work hard furling sails, washing the deck, and coiling the heavy lines. Eight seamen raise a staysail by turning the capstan. As they go round and round, they sing a sea chantey to stay in rhythm.

Gloucester girls, they have no combs.
Heave away! Heave away!
They comb their hair with codfish bones.
We're bound for Californ-i-a!

The *Star of India* is under sail.

Below deck, another team hoists a heavy wooden barrel of cargo, using pulleys and ropes called "block and tackle."

The galley (kitchen) crew prepares beef stew. Fresh carrots and potatoes are washed in a tin pail on deck. Breakfast will be oatmeal porridge.

The crew takes turns "standing watch" during the night. They search the ocean for possible dangers, including icebergs, reefs, whales, and pirates. While a cold wind rattles the rigging, the salty smell of the sea tickles noses.

By the end of the voyage, the "men" have tasted life in the past. Do you think they are happy to return to the present?

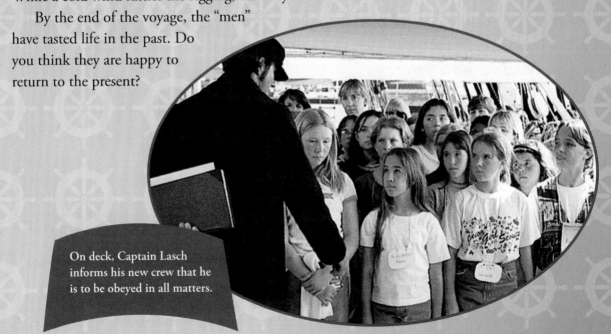

On deck, Captain Lasch informs his new crew that he is to be obeyed in all matters.

291

Connections

Comparing Texts

1. Which story character are you more like, Albert or Matilda? Explain.

2. Compare the experiences of the characters in "Sailing Home: A Story of a Childhood at Sea" to the experiences of the kids in "Voyage into the Past."

3. In what ways was the school aboard the *John Ena* similar to schools in the United States today? In what ways was it different?

Vocabulary Review

Word Webs

Work with a partner. Choose two Vocabulary Words. Create a web for each word. In the outer circles, write words and phrases that are related to the Vocabulary Word. Explain how each word or phrase is related to the Vocabulary Word.

broached — afraid — tipped over — rough waves

inflammable

dignified

rowdy

seldom

conducted

shatter

broached

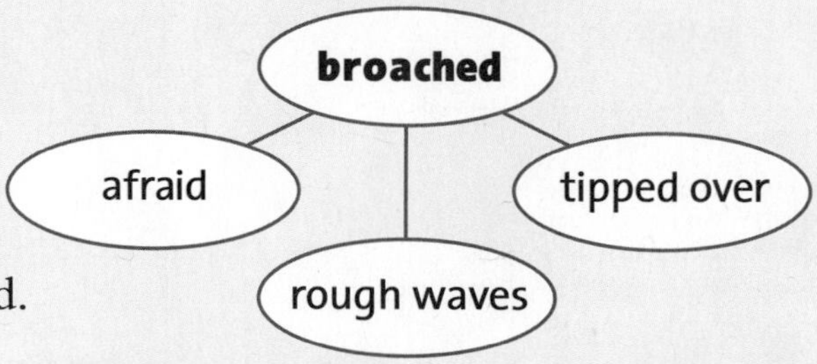

Fluency Practice

Partner Reading

Work with a partner. Find your favorite part of the selection. Read that section aloud with proper intonation, while your partner listens and follows along. When you finish reading, ask your partner for feedback. Then switch roles and repeat the activity.

Writing

Write a Paragraph

Imagine that you are taught by a governess in your home instead of by a teacher at school. Write a paragraph comparing and contrasting how your learning experience might be different.

Home   Both   School

My Writing Checklist

Writing Trait → Sentence Fluency

✔ I used a Venn diagram to plan my writing.

✔ I used a variety of complete sentences in my paragraph.

✔ I included details to compare and contrast the ideas.

Reading-Writing Connection

Analyze Writer's Craft: Expository Nonfiction

Expository nonfiction gives information about a topic. It may include **photographs** and **captions**. When you write expository nonfiction, you can use the works of writers such as Ann Collins as writing models. Read the paragraphs below from "Voyage into the Past," and notice how the author used **sentence fluency** and **organization**.

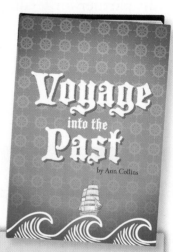

Writing Trait

SENTENCE FLUENCY
Each of the author's sentences builds on the one before it. This is how she connects her ideas.

Writing Trait

ORGANIZATION
The author begins the paragraph with a **topic sentence. Details** support the topic sentence.

The galley (kitchen) crew prepares beef stew. Fresh carrots and potatoes are washed in a tin pail on deck. Breakfast will be oatmeal porridge.

The crew takes turns "standing watch" during the night. They search the ocean for possible dangers, including icebergs, reefs, whales, and pirates. While a cold wind rattles the rigging, the salty smell of the sea tickles noses.

Expository Composition

In an **expository composition** the writer gives information about a topic. To make a topic more interesting, writers may use examples and details from their own lives. Read this expository composition written by a student named Elena. Notice how she used different types of **sentences** to connect her ideas.

Student Writing Model

What We Learn from Animals
by Elena O.

Our classroom used to be like most other fifth-grade classrooms. Then we started collecting animals. Now we have fish, snails, a rabbit, and a hamster. Those are just the creatures that live in our room. Many more come to visit us each month. The animals aren't there just for fun, though; they help us learn.

I like to take care of the aquarium. The rocks, water, plants, animals, and fish in our aquarium make up an entire community. Snails help clean the bottom of the tank. If each part of the community isn't working together just right, the fish may die. We take turns feeding the fish and cleaning the tank.

Writing Trait

ORGANIZATION
The topic of Elena's composition is animals. Each paragraph has a **main idea** and **details**. Elena makes her topic interesting by using examples and details from her own life.

Writing Trait

SENTENCE FLUENCY
Elena uses a mix of **simple**, **compound**, and **complex sentences**. This keeps the writing interesting.

We love to watch Hector, our hamster, race around his cage and turn his exercise wheel. One day, Ruby, our rabbit, got loose and hid under a cabinet in the corner of the room. We had to coax her out with carrots. Observing these animals helps us learn about their traits. Caring for them helps us learn to be responsible.

Writing Trait

ORGANIZATION
Elena gives **examples** of visiting animals and what they help students learn.

Elena's **conclusion** paragraph sums up the important ideas of her composition.

Twice a month, we have Visiting Animal Day. One time, a police officer brought his K-9 dog to our classroom. On another day, we had a visit from a guide dog trainer. We learned a lot about how animals help people. We have posted pictures of our animal visitors.

Animals teach us many things. We learn about their care and feeding and about how helpful they can be to people. Most importantly, animals make our classroom a very interesting place.

A police officer and his K-9 dog ▶

Now look at what Elena did to prepare to write her expository composition.

Organizing Ideas

After Elena chose her topic, she used a chart to help her brainstorm facts and details for her composition. First, she listed the animals she wanted to write about. Then she listed what she and her classmates learned from each animal.

FACTS AND DETAILS	
Animals	What We Learned
fish	about animal communities
hamster, rabbit	about mammals and their traits
visiting animals	how animals help people

Outline

Then Elena created an outline to organize the parts of her composition. The outline shows the order of main ideas that Elena followed as she wrote her composition.

Title: What We Learn from Animals

I. Introduction:

II. Aquarium

    A. The animals in it

    B. What we learn from them

III. Mammals

    A. Rabbit

    B. Hamster

    C. What we learn from them

IV. Visiting animals

    A. Working dogs

    B. What we learn from them

V. Conclusion

Big  Idea

In informational narratives, writers can use compare and contrast as one type of text structure.

Enduring ! Understanding

Readers can better understand text when they recognize compare-and-contrast text structure.

Essential ? Question

Why do readers use the compare-and-contrast text structure?

Spelling Words

Words with Prefixes
re-, un-, non-

reenter	unable
refried	uninformed
reconsider	undesirable
repaint	untold
reform	unwise
replay	nonconductor
retake	nonproductive
remake	nonexistent
reclaim	nonflammable
replant	nondairy

Challenge

rewrap	reassemble
unspeakable	unsightly
nonessential	

Fluency

Intonation

Comprehension

 Text Structure: Compare and Contrast

 Monitor Comprehension: Self-Correct

Robust Vocabulary

adjust

residents

specimens

recoil

pesky

debris

internal

Writing

- Compare-and-Contrast Composition
- Sentence Fluency

Lesson 12

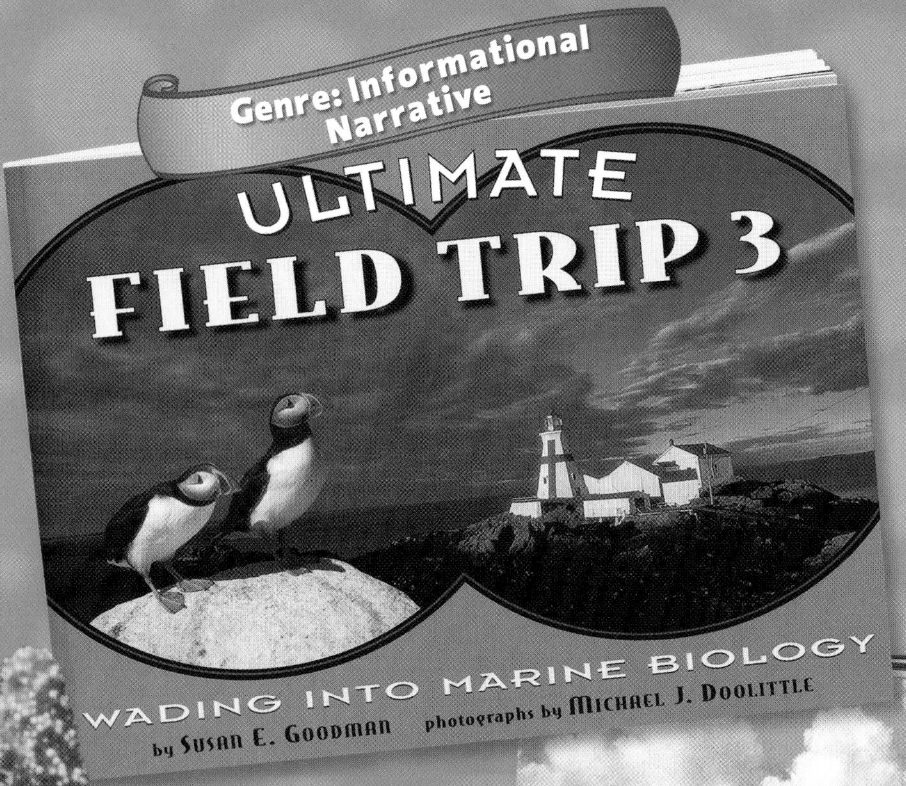

Genre: Informational Narrative

ULTIMATE FIELD TRIP 3

WADING INTO MARINE BIOLOGY

by Susan E. Goodman   photographs by Michael J. Doolittle

The Florida Everglades

by Kelly Strykul
illustrated by Robert Hynes

Genre: Expository Nonfiction

Text Structure: Compare and Contrast

You have learned that authors of nonfiction texts organize their ideas in certain ways called **text structures**. One kind of text structure is **compare and contrast**. In this text structure, the author shows how two or more ideas are alike and different. When you recognize this text structure in nonfiction text, you can better understand what you read.

Both

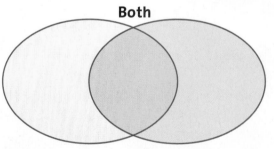

Tip In nonfiction text, use the headings to help you see how the author compared and contrasted information.

Read the paragraph below. Then look at the graphic organizer. It shows some of the similarities and differences the paragraph describes. The clue words *however* and *instead* signal a contrast.

Land snails and sea snails look similar. Both types of snails have spiral shells that protect their soft bodies. However, land snails have lungs instead of gills, which let them breathe air. Sea snails and land snails both need moisture to survive. Land snails produce mucus that keeps them from drying out, but sea snails get the moisture they need from the ocean.

Land Snails   **Both**   **Sea Snails**

have lungs | have spiral shells and soft bodies | have gills

 Try This!

Look back at the paragraph. Find another way in which land snails and sea snails are alike and another way they are different. What clue words helped you?

GO online www.harcourtschool.com/storytown

Vocabulary

Build Robust Vocabulary

residents

specimens

debris

recoil

internal

adjust

pesky

Seaside Surprises

The **residents** of Turtle Island are working hard to clean up area beaches after last weekend's storm. Local scientists, however, see it as an unexpected opportunity. Today, I'm walking on the beach with Dr. Diane Sabo, a marine biologist.

"During a storm such as the one last weekend, things get washed ashore that we'd normally never see on the beach," she says. She moves aside a strand of seaweed. "I've been collecting **specimens** of reef fish."

The storm washed up some **debris**. Dr. Sabo is impressed with what she finds.

302

Dr. Sabo is studying the ecosystem of the offshore reefs. "We learn a lot from the condition of the animals that wash up. Our ultimate goal is to use this knowledge to protect the reefs."

Dr. Sabo points to a dead fish in the sand. I try not to **recoil** at the sight. "It's not normally so bloated," she says. "Its swim bladder has expanded—that's an **internal** gas-filled sac that helps the fish **adjust** to changing water pressure."

As we walk, I wonder what she will point out next. The piles of debris, a **pesky** cleanup chore for some, hold many exciting clues for Dr. Sabo.

 www.harcourtschool.com/storytown

Word Detective

 This week, search for the Vocabulary Words in the world around you. Be alert for them as you listen to people talk and as you read magazine articles. Also, look for the Vocabulary Words in books about the natural environment. In your vocabulary journal, write the words you find and list where you found each one.

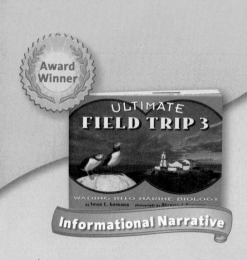

ULTIMATE
FIELD TRIP 3
WADING INTO MARINE BIOLOGY
by Susan E. Goodman   photographs by Michael J. Doolittle

Informational Narrative

Genre Study

An informational narrative is a story that presents factual information. As you read, look for

- headings that begin sections of related information.

- a story that involves real people or events

- information about a topic.

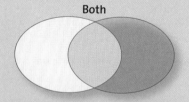

Both

Comprehension Strategy

Monitor comprehension as you read. Stop and **self-correct** reading mistakes that change the meaning of text.

Ultimate Field Trip 3:
Wading into
Marine Biology

by Susan E. Goodman

photographs by Michael J. Doolittle

LIFE IN THE TIDAL ZONE

Imagine living in a world that changes every six hours. First it sits underwater, then in open air. The temperature jumps from cold to steaming within minutes and from cool to freezing just as quickly. This world can be calm. And it can be battered by walls of water crashing down at twenty-five miles an hour.

This is the tidal zone—land covered and uncovered by the ocean as the tide climbs up and down the shore. To survive, the plants and animals of the tidal zone must be able to adjust to many different conditions. Snails creep along, for example, until the waves roll in. Then they attach themselves to rocks, using their single foot like a suction cup. Barnacles also avoid being swept out to sea by cementing themselves to rocks. Then, when the tide retreats, these barnacles close their shells tight to keep their wet world safely inside. Clams dig into the sand and wait for the water's return.

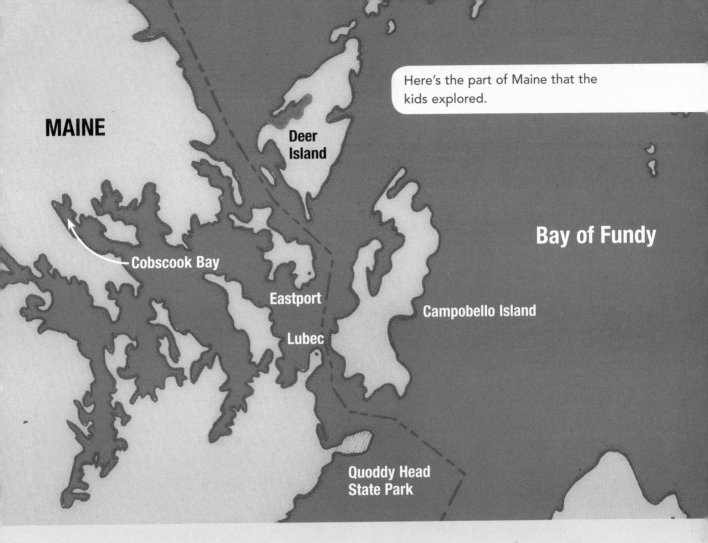

MAINE

Deer Island

Bay of Fundy

Cobscook Bay

Eastport

Lubec

Campobello Island

Quoddy Head State Park

Here's the part of Maine that the kids explored.

Every beach has a tidal zone, but the one in Cobscook Bay, Maine, is special. Its tides are among the highest in the world. In some places, the water climbs a mile onto shore. The bay's tidal zone is so big that the plants and animals living at its top are completely different from the ones closest to the ocean. Many marine biologists, scientists who study life in and around the sea, come to Cobscook Bay to learn how its creatures adapt to such a complicated life.

And they aren't alone. A group of middle-school kids came up to Suffolk University's Friedman Field Station. During their one-week program, they braved cold water and crab claws, searched for rock eels, and sailed the ocean to explore this amazing world.

TIDAL ZONES

The tidal zone has many subzones on its way from dry land to ocean. Each subzone's set of plants and animals is determined by how long they can survive in air and underwater. Some animals, like crabs, travel between different zones. Others, like mussels, may use one zone as a nursery and another to live their adult lives.

THE BLACK ZONE, just below dry land and above the highwater mark, occasionally gets wet from the spray of waves and the highest of high tides. Blue-green bacteria coat its rocks like black paint. A jellylike covering keeps this bacteria from drying out. But it can't save the bacteria from rough periwinkles that scrape it off the rocks for food.

THE UPPER ZONE is only underwater at high tide. Here, barnacles glue themselves to rocks and wait for high tide to bring them food. But these barnacles are food for dog whelks that drill holes into a barnacle's shell or force open its "trap door" with their foot and eat what's inside.

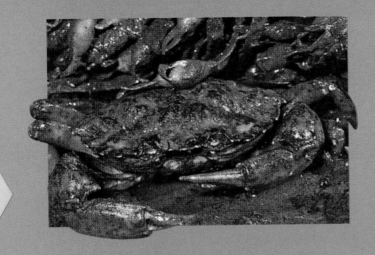

THE MIDDLE ZONE is both underwater and exposed to air during every tidal cycle. Here, seaweeds called rockweed and wrackweed use air bladders to stay afloat so they can catch the sunlight when they are in water. At both high tide and low, the seaweed provides cover for animals like mussels, smooth periwinkles, limpets, and this hiding crab.

THE LOWER ZONE is only exposed to air briefly, during low tide. Here, seaweeds like this Irish moss and sea lettuce protect the zone's residents—crabs, sea urchins, and sea stars—from drying out or being pounded by waves.

THE SUBTIDAL ZONE, always underwater, is home to larger seaweed called kelp. This busy zone is filled with familiar creatures like crabs, sea urchins, sea stars, fish, and lobsters. It is also inhabited by jellyfish, marine worms, anemones, and sea squirts like the sea vase pictured here.

This anemone may look like a flower, but it's actually a hollow relative of the jellyfish. Its "petals" are a ring of tentacles that first sting its prey, then drag the food toward a mouth in its center.

Dog whelks are the terrors of the tide pool. They hunt mussels, snails, and barnacles.

MEETING THE TIDAL RESIDENTS

A good way to learn about the tidal zone is to meet the animals that live there. On their first day in Maine, the kids put on their old sneakers or rubber boots. They were off to the bay for a look at its tidal residents—up close and personal.

"Soon it will be low tide, when the water's at its lowest point on the shore. That's the best time to find specimens," announced Dr. Carl Merrill, the marine biologist in charge of the field station. "In fact, we'd better get going; we don't have much time. Our tide comes back in fast, about one vertical foot every fifteen minutes."

"In other words, the tide climbs from your foot to your calf in about fifteen minutes," explained Chery Gibson, another instructor. "But since most beaches are set at an angle, the water could travel three, four feet up the shore in that same amount of time.

"The first time I was here, somebody asked me a question," Chery continued. "I needed my hands to answer, so I put my camera in a bucket beside me on the beach. By the time I'd finished, the bucket had already started floating and tipped over. My camera was ruined, but I learned to respect the tides."

"Wow," said Ben, "can they be dangerous?"

"You have to be careful," said Carl. "I've heard of plenty of hikers whose paths home were covered by water. Here, our rule is you don't go by the bay unless you're with a counselor. Another rule—after you've looked at a specimen, put it back exactly where you found it. Placing it just a few feet away could put it into another environment where it might not survive."

"I just found some mussels all together in a group," said Greg. "I wonder if they stick together for safety."

"While you're looking at something, try to notice how it has adapted to its place in the tidal zone," said Chery. "How does it stay wet during low tide? How does it avoid being eaten? What makes this animal special?"

Lugging their buckets, the kids trampled down to a part of the bay called the Narrows. Before he set them loose, Carl put a thermometer in the water. "Right now the water is about sixty-four degrees, a bit warmer than at high tide," he said. "It has heated up while sitting on shore."

"You call this warm?" Amie said as she waded in.

"No problem, I'm wearing two pairs of socks inside my boots," said Bill.

Soon, however, the kids forgot about their cold feet and goose bumps.

"Mussels by the millions!" said Kendra.

"Here's a whole city of them," said Roger. "They're crunching under my feet."

"They certainly couldn't get out of your way," said Chery, as they kneeled for a closer look. "Mussels tie themselves to rocks and seaweed using strings they make called byssal threads. That way, waves can't carry them out to sea. If you were stuck in one place like these mussels, how could you get your food?"

"Take-out?" Katelyn said, laughing.

"Try filtration," said Chery. "When it's covered with water, the mussel opens its shell. As water flows past its mouth, the mussel filters out tiny one-celled creatures and eats them."

Rock gunnels hide in crevices and under seaweed. They are also called "butterfish" because they're so hard to catch.

"I found an eel," Rand shouted as she lifted a rock. "Will it bite me?"

"I got one too," said Matt. "It feels so funny in your hand."

"It squirms like an eel, so people call it a 'rock eel,'" explained an instructor named Jennifer Kelly. "Actually, it's a fish called a rock gunnel. And don't worry, Rand, it eats shrimp and worms—not kids."

"Carl said they can't live out of water very long," said Richard. "We'd better put them back under their rocks."

At 1:45 P.M., Carl announced, "The current has stopped going out. Notice how still the water is. In just a minute, it will start coming back in."

The kids paused, but just for a moment. They were much more interested in their treasure hunt.

"Chery, check out this huge shell," said Hannah.

"That belonged to a moon snail, a fierce predator," said Chery. "Have you ever seen shells with a hole in them?"

"Aren't those holes there so you can make necklaces?" joked Laila.

"The moon snail holds a clam down with its foot and uses its radula, or tongue, to drill a hole in the shell," Chery explained. "Then it sucks the clam out and eats it."

"Starfish!" said Nicole, as she turned a common sea star over to examine its underside. "Look at all those little things. Are they teeth?"

"They're tube feet," said Carl. Then he explained how the starfish, or sea star, walks by pumping those tubes full of water and attaching the little suction cups at their tips onto something solid. When the sea star lets the water out, its feet recoil, pulling the animal forward.

At 2:03 P.M., Chery told the kids to watch the current. "The water's really coming in now," she said.

Carl placed his thermometer in the water. "The water coming in from the ocean is colder," he said. "The temperature has already dropped to sixty-one degrees."

"Start back in," Chery called to the group who had walked across low-tide mud to a nearby island. "I don't want to have to get you in the boat."

A few minutes later, Mary K. was looking for sea stars. "Hey, I'm sinking," she said.

"No you aren't," Amie replied, "the water's rising."

"That's cool!" Nicole exclaimed.

"No, it's scary," said Mary K.

The tide was covering their hunting grounds; it was time to leave. As she walked back, Mary H. said, "We're stepping on so many little mussels."

"I know," said Laila. "Everytime I hear a crunch I feel guilty now."

"They are gripping on my fingers," said Jen B. "I'm the Starfish Queen!"

313

HOW TIDES WORK

Long ago, people thought tides rose and fell as a sea god swallowed and spit out water. The real cause is up in space, not down at the bottom of the sea. The moon's gravity acts like a magnet pulling the earth's oceans. So the water level in the ocean closest to the moon rises up into high tide. At the same time, the water on the opposite side of Earth rides high as well. Meanwhile, the rest of Earth's oceans sink to a lower level. Since Earth rotates, the moon's pull upon the oceans moves across the globe. Most spots have two high tides and two low tides just about every day.

All beaches have tides, but the ones at Cobscook Bay are special. Cobscook Bay is part of the Bay of Fundy, which has the highest tides in the world. Most other bays have shallow, sloping sides, but this bay is steep-sided like a bathtub. When water rushes from the wide ocean into this narrow, steep place, there's nowhere to go but up. In some places, the difference between high and low tide can be as much as forty-eight vertical feet, the height of a four-story building!

Here's Katelyn standing on the shore at 4:05 P.M. . . .

. . . and in the same spot forty-five minutes later.

LIFE IN A TIDE POOL

Even at low tide, parts of the tidal zone keep their seawater. These tide pools can be little water-filled caves under rocks or even ponds twenty feet across. They are nature's aquariums, home to a semipermanent community of sea plants and animals.

Under a tide pool's seaweed, a hermit crab trades its outgrown shell for a bigger one. A sea star holds up the light-sensitive tip of its arm to "look" for a dark, safe corner. Water flows in and out of holes in a purple sponge's body, bringing in tiny bits of food.

"People often say, 'Life's a beach,' because they think being on a beach is free and easy," said Chery. "But it's no vacation for the creatures living there. Life can actually be dangerous for animals in a tide pool."

Winter can turn a small tide pool icy cold. The summer sun makes it too hot for comfort. And, as the temperature rises, oxygen bubbles out of the water, leaving less for animals to breathe. A tide pool's water can evaporate, too, making the water that remains much too salty. Rain can make the water not salty enough.

The kids kept all this in mind when they checked out a tide pool. But their real interest was finding animals that lived there. At first glance, a tide pool can look empty or just, as one kid called it, "Seaweed City." But with patience . . .

"Hey," said Bill. "I was feeling around under a rock and this sea urchin pricked me."

"That sure is a big one," said Chery. "Remember those tube feet sea stars have on their undersides? The urchins have them, too. This one's using its tube feet to hold pieces of shell against its body for camouflage."

"Here's a little starfish," said Vlad, holding up his find.

"That's actually called a blood star," said a counselor named Lila Austin.

"Will it suck my blood?"

"Actually, its name comes from its bright red color," she answered as she examined the tiny sea star. "Look, one of its arms has been eaten off."

"Is it going to die?" Vlad asked.

"Nope," said Lila, "its arms grow back. If one is crushed, the sea star gets rid of it and grows another."

Now scientists know that even one sea star arm can grow four new ones—as long as it remains attached to part of the disk in the animal's center. Fishermen used to think sea stars were pests but didn't know about this unusual ability. So whenever they found sea stars in their nets, they'd cut them in half and throw them back into the sea. The joke was on the fishermen. Instead of destroying one pesky sea star, they produced two!

Laila and Vlad put the blood star back into the water and watched it settle onto a rock. But Laila couldn't stop thinking about the sea star's amazing trick. "Wouldn't it be great if we could do the same thing?" she said. "We'd never wear casts or use crutches again."

A type of sea star called a sun star typically has eight to twelve legs, but when Paul first saw it, he asked, "Is this a radioactive mutant?"

Tide pools near the waterline are nurseries for young lobsters.

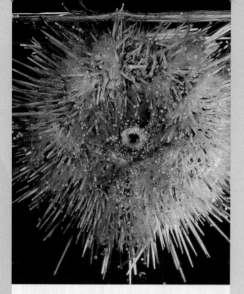

Urchins also use their tube feet to move around to graze on algae.

The distance high tide climbs onto the shore changes over the course of a month. Since each high tide marks the shore by leaving debris, this picture shows a part of the cycle when the high tides are getting lower.

OUT WITH THE TIDE

Right before high tide, the kids returned to the shore—what was left of it. In the six hours since low tide, water had swallowed most of the beach. Now safely underwater, the animals of the tidal zone were busy feeding.

Carl had everyone sit on the rocks that remained so they could put their feet in the water and feel the tide turn.

"In exactly three minutes, the water will come to a dead stop. That will be high tide," said Jennifer. "A few minutes later, it will start going out again."

"Sh-h-h," said Carl. "Let's see if you can *hear* the water turn as well."

The kids didn't say a word. They looked across the still waters. They listened to crickets chirping. Matt picked up a sea urchin and felt its sharp spines. Roger found a flat stone and cheated by skipping it across the silent bay.

"Are our feet supposed to be getting numb?" asked Andrew.

"Take them out of the water if you're cold," said Carl, "but think about how lucky it is that you can. When you're cold, you can move your feet or put on a sweater. And since you're warm-blooded, you have an internal thermometer that helps you adjust and keep warm.

"Imagine life as a barnacle or mussel. Imagine being cold-blooded so that your body temperature depended upon the surrounding environment. These animals can be sitting in sixty-degree water and suddenly, when the tide drops, they are hit with an eighty-five-degree day. With the sun pounding on the rocks, it could be hotter than that."

"Listen," Mary H. called excitedly, "I can hear it now!"

The water had started its rush toward the ocean. Within moments, Amie saw her ankle bracelet peek out of the bay. Matt put his sea urchin back in the water and the outgoing current pushed it toward the sea.

The tide's endless cycle had once more begun.

Think Critically

1. What does the author of "Ultimate Field Trip 3: Wading into Marine Biology" want readers to understand about the tidal zones? AUTHOR'S PURPOSE

2. In your opinion, why is it important to disturb wild creatures as little as possible? DRAW CONCLUSIONS

3. Explain what happens to a tidal zone over the course of one day? SUMMARIZE/SEQUENCE

4. Why do you think the author used a compare-and-contrast text structure to organize the information in this selection? TEXT STRUCTURE: COMPARE AND CONTRAST

5. **WRITE** How do plants and animals of Cobscook Bay survive in a harsh environment? Use information and details from the selection to explain your answer. SHORT RESPONSE

About the Author
Susan E. Goodman

From an early age, Susan Goodman knew she wanted to become a writer. A teacher gave her this advice: *First* a writer figures out what to say and *then* finds the right words to express the ideas. Susan Goodman's life as a writer has taken her on many adventures, such as to the Amazon rain forest to write about an underwater hotel. Her advice to young writers is this: "Read a lot—and then read some more. Think a lot—and then think some more . . . . And imagine a lot—and then imagine some more."

About the Photographer
Michael J. Doolittle

Whether Michael J. Doolittle is exploring a rain forest in Peru, a skyscraper in New York, or a tidal zone in Maine, it's just another day at the office for this adventurous photographer. No matter where he travels, he likes photographing children, and his pictures can be found in many books and magazines. Michael J. Doolittle lives with his wife and two daughters in Connecticut.

GO online www.harcourtschool.com/storytown

321

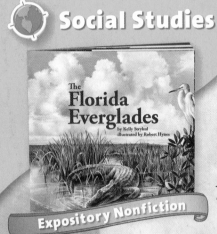

The Florida Everglades
by Kelly Strykul
illustrated by Robert Hynes

Expository Nonfiction

The Florida

A Fragile Ecosystem

The Everglades is an area of great natural beauty that spreads across much of southern Florida. It is an ecosystem that includes plants, animals, and water. An ecosystem is all the living and nonliving things in an environment and how they interact with one another.

The Miccosukee (mik•uh•soo•kee) Indians of Florida call the Everglades *Pa-hay-okee,* which means "River of Grass." For thousands of years, the waters of the Everglades flowed from the Kissimmee (ki•sih•mee) River Basin into Lake Okeechobee and then to Florida Bay. The plants and animals living in the Everglades depended on the food and water provided by this large wetland area.

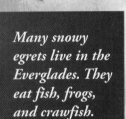

Many snowy egrets live in the Everglades. They eat fish, frogs, and crawfish.

The three maps below show how the flow of the Everglades has changed.

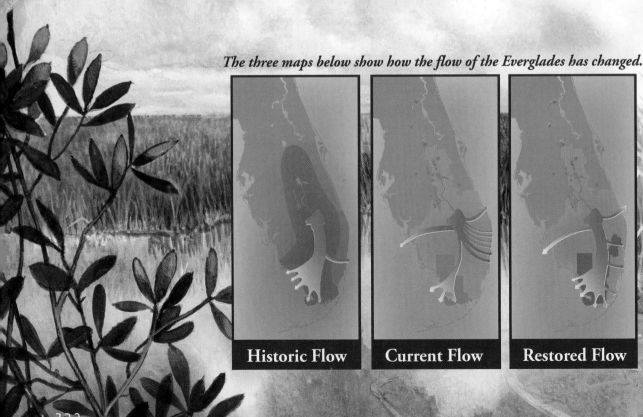

Historic Flow **Current Flow** **Restored Flow**

Everglades

by Kelly Strykul   illustrated by Robert Hynes

Human Impact

Some people saw the Everglades as a chance to create land where there was none. Land developers built canals that drained the swampy water. This changed large areas of wetland into land that people could use for farming.

In the 1920s northern tourists visited Florida. They liked the warm winter climate. Some of them decided to settle in the Everglades, and they drained even more parts of it. Farms and towns replaced much of the river water in the Everglades. This changed the natural flow of water and left less water for the plants and animals. Over time, fertilizers used on farm crops polluted the waters of the Everglades. Today, the Everglades is only half as big as it was one hundred years ago.

Protection and Restoration

Many people have worked to protect the Everglades. Marjory Stoneman Douglas was one of them. For much of her life, she taught others that it was important to save the Everglades. Because of her work and the efforts of others, part of the Everglades became a national park in 1947. In Everglades National Park, the fragile ecosystem has been protected.

The Miccosukee and other concerned people have worked together to help stop the pollution in the Everglades. In 1994, the state government of Florida passed the Everglades Forever Act. As part of the act, six treatment marshes were built. These marshes filter pollution from water before it flows into the Everglades.

In 2000 the state of Florida, the federal government, Native American groups, and other groups developed a plan to protect the Everglades ecosystem. This plan, called the Comprehensive Everglades Restoration Plan, includes projects to restore the natural flow of water through the Everglades. The projects will take more than thirty years to complete, but the result will be the preservation of the Everglades for future generations.

The alligator is a famous resident of the Florida Everglades.

Connections

Comparing Texts

1. Imagine you are on the field trip to Cobscook Bay. What is your favorite part of the trip? Why?

2. How are the ideas in "Wading into Marine Biology" and "The Florida Everglades" alike and different?

3. The students in "Wading into Marine Biology" visit a unique setting. What interesting setting could students at your school visit?

Vocabulary Review

Residents of a tide pool must adjust to changes in temperature.

Word Pairs

Work with a partner. Write the Vocabulary Words on separate index cards. Place the cards face down. Take turns flipping over two cards and writing a sentence that uses both words. Read the sentence aloud to your partner. You must use the words correctly to keep the cards. The player with more cards at the end wins.

adjust

residents

specimens

recoil

pesky

debris

internal

Fluency Practice

Repeated Reading

Choose a page to read aloud from "Wading into Marine Biology." Read to the end of the page. Think about how you would use correct intonation. Then reread the page using correct intonation.

Writing

Write a Letter

Imagine that you are a marine biologist. A student has written you a letter asking whether rock crabs are different from hermit crabs. Write a letter that summarizes the differences between these animals.

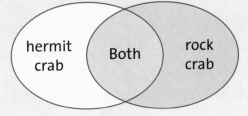

My Writing Checklist

Writing Trait ▸ Sentence Fluency

✔ I used a Venn diagram to plan my writing.

✔ I used a variety of sentence types to match my purpose.

✔ I used the correct form for a letter.

Big Idea
In tall tales, the qualities of the characters cause impossible events to occur.

Enduring Understanding
Readers recognize that impossible events in tall tales happen because of the characters' exaggerated qualities.

Essential Question
How does the reader determine exaggeration in tall tales?

Spelling Words

Words with Suffixes
-able, -ible, -ment, -less

development	amazement
dispensable	priceless
enjoyable	judgment
digestible	resentment
divisible	embarrassment
irresistible	boundless
admissible	ageless
appointment	aimless
argument	motionless
payment	worthless

Challenge

meaningless	gullible
dependable	credible
portable	

Fluency
Pace

Comprehension
Cause and Effect

Use Graphic Organizers

Robust Vocabulary
bellowing
outcast
reputation
betrayed
yearning
withered
escapades
unfathomable

Writing
- Descriptive Paragraph: Character
- Conventions

Lesson 13

Genre: Tall Tale

Stormalong
from American Tall Tales
by Mary Pope Osborne   illustrated by Greg Newbold

PAUL BUNYAN
Makes Progress
BY PLEASANT DeSPAIN

Genre: Tall Tale

Focus Skill

 ## Cause and Effect

A **cause** is the reason that something happens. An **effect** is what happens as a result. In a story, one event often causes another event to happen. A cause may have more than one effect, and an effect may have more than one cause. The words *because*, *when*, *then*, and *so* may signal a cause-and-effect relationship.

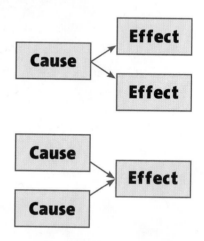

Tip

Asking yourself the question *Why did this happen?* can help you figure out the cause or causes of an event.

328

Read the paragraph below. Think about how the events are related. Then look at the graphic organizer, which shows one cause-and-effect relationship from the paragraph.

Strong winds blew across the ocean, rocking the ship violently. Then a huge wave, whipped up by the storm, crashed onto the deck. "Take down the sails!" the captain shouted. The sailors worked fast to get control of their ship. When the last sail was down, the rocking slowed. The soaked crew members breathed a sigh of relief.

Cause	**Effect**
Strong winds blew.	The ship rocked violently.
	A huge wave crashed on the deck.

Try This!

Look back at the paragraph. When the crew members took down the sails, what effect did this have on the ship?

 www.harcourtschool.com/storytown

329

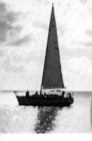

Vocabulary

Build Robust Vocabulary

- reputation
- yearning
- escapades
- bellowing
- betrayed
- outcast
- withered
- unfathomable

Life on the Sea Eagle

May 14, 1847

From the first time I saw her in the harbor, I wanted to sail on the *Sea Eagle.* Her **reputation** as the fastest clipper ship around made my **yearning** stronger. Finally, today, this wonderful day, I joined the ship's crew!

May 19

These first days aboard, I've been hearing stories about the ship's **escapades** on the high seas. Old Barton told me about the night he heard a horrible **bellowing** in the darkness. He peered over the side to discover a whale-sized walrus with spear-length tusks, swimming alongside the ship!

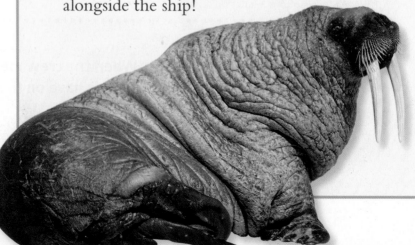

June 9

The winds have **betrayed** us! For the past week, there hasn't been even the softest breath of wind. The ship is like an **outcast**, drifting lazily in the vast ocean. Our once-mighty sails hang like **withered** leaves at the end of autumn. No one on the ship can believe our misfortune. It is **unfathomable** that our mighty ship has not moved in so many days.

June 12

The winds have picked up. We are once again speeding across the sea. Soon we will arrive at our destination, Boston Harbor.

 www.harcourtschool.com/storytown

Word Champion

 Make it one of your goals this week to use Vocabulary Words outside of your classroom. Keep the words in mind as you talk to your family and friends. For example, you might ask a family member to tell you about an escapade he or she had. In your vocabulary journal, write the sentences you spoke or heard that contained the Vocabulary Words.

Tall Tale

Genre Study

A tall tale is a humorous story about impossible or exaggerated events. As you read, look for

- exaggerations about the strength and abilities of a character.

- stories and legends about American folk heroes.

Cause → Effect

Comprehension Strategy

Use graphic organizers like the one above to keep track of causes and effects in the text.

Stormalong

by Mary Pope Osborne   illustrated by Greg Newbold

One day in the early 1800s a tidal wave crashed down on the shores of Cape Cod in New England. After the wave had washed back out to sea, the villagers heard deep, bellowing sounds coming from the beach. When they rushed to find out what was going on, they couldn't believe their eyes. A giant baby three fathoms tall—or eighteen feet!—was crawling across the sand, crying in a voice as loud as a foghorn.

The villagers put the baby in a big wheelbarrow and carried him to town. They took him to the meetinghouse and fed him barrels and barrels of milk. As ten people patted the baby on the back, the minister said, "What will we name him?"

"How about *Alfred Bulltop Stormalong*?" a little boy piped up. "And call him Stormy for short."

The baby smiled at the boy.

"Stormy it is!" everyone cried.

As he grew older Stormy was the main attraction of Cape Cod. He didn't care for all the attention, however. It reminded him that he was different from everyone else. After school he always tried to slip away to the sea. He liked to swim out into the deep water and ride the whales and porpoises. Stormy's love for the ocean was so strong that folks used to say he had salt water in his veins.

By the time Stormy was twelve, he was already six fathoms tall—or thirty-six feet! "I guess you're going to have to go out into the world now," his friends said sadly. "The truth is, you've grown too big for this town. You can't fit in the schoolhouse, and you're too tall to work in a store. Maybe you should go to Boston. It's a lot bigger than Cape Cod."

Stormy felt like an outcast as he packed his trunk, hoisted it over his shoulder, and started away. And when he arrived in Boston, he discovered something that made him even sadder. Although the city had more buildings than Cape Cod, they were just as small. Worse than that, his huge size and foghorn voice scared the daylights out of everyone he met.

"A sailor's life is the only one for me," he said, staring longingly at Boston Harbor. "The sea's my best friend. It's with her that I belong." And with his back to Boston, Stormy strode toward the biggest Yankee clipper docked in the harbor, *The Lady of the Sea*.

"Blow me down!" said the captain when Stormy stood before him. "I've never seen a man as big as you before."

"I'm not a man," said Stormy. "I'm twelve years old."

"Blow me down again!" said the captain. "I guess you'll have to be the biggest cabin boy in the world then. Welcome aboard, son."

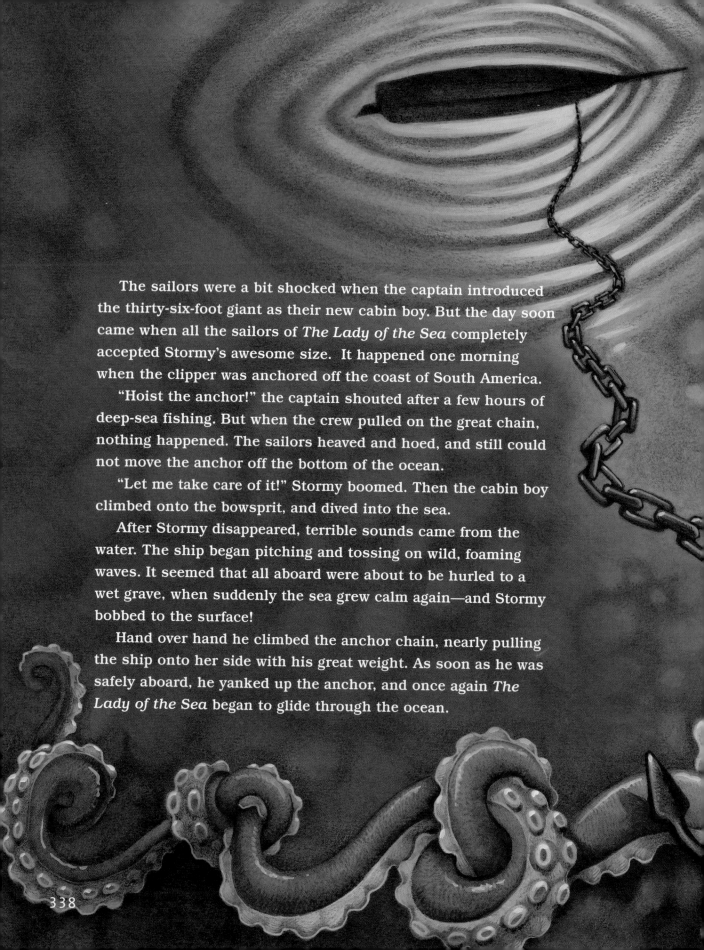

The sailors were a bit shocked when the captain introduced the thirty-six-foot giant as their new cabin boy. But the day soon came when all the sailors of *The Lady of the Sea* completely accepted Stormy's awesome size. It happened one morning when the clipper was anchored off the coast of South America.

"Hoist the anchor!" the captain shouted after a few hours of deep-sea fishing. But when the crew pulled on the great chain, nothing happened. The sailors heaved and hoed, and still could not move the anchor off the bottom of the ocean.

"Let me take care of it!" Stormy boomed. Then the cabin boy climbed onto the bowsprit, and dived into the sea.

After Stormy disappeared, terrible sounds came from the water. The ship began pitching and tossing on wild, foaming waves. It seemed that all aboard were about to be hurled to a wet grave, when suddenly the sea grew calm again—and Stormy bobbed to the surface!

Hand over hand he climbed the anchor chain, nearly pulling the ship onto her side with his great weight. As soon as he was safely aboard, he yanked up the anchor, and once again *The Lady of the Sea* began to glide through the ocean.

"What happened?" cried the crew.

"Just a little fight with a two-ton octopus," said Stormy.

"Octopus!"

"Aye. He didn't want to let go of our anchor."

"What'd you do to him?" the others cried.

"Wrestled eight slimy tentacles into double knots. It'll take a month o' Sundays for him to untie himself."

From then on Stormy was the most popular sailor on board. Over the next few years his reputation spread too, until all the Yankee clipper crews wanted him to sail with them.

But Stormy still wasn't happy. Partly it was because
no ship, not even *The Lady of the Sea*, was big enough
for him. She would nearly tip over when he stood close
to her rail. All her wood peeled off when he scrubbed
her decks. And giant waves rolled over her sides when
he sang a sea chantey.

Worst of all, Stormy was still lonely. The clipper's
hammocks were so small that at night he had to sleep
by himself in a rowboat. As he listened to the other
sailors singing and having a good time, he felt as if his
best friend, the sea, had betrayed him. Maybe it was
time for the giant sailor to move on.

One day, when *The Lady of the Sea* dropped anchor in Boston, Stormy announced to his friends that he'd decided to give up his seafaring life. "I'm going to put an oar over my shoulder and head west," he said. "I hear there's room enough for any kind of folks out there, even ones as big as me."

"Where will you settle down, Stormy?" a sailor asked.

"I'm going to walk till the first person asks me, 'Hey, mister, what's that funny thing you got on your shoulder there?' Then I'll know I'm far enough away from the sea, and I won't ever think about her again."

Stormy walked through the cities of Providence and New York. He walked through the pine barrens of New Jersey and the woods of Pennsylvania. He crossed the Allegheny Mountains and floated on flatboats down the Ohio River.

Pioneers often invited Stormy to share their dinner, but these occasions only made him homesick, for folks always guessed he was a sailor and asked him questions about the sea.

It wasn't until Stormy came to the plains of Kansas that a farmer said, "Hey, mister, what's that funny thing you got on your shoulder?"

"You asked the right question, mate," said Stormy. "I'm going to settle down on this spot and dig me some potatoes!"

And that's just what Stormy did. Soon he became the best farmer around. He planted over five million potatoes and watered his whole crop with the sweat of his brow.

But all the time Stormy was watering, hoeing, picking, and planting, he knew he still had not found a home. He was too big to go square dancing in the dance hall. He was too big to visit other farmhouses, too big for the meetinghouse, too big for the general store.

And he felt a great yearning for the sea. He missed the fishy-smelling breezes and salt spray. Never in the prairies did a giant wave knock him to his knees. Never did a hurricane whirl him across the earth. How could he ever test his true strength and courage?

One day, several years after Stormy's disappearance, the sailors of Boston Harbor saw a giant coming down the wharf, waving his oar above his head. As he approached, they began to whoop with joy. Stormy was back!

But as happy as they were to see him, they were horrified when they discovered how bad he looked. He was all stooped over. His face was like a withered cornstalk, and there were pale bags under his eyes.

After word spread about Stormy's condition, thousands of sailors met to talk about the problem.

"We've got to keep him with us this time," one said.

"There's only one way to do it," said another. "Build a ship that's big enough."

"Aye!" the others agreed. "We can't be having him trail behind us at night in his own rowboat!"

So the New England sailors set about building the biggest clipper ship in the world. Her sails had to be cut and sewn in the Mojave Desert, and after she was built, there was a lumber shortage all over America. It took over forty seamen to manage her pilot's wheel—unless, of course, the captain happened to be Alfred Bulltop Stormalong, who could whirl the ship's wheel with his baby finger!

Stormalong named the clipper *The Courser*. On her maiden voyage, he clutched *The Courser*'s wheel and steered her out of Boston Harbor. As he soared over the billowing waves, his cheeks glowed with sunburn, his hair sparkled with ocean spray, and the salt water began coursing through his veins again.

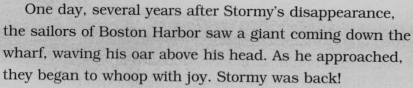

Soon Stormy and *The Courser* were taking cargoes all over the world—to India, China, and Europe. It took four weeks to get all hands on deck. Teams of white horses carried sailors from stem to stern. The ship's towering masts had to be hinged to let the sun and the moon go by. The tips of the masts were padded so they wouldn't punch holes in the sky. The trip to the crow's nest took so long, the sailors who climbed to the top returned with gray beards. The vessel was so big that once, when she hit an island in the Caribbean Sea, she knocked it clear into the Gulf of Mexico!

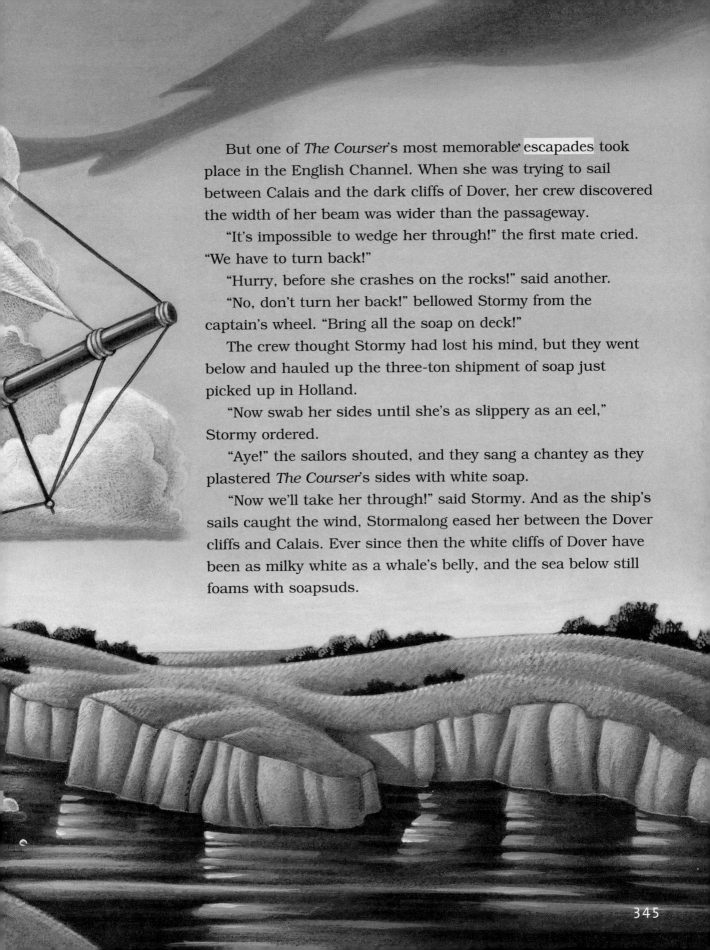

But one of *The Courser*'s most memorable escapades took place in the English Channel. When she was trying to sail between Calais and the dark cliffs of Dover, her crew discovered the width of her beam was wider than the passageway.

"It's impossible to wedge her through!" the first mate cried. "We have to turn back!"

"Hurry, before she crashes on the rocks!" said another.

"No, don't turn her back!" bellowed Stormy from the captain's wheel. "Bring all the soap on deck!"

The crew thought Stormy had lost his mind, but they went below and hauled up the three-ton shipment of soap just picked up in Holland.

"Now swab her sides until she's as slippery as an eel," Stormy ordered.

"Aye!" the sailors shouted, and they sang a chantey as they plastered *The Courser*'s sides with white soap.

"Now we'll take her through!" said Stormy. And as the ship's sails caught the wind, Stormalong eased her between the Dover cliffs and Calais. Ever since then the white cliffs of Dover have been as milky white as a whale's belly, and the sea below still foams with soapsuds.

For years Stormalong was the most famous sea captain in the world. Sailors in every port told how he ate ostrich eggs for breakfast, a hundred gallons of whale soup for lunch, and a warehouseful of shark meat for dinner. They told how after every meal he'd pick his teeth with an eighteen-foot oar—some said it was the same oar he once carried to Kansas.

But it was also said that sometimes when the crew sang chanteys late at night, their giant captain would stand alone on the deck, gazing out at the sea with a look of unfathomable sorrow in his eyes.

After the Civil War, steamships began to transport cargo over the seas. The days of the great sailing ships came to an end, and the courageous men who steered the beautiful Yankee clippers across the oceans also began to disappear.

No one remembers quite how Stormalong died. All they recollect is his funeral. It seems that one foggy twilight thousands of sailors attended his burial. They covered him with a hundred yards of the finest Chinese silk, and then fifty sailors carried his huge coffin to a grave near the sea. As they dug into the sand with silver spades and lowered his coffin with a silver cord, they wept tears like rain.

And for years afterward they sang about him:

*Old Stormy's dead and gone to rest—
To my way, hey, Stormalong!
Of all the sailors he was the best—
Aye, aye, aye, Mister Stormalong!*

Ever since then seamen first class put "A.B.S." after their names. Most people think it means "Able-Bodied Seaman." But the old New England seafaring men know different. They know it stands for the most amazing deep-water sailor who ever lived, Alfred Bulltop Stormalong.

Think Critically

1. Why does Stormalong decide to give up the seafaring life? CAUSE AND EFFECT

2. Why does Stormalong yearn to return to sea after he becomes a successful farmer? CHARACTER'S MOTIVATIONS

3. What do you think is the theme in "Stormalong"? THEME

4. How does the author's use of exaggerated details help influence the way readers see Stormalong? AUTHOR'S CRAFT/IMAGERY

5. WRITE Stormalong's size has advantages and disadvantages. Use details and information from the story to explain both the benefits and the challenges of being so big. SHORT RESPONSE

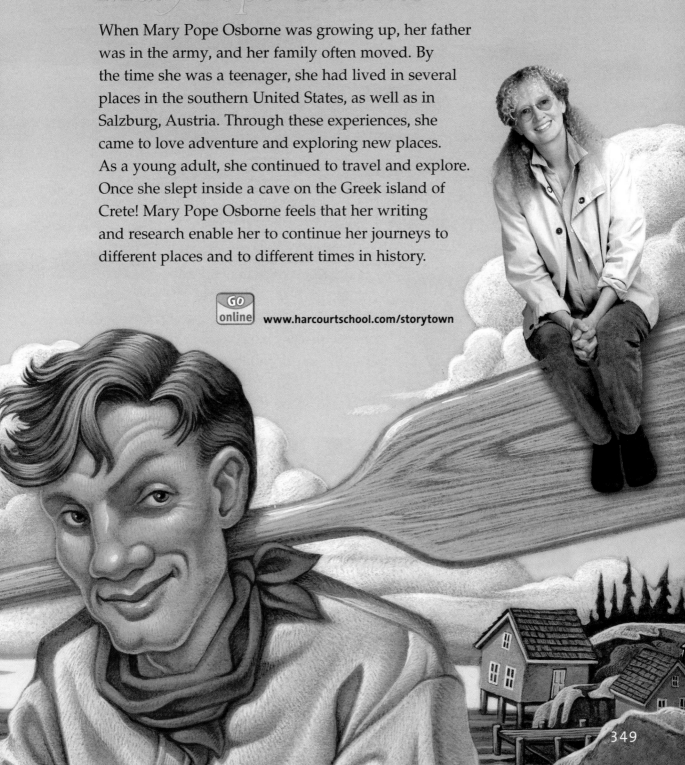

About the Author

Mary Pope Osborne

When Mary Pope Osborne was growing up, her father was in the army, and her family often moved. By the time she was a teenager, she had lived in several places in the southern United States, as well as in Salzburg, Austria. Through these experiences, she came to love adventure and exploring new places. As a young adult, she continued to travel and explore. Once she slept inside a cave on the Greek island of Crete! Mary Pope Osborne feels that her writing and research enable her to continue her journeys to different places and to different times in history.

GO online www.harcourtschool.com/storytown

PAUL BUNYAN Makes Progress

BY PLEASANT DeSPAIN
ILLUSTRATED BY JON FLAMING

Tall Tale

Paul Bunyan, the Hercules of lumberjacks, was born in the Maine woods. A rambunctious baby, he leveled an acre of trees while learning to crawl. On the day that he turned seven, he used his daddy's saw to harvest three square miles of standing timber before lunchtime.

A strange blue snow fell one frozen winter morning a few years later. Everything was buried under a cold blanket of bright blue! Young Paul strapped on his snowshoes to explore this new landscape. Upon hearing the cry of a lost calf, he found a tiny blue ox stuck in a snowdrift. He pulled him out and took him home.

Paul named him Babe and fed him plenty of hay. The ox grew large, right along with Paul. Full grown, Babe measured seven axe-handles between his eyes.

Paul trained Babe to help him log the Maine woods. He would pull giant trees from the forest with ease. If a crooked road made it difficult to haul logs down to the river, Paul would attach one end of a thick chain to the road and the other end to Babe. Babe pulled so hard that the road would straighten right out.

After cutting down most of the tall trees in Maine, Paul and Babe moved to Minnesota. Then they took care of the forests in Michigan and Wisconsin. When they finished their work in the great North Woods, they traveled to the Far West, ending up in Oregon and Washington.

Paul marveled at this region's two-hundred-foot fir trees. Their enormous brown-bark trunks had taken five hundred years and more to grow. It was the first time he'd seen trees taller than he was. Paul showed Babe the majestic Olympic Mountain Range that led to the edge of the Pacific Ocean. He thought it wonderful that the snow-capped Cascade Mountains cut through the center of this lush region. And he was delighted by all the timberwolves, grizzly bears, and long-eared jack rabbits.

"I'm a woodsman and a logger," he said to Babe. "I'm the lumberjack of all lumberjacks! I'm as old as time, as tall as a mountain, and as powerful as an earthquake. My axe will fell these trees. My saws will cut this lumber. To progress is to build. Let's help build the great Northwest!"

Connections

Comparing Texts

1. Stormalong loves the sea so much that people say, "He has salt water in his veins." Give a vivid description of a place you love.

2. How did the events in the lives of Stormalong and Paul Bunyan lead to their accomplishments?

3. Stormalong did not feel at home in many places in North America in the 1800s. How might he feel today?

Vocabulary Review

Rate a Situation

With a partner, read aloud each sentence below. Point to a spot on the line to show how comfortable you would feel in each situation. Explain your choices.

Least Comfortable ——————————— Most Comfortable

- You heard **bellowing** coming from the next room.
- Your friend planned new **escapades**.
- You have a **reputation** for being funny.
- There was only a **withered** apple for a snack.

bellowing

outcast

reputation

betrayed

yearning

withered

escapades

unfathomable

Fluency Practice

Partner Reading

Work with a partner. Choose from "Stormalong" several paragraphs to read. Reread the paragraphs aloud as your partner listens and follows along. When you finish reading, ask your partner to give you feedback about your pace. Your partner should say "too fast," "too slow," or "just right." Then switch roles.

Writing

Write a Poem

Think about some of the amazing feats Stormalong accomplishes. Write a poem describing the cause and effect of one of these feats.

Cause → Effect

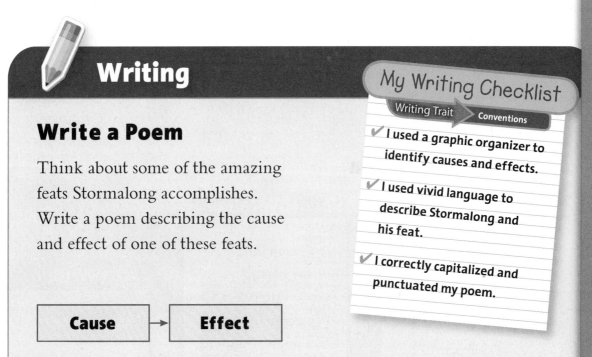

My Writing Checklist

Writing Trait ▸ Conventions

✔ I used a graphic organizer to identify causes and effects.

✔ I used vivid language to describe Stormalong and his feat.

✔ I correctly capitalized and punctuated my poem.

Big 💡 Idea

Writers of expository nonfiction use a causal chain when writing about a series of causes and effects.

Enduring ❗ Understanding

Readers recognize a causal chain by using cause-and-effect clues while reading.

Essential ❓ Question

How do readers know that the author has used a cause-and-effect text structure?

Spelling Words

Words with Endings /ən/, /əl/, /ər/

barrel	mayor
cannon	pepper
capitol	polar
civil	proper
clever	sandal
discover	saucer
frozen	original
general	theater
hidden	tutor
inventor	musical

Challenge

cinnamon	factual
accidental	intentional
elevator	

Fluency

Pace

Robust Vocabulary

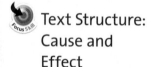

- elongates
- elastic
- rigid
- accumulate
- underlying
- intricate
- vanish
- replenishing

Comprehension

 Text Structure: Cause and Effect

Use Graphic Organizers

Writing

- Cause-and-Effect Paragraph
- Conventions

Lesson 14

Genre: Expository Nonfiction

A
DROP
OF
WATER

A BOOK OF SCIENCE AND WONDER BY

WALTER WICK

RAIN, DANCE!
STEAM
ICE CYCLE

Genre: Poetry

Text Structure: Cause and Effect

Authors of nonfiction texts may organize information in a **cause-and-effect text structure**. In texts with this structure, a cause may have an effect that then becomes the next cause. A series of causes and effects is called a **causal chain**. You can use a graphic organizer like this one to keep track of the cause-and-effect relationships in the text.

| Cause | → | Effect/Cause | → | Effect |

Tip

Look for clue words such as *when, then, so,* and *because* in nonfiction text to help you identify cause-and-effect relationships.

Read the paragraph below. Then look at the graphic organizer, which shows a causal chain. The paragraph states that falling rain caused the water level in the river to rise. The rising water then caused fallen logs and branches to be lifted from the shore.

Rain fell for six days, raising the water level of the river. When the water rose, it lifted fallen logs and branches from the shore. Then the swift water carried this debris downstream, to the place where the flooded river widened. When the rushing water slowed down, it deposited logs and branches on the river's banks there, miles from where they had fallen.

Cause	**Effect/Cause**	**Effect**
Rain fell for six days.	The water in the river rose.	The water lifted logs and branches from the shore.

Try This!

Look back at the paragraph. Identify another event that could be added to the causal chain. Where in the graphic organizer would you place this event?

 www.harcourtschool.com/storytown

Vocabulary

Build Robust Vocabulary

- elongates
- replenishing
- intricate
- rigid
- accumulate
- elastic
- vanish
- underlying

Water Striders

The water strider is an insect that travels on the surface of ponds and slow-moving streams. Like other insects, it starts life as an egg. The egg hatches into a nymph. As the nymph eats, its body **elongates**. The water strider sheds its hard external skin several times before it reaches adult size. An adult female may lay hundreds of eggs, **replenishing** the water strider population in the pond.

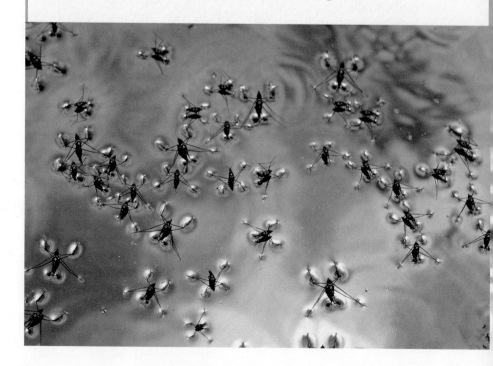

Water striders often skate in groups.

A water strider's legs are covered with an **intricate** arrangement of tiny, **rigid** hairs. These hairs **accumulate** air bubbles around them. The bubbles keep the insect from sinking and let it move in a way that looks as if it's skating.

If you look carefully, you can see that the water strider's legs press into the water, making dimples on the **elastic** surface of the pond. If you disturb a water strider, it quickly skates away, seeming to **vanish** among the reeds.

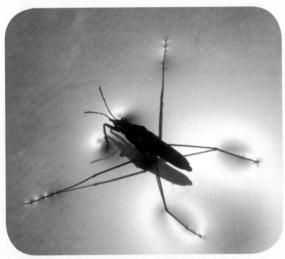

The water strider's legs stretch the surface of the water but don't break it. Surface tension is the **underlying** property of water that makes this possible.

 www.harcourtschool.com/storytown

Word Scribe

This week, use the Vocabulary Words in your writing. In your vocabulary journal, write sentences to show you understand the meanings of the words. You could write about an intricate design you've seen in an art book. Write about as many of the Vocabulary Words as you can.

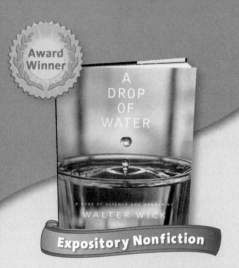

A DROP OF WATER

A BOOK OF SCIENCE AND WONDER BY WALTER WICK

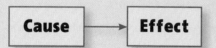

Expository Nonfiction

Genre Study

Expository nonfiction gives facts and information about a topic. As you read, look for

- headings that begin sections of related information.

- text structure—the ways the ideas and information are organized.

Cause	→	Effect

Comprehension Strategy

Use graphic organizers like the one shown above to write causes and effects.

A
DROP
OF
WATER

written and photographed by Walter Wick

WATER'S SMALLEST PARTS

A drop of water falls through the air. Down it splashes,
breaking apart into tiny droplets. What would you see
if you could break water into even smaller bits?

No matter how closely you look, you can't see water's
tiniest parts. Like every other substance in the world, water
is made of very tiny particles called molecules. On the pin
below, the smallest droplet contains more than three hundred
trillion water molecules.

PIN
ACTUAL SIZE

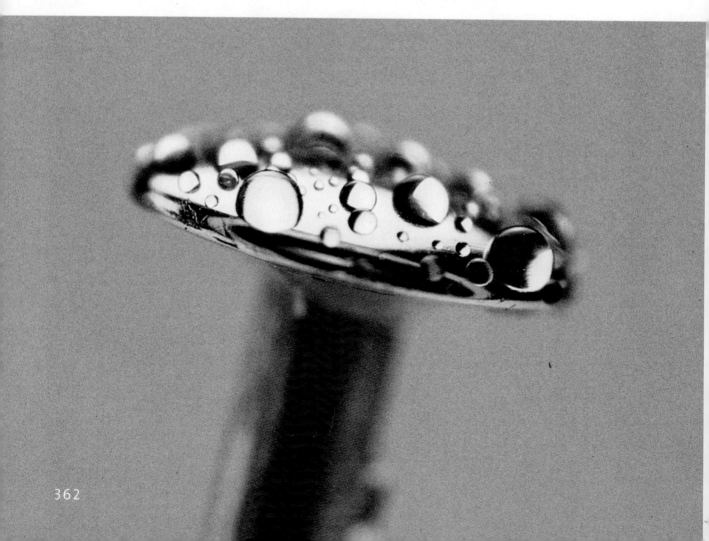

WATER'S ELASTIC SURFACE

Step by step, a camera reveals the curious changing shape of a drop of water as it falls from a spout.

The drop grows heavy and begins to fall. As it breaks from a strand of water, the drop shrinks itself into a round ball, or *sphere*. The drop flattens then elongates as it falls.

The strand, meanwhile, breaks into tiny droplets. The impact of the drops hitting the water causes a new strand to bounce back out as another drop breaks away.

Because water molecules cling to each other like tiny magnets, a drop of water can stay in one piece, even as it falls through the air. But the molecules at the water's surface cling with a force that causes the surface to shrink. This force is called *surface tension*.

When the surface of a drop of water shrinks to its smallest size, the drop forms a sphere. The sphere stretches because of the drop's weight and motion, but surface tension helps keep the drop together, as if it were held in an elastic skin.

MOLECULES IN MOTION

If a drop of water is added to a jar of still water, and if the water in the jar is not stirred, where will the new drop go? Will it stay near the top or sink to the bottom? A simple experiment reveals the answer.

A drop of blue water enters a jar of clear water. It begins to split up. Parts of the drop sink and swirl in different directions. At last, the colored drop breaks into so many parts that it has become part of the whole jar of water.

The molecules in a liquid are moving all the time, pushing and pulling each other, attaching to and breaking away from neighboring molecules. The molecules in the blue drop break apart because they are pushed and pulled all over the jar by other water molecules. The energy that keeps the molecules moving is heat. This heat can come from the sun or the room in which the jar is standing. Without heat, water would not remain a liquid.

ICE

When water cools, it loses energy. The molecules slow down and eventually stop swirling and pushing each other. When water freezes, the molecules lock together, forming a rigid structure. A drop of blue water no longer moves. The water has changed from a liquid to a solid—ice.

Ice is a solid, like metal or rock. But, unlike metal or rock, ice is solid only at temperatures of 32 degrees Fahrenheit (0 degrees Celsius) or colder. At room temperature, ice melts, changing back to a liquid.

WATER VAPOR

Water always seems to be disappearing: from wet clothes on a line, from puddles on the ground, and from dishes on a draining board. We say it has dried up, but where has the water gone?

Just as water can be a liquid or solid, it can also be a gas. The water from the wet dishes *evaporates*. That is, it turns into a gas called *water vapor*. Molecule by molecule, the water from the drops on the wet dishes drifts invisibly into the air.

Heating water in a kettle speeds evaporation. Heat from the stove makes the water turn to steam, which is extremely hot water vapor. When the steam hits the cooler air, tiny droplets form, and we see a cloud just beyond the kettle's spout. Almost immediately, the droplets evaporate and change back to invisible vapor. Then the water molecules mingle with other molecules that make up air.

CONDENSATION

The air around us always contains some water vapor. Water molecules move rapidly through the air and hit everything in their paths. The molecules bounce off most warm surfaces, but stick to surfaces that are cold. In these photographs, molecules of water vapor stick to the coldest part of the glass. Gradually, droplets form on the glass as the molecules accumulate. Water vapor changes from a gas to a liquid; that is, it *condenses*.

EVAPORATION VERSUS CONDENSATION

In the photographs below, why do the water drops outside this glass disappear, while the drops inside remain?

Outside the glass, the water evaporates and spreads throughout the room as vapor. In time, the drops disappear. Inside the glass, water also evaporates, but the vapor is trapped. The air inside the glass becomes *humid*, which means that the air is full of water vapor. And that vapor condenses back onto the water drops as quickly as water molecules can evaporate. Therefore, the drops remain.

Remove the glass, and the vapor expands throughout the room. Evaporation continues, but condensation slows down. In time, the uncovered drops will disappear.

ENDLESS VARIETY

Many ice crystals grow into shapes that are just tiny slivers, rods, or clumps of ice. Of these, the underlying six-sided structure may not always be visible. But when weather conditions are just right, the crystals will grow into an astonishing variety of elaborate six-sided designs.

All the snowflakes on this page were photographed on the same day. All share the same angles, but vary in design. One has six branches of unequal length, giving the appearance of a three-sided snowflake. Another snowflake has only four branches. Apparently, two of its branches didn't grow. Odd variations like these are typical. Because different conditions of humidity, wind, and temperature affected the growth of each snowflake as it fell, each design holds secrets of its unique journey to earth.

When a snowflake melts, its intricate design is lost forever in a drop of water. But a snowflake can vanish in another way. It can change directly from ice to vapor.

FROST AND DEW

On some days, when the air is humid, a sudden drop in temperature during the night will cause water vapor to condense on cold surfaces. By morning, the landscape is covered in sparkling drops of water—dew. If temperatures fall below freezing, the cold-weather relative of dew appears—frost.

On windows, frost forms along tiny scratches and other imperfections in the glass. As with snowflakes, frost is the result of water vapor changing from a gas to a solid. That's why the angular structure of ice crystals is evident in the fern-like patterns of frost.

When dew forms, a short walk through the grass will soak your feet. On spider webs, dewdrops appear like glistening pearls.

THE WATER CYCLE

The sun's heat and the earth's gravity keep water in constant motion. Water evaporates from puddles, ponds, lakes, and oceans; from plants and trees; and even from your skin. Water vapor moves invisibly through the air, but it is always ready to condense on a cool blade of grass or the surface of a pond. Massive clouds form as vapor condenses on tiny particles of dust in the air. Then, and only then, can water fall from the sky as rain, replenishing lakes, rivers, and oceans. Hard to predict, impossible to control, water cycles around the earth.

And water is precious. Without it, not a single living thing could survive. No plants would grow, not even one blade of grass. No animals would roam the earth, not even a spider. But somewhere in the world right now, snow drifts on a mountaintop and rain falls in a valley. And all around us, we are reminded of the never-ending journey of a drop of water.

THINK CRITICALLY

1 What conditions must be present for frost to form? NOTE DETAILS

2 How would your life be different if fresh water were limited? SPECULATE

3 What would happen on a humid day if you took an empty metal cup out of a freezer and put it on a napkin? CAUSE AND EFFECT

4 How does the text's structure help you understand and remember the information?  TEXT STRUCTURE: CAUSE AND EFFECT

5 **WRITE** What happens to the molecules in an ice cube when the ice melts? Use details and information from the selection to support your answer. SHORT RESPONSE

WALTER WICK

As a boy, Walter Wick loved exploring the woods near his home in Connecticut. He became interested in both art and photography in high school. He took his first famous photograph while cleaning out his studio. The photograph of screws, paper clips, safety pins, and other items launched a series of "photographic puzzles" that were published in magazines.

While taking the photographs for *A Drop of Water*, Walter Wick learned how to photograph a snowflake. First, he caught a snowflake on a piece of black cardboard. Then, he used a feather to lift the snowflake off the cardboard and place it under his camera lens. By working in an unheated barn, he could photograph the snowflake before it melted!

GO online www.harcourtschool.com/storytown

RAIN, DANCE!
STEAM
ICE CYCLE

Poetry

RAIN, DANCE!

Rain,
you cloud head,
Wake up!

Stretch those mile-long legs
down here and dance.
Shuffle your nimble feet
over leaf tops.
Do the grass-tap;
do the petal-patter.
Make your drizzle sizzle!

We green things
are bored here,
way
deep
to
our
roots.

C'mon, let's celebrate.
Make Thunder
clap!

—Constance Levy

Steam

S
t
e
a
m

S
t
e
a
m

S
t
e
a
m

boil, boiling, bubbling pot
looks like it's sweaty hot
once was water, now is not
cooking is a clever shaper
turned it into water vapor

—Joan Bransfield Graham

ICE

CYCLE

I've always thought it rather nice
That water freezes into ice.
I'm also pleased that it is true
That ice melts back to water, too.
But even so I find it strange
The way that ice and water change
And how a single water drop
Can fathom when it's time to stop
Its downward drip and go ahead
And start an icicle instead.

—Mary Ann Hoberman

Connections

Comparing Texts

1. We usually think of water as a liquid. Name two everyday ways you experience water as a gas.

2. Compare the descriptions of water in "A Drop of Water" and the three poems.

3. You've learned how the behavior of molecules gives water its properties. Does this change the way you think of the water around you? Explain.

Vocabulary Review

Word Sort

Work in a small group to sort the Vocabulary Words into categories. For example, you might sort the words into adjectives and verbs. Then choose at least one Vocabulary Word from each category, and write a sentence for each.

Adjectives	Verbs

elongates

elastic

rigid

accumulate

underlying

intricate

vanish

replenishing

Fluency Practice

Repeated Reading

Good readers slow down when a text includes ideas that may be difficult for listeners to understand. Choose one page from "A Drop of Water." Read the page aloud. Then reread the page, choosing a pace that will be easy for listeners to follow.

Writing

Write a Cause-Effect Paragraph

Use facts from the selection to write a paragraph that describes a change in the surface of water. Tell what causes the change you are describing.

My Writing Checklist

Writing Trait ▸ Conventions

✓ I used a graphic organizer to plan my writing.

✓ I used signal words to show cause-and-effect relationships.

✓ I correctly capitalized and punctuated my sentences.

| Cause | → | Effect/ Cause | → | Effect |

Big 💡 Idea

Myths and realistic fiction stories have different purposes and characteristics.

Enduring ❗ Understanding

Readers recognize specific vocabulary to identify the differences between myths and realistic fiction.

Essential ❓ Question

How do readers distinguish the differences and similarities between myths and realistic fiction?

Spelling Words

Review

enemy	digestible
fanatic	enjoyable
honest	admissible
ocean	argument
slogan	amazement
reclaim	priceless
reconsider	capitol
uninformed	general
unwise	mayor
nonexistent	theater

Fluency

Review Intonation, Pace

Comprehension

Review

 Compare and Contrast, Cause and Effect

 Monitor Comprehension: Self-Correct, Use Graphic Organizers

Robust Vocabulary

- recount
- uninhabitable
- sustain
- monotonous
- endeavor
- dwell
- brimming
- teeming
- parched
- sorrowful

Writing

- *Review* Sentence Fluency, Conventions
- Revise and Publish

Lesson 15
Theme Review and Vocabulary Builder

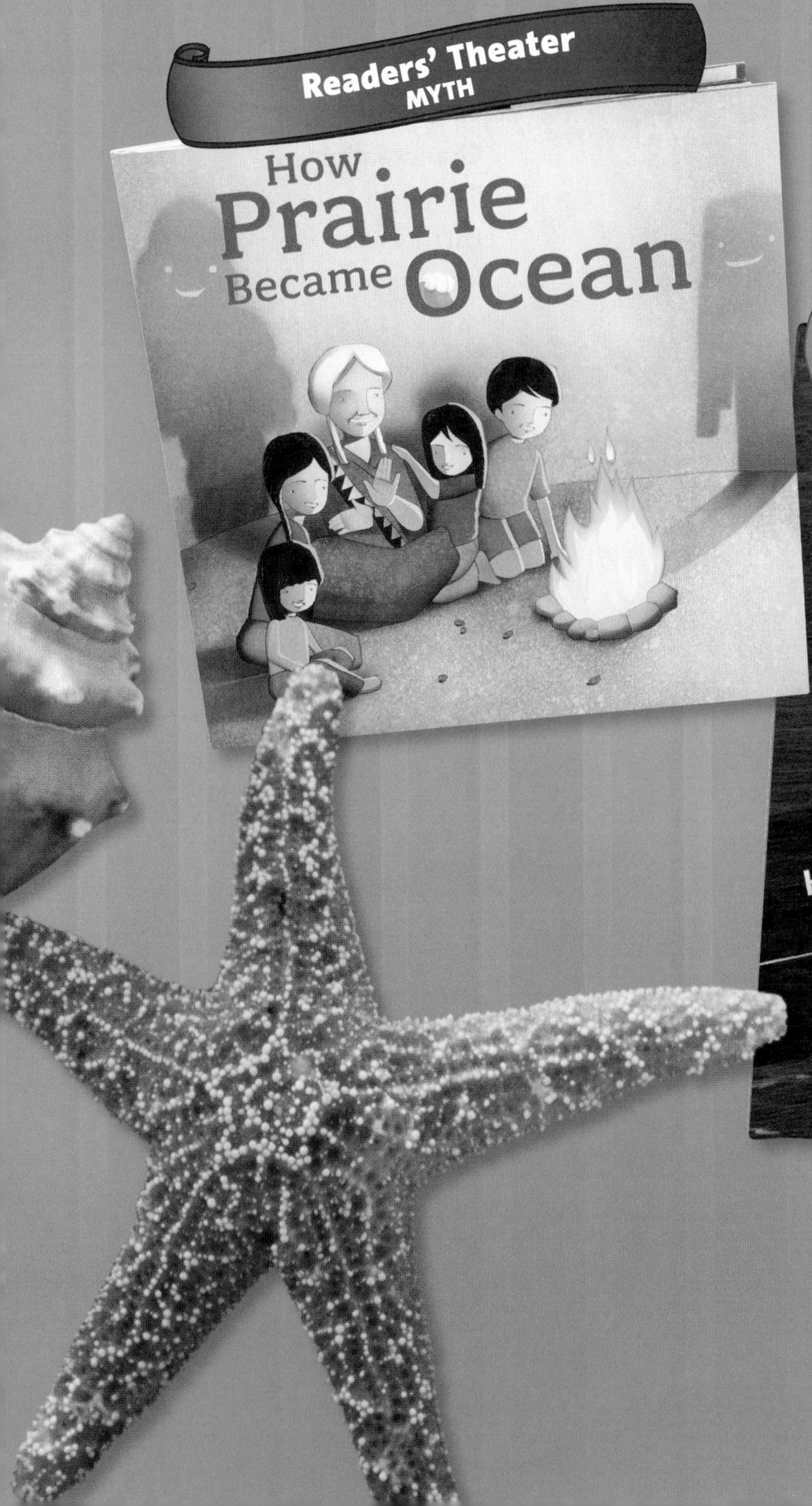
Readers' Theater
MYTH
How Prairie Became Ocean

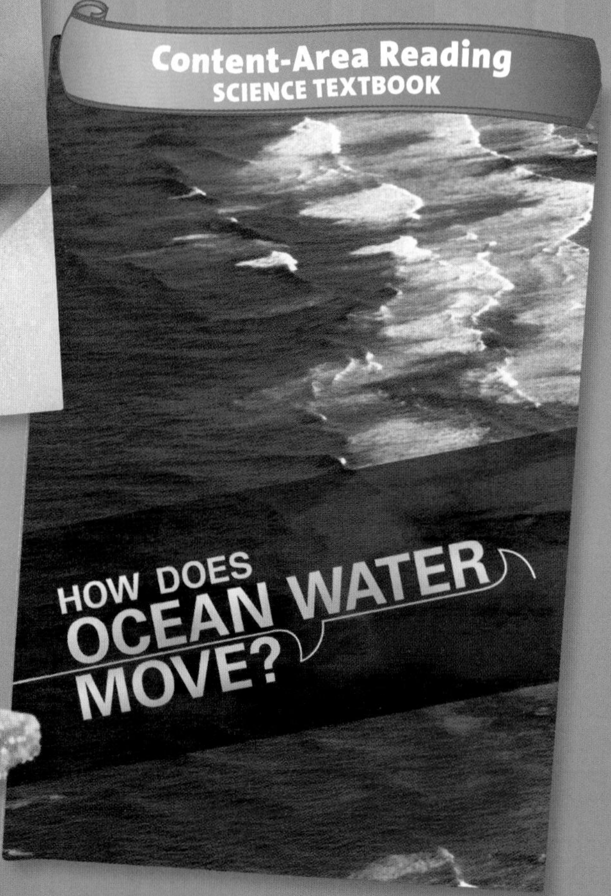
Content-Area Reading
SCIENCE TEXTBOOK
HOW DOES OCEAN WATER MOVE?

recount

uninhabitable

sustain

monotonous

endeavor

dwell

brimming

teeming

parched

sorrowful

Reading for Fluency

When reading a script aloud,

- Change your intonation by raising and lowering your voice to show your audience how your character is feeling.

- Adjust your pace to match the characters' actions.

Characters:
Narrator
Eldest granddaughter
Eldest grandson
Chorus
Grandmother
Thunder
Earthquake
Kingfisher

How Prairie Became Ocean

illustrated by Alan Flinn

Narrator: Several Yurok children are awake on this stormy night inside their cedar plank lodge. After whispering among themselves, they get up quietly and tiptoe over to the fire, where their grandmother sits.

Eldest granddaughter: Grandmother, I'm glad you're awake. The storm is so loud that none of us can sleep.

Eldest grandson: The waves have been crashing against the shore all night! It's impossible to sleep. May we join you by the fire?

Chorus: We can't sleep a wink, Grandmother!

Grandmother: Sit down, my children. We will keep each other company.

Eldest granddaughter: Will you tell us a story, Grandmother?

Chorus: Yes, Grandmother, please tell us a story!

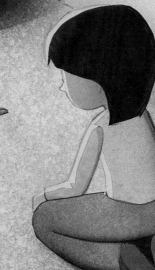

Grandmother: I have the perfect tale for stormy evenings. I will recount a story about a time when Thunder rumbled and Earthquake changed the land.

Narrator: The children huddle close together. Shadows and light cast by the fire dance along the lodge walls.

Grandmother: This story comes from a long-ago time, when no people lived in this place we call home. Then, the land looked different. We would not recognize it as our own.

Eldest granddaughter: How was the land different, Grandmother?

Grandmother: Long ago, there was no ocean here.

Chorus: No ocean? That's impossible!

Eldest granddaughter: Without the ocean, there would be no salmon entering our rivers for us to catch.

Eldest grandson: I could not adjust to life without the ocean.

Chorus: Life would be impossible without the ocean!

Grandmother: There was only a treeless prairie as far as the eye could see. The land was flat, empty, and dusty. With no ocean, this place was bleak and uninhabitable. Because no one could live here, no one did. Then one day, everything changed.

Chorus: What happened, Grandmother?

Grandmother: Two friends, Thunder and Earthquake, came upon this barren landscape. While wandering across its vast emptiness, they talked.

Narrator: As Grandmother speaks, she gestures with her hands, which swoop and bend in the light of the fire. The shadows elongate, forming images on the wall behind her that resemble the characters in her tale.

Fluency Tip

Use a different intonation for Grandmother's lines than for those of her grandchildren.

Thunder: This land cannot sustain life. The few plants that survive in the barren earth are brown and withered. Without plants, the animals refuse to come. And without plants and animals, it is unfathomable that people will populate the land.

Earthquake: This land does not please me. The endless brown plains are monotonous. There are no majestic mountains or beautiful valleys.

Thunder: We should change this place so that plants will grow and so that animals and people will come and thrive. But how?

Earthquake: My friend, we need water. With water, you and I can make this desolate land fertile.

Thunder: But where will we find water? This dry prairie stretches without relief in every direction.

Earthquake: Let us summon our wise friend Kingfisher, the greatest traveler of all. If water can be found, Kingfisher will know its whereabouts.

Grandmother: Thunder and Earthquake called to Kingfisher. Swift as the wind, he flew to them. Solemn and dignified, he greeted his friends.

Kingfisher: Earthquake and Thunder, you have called me, and I have come. Tell me, what are you doing in this barren place?

Thunder: This land is precisely why we have called you. Earthquake and I wish to transform this place into a land where plants, animals, and people can live, but we need your help.

Earthquake: If we can bring water here, plants will grow, animals will come, and people will be able to live on this land. Can you help us find water?

Kingfisher: Ah, yes, I think I can help with your endeavor. Hundreds of miles from here, at the very edge of the land, I have glimpsed a great body of water. Huge schools of salmon swim in the water, and mighty whales dwell in its depths. Thunder, climb on my back. Together we will journey to the water. Earthquake, please wait for us.

Grandmother: Thunder climbed onto Kingfisher's back, and together they flew away. Earthquake stood alone on the prairie, watching until his friends vanished into the horizon, and he awaited their return.

Narrator: Grandmother holds her hands like a pair of wings. In the shadows, they create the shape of Kingfisher flying.

Chorus: See Kingfisher flying in the shadows!

Grandmother: They traveled for three days and three nights. By the third night of their journey, both Kingfisher and Thunder yearned for rest. Finally, they reached the place where the land met the water.

Kingfisher: Here is the body of water I told you about. There is much life here. Look at the salmon! Look at the sea lions and the whales!

Thunder: How will we carry the water back to the land?

Grandmother: Thunder scooped up the water in his hands, but it spilled out. Kingfisher filled his beak, but his beak did not hold much water.

Chorus: How will they get the water back to Earthquake?

Grandmother: It was then that Thunder came across two enormous abalone (a•buh•LOH•nee) shells lying in a pile of seaweed and debris. He filled the pearly shells until they were brimming with water.

Thunder: Now we can return to Earthquake.

385

Grandmother: For three days and three nights, Kingfisher flew, with Thunder sitting on his back carefully balancing the abalone shells.

Eldest granddaughter: It must have been difficult to carry the water for three days and three nights!

Chorus: Did Thunder spill any water?

Grandmother: Thunder was very careful and did not spill a drop. Finally, Thunder and Kingfisher arrived at the prairie where Earthquake waited.

Earthquake: Welcome back, my brave friends! I see you have succeeded in bringing the water. Now we can transform this lifeless land into a bountiful place.

Kingfisher: Where should we put the water?

Thunder: Before we pour out the water, let us make a channel so the water can flow. We should also dig a deep place where the water can collect.

Earthquake: Leave it to me!

Grandmother: Earthquake sprinted across the entire length of the prairie. The quaking earth rocked wildly to and fro.

Kingfisher: Run, Earthquake, run! Make a place for the water to flow.

Thunder: Go, Earthquake, go! The land changes with your every step.

Narrator: The children spring up and run around the campfire, stomping their feet in imitation of Earthquake. Their grandmother laughs at the sight. At last, the rowdy children settle down to listen once more.

Grandmother: Earthquake's heavy footsteps shook the ground so much that it sank, forming a wide, deep trench that stretched for miles.

Thunder: Now we can pour the water onto the land.

Grandmother: Kingfisher and Thunder poured out the water from the abalone shells. With a roar, it cascaded into the trench. Bellowing sea lions, fish of every color and size, and mighty whales poured out of the shells as well. Just like that, part of the prairie disappeared, and an ocean took its place.

Earthquake: We did it, my friends! We transformed the barren prairie into an ocean teeming with life.

Thunder: The waves are full of silver-scaled trout and powerful salmon. Mussels and clams encrust the rocky tide pools along the shore.

Eldest granddaughter: I am grateful to Thunder and Earthquake for their gift of the ocean.

Chorus: Thank you, Thunder and Earthquake!

Eldest grandson: They could not have succeeded if Kingfisher had not found the water.

Chorus: Thank you, Kingfisher.

387

Chorus: What happened next, Grandmother?

Grandmother: The three friends saw that Earthquake's rowdy stomping had changed other parts of the land as well.

Thunder: Look! The land alongside our new ocean is no longer flat. Earthquake reshaped it into hills, mountains, and rivers.

Kingfisher: Now that the land is no longer parched with thirst, forests will flourish here. Deer, foxes, rabbits, and elk will find shelter and nourishment under the trees.

Earthquake: With the abundant plants and animals, people are sure to come. Hunters will track the animals among the trees. Lumberjacks will carve the largest tree trunks into great boats. Children will play in the forests' shade.

Grandmother: Earthquake and Thunder were pleased with their handiwork, but their hearts were sorrowful at the thought of leaving the beautiful land they created.

Earthquake: I could live happily here forever. Thunder, let us stay and make our home on this land.

Thunder: We will live alongside the people and watch over them.

Kingfisher: The people will never forget that you gave them the bountiful ocean that sustains their lives. The beauty of the ocean will replenish their spirits when they are sad. They will gaze at the misty horizon and find comfort in its beauty.

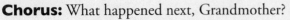

Fluency Tip

Practice reading your lines with different intonation to decide which tone best expresses the character's personality and feelings.

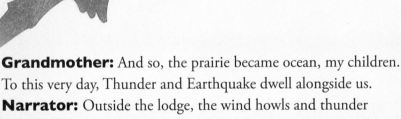

Grandmother: And so, the prairie became ocean, my children. To this very day, Thunder and Earthquake dwell alongside us.

Narrator: Outside the lodge, the wind howls and thunder booms. Ocean waves slap against the rocky shore. Grandmother and the children pause to listen.

Eldest granddaughter: What a wonderful tale. I'm glad that Thunder and Earthquake decided to live with us, near the ocean.

Eldest grandson: Whenever I hear thunder boom, I'll remember your story, Grandmother! And someday, perhaps, I will tell it to my own grandchildren.

Narrator: A terrific thunderclap outside makes everyone recoil.

Grandmother: Maybe Thunder was listening to our story, too!

COMPREHENSION STRATEGIES
Review

Reading a Science Textbook

Bridge to Content-Area Reading Textbooks give facts and information about a topic. The notes on page 391 point out text features of science textbooks, including headings, charts, and diagrams. These features provide information that can help you better understand the topic.

Review the Focus Strategies

If you do not understand what you are reading, use the strategies you learned about in this theme.

Monitor Comprehension: Self-Correct

It is important to monitor your own comprehension as you read. Use self-correction strategies such as decoding longer words to improve your understanding.

Use Graphic Organizers

Use graphic organizers to show how authors organize important ideas into text structures, such as cause and effect, compare and contrast, or sequence.

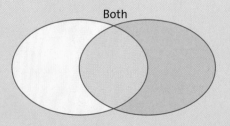

As you read the science textbook lesson on pages 392–395, think about where and how to use comprehension strategies.

CAPTIONS
Captions give information about photographs, diagrams, and charts.

Reading in Science

VOCABULARY
wave p. 376
current p. 378
tide p. 380

SCIENCE CONCEPTS
▶ how waves form
▶ what causes currents and tides

READING FOCUS SKILL

COMPARE AND CONTRAST Look for ways waves and currents are alike and different.

alike ——— different

Waves

Have you ever stood on a beach and watched the waves? From a distance, waves look like traveling ridges of water. But the water in waves doesn't move across the ocean. The water actually moves up and down. A **wave** is the up-and-down movement of surface water.

You know that air blowing across water makes waves. Energy from the moving air moves the water. When wind blows across the ocean, it pushes the water up, forming ripples. When wind blows on the ripples, more water moves up. Soon, the ripples form waves.

A wave carries energy, not water, across the ocean. Inside the wave, water turns in small ovals. After the water moves around the ovals, it returns to about the place where it started. The energy, however, travels forward.

Water moves up and down and energy moves forward until waves approach a

Modern surfing began in Hawai`i in the 1800s. ▼

A tsunami, like the one that caused this damage in Sri Lanka in 2004, is the most destructive of all ocean waves. ▶

shore. As the water becomes shallow, the waves slow down. They also become higher and closer together.

The bottom of the wave slows the most, so the top moves ahead of the bottom. When the top gets far enough ahead, the wave falls over, or *breaks*. It's like tripping over something. Your foot stops moving, but the rest of you keeps going, causing you to fall forward. Breaking waves are what people see crashing onto the shore at the beach.

Some waves are caused by more than ordinary winds. A hurricane or other strong storm moving over the ocean pushes water forward. This adds to the usual height of the waves. The mound of water that pushes onto shore in a hurricane is called a *storm surge*. Storm surges are highest in places where the continental shelf is nearly flat.

The biggest waves are not caused by winds. The great energy of an earthquake or a volcanic eruption can produce a wave called a *tsunami* (tsoo•NAH•mee). In the open ocean, a tsunami isn't a high wave, but it is long and moves very fast. When a tsunami approaches the shore, it slows down. This makes it become much higher. In 1958, an earthquake near Alaska produced a tsunami that was 524 m (1719 ft) high!

COMPARE AND CONTRAST How is a tsunami different from other waves?

Wave Movement

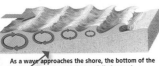

As a wave approaches the shore, the bottom of the wave slows down and the top falls forward.

Math in Science
Interpret Data

Waves Around the World

Scientists use the movement of buoys offshore to calculate how high waves will be and how fast the wind is moving. These are the predictions for one week. Why do you think the waves were predicted to be higher near Australia than near Florida?

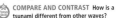

Waves Around the World		
Location	Open Ocean Wave Heights (m)	Wind Speeds (km/hr)
Capetown, South Africa	2–7	11–45
Long Beach, California	1–2	3–21
Port Orange, Florida	0–1	3–11
Hilo, Hawai`i	2–4	6–27
Gold Coast, Australia	1–8	5–39

DIAGRAMS
Diagrams present information visually.

CHARTS
Charts sort and categorize kinds of information.

Apply the Strategies Read this textbook lesson about how ocean water moves. As you read, use different comprehension strategies such as self-correcting to help you understand.

Reading in Science

VOCABULARY
wave p. 376
current p. 378
tide p. 380

SCIENCE CONCEPTS
▶ how waves form
▶ what causes currents and tides

READING FOCUS SKILL

COMPARE AND CONTRAST Look for ways waves and currents are alike and different.

> alike ——— different

Waves

Have you ever stood on a beach and watched the waves? From a distance, waves look like traveling ridges of water. But the water in waves doesn't move across the ocean. The water actually moves up and down. A **wave** is the up-and-down movement of surface water.

You know that air blowing across water makes waves. Energy from the moving air moves the water. When wind blows across the ocean, it pushes the water up, forming ripples. When wind blows on the ripples, more water moves up. Soon, the ripples form waves.

A wave carries energy, not water, across the ocean. Inside the wave, water turns in small ovals. After the water moves around the ovals, it returns to about the place where it started. The energy, however, travels forward.

Water moves up and down and energy moves forward until waves approach a

Modern surfing began in Hawai`i in the 1800s. ▼

Wave Movement

As a wave approaches the shore, the bottom of the wave slows down and the top falls forward.

As you read, correct any mistakes that change the meaning of the text. **MONITOR COMPREHENSION: SELF-CORRECT**

A tsunami, like the one that caused this damage in Sri Lanka in 2004, is the most destructive of all ocean waves. ▶

shore. As the water becomes shallow, the waves slow down. They also become higher and closer together.

The bottom of the wave slows the most, so the top moves ahead of the bottom. When the top gets far enough ahead, the wave falls over, or *breaks*. It's like tripping over something. Your foot stops moving, but the rest of you keeps going, causing you to fall forward. Breaking waves are what people see crashing onto the shore at the beach.

Some waves are caused by more than ordinary winds. A hurricane or other strong storm moving over the ocean pushes water forward. This adds to the usual height of the waves. The mound of water that pushes onto shore in a hurricane is called a *storm surge*. Storm surges are highest in places where the continental shelf is nearly flat.

The biggest waves are not caused by winds. The great energy of an earthquake or a volcanic eruption can produce a wave called a *tsunami* (tsoo•NAH•mee). In the open ocean, a tsunami isn't a high wave, but it is long and moves very fast. When a tsunami approaches the shore, it slows down. This makes it become much higher. In 1958, an earthquake near Alaska produced a tsunami that was 524 m (1719 ft) high!

 COMPARE AND CONTRAST How is a tsunami different from other waves?

Math in Science
Interpret Data

Waves Around the World

Scientists use the movement of buoys offshore to calculate how high waves will be and how fast the wind is moving. These are the predictions for one week. Why do you think the waves were predicted to be higher near Australia than near Florida?

Waves Around the World		
Location	Open Ocean Wave Heights (m)	Wind Speeds (km/hr)
Capetown, South Africa	2–7	11–45
Long Beach, California	1–2	3–21
Port Orange, Florida	0–1	3–11
Hilo, Hawai`i	2–4	6–27
Gold Coast, Australia	1–8	5–39

▲ On this satellite image, the warm water of the Gulf Stream is shown in orange. Cooler water is yellow, green, and blue.

Currents

Would you be surprised to learn that the sun causes ocean water to move? Air around the equator is heated by the sun. This air moves north, toward the poles. As it moves, the air pushes ocean water forward. The result is a **current**, a stream of water that flows like a river through the ocean.

Large currents in the open ocean are known as surface currents. These carry water great distances across the surface.

The Gulf Stream is a surface current that flows all the way across the Atlantic Ocean. The current begins in the Gulf of Mexico and flows north along the eastern coast of the United States. Then it turns east and flows across the Atlantic Ocean to Europe.

Oceans also have smaller currents that stay near coasts. These currents erode and deposit sand, helping shape beaches.

Sometimes people coming out of the ocean after a swim have trouble finding their beach towels. A current, called a longshore current, sometimes flows along the shore. It carries swimmers away from the place where they entered the water.

Another kind of current along some shores is a rip current. Rip currents carry water away from the beach. This makes them dangerous for swimmers. A rip current can flow faster than 2.4 m/sec (7.9 ft/sec). That's faster than even an Olympic swimmer can swim back to shore.

The gaps in these waves are caused by rip currents. The water on either side of them flows toward shore. If you get caught in a rip current, don't swim against it. Swim parallel to the shore until you leave the rip current.

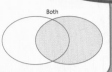

Stop and Think

Use graphic organizers, such as a Venn diagram, to show the relationship among ideas. **USE GRAPHIC ORGANIZERS**

The huge red-and-white areas in the Pacific show warmer waters caused by an El Niño. The purple area shows water kept cool by the El Niño. ▼

▲ Rain from an El Niño has caused many landslides along the California coast.

Some currents flow deep in the ocean. Off the west coast of South America, for example, winds blow warm surface water away from the land. Deep ocean currents then carry cooler water up toward the surface near the coast.

Changing winds can affect these currents. If the winds don't blow toward the west, the warm surface water stays near the coast. The deep, cold currents don't reach the surface, and the coastal water stays very warm. This warm water causes an *El Niño* (EL NEEN•yoh), a change in the weather patterns over the Pacific Ocean.

How does the warm water affect the weather? Warm water evaporates faster than cool water does. Where the ocean is warm, clouds form and bring rain. In most years, the wind pattern pushes the warm water to the west. As a result, Australia gets rain, and South America and the west coast of North America have dry weather.

During an El Niño, however, the weather pattern reverses. Australia has very dry weather, and the west coasts of South America and North America get storms and huge amounts of rain.

 COMPARE AND CONTRAST How is a surface current different from a current near a coast?

A Kitchen El Niño

Fill a large container with very warm water. Fill a small cup with very cold water, and add a few drops of food coloring. Use tongs to gently lower the cup straight down into the warm water, below the surface. Observe what happens. How is this similar to what happens during an El Niño?

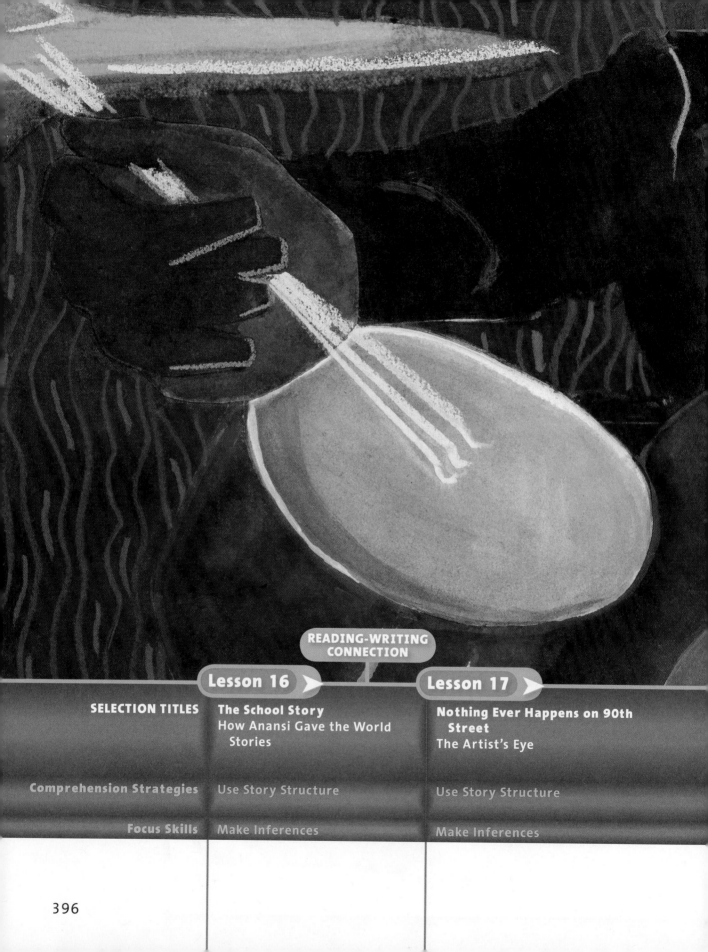

Theme 4 Dare to Be Great

Drummer, Gil Mayers

Lesson 18	Lesson 19	Lesson 20 Review
Project Mulberry Journey on the Silk Road	**Inventing the Future: A Photobiography of Thomas Alva Edison** Letter from Thomas Edison to Henry Ford	**The Invention Convention** **When Our Family Bands Together**
Monitor Comprehension: Adjust Reading Rate	Monitor Comprehension: Adjust Reading Rate	Review Skills and Strategies
Main Idea and Details	Main Idea and Details	

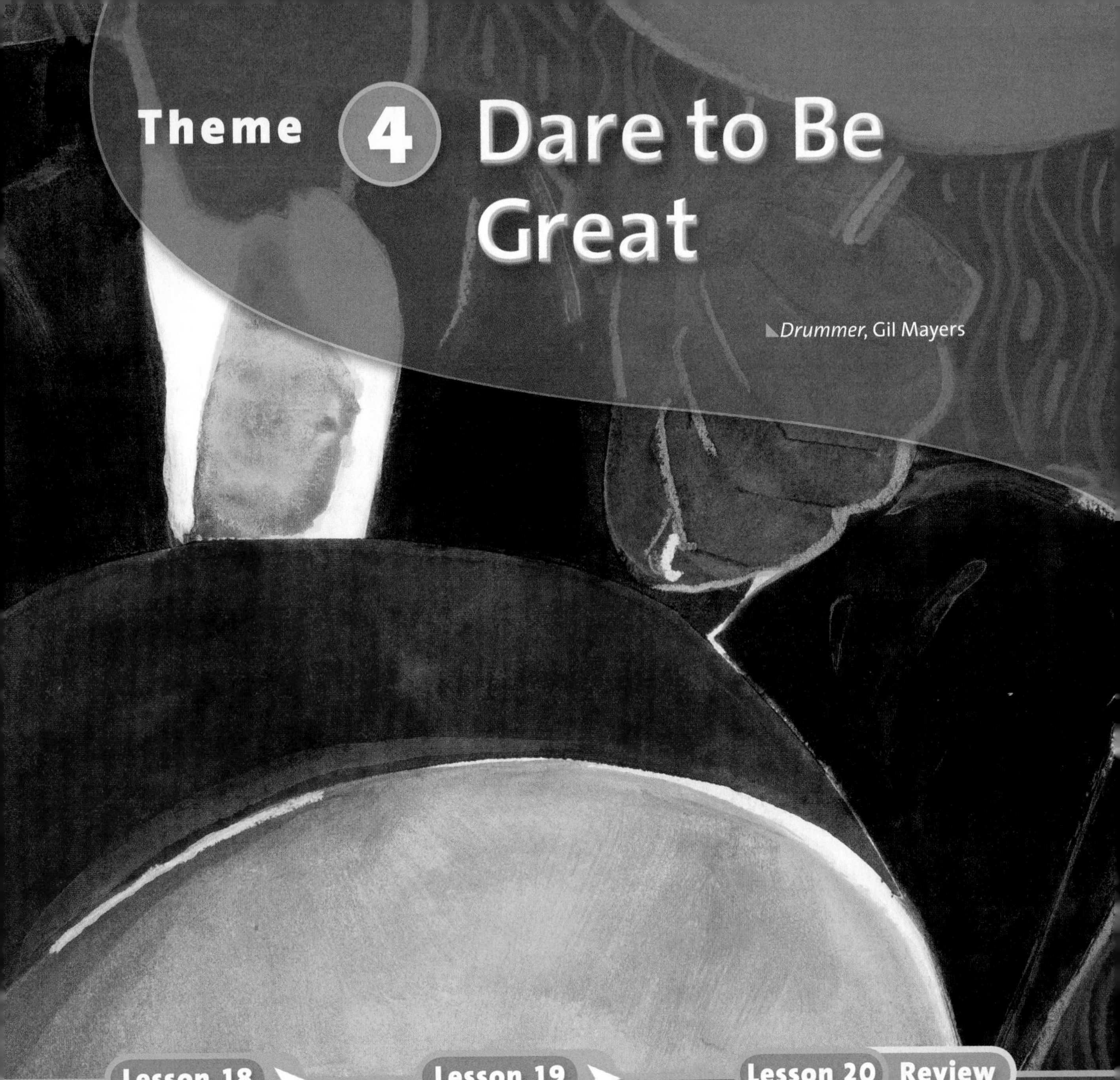

Big 💡 Idea
Authors of realistic fiction may leave clues for readers to use as they read the text.

Enduring ❗ Understanding
Readers make inferences when they use story clues and their own experiences to understand text.

Essential ❓ Question
How do authors leave clues in the text?

Spelling Words

Words with Prefixes
im-, in-, ir-, il-

inactive	illegal
inaccurate	illiterate
irregular	illegible
irrelevant	inaction
ineffective	independent
imbalance	invalid
immature	indefinite
impatient	injustice
imperfect	irreplaceable
impossible	impolite

Challenge

irreconcilable	immaterial
inanimate	impassable
inconsistent	

Fluency

Intonation

Comprehension

 Make Inferences

 Use Story Structure

Robust Vocabulary

tempted
insights
essence
indication
proposed
instinct
baffled

Writing

• Narrative
• Voice

Lesson 16

Genre: Realistic Fiction

THE SCHOOL STORY

ANDREW CLEMENTS
Best-selling Author of FRINDLE

How **Anansi Gave** the **World Stories**

illustrated by Jaime Zollars

Genre: Folktale

Make Inferences

Authors of fiction do not always state directly everything
that is happening in the story. Sometimes an author just gives
information that the reader can use to **make inferences** about
what is not stated directly. An inference is a connection that a
reader makes between information the author gives and what
the reader already knows.

What the Author Says	What I Already Know	Inference

Tip

To make an inference about
how a character feels, think about what
the character says and does. Connect
that to what you already know about
people.

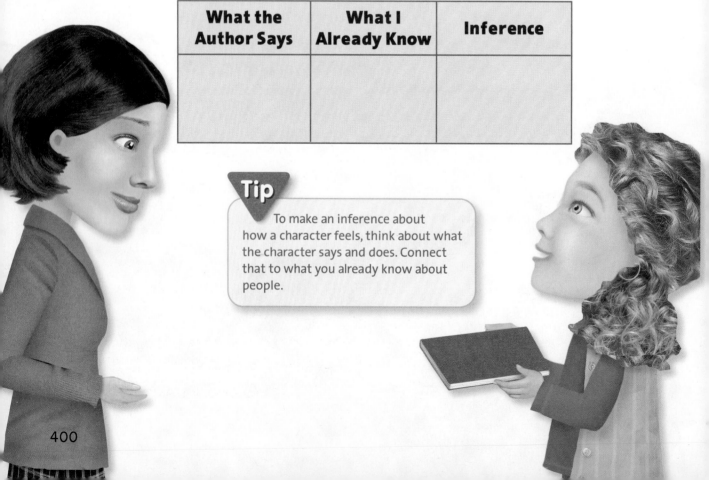

Read the paragraph below. Then look at the graphic organizer. It shows information the author provides in the text. It also shows the knowledge and experience a reader might use to make an inference.

Linda read the magazine advertisement for the poetry contest again. On her desk was the poem she had written about her favorite aunt. Linda decided to show the poem to Ms. Small. It was the first time Linda had shown anyone her poetry. Ms. Small smiled and said, "Linda, this poem is beautiful. I feel as though I know your aunt."

What the Author Says	What I Already Know	Inference
It was the first time Linda had shown anyone her poetry.	When you share something with someone, it is usually because you trust him or her.	Linda trusts Ms. Small and values her opinion.

Try This!

Why does Linda read the ad again? What does Linda want to do? Connect the clues in the paragraph with what you know to make another inference about Linda's feelings.

www.harcourtschool.com/storytown

Vocabulary

Build Robust Vocabulary

indication

baffled

proposed

instinct

tempted

insights

essence

Bad Book Ideas

April 16—Today, I told Mr. Jones, the editor at Kid Zone Books, about my idea for a children's book: 101 ways to make a bed. He listened very quietly. I hope that was an **indication** that he is interested.

April 18—I'm **baffled** that I haven't heard back from Mr. Jones.

April 21—Mr. Jones called—with terrible news. He said kids would think the book idea I **proposed** was boring. I don't care *what* he thinks! I trust my **instinct**. I'm going to try a different editor.

I was **tempted** many times to call Mr. Jones.

April 25—I can't find one book editor in New York City who is interested in my **insights** about making a bed! Personally, I think it is a fascinating subject. There are dozens of ways to fluff pillows and fold blankets, and there are even more ways to tuck sheets tight. I believe there must be thousands of kids who would want to read about the art of making a bed!

April 29—I have a new idea for a children's book: the history of homework. After all, isn't homework the **essence** of a good education? I'm sure it will be a best–seller!

A well-made bed can really help you get a good night's sleep!

 www.harcourtschool.com/storytown

Word Champion

Your challenge this week is to use the Vocabulary Words outside your classroom. Post the list of words at home. Use as many of the words as you can with family members and friends. For example, you might ask your sister if she is tempted to have a snack at a certain time every day. In your Vocabulary journal, write the words you used and tell how you used them.

Award Winner

THE SCHOOL STORY

Realistic Fiction

Genre Study

Realistic fiction has characters and events that are like people and events in real life. As you read, look for

- characters who have feelings that real people have.

- conflicts that might happen in real life.

Characters	Setting

Conflict

Plot Events

Resolution

Comprehension Strategy

Use story structure to identify and remember how plot events lead to the resolution of the story's conflict.

The School Story

by Andrew Clements

illustrated by Elizabeth Brandt

Natalie Nelson is young, but she has written her first novel,
The Cheater, *about a student accused of cheating. Her best friend,
Zoe, and Natalie's English teacher, Ms. Clayton, encourage Natalie
to submit her work to Shipley Junior Books. However, Natalie's
mother, Hannah, works for this publisher, and Natalie doesn't want
any special treatment. To keep her identity secret, Natalie uses the
pen name Cassandra Day. When her story is accepted, Natalie has
a problem. How will she keep her mom from discovering the true
identity of Cassandra Day?*

During four weeks of revisions the book got steadily better. Every day, and especially during their bus rides home, Natalie was tempted to ask her mom about the book she was editing. But she didn't. Natalie felt like that would have been unfair . . . like cheating.

She also learned that the editing process was when an author and an editor got to know each other. When one said, "Let's cut this out of the book," and the other said, "No, I really think it should stay," each learned something new about the other. It was like a very long conversation about . . . about life. Natalie felt she was getting to know her mom in a way she never had before. When a note from her mom asked Cassandra Day, "Does Sean really have to seem so mean at this part of the story?"—Natalie could hear her mom and dad telling her how important it was to be kind.

And when Cassandra Day wrote back and said, "Sean's not really being mean here, it's just that his feelings are hurt, and the narrator hasn't figured it out yet," Hannah read the note and smiled, and suggested a way to make that clearer to the reader without giving too much away too soon.

And during the editing process the author and the editor came to respect each other's ideas and insights more and more.

Near the end of the manuscript there was a note from the editor about Angela's father. Of all the notes, it was the one that meant the most to Natalie.

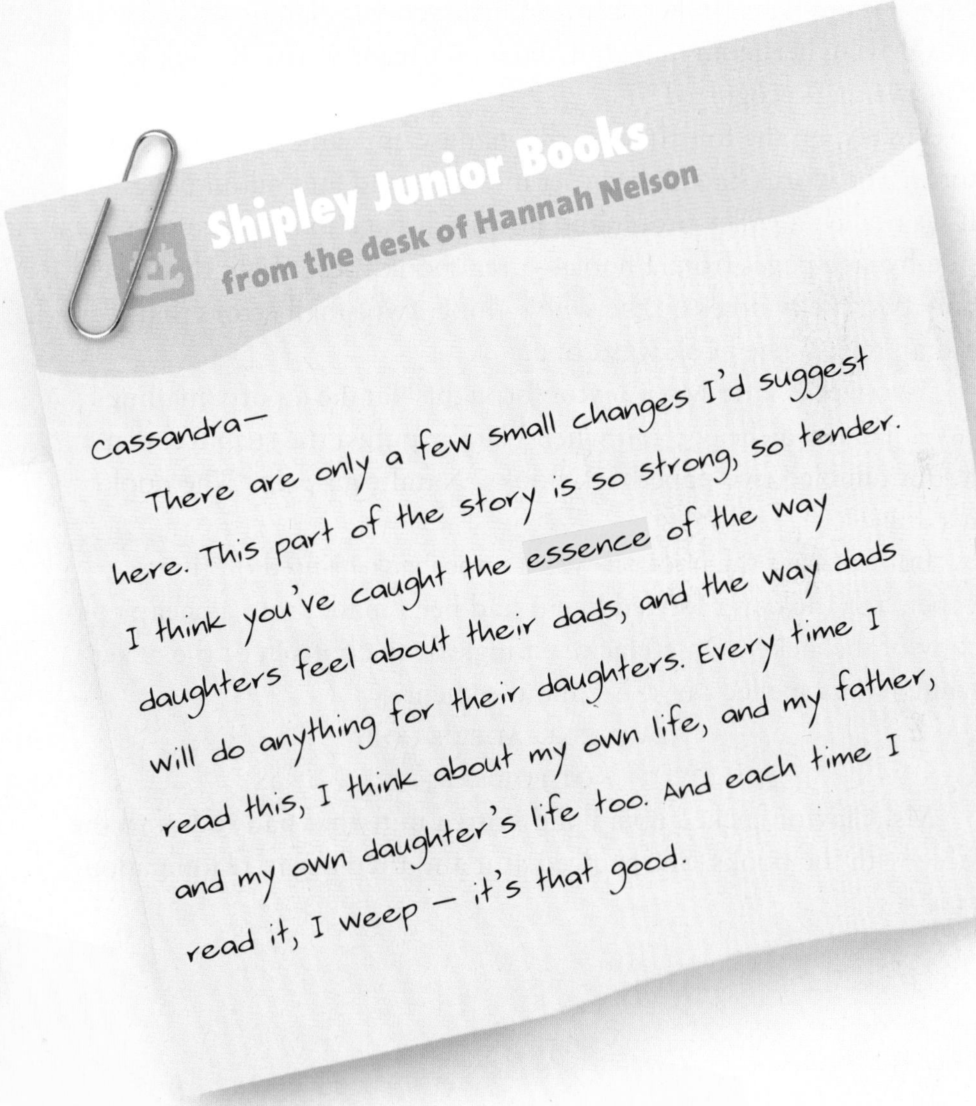

Shipley Junior Books
from the desk of Hannah Nelson

Cassandra—

There are only a few small changes I'd suggest here. This part of the story is so strong, so tender. I think you've caught the essence of the way daughters feel about their dads, and the way dads will do anything for their daughters. Every time I read this, I think about my own life, and my father, and my own daughter's life too. And each time I read it, I weep — it's that good.

Several times during the editing Hannah Nelson invited Cassandra Day to drop by the office if she was in the area, or just pick up the phone anytime something wasn't clear. Each invitation to visit was politely refused, and the author continued to communicate only by mail.

Hannah also found Cassandra's handwriting hard to read. Cassandra's notes were written with a thin pencil in tiny letters, and the writing had an unusual slant. They looked like that because Zoe was a lefty. After Natalie wrote each note and comment, Zoe copied it out again in her cramped little scrawl. Natalie was sure it was driving her mom nuts, but she didn't want to risk having her handwriting recognized.

Finally, on the fourth pass, the manuscript came back in a new form. The words had all been set into type and laid out in pages. It was called a galley proof, and now each page looked like two side-by-side pages from a book—a real book! Best of all, there were only two sticky notes on the whole thing, two small errors that were a snap to fix. The book was done.

Two weeks later Ms. Clayton brought Natalie a puffy mailing envelope. It was heavy, and when Natalie pulled the strip to open it, out tumbled two paperback books. Natalie gasped. "The book! It's done!"

But it wasn't the book. It was a paperback printed on flimsy paper, and the cover looked like it had been made from a cheap color copy of the jacket. On a black rectangle at the bottom of the cover white letters spelled out this announcement:

ADVANCE READER'S COPY

NOT FOR SALE

Ms. Clayton picked up a handwritten note that had slid onto the table with the books. She glanced at it and then began reading aloud.

Dear Cassandra:

Our marketing department is excited about your book, so we've printed up five hundred of these advance reader's copies. So far, our salespeople have been using our catalog to tell booksellers about your book, and now they will send these ARCs to all their key bookstore accounts. The subsidiary rights department will be sending them to the book clubs, the specialty markets, and our overseas agents. Also, the publicity department will be sending out more than two hundred ARCs to the trade, institutional, and consumer review media. I'll let you know when we start getting reviews. The hardcover is already in production, and we'll be shipping the advance orders by mid-May. The advance orders aren't great, but a few good reviews should give the sales a boost. I know we rushed a little on the revisions to meet the deadlines, but the book turned out great. You should be very proud.

Yours truly,

Hannah

409

Natalie held one of the paperbacks with both hands. She *was* proud. It wasn't the real book yet, but it was so close.

Zoe held the other reading copy. She was proud too, but she was also indignant. "What does she mean, the orders aren't so great? What's the matter with these people? They should be selling these books like crazy. Their publicity people must stink, that's all I can say."

Natalie said, "Remember how my mom said that every year there are more than five thousand new children's books published in the United States? They can't all be bestsellers, Zoe. It's amazing to get one published at all."

Zoe made a face and shrugged. Actually, Zoe had heard only about half of what Natalie had said. Natalie and Ms. Clayton kept talking, but Zoe was busy. She was having a brainstorm. It took only about thirty seconds for the whole idea to take shape, and when it had, Zoe held up the reading copy and said, "Can I have this one, Natalie?"

Natalie smiled and said, "Of course you can." Then Natalie handed her copy to Ms. Clayton and said, "And I want you to have this one. I'll ask my editor to send another one for me."

Ms. Clayton felt choked up, but she swallowed hard and said, "Thank you, Natalie. I'm going to treasure this my whole life."

Absentmindedly Zoe said, "Yeah . . . me too, Natalie." But Zoe's thoughts were elsewhere. She had just decided it was time for Zee Zee Reisman to develop some new skills. Zoe thought, *I mean, being an agent was fun, but now my client needs something else. What she* really *needs is . . . publicity!*

Most books are published quietly. They don't get big ads in the newspaper, they don't get written about in *Time* magazine, and they don't get a publication party. If it's a book by a famous author, or by an author that the publisher wants to impress, then the publisher might send out some invitations and throw a little party. Publishers do this to create some news and, hopefully, sell some books.

So when Zee Zee Reisman—Zoe's name when she was acting as Cassandra Day's agent—called Hannah in mid-April to suggest that Shipley Junior Books might want to throw a little publication party to launch *The Cheater*, Hannah's first reaction was, "It's a nice idea, but I don't think it makes sense."

But then her curiosity took over. All through the negotiations and the editing Cassandra Day and Hannah Nelson had never sat at a worktable together, never gone out to lunch, never even talked on the phone. She felt close to Cassandra Day and had loved their little exchanges about the manuscript. So she thought, *Zee Zee's right. A little party might be nice—and then I'll finally get to meet this lady.*

But Hannah had so much to do that she never focused on the idea. Letha, her boss, had been piling extra work on her ever since the day she'd been appointed as Cassandra Day's editor.

Then, three days after Zee Zee's call, the first review arrived. It was from *Kirkus Reviews*, and the reviewer gave *The Cheater* special notice with a "star," which is like giving a book an A++. Hannah liked the last three sentences best: "*The Cheater* grabs hold of your heart and never lets go. This writer speaks with a fresh and honest voice, something always welcome in middle-grade fiction. If this first novel is an indication of things to come, then Cassandra Day could emerge as a major new talent."

With the review in her hand Hannah went upstairs to talk to Tom Morton, president and publisher of Shipley Junior Books. Hannah read him the review, and then she proposed a simple publication party on a Friday afternoon in June. Tom Morton agreed instantly, and that was that.

Getting back on the elevator, Hannah had second thoughts. Letha would not be happy about this party, and she'd be furious that Hannah had asked Tom instead of coming to her first.

Hannah almost stepped out of the elevator to go back and call it off. But then she stopped and let the doors glide shut. On the short ride from the sixteenth down to the fourteenth floor, she realized something: Letha was not as scary as she used to be. And then Hannah said to herself, No, *that's not it. Letha is actually scarier than ever. It's just that I'm not afraid of her anymore.*

413

Back in her office Hannah called and left a message for Zee Zee. She said there would be a small "pub party" in honor of Cassandra Day's first novel. It would be on the sixteenth floor of the Shipley Publishing Company building on the second Friday in June. Zee Zee was free to invite anyone she'd like to be there. And everyone was very excited about actually getting to meet the author.

When Zoe got the phone message, she was excited, too. But she kept it to herself.

414

Natalie had finally gotten Zoe to shut up. For a solid week Zoe had bugged her and begged her and driven her batty. She wanted Natalie to ask her mom if she could bring Zoe and Ms. Clayton to see Shipley Junior Books—just to have a look around.

Natalie thought it wasn't such a good idea, but Zoe wouldn't let up. "It'll be like a field trip for the Publishing Club—and besides, school's almost over. Ms. Clayton probably won't even be our teacher next year."

Finally Natalie agreed to ask her mom if she could bring Zoe and her English teacher to see the publishing office—it wouldn't be a long visit, just in and out.

And her mom said, "Of course you may, sweetie. Just bring them with you after school one day. If I'm too busy to show you around, my assistant, Ella, can do the honors."

So it was all settled. They had an open invitation, and Zoe stopped pestering Natalie. And the day that looked the best for everyone was a Friday afternoon—the second Friday in June.

At three thirty on Friday, June 12, the editorial staff of Shipley Junior Books started straggling up to the sixteenth floor for the publication party. The manuscript had floated around a little, and there was a definite buzz about this book—and early in the day the third starred review had arrived. Everyone was excited about meeting Cassandra Day.

Hannah had already been up to the large conference room twice, once to check on the caterers, and once to be sure that the big banner had been hung up. When Hannah got off the elevator the third time, she could hear that the party had begun. As she walked into the room the first thing she noticed was the camera crew. A woman with a large video camera was taking a shot of the banner while a skinny young man behind her held up a bright light. The young man wore a jacket labeled NEWS. A man with perfect hair, perfect teeth, and a pinstriped suit was talking with Tom Morton. Glancing across the room, Hannah caught the eye of Jody Cross, the publicity director. Jody nodded toward the camera crew, smiled, and gave Hannah a thumbs-up. Hannah smiled and nodded back. She was impressed that Jody had managed to get some news coverage of such a small event.

When Zoe and Natalie and Ms. Clayton arrived at the fourteenth-floor reception area, they were buzzed right in. Her mom wasn't in her office, so Natalie just started walking her guests around the floor. Natalie had been dreading Zoe's little field trip, but now that they'd arrived, she began to enjoy herself.

They started in the art department and slowly worked their way clockwise from area to area. It struck Natalie as odd that there were so few people around, but she just figured that people had left early on a Friday afternoon. It was nice because they didn't have to be as quiet.

Natalie was showing them the stages of a book's cover art, but Zoe interrupted her. "Let's go find your mom, Natalie. You know, so we can ask her some questions too."

Natalie shook her head. "If she's not in her office, it means she's busy. We'll find her later."

Natalie really understood the publishing process now, and Ms. Clayton had a lot of questions. It was fun to teach her teacher, and it would have been perfect, except that Zoe was so impatient.

They were almost back to her mom's office, and Natalie was standing in Ella's cubicle pointing at the huge pile of envelopes on her worktable. "And that's the slush pile. I've seen it when it was even bigger." Turning around, Natalie said, "And over there in Tim's, an assistant editor's, office—" She stopped midsentence. Letha stood in the corridor outside her office, ten feet away.

Crossing her arms, Letha walked toward them. She smiled faintly and said, "Well, this is a cheery little group . . . and I see you have a tour guide."

Natalie gulped and said, "This is my friend Zoe and my English teacher, Ms. Clayton—and this is my mom's boss, Letha Springfield."

Ms. Clayton stepped around Natalie and held out her hand. "Pleased to meet you, Ms. Springfield."

Letha looked at Ms. Clayton's hand and then shook it briefly. "Yes. Well. We're happy to have you visit us."

Natalie said, "We . . . I was going to wait for my mom, but I don't think she's back yet. If she's not back in a few minutes, then we'll just go. We don't want to bother anyone."

Letha said, "Actually, your mother is . . . just upstairs." Then with an amused smile she added, "But I know she'd want to see you . . . and your friends, too. Just take the elevator up to the sixteenth floor. And be sure to tell her that I sent you to see her."

Natalie nodded and said, "Sure . . . okay. Thanks."

And Letha said, "Oh, you're quite welcome."

The Cheater by Cassandra Day
Congratulations to our newest author!

As the elevator door opened onto the sixteenth floor an alarm went off in Natalie's head. It didn't sound right. It sounded like . . . like a convention or something. Her first instinct was to push another button—any button—and get away fast. Before she could act, Zoe grabbed her hand and pulled her out of the elevator. Ms. Clayton followed, and Zoe headed right toward the open double doors of a large room where fifty or sixty people were standing around in small groups, talking loud enough to be heard over the talking of everyone else.

Natalie said, "Zoe! I don't think we'd better—"

But Zoe said, "Look, there's your mom," and she tightened her grip on Natalie's hand and headed straight toward Hannah Nelson like a locomotive. Ms. Clayton stopped in the doorway, just barely overcoming her urge to flee.

Halfway across the floor Natalie saw the banner:

The Cheater by Cassandra Day
Congratulations to our newest author!

The camera operator swung to face Zoe and Natalie, and her assistant turned on the lights. All but a few of the people at the edges of the room stopped talking. Everyone craned their necks to see what the camera was targeting. Natalie tried to make sense of the scene around her, but it was happening too fast. In another three seconds Zoe was standing in front of Hannah Nelson.

Hannah had been talking to Tom Morton, trying to act completely at ease. So what if the guest of honor was already thirty minutes late? The lights from the camera suddenly blinded her, and when she looked again, Zoe and Natalie were standing right in front of her.

Zoe looked up into her face and said, "Mrs. Nelson, I know this is going to be a shock, but I want to introduce you to Cassandra Day."

Hannah looked from Zoe to Natalie and then over their heads. Standing in the doorway of the room was a shy-looking young woman wearing a black skirt and a green cardigan sweater. Hannah's face broke into a relieved smile, and she said, "Well, this is . . . great. Come on, Tom, let's go welcome her."

Zoe looked over her shoulder and then turned back and said, "Mrs. Nelson, that's not her." Putting her arm gently around Natalie's waist, Zoe said, "*This* is Cassandra Day. That's her pen name. Cassandra Day is Natalie Nelson."

The camera operator saw it all. As the tape rolled she thought, *It doesn't get better than this*. And she was right.

The camera saw everything so clearly. It saw the woman look at the girl, completely baffled. It saw the mother's eyes widen, her eyebrows furrow into a question mark and then smooth to understanding. It recorded the ballet of emotions that danced across both faces.

The microphone heard the woman's sharp intake of air, almost a gasp, and then the long breathing out, almost a sigh. And it heard the girl whisper, "It's true, Mom."

Mother and daughter looked at each other for a long moment, and when they hugged, the people and the room and the building and the city around them disappeared.

Pulling away, Natalie looked around and then reached out to take Zoe's hand. "And Mom, this is Zee Zee Reisman." The woman's face did another dance, and then the hug held three.

And standing over in the doorway, tears streaming down her cheeks, Ms. Clayton felt as if she'd just won the New York Marathon.

Think Critically

1 Does Natalie make the right decision in keeping her identity secret from her mother? Why or why not? MAKE JUDGMENTS

2 Why does Zoe decide it is time for Zee Zee Reisman to develop some new skills? MAKE INFERENCES

3 Based on what you know about Zoe, is it believable that she persuades the publisher to organize a publicity party? Explain. CHARACTER'S TRAITS

4 What would you enjoy most about the process of writing a book? Why? EXPRESS PERSONAL OPINIONS

5 **WRITE** How is Natalie's relationship with her mother DIFFERENT by the end of the story? Use information from the story to support your answer. EXTENDED RESPONSE

About the Author
Andrew Clements

As a child, Andrew Clements loved to read mystery and adventure stories. He says that he never dreamed of becoming an author, but he remembers that sometimes after reading a book, he thought, "Ah, I wish I had written this." Now Andrew Clements has written many books and often visits schools to talk about them. He tells young writers, "You don't have to do everything at once. You don't have to know how every story is going to end. You just have to take that next step, look for that next idea, write that next word."

About the Illustrator
Elizabeth Brandt

Elizabeth Brandt became an illustrator not only because she loves to create, but also because she likes to learn new things. For one illustration, she might spend hours learning what children in the 1900s wore or how monks live in Vietnam. She developed her collage look when she wanted her art to look wackier. Elizabeth Brandt lives with her husband in Holland, Michigan. They love to travel—they planned a two-year trip on their boat that would take them through the United States, the Bahamas, and Canada.

GO online www.harcourtschool.com/storytown

425

How
Anansi Gave
the World Stories
Illustrated by Jaime Zollars

Folktale

How
Anansi Gave

In the beginning, the Ruler of the Sky hoarded all of the world's stories in a box of pure gold. Anansi the Spider wanted those stories, and whatever Anansi desired, he attained.

"What would you like in exchange for the stories?" Anansi asked the Ruler.

The Ruler contemplated Anansi's request. Then the skies lightened at his smile, for he knew the payment he wanted was difficult to acquire. "Bring me Onini, the python with the devastating squeeze; Osebo, the panther with the spearlike teeth; and the Mmoboro, the hornets whose stings ache like fire."

Anansi bowed and journeyed home to gather the payment.

Anansi collected a long branch and a coil of vines and went to the stream where Onini rested. Back and forth Anansi strolled in front of the python, all the time chuckling with satisfaction.

the World Stories

illustrated by Jaime Zollars

When he had the python's attention, he said, "My wife says you are a mammoth among pythons, longer even than this branch, but I told her that was impossible. I see now that I was correct."

Onini took pride in his size, and he was insulted. To prove his remarkable length, the python stretched himself alongside the branch and said, "You were mistaken to think the branch was longer than me."

"I was indeed," Anansi said, binding Onini to the branch.

Anansi obtained a sack and went to the area of the forest Osebo the panther favored. Anansi paced in front of him, pausing every few moments to laugh enthusiastically.

When he had attracted the panther's attention, Anansi said, "My son is positive you can fit into this sack, but I told him that too many rich meals had made your belly stout. It is apparent that I was correct."

While it was true that Osebo enjoyed dining plentifully, he insisted that he could fit into the sack. To demonstrate this, he crawled inside. He said, "I may be robust, but I can certainly fit in this sack."

"You fit perfectly," Anansi agreed, gleefully securing the sack.

Anansi filled a gourd with water and climbed
the tree where the Mmoboro had their home. He
doused himself with water and poured the rest over
the hornets' nest. Then he plucked a leaf from the
tree and held it over his head, as he strutted back and
forth, laughing loudly.

When Anansi had the hornets' attention, he said,
"My wife believes that you are clever creatures, yet
look at all of you flying around in the rain! I knew
you didn't have enough sense to stay dry. As for me,
I'm going to take shelter in that gourd."

The hornets thought themselves clever creatures
indeed. They did not want Anansi to be dry while
they were soaking wet, so they swarmed into the
gourd. They buzzed, "You were mistaken to think we
weren't clever. Now we shall stay dry."

"So you shall," Anansi said, sealing the gourd shut.

The Ruler of the Sky was impressed when Anansi delivered Onini, Osebo, and the Mmoboro. He presented him with the box, saying, "You are worthy of these stories, Anansi the Spider. From now on, they belong to you."

Anansi shook his head. "No one creature should hold so many riches." He opened the box, allowing the stories to escape to all parts of the world, and that is how the world got its stories.

Connections

Comparing Texts

1. Natalie could not have published her book without help. What is a project you are proud of that you could not have completed without help?

2. Compare the way Anansi and Natalie share their stories.

3. Should more children have their stories published? Why or why not?

Vocabulary Review

Word Sort

Work in a group. Sort the Vocabulary Words into categories. Compare your sorted words with those of your group. Explain your choices. Then choose at least one Vocabulary Word from each category. Write a sentence for each word.

Nouns	Verbs

tempted

insights

essence

indication

proposed

instinct

baffled

Fluency Practice

Recorded Reading

Listen to "The School Story" on *Audiotext 4,* and follow along in your *Student Edition.* Pay attention to the reader's intonation, noting where the reader's voice rises and falls. Then choose a page from "The School Story" to read aloud quietly. Practice reading it until your intonation matches the recording you heard.

Writing

Write a Story Proposal

Imagine you have an idea for a story that you want to write. Write to an editor, proposing your book idea and why the editor should publish it.

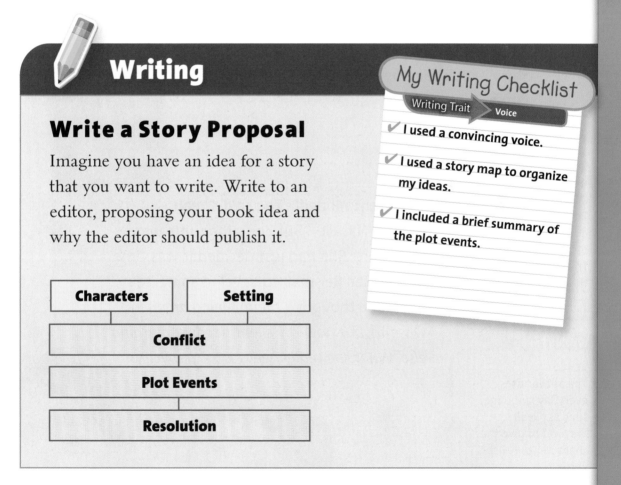

My Writing Checklist

Writing Trait ➤ Voice

✔ I used a convincing voice.

✔ I used a story map to organize my ideas.

✔ I included a brief summary of the plot events.

Characters	Setting

Conflict

Plot Events

Resolution

Reading-Writing Connection

Analyze Writer's Craft: Narrative

A narrative is a work of fiction that tells a story. It has **characters**, a **setting**, and a series of **plot events**. Often, one event causes another event to happen. When you write narratives, you can use the works of authors such as Andrew Clements as writing models. As you read this paragraph from "The School Story," look for ways to express your personal **voice** in your story.

Writing Trait

CONVENTIONS
The writer uses **quotation marks** to set off **spoken dialogue**. The character's **thoughts** are in italic print.

Writing Trait

VOICE
The author uses everyday language, such as "*Yeah . . . me too,*" to give the character a realistic **voice**.

Absentmindedly Zoe said, "Yeah . . . me too, Natalie." But Zoe's thoughts were elsewhere. She had just decided it was time for Zee Zee Reisman to develop some new skills. Zoe thought, *I mean, being an agent was fun, but now my client needs something else. What she really needs is . . . publicity!*

Narrative

In a **fictional narrative**, the characters, settings, and plot events are like people, places, and events in real life. As you read this fictional narrative by a student named Julia, notice the enthusiasm and humor in the writer's **voice**.

Student Writing Model

Double Bubble Trouble
by Julia Y.

> Julia introduces the **conflict** at the beginning of her narrative.

It was raining outside, so Lena and Sophie were trapped inside. They were bored. Lena rummaged through her closet, looking for a CD. She discovered some packs of bubble gum and had an idea. She held up the CD and the bubble gum and said, "Let's have a contest!"

"What kind of contest?" Sophie asked.

> **Writing Trait**
>
> **VOICE**
> The writer uses short sentences and exclamation marks to create an energetic **voice** for Lena and Sophie.

"We each chew a piece of gum and chomp to the beat of the music," said Lena. "The first person to chew off the beat loses."

"You're on!" said Sophie.

Lena started the music. The girls stared at each other and chewed in rhythm. The next song had a fast beat. Lena and Sophie twirled and bounced around the room, chewing furiously.

> **Writing Trait**
>
> **CONVENTIONS**
> The writer begins a new paragraph each time the speaker changes. **Punctuation marks** are placed inside the quotation marks.

433

Lena burst into laughter. Sophie started laughing, too. Suddenly, the wad of gum shot out of Sophie's mouth and landed in Lena's hair. When Sophie reached forward to untangle the gum, she stumbled into Lena, and the girls tumbled to the carpet. When they stood up, they were stuck together by their hair.

"What do we do?" asked Sophie, horrified. They walked into the kitchen to tell Lena's mother. Her jaw dropped when she saw the girls' heads attached in a gummy web.

An hour later, at the hair salon, the stylist tried not to laugh. Large chunks of Lena's and Sophie's hair fell on the floor, along with the gum.

"I've always wanted short hair," Lena said.

"Looks like our boring, rainy day turned into a great, make-over day," Sophie said. Lena looked at her reflection in the salon window, and agreed.

Thirty minutes later, the girls happily emerged from the salon with their new haircuts.

Now look at what Julia did to prepare to write her narrative.

Brainstorm Ideas

Julia used a web to brainstorm story ideas. She chose the story idea she thought she would have the most fun writing about.

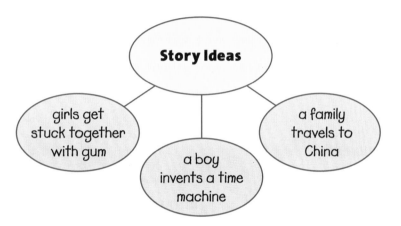

Organize Ideas

Julia used a graphic organizer to plan her narrative. She thought about the characters, the setting, the conflict, and the resolution.

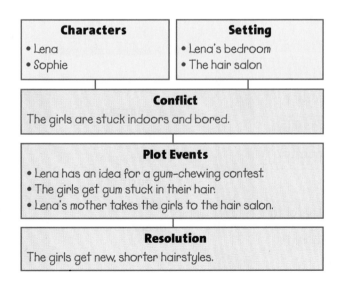

Big 💡 Idea
Readers of realistic fiction can "read between the lines."

Enduring ❗ Understanding
Readers can recall the characters' actions and feelings to make inferences about text.

Essential ❓ Question
How do the characters' motivations and traits help readers "read between the lines"?

Spelling Words

Words with Suffixes
-ant, -ent, -eer, -ist, -ian

accountant	dependent
applicant	indulgent
attendant	insistent
defiant	urgent
mutineer	auctioneer
expectant	accompanist
hesitant	artist
quadrant	cellist
resistant	technician
servant	novelist

Challenge

descendant	beautician
mountaineer	geologist
significant	

Fluency

Intonation

Comprehension

 Make Inferences

 Use Story Structure

Robust Vocabulary

- hiatus
- embarked
- unimaginable
- extravagant
- gourmet
- throng
- precarious

Writing

- Skit
- Voice

Lesson 17

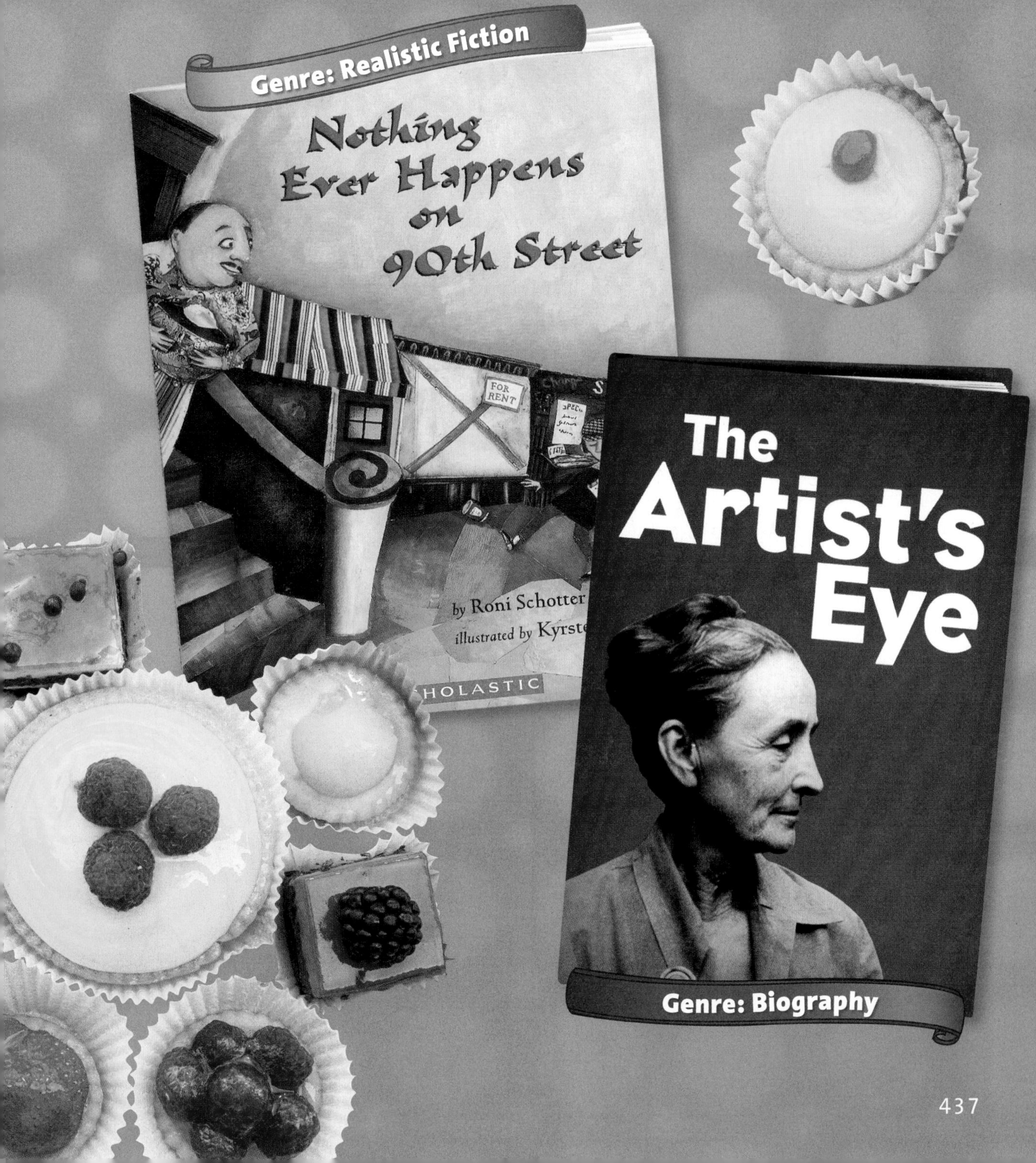

Genre: Realistic Fiction
Nothing Ever Happens on 90th Street
FOR RENT
by Roni Schotter
illustrated by Kyrste
HOLASTIC
The Artist's Eye
Genre: Biography

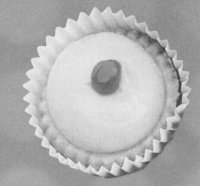

Focus Skill

Make Inferences

You know that authors do not always directly state everything necessary for understanding a story. Sometimes authors just leave clues so that readers can **make inferences** about something in the text. Making inferences is also known as "reading between the lines." To make an inference, you should

- use the clues the author gives you, such as how characters act or feel.
- connect the author's clues to your own experience.

What the Author Says	What I Already Know	Inference

Tip

Readers may draw different inferences from the same text. After reading, compare your inferences with those of a classmate.

438

Read the paragraph below. Then look at the graphic organizer. It shows a clue that the author provides in the text. It also shows the knowledge and experience a reader may use to make an inference about the character.

Min looked at the drum set in the photo she had tacked above her bed three months earlier. Then she looked at the jar on her bookshelf. It was full of coins and bills—the money she had made from washing cars every weekend. She was too nervous to count it. What if it wasn't enough? Min looked at her carwash supplies and scowled.

What the Author Says	What I Already Know	Inference
Min looked at her carwash supplies and scowled.	Sometimes, when I am frustrated or upset, I scowl.	Min does not want to wash any more cars.

Why is Min saving money? How do you know? Make another inference about the paragraph. What would you put in the chart to show how you made the inference?

GO online www.harcourtschool.com/storytown

439

Vocabulary

Build Robust Vocabulary

- extravagant
- unimaginable
- gourmet
- throng
- embarked
- precarious
- hiatus

Between Two Lives

Mila had already said good-bye to her friends with **extravagant** hugs. The neighbors had given her family a big, noisy farewell party at the corner restaurant. Its chef had prepared a dinner of **unimaginable** delights, with every dish fit for a **gourmet** meal. The **throng** of partygoers had cheered as Mila and her family posed for a last photo.

Now the movers had left, and the apartment was empty and cold. The family hadn't **embarked** on their journey to a new life in Michigan yet, because their new home was not ready. Mila felt stuck in the **precarious** position of having said goodbye to her old life while still being inside it. She had looked forward to the **hiatus** in going to school, but now she missed being in class. To keep her mind occupied, Mila calculated the number of hours until the airport shuttle would arrive. "Sixty-seven," she said out loud, "and that van better not be a minute late!"

 www.harcourtschool.com/storytown

Word Detective

Your challenge this week is to find Vocabulary Words outside your classroom. Look for the words in advertisements, in the newspaper, or on television. You might find that there is a hiatus in your favorite TV series. When you find a Vocabulary Word, remember to write in your vocabulary journal where you found the word and how it was used.

441

Nothing
Ever Happens
on
90th Street

by Roni Schotter
illustrated by Kyrsten Brooker

Realistic Fiction

Genre Study

Realistic fiction has characters and events that are like people and events in real life. As you read, look for

- characters who behave like real people.

- characters with problems that might happen in real life.

Comprehension Strategy

Use story structure to identify and remember how plot events lead to the resolution of the story's conflict.

NOTHING EVER HAPPENS ON 90TH STREET

by Roni Schotter

illustrated by Kyrsten Brooker

Eva unwrapped a cinnamon Danish, opened her notebook, and stared helplessly at the wide, white pages. "Write about what you know," her teacher, Mrs. DeMarco, had told her. So Eva sat high on the stoop and looked out over 90th Street waiting for something to happen. A horn honked. A radio rapped. A kid cried. The usual. "Nothing ever happens on 90th Street," Eva scribbled in her notebook.

A few doors down, Mr. Chang was arranging fish fillets in his newly opened Seafood Emporium. No one was buying, and his shop looked as empty and ignored as the tiny, boarded-up store next door to it. He nodded to a woman passing by and called hello to Eva.

Out the door of Eva's building came Mr. Sims, the actor, carrying his enormous cat, Olivier. Mr. Sims was "on hiatus again," which meant out of work, in between shows, and so, every day, dressed in his finest, he embarked on a daily promenade with Olivier under his arm. "Writing?" he asked.

"Trying to," Eva answered, "but nothing ever happens on 90th Street!"

"You are mistaken, my dear," Mr. Sims said. "The whole world's a stage—even 90th Street—and each of us plays a part. Watch the stage, observe the players carefully, and don't neglect the details," he said, stroking Olivier. "Follow an old actor's advice and you will find you have plenty to write about."

"Thanks," Eva said, and fast as she could, using as many details as she could recall, Eva described Mr. Sims in her notebook—his felt fedora hat, his curly gray hair, his shiny button shoes. When she looked up, he was halfway down the street and Mr. Morley, the mousse maker, was at his window.

Just as he did every day, Mr. Morley set his chocolate pot and coffee urn out on his ledge with a sign. Mr. Morley dreamed of having a catering business where the fanciest people demanded his dessert. But the trouble was . . . Mr. Morley's mousse was missing something. No matter how he tried, his mousse never had much taste, and Mr. Morley never had many customers.

"Writing?" he asked.

"Um. Hmmm," Eva answered, chewing on her pencil.

"Try to find the poetry in your pudding," Mr. Morley said softly. "There's always a new way with old words."

"You're right," Eva said, wishing Mr. Morley would one day find the poetry in *his* pudding. Taking his advice, she tried to think up a new way to describe the look of Mr. Morley's mousse. Smooth and dark as midnight. Or maybe more like mink! Yes, that was it! Eva thought, writing in her notebook.

PRIME CUTS

The door to the building slammed and a gust of wind sent dead
leaves soaring and dipping like crazy kites. Alexis Leora nodded to Eva
and stepped gracefully down the steps to do her warm-up exercises.
Alexis was a dancer. When she wanted to, she could hold an extremely
long leg straight up against her ear like a one-legged woman with three
arms. But she couldn't smile. Eva decided it was because Alexis Leora
was lonely.

"Writing?" Alexis Leora asked Eva.

"Yes," Eva answered.

Alexis Leora did six deep knee bends and then sighed. "Stretch,"
she said sadly. "Use your imagination. If your story doesn't go the way
you want it to, you can always stretch the truth. You can ask, 'What
if?' and make up a better story."

"You're right," Eva said, thinking "What if?" What if Alexis Leora
met someone? Would she smile then? What would that look like? Eva
closed her eyes to try to picture it, but all she could picture was soup—
Spanish soup—rich and brown and so spicy it seemed as if she could
actually smell it.

She could! When Eva opened her eyes, Mrs. Martinez was standing beside her. She nodded to Alexis Leora as she handed Eva a bowl of soup. "Have some," she said. "Writers *need* soup. What's your story about?"

"Nothing much." Eva sighed. "Nothing ever happens on 90th Street."

"Add a little action," Mrs. Martinez said. "Like soup. A little this. A little that. And don't forget the spice. Mix it. Stir it. Make something happen. Surprise yourself!" She nodded again to Alexis Leora and went inside.

Eva put down her pencil and tasted Mrs. Martinez's wonderful, surprising soup. She thought about her story. It wasn't wonderful. It wasn't surprising. But what could she do? Nothing ever happened on 90th Street. How could she possibly "add a little action" and "make something happen"? Eva had no ideas. She was stuck!

Then Mrs. Friedman from up the block came wheeling Baby Joshua in his stroller. He was holding a bright red ball in two tiny, fat hands. "Bird!" he called out to a pigeon hunting for something to eat. "Bird. Hungry!"

"Pigeon," Mrs. Friedman told him.

Eva sighed and looked down at her half-eaten Danish, then at her notebook. She looked at Baby Joshua, then at the pigeon. She remembered Alexis Leora's words of advice. "What if?" Eva thought. Suddenly she had an idea.

What if she stood up, broke her Danish into dozens of tiny pieces, and scattered them wide and wild into the street? What would happen? Eva laughed to think of it . . . .

From lampposts and ledges dozens of pigeons swooped down to dine on Danish. Eva eagerly picked up her pencil and began to write again. "Bird!" Baby Joshua called out, pointing. "More bird!" he cried, panting. The bright red ball dropped out of his tiny, fat hands and bounced onto the sidewalk. "Bye, bye, ball!" Baby Joshua screamed.

The ball rolled off the curb, into the street, and straight into the path of a pizza delivery man on his bicycle!

Everyone gasped in horror. Alexis Leora paused in mid-plié and leaped to the rescue. She got there just as the pizza delivery man landed, right side up, at her feet. Alexis Leora looked down at the pizza man and he looked up at her. And then something almost unimaginable happened: Alexis Leora smiled! "Are y-y-you all right?" she asked, shyly. Her smile was sweet and bright. Her teeth were straight and white. (It was the first time Eva or anyone on 90th Street had seen them!)

"Yes," said the pizza man, smiling up at her. It was love at first sight. Pepperoni and peppers rained down on the happy couple. The pizza man pulled a pepper out of his hair as horns began to honk.

Eva added this to her notebook and wondered what could possibly happen next . . . .

A long, white limousine was honking its horn loudest of all. The limo driver rolled down his window. "Whad'ya wanna block traffic for?" he called out. The back door of the limo opened and out stepped a woman in sunglasses, wearing a turban and a coat the color of a taxi.

"There seems to be a problem, Henry," she said in a fake English accent. "There's some sort of accident here. Perhaps—"

"It's *Sondra!*" someone suddenly screamed, interrupting her. "Sondra! Can I have your autograph?" Mrs. Martinez called out.

"Sondra Saunderson!" Mr. Morley blushed.

Was Eva dreaming? There, in the middle of 90th Street, larger than life, stood Sondra Saunderson, star of stage, screen, and the sensational soap opera "One World To Live In."

"Darlings, what's happening here? I'm sure I . . . *Lar*-ry!" she called out suddenly, and stretched her arms toward Mr. Sims, who had just returned from his promenade. "It's been an age since we saw each other!"

Mr. Sims' cat, about to be crushed in an extravagant embrace, leaped out of Mr. Sims' arms to chase after Baby Joshua's ball.

"Olivier!" Mr. Sims called out. "Come back!"

Everyone raced into the street after the ball, but it was the limo driver who, in the right place at the right time, leaned into the gutter and picked it up.

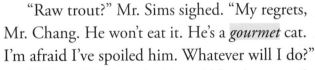

With a flick of the wrist, he tossed the ball to Mrs. Friedman, who presented it to a drooling but grateful Baby Joshua.

"How's that for a throw?" the limo driver proudly asked the crowd.

No one, not even Baby Joshua, had a chance to answer. Olivier, frightened by so many people, raced past Eva, scrambled onto Mr. Morley's ledge, where he knocked over his coffee urn, spilling all the coffee into his mousse pot.

"Ruined!" Mr. Morley cried, wringing his hands.

At that, Olivier bounded to the top of a ginkgo tree, where he swayed dangerously like a heavy, white balloon.

"Now he'll *never* come down!" Mr. Sims lamented. "He's terribly stubborn."

"There, there, Larry," Sondra Saunderson comforted him. "I'm sure someone on 90th Street will have a solution."

Eva tried to imagine who that could possibly be . . . .

"I have one!" she heard Mr. Chang call out. Generously, he offered trout, fresh from his store, to Olivier.

High up in the tree, Olivier barely blinked.

"Raw trout?" Mr. Sims sighed. "My regrets, Mr. Chang. He won't eat it. He's a *gourmet* cat. I'm afraid I've spoiled him. Whatever will I do?"

"What if?" Eva asked herself for the second time that day, and suddenly she had another idea. A truly great one! She whispered it to Mr. Morley, Mrs. Martinez, and Mr. Chang.

"Brilliant!" Mr. Morley exclaimed. And with that he, Mrs. Martinez, and Mr. Chang, still clutching his trout, vanished into the building.

Eva righted Mr. Morley's coffee urn and stuck her finger into his ruined mousse, then into her mouth to determine the degree of damage. "Mocha!" she called out in surprise. "Mr. Morley's mousse is mocha now and . . . ." She paused, trying to find the perfect word. "*Magnificent!*" she announced to the assembled throng. And, giving the pot a stir, she dished out samples to all assembled.

"Delicious!" Alexis Leora said, spooning some into the pizza man's mouth.

"Poetry!" Sondra Saunderson pronounced.

Now on 90th Street, people who had never spoken to one another before were speaking at last. The pizza delivery man and the limo driver shook hands, and everyone tried to tempt Olivier down from his precarious perch.

And then . . . Mr. Morley appeared on the steps, followed by Mrs. Martinez and Mr. Chang. Mrs. Martinez carried a large pot of her surprising soup, while Mr. Morley carried a platter of Mr. Chang's trout, now surrounded by many tiny vegetables and cooked to perfection. With the addition of a cup of Mr. Morley's cat-created mocha mousse—it was a meal worthy of the finest culinary establishment.

"Do you smell that, Olivier?" Mr. Sims called, fanning the steam so it rose up the ginkgo tree.

Olivier took one deep sniff and bolted down the tree to dine!

Everyone on 90th Street sampled each course and everyone on 90th Street sighed with delight. "Superb!" "*Fantastico!*" "Yum!"

Eva smiled and glanced up from her notebook. For the third time that day she asked herself, "What if?"

"Mr. Chang," she began, "you and Mr. Morley and Mrs. Martinez are such great cooks. The boarded-up store next to your Seafood Emporium, what if all of you used it for a restaurant?"

"A restaurant?" The three chefs looked at one another. "What a wonderful idea," they said, shaking Eva's hand. "Everyone on 90th Street could be our customers. You too, Sondra."

"Everyone but me," Mr. Sims said regretfully. "Just now, I'm between jobs and a bit low on cash."

"No longer!" Sondra called out. "You'll be on my show! I'll arrange it." Mr. Sims kissed Sondra's hand, and everyone cheered.

"What an amazing day!" Mrs. Martinez said. "Who would believe it? If only someone had written it all down."

"I did," Eva announced, and she opened her notebook and began to read her story (the same story you're reading now) about how *nothing* ever happened on 90th Street.

"What a story!" Sondra exclaimed. "Full of detail. Dialogue. Suspense. A bit of poetry. A hint of romance. Even a happy ending. Why, you'd almost think some of it was made up!"

Eva smiled mysteriously. "Thanks," she said proudly. "But just wait. It'll be even better . . . after I rewrite it."

THINK CRITICALLY

1 When Baby Joshua's ball rolls into the street, there are many consequences. List the chain of events this incident triggers.
CAUSE AND EFFECT

2 How do you think Mr. Sims and Sondra know each other?
MAKE INFERENCES

3 If you could make up a story about someone you know, who would you write about? What characteristics about that person would make you want to include him or her? CHARACTER'S TRAITS

4 What finally gets Olivier out of the tree? NOTE DETAILS

5 **WRITE** Write a short article for a local newspaper describing the 90th Street Café. What kinds of food are on the menu? Who are the customers? Use information and details from the selection to support your descriptions. SHORT RESPONSE

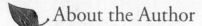

Roni Schotter

Roni Schotter lives in a small town north of New York City. As a child, she loved words, but she never imagined she would grow up to be a writer. Like Eva, Roni Schotter writes in her notebook about what puzzles and excites her. She uses her imagination to craft her stories. Roni Schotter has written more than twenty children's books.

GO online www.harcourtschool.com/storytown

About the Illustrator

Kyrsten Brooker

Kyrsten Brooker studied art in New York City, which she calls "the most energizing and inspiring place" she's ever been. In her career as an illustrator, she has had her work published in several books for young readers and magazines for adults. Kyrsten Brooker lives with her husband and son in Edmonton, Alberta, Canada.

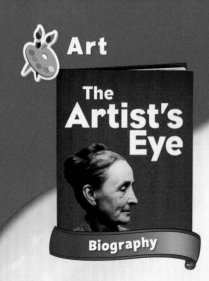

The Artist's Eye

Biography

The Artist's Eye

by Joan T. Zeier

Did you ever think you might like to be an artist? Perhaps you have done a drawing that everyone praised. What was it that made your drawing special?

Could it be that you saw the subject more clearly than most people? You may have noticed a detail like a shadow or the contrast between an object and its background. These things make the difference between an ordinary drawing and one that is really exciting.

Some people seem to be born with the gift of vivid sight. Sometimes they are able to store images in their minds for a long time.

Born on November 15, 1887, Georgia O'Keeffe grew up in Sun Prairie, Wisconsin. In her autobiography, she recalls herself as a baby, sitting in the sun on a red-white-and-black-patterned quilt, surrounded by white pillows. Nearby were her mother and a visiting aunt. A few years later when she was able to talk, Georgia described her memory of the scene, including her aunt's hairstyle and the design of her aunt's dress. Her mother was amazed because that event had taken place when Georgia was only nine months old! Yet everything she described was exactly right.

It is interesting that O'Keeffe remembered her aunt's unusual hairstyle and fashionable costume in sharp detail but did not recall at all what her mother wore that day. Often we do not notice the details of things we see every day.

As a young woman, O'Keeffe studied many artists and learned their styles and techniques. One way to learn how to do something is to copy the work of others who do it well.

Canna Red and Orange (1922)

Georgia O'Keeffe

Everyone thought Georgia O'Keeffe did fine work. But she was unhappy. She felt the paintings that she did were similar to those of other artists. She wanted to do something all her own. She even stopped painting for a while. Then she slowly began to work by herself. She knew that her "artist's eye" had always seen things differently. She needed to be free to put her ideas on canvas in that fresh, new way.

Some people did not like her new paintings at first, but she did not let that bother her. As long as she painted her own visions, she was happy. After a while, people began to appreciate the unique qualities of her style.

Georgia O'Keeffe has been recognized as one of America's most important artists. She continued to create art with her own personal touch throughout her long life, stopping only when her health failed at age 96. O'Keeffe died in 1986, but the different view of the world she captured in her paintings can still be enjoyed in museums around the world.

Artist's Eye Activities

See if you can draw a picture of your toothbrush without looking at it. How is the handle shaped? Is the end round or pointed? Are the rows of bristles long or short? Is it hard to remember details about something so familiar?

Try hard to give your next drawing your personal touch. Choose a subject you would like to draw. Combine close observation with an unlimited imagination. Develop your "artist's eye" by drawing your subject the way *you* see it.

459

Connections

Comparing Texts

1. Eva receives advice from her neighbors about writing. What is a valuable piece of advice you have received from someone?

2. Compare how Eva and Georgia O'Keeffe use details of everyday life in their work.

3. At the end of "Nothing Ever Happens on 90th Street," Eva's neighbors open a café. What is another way people in a community can work together for a common goal?

Vocabulary Review

I prepared an extravagant gourmet meal.

Word Pairs

Work with a partner. Write the Vocabulary Words on index cards. Place the cards face down. Take turns flipping over two cards and writing a sentence that uses both words. Read aloud the sentence to your partner. You must use the words correctly to keep the cards. The student with the most cards at the end wins.

hiatus

embarked

unimaginable

extravagant

gourmet

throng

precarious

Fluency Practice

Partner Reading

Work with a partner. Silently reread the first five paragraphs on page 450. How does the mood of the story change in this section? Read the paragraphs aloud. Use intonation to reflect the mood of the story. Ask your partner to give you feedback. Then switch roles and repeat the activity.

Writing

Write an E-mail

Think about something ordinary that happened in your day, such as eating breakfast. Use your imagination to write an e-mail to a friend describing the event more dramatically than it actually happened.

Characters	Setting
Plot Events	

My Writing Checklist

Writing Trait ▸ Voice

✓ I used a story map to plan my writing.

✓ I used my personal voice to connect with the reader.

✓ I included imaginative details to make the event come alive.

Big Idea

The main idea is the focus of a selection.

Enduring Understanding

Readers look for the most important details to understand the main idea of a selection.

Essential Question

Why do readers use details to find the main idea?

Spelling Words

Words with Suffixes -ous, -eous, -ious

courteous	gracious
hazardous	ambitious
humorous	discourteous
monstrous	dangerous
porous	anxious
curious	spontaneous
furious	religious
glorious	delicious
delirious	mountainous
fictitious	ridiculous

Challenge

frivolous	igneous
melodious	nutritious
aqueous	

Fluency

Reading Rate

Robust Vocabulary

- compartments
- swayed
- phobia
- invasion
- vetoed
- wispy

Comprehension

 Main Idea and Details

 Monitor Comprehension: Adjust Reading Rate

Writing

- Suspense Story
- Word Choice

Lesson 18

a novel by
Linda Sue Park

PROJECT
MULBERRY

Julia Song

JOURNEY
on the
SILK ROAD

by Luann Hankom
Illustrated by Fiona White

TURKEY

SYRIA

Tyre

Main Idea and Details

The **main idea** is what a text is mostly about. **Details** tell more about the main idea. The main idea is often stated in a **topic sentence**. It may appear at the beginning, in the middle, or at the end of a text. As you read, look for the main idea and details to help you better understand the text.

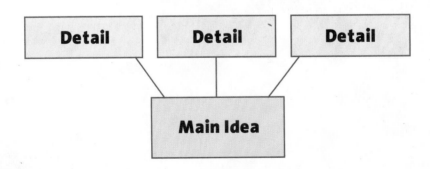

| Detail | Detail | Detail |

Main Idea

Tip
Read the whole text to find its main idea. Then look for the details that support the main idea.

Read the paragraph below. Then look at the graphic organizer. It shows the main idea of the paragraph and three details that support the main idea.

Silk has been an important material for many centuries. Hundreds of years ago in China, silk was so valuable that it was used as money. Farmers used silk to pay their taxes. The government gave workers silk instead of money. People also used silk to trade with foreign countries for other items. The Chinese kept the process of producing silk a secret for almost 3,000 years.

Detail	**Detail**	**Detail**
Chinese farmers used silk to pay their taxes.	The Chinese government paid workers with silk.	China kept the process of producing silk a secret.

Main Idea
Silk has been a highly prized material for many centuries.

Try This!

Look back at the paragraph. What other detail could you add to the graphic organizer?

 www.harcourtschool.com/storytown

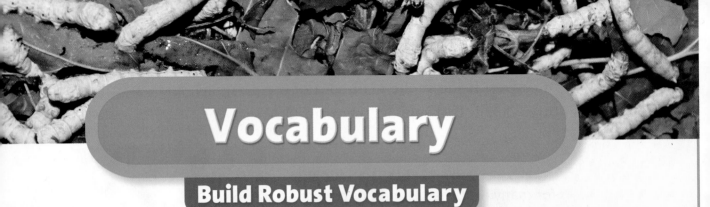

Vocabulary

Build Robust Vocabulary

phobia

wispy

compartments

invasion

swayed

vetoed

Mouse in a Maze

January 3

Dear Diary,

You know I've always had a **phobia** about mice. I don't like their thin, **wispy** whiskers or their shrill squeaks. Imagine my horror when I walked into science class this morning. Four mouse mazes were sitting on a table! Each maze had two small **compartments**, one at each end. The mice were in one compartment, and a reward was in the other. Jerry peeked inside the mouse compartment. They squeaked in protest over the **invasion** of their privacy.

Four mice seem like a lot, when you're afraid of them.

January 4

Dear Diary,

Today we timed the mice going through the mazes. When the mice left their compartments, they stood on their hind legs and **swayed** side to side. For a moment I forgot my fear. I was too busy wondering which one would be the fastest.

Every mouse managed to find its reward, though some were much quicker than others. I was hoping that my group's mouse would be the fastest. The teacher **vetoed** my suggestion that we let the mice try again.

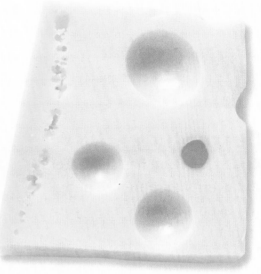

At least the mice got a treat for their efforts.

 www.harcourtschool.com/storytown

Word Scribe

 This week your task is to use the Vocabulary Words in your writing. In your vocabulary journal, write sentences to show the meanings of the words. For example, you could write some ideas for people who want to get over a phobia, or explain what is in each of the compartments of your backpack. Write about as many of the Vocabulary Words as you can. Share your writing with your classmates.

a novel by
Linda Sue Park

PROJECT MULBERRY

Realistic Fiction

Genre Study

Realistic fiction has characters and events that are like people and events in real life. As you read, look for

- characters that have feelings that real people have.

- characters with problems that might happen in real life.

Comprehension Strategy

Monitor comprehension while you read by **adjusting your reading rate.** When you come to difficult sections of text, read them more slowly.

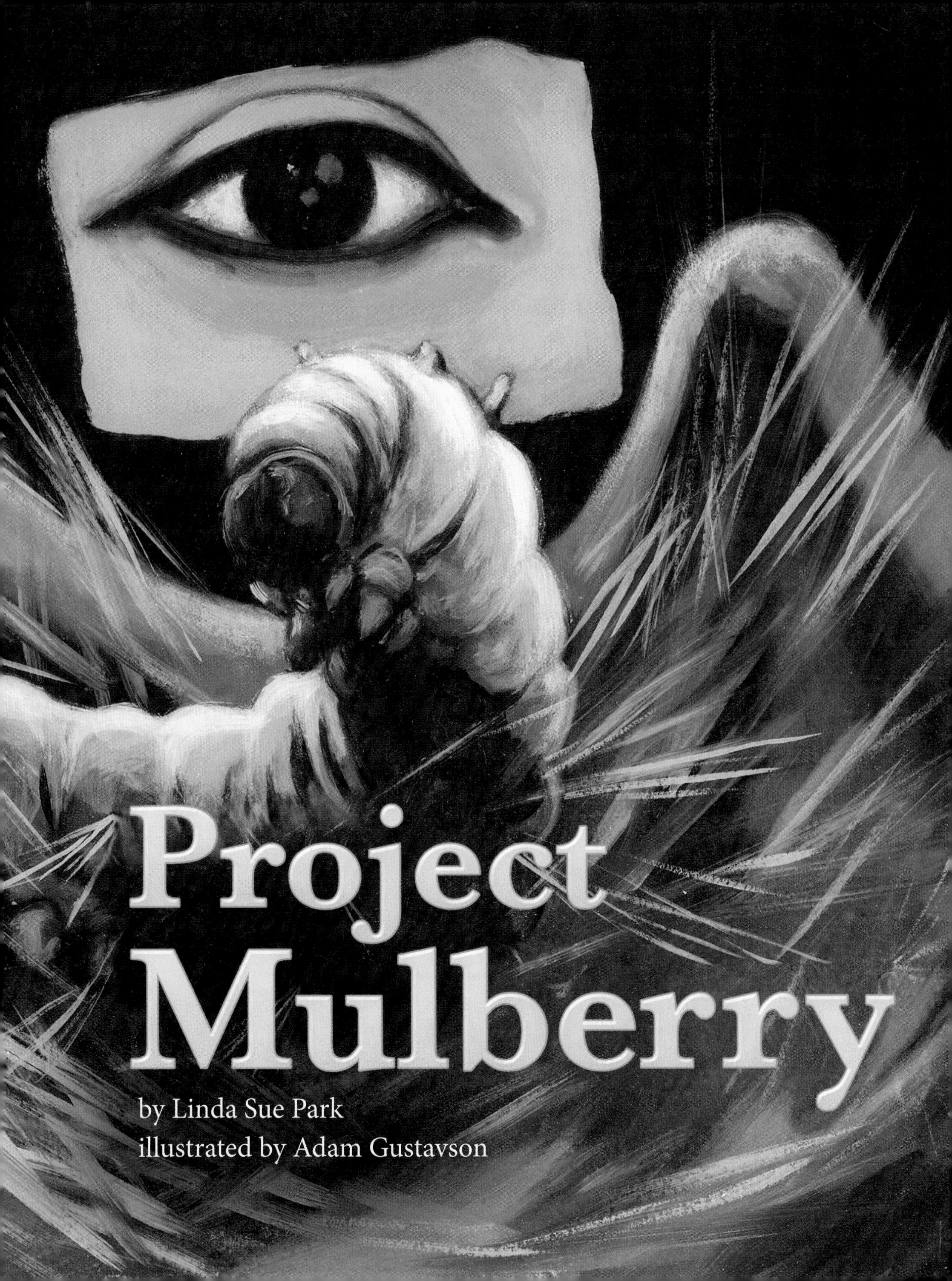

Project Mulberry

by Linda Sue Park

illustrated by Adam Gustavson

Julia Song and her best friend, Patrick, are entering projects in two categories at the state fair. Together the friends have decided to raise silkworms and document the process for the contest. Then Julia will use the silk thread spun by the worms in an embroidery project, but she hasn't decided on a design. Halfway through their project, Julia and Patrick have videotaped the worms' life cycle from eggs to caterpillars. They have also overcome several challenges, including keeping their pesky younger brothers—Kenny, Hugh, Ben, and Nicky—from getting in the way. However, Julia has just learned about Patrick's fear of worms.

When they were twenty-four days old, the caterpillars stopped eating. I didn't panic because Patrick had warned me it would happen. "They'll stop eating and change color—they'll turn yellowish," he'd said. "That means they're getting ready to spin their cocoons. Tomorrow we should move them into egg cartons."

Patrick had read that the caterpillars liked to have their own little compartments to spin in. The brochure suggested toilet-paper tubes cut in half or egg cartons. I'd saved two egg cartons, and Patrick brought over a third from his house.

There were twenty-six worms. "I'm not going to put them twelve, twelve, and two in the cartons," I said. "I think they'd like it better to be divided up more evenly. I'm going to put them eight, nine and nine instead."

The next day we cut through the hinges of the egg cartons so the tops would be easier to take off and put back on. Patrick's research said the caterpillars liked to spin in the dark, so we'd be leaving the tops on most of the time, but we still wanted to be able to watch them once in a while.

I picked up each caterpillar carefully and let it crawl on my hand for a few seconds. Then I put it into an egg pocket.

Some of the caterpillars sort of stood up halfway and swayed around like they were investigating their new homes. Then they coiled themselves up neatly. We cleaned out the old leaves one last time and put the egg cartons into the aquarium.

Now that I knew about Patrick's phobia, I couldn't believe I'd never noticed it before. If he wasn't shooting tape, he was fussing with the focus or playing back what he'd taped or switching to the regular camera. He *never* looked at the caterpillars straight on. The only way he ever looked at them was through a lens.

I could tell he was still really creeped out by them. I tried to think of something that scared me the same way. I didn't like spiders very much. . . . When I was little, I slept with a night-light on. . . . But I knew neither of those was really a phobia, not like Patrick's.

I couldn't imagine what it felt like, to be *that* scared of something. Sometimes I wanted to talk him out of it again, make him hold one, stuff like that. But that didn't seem fair. I just had to try to understand in other ways. Like by thinking how it was very brave of him to want to do a worm project at all. And how he'd decided to do it both to try to get over his phobia and because he thought it was what I wanted.

My best friend had a phobia. If he could deal with it, so could I.

• • • • • • • •

The next morning I went to check on the caterpillars. The egg cartons wouldn't open. Somehow they had gotten stuck closed. I showed Patrick when he came over.

"I can only get them open a little," I said. "Wait, let me try again."

I held one of the cartons at eye level, pulled at the top, and managed to open it a crack so I could peek in.

"Wow!"

"What is it?" Patrick asked. "What do you see?"

"They're going nuts!" I said. "They're moving their heads around like crazy. I can't see very well, but they're all, like, frantic. Do you think something's wrong? Maybe they don't like it in there."

"No, I think they're okay," Patrick said. "The silk comes out of their mouths, and the book said they're constantly in motion while they're weaving their cocoons. That's gotta be what they're doing. But why can't you open the carton?"

There's all this webbing. It's stuck to the top and bottom—it's like they've glued the carton shut. Maybe they want to make their cocoons in private."

"That's not it," Patrick said. "They make a little sort of hammock thing first, to hold the cocoon. And they have to string it up somehow. So they're doing it from top to bottom. They're not gluing the carton shut on purpose."

I watched for another few seconds. Then I closed the carton gently and put it back in the aquarium.

Patrick flapped his arms. "There's no way I can film through that crack," he said. "What a bummer—this would be the most interesting part."

On the way to school we talked it over some more. "There's gotta be some way to film them," Patrick kept saying.

We were in luck—it was a Friday, so we had the whole weekend to work on the problem.

First we tried cutting a window into one of the cartons. This was a little scary. I picked the carton that held eight caterpillars—I knew I'd left the corner egg pockets empty, so that was where I cut the window. I used nail scissors and poked a hole with the point, then made tiny tiny snips to cut a square. All the while I was praying that none of the caterpillars had moved into that space overnight.

I pulled out the little cardboard square and let out a huge breath. It was fine—there wasn't any caterpillar under it. But I couldn't really see any of the other ones either, unless I put my eye right up to the window and tilted the carton a little.

Patrick shook his head. "We gotta make the window bigger," he said.

So I did that next. I cut more of the carton, so three egg pockets would be exposed. But when I lifted off the flap of cardboard, a caterpillar came with it, trailing a little cloud of webbing.

Patrick jumped back in alarm.

"Oh no!" I cried out, then rescued the poor thing as it dangled in the air.

I pulled the caterpillar off the flap—the webbing was *really* sticky—and put it back into the carton. Then I checked it over anxiously. It seemed fine, but the first thing it did was try to wiggle away from the open window.

"This isn't working," I said. "See, it doesn't like being out in the open."

I ran into the house and found a roll of masking tape. Then I ran out to the porch again, taped the bits of cardboard together, and stuck them back onto the carton.

I felt much better once I'd done that. It had made me quite panicky—the caterpillar was obviously upset by our invasion of its privacy.

"Gak," Patrick said. "Now what?"

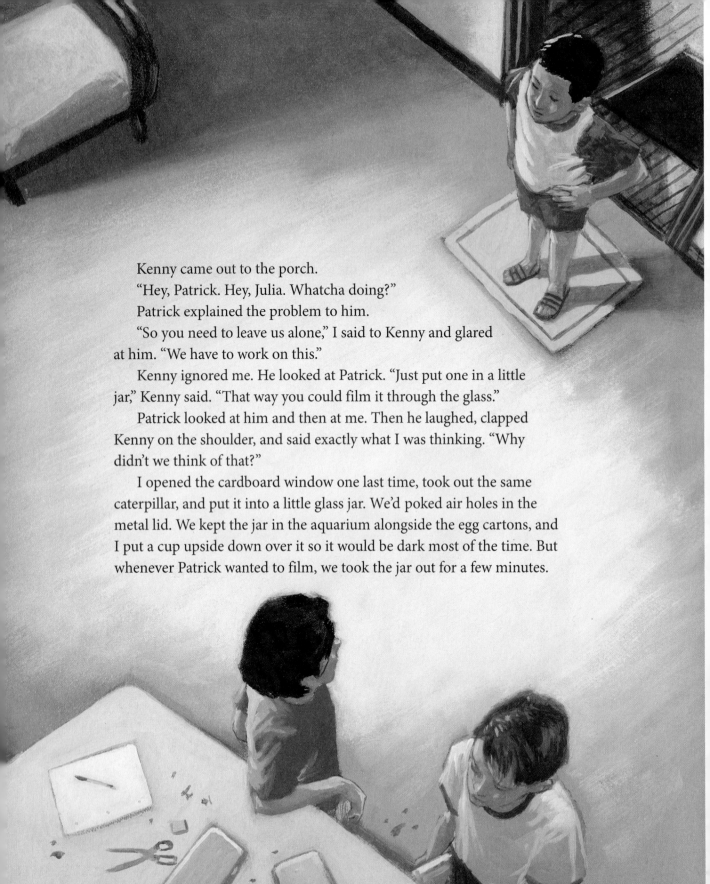

Kenny came out to the porch.

"Hey, Patrick. Hey, Julia. Whatcha doing?"

Patrick explained the problem to him.

"So you need to leave us alone," I said to Kenny and glared at him. "We have to work on this."

Kenny ignored me. He looked at Patrick. "Just put one in a little jar," Kenny said. "That way you could film it through the glass."

Patrick looked at him and then at me. Then he laughed, clapped Kenny on the shoulder, and said exactly what I was thinking. "Why didn't we think of that?"

I opened the cardboard window one last time, took out the same caterpillar, and put it into a little glass jar. We'd poked air holes in the metal lid. We kept the jar in the aquarium alongside the egg cartons, and I put a cup upside down over it so it would be dark most of the time. But whenever Patrick wanted to film, we took the jar out for a few minutes.

It was *so* cool. My parents came out to see, and Patrick's parents brought Hugh-Ben-Nicky over that evening to have a look. The porch was very crowded; I worried that all those people would upset the caterpillar. But it didn't seem to care, not even when both the twins started jumping up and down and screeching with excitement.

The caterpillar moved its head constantly. Sometimes fast, sometimes a little slower, but never stopping—it looked like really hard work. The silk came out of its mouth just as Patrick had said.

At first the silk was almost invisible. You could see the strands only if you looked really hard.

By the next morning, though, the caterpillar had already wrapped itself in a layer of silk. It looked like it was living inside a cloud. We could see its black mouth moving, moving, busy, busy, busy. Patrick wanted to stay up all night to film it, but both our moms vetoed that idea. The following morning he was at our house in his pajamas again. The silk was almost solid; now we could barely see the black mouth moving inside.

I was glad Patrick was taping it; I'd be able to watch it again as many times as I wanted. But I knew it would never be as special on tape as it was now, happening right in front of me, those wispy threads at first barely more than air, and then like a cloud, the caterpillar spinning layer after layer after layer, each layer made of one hundred percent real silk thread.

I stood with a piece of paper held behind my back. "I am a genius," I said to Patrick.

It was the afternoon of the third day of the spinning, a Sunday. Patrick was sitting on the couch in our living room. I'd told him to sit there while I went and got the paper from my room. He raised his eyebrows at me but didn't say anything.

"I've decided what I'm going to embroider. I'm going to do"—I paused dramatically, then whipped out the paper—"the Life Cycle of the Silkworm."

I held up the sketch I'd drawn.

"Egg. Worm. Cocoon. Moth." I pointed to the drawings one by one. "And wait till you hear the best part. I'm going to use regular embroidery floss to do the egg and the worm. And the moth, too. But for the cocoon, I'm going to use the thread we make. The cocoon is made of silk in real life, and it will be made of silk in the picture too, get it?"

Patrick grinned, a really huge grin.

He got it, all right. I almost felt like hugging him. He put his hands up in the air and bent forward a few times like he was bowing to me.

"Julia Song, you *are* a genius. We are absolutely, positively, going to win a prize at the fair."

I made a silly curtsy back at him. "Thank you, thank you." I'd thought of doing the life cycle a while back. But it was the caterpillar that had given me the idea for the cocoon part. I'd watched it spin for a while right before I went to bed, and I'd woken up that morning with my genius plan.

I had known right away that it was perfect.

Think Critically

1 How do caterpillars weave their cocoons? SUMMARIZE

2 Read the paragraph on page 471 that begins "Now that I knew about Patrick's phobia, ..." What is the main idea of the paragraph? What is the most important detail that supports the main idea?

MAIN IDEA AND DETAILS

3 From what you know about Patrick, is it believable that he would show up in his pajamas to film the caterpillars? Explain your answer.

MAKE JUDGMENTS

4 What kind of science project would you be most interested in doing? Explain your choice. EXPRESS PERSONAL OPINIONS

5 **WRITE** Many science contests require a written explanation of the steps involved in a project. Imagine that you are Julia or Patrick. Write an outline of the steps in your project. Use information and details from the selection in your answer. SHORT RESPONSE

About the Author
Linda Sue Park

Linda Sue Park was raised with little connection to her Korean roots. After college, she studied and worked in Great Britain. When she moved back to the United States with her husband and children, she wanted to introduce her children to their Korean heritage. She began to research Korean history, and from that research came her first four books for children.

About the Illustrator
Adam Gustavson

Adam Gustavson has never had a phobia involving worms or caterpillars but thinks he may have developed one while working on the illustrations for this story. He began drawing somewhere around the age of two, and is the illustrator of several books for children. He lives in New Jersey with his family.

GO online www.harcourtschool.com/storytown

Historical Fiction

JOURNEY
on the
SILK ROAD

by Luann Hankom
illustrated by Fiona White

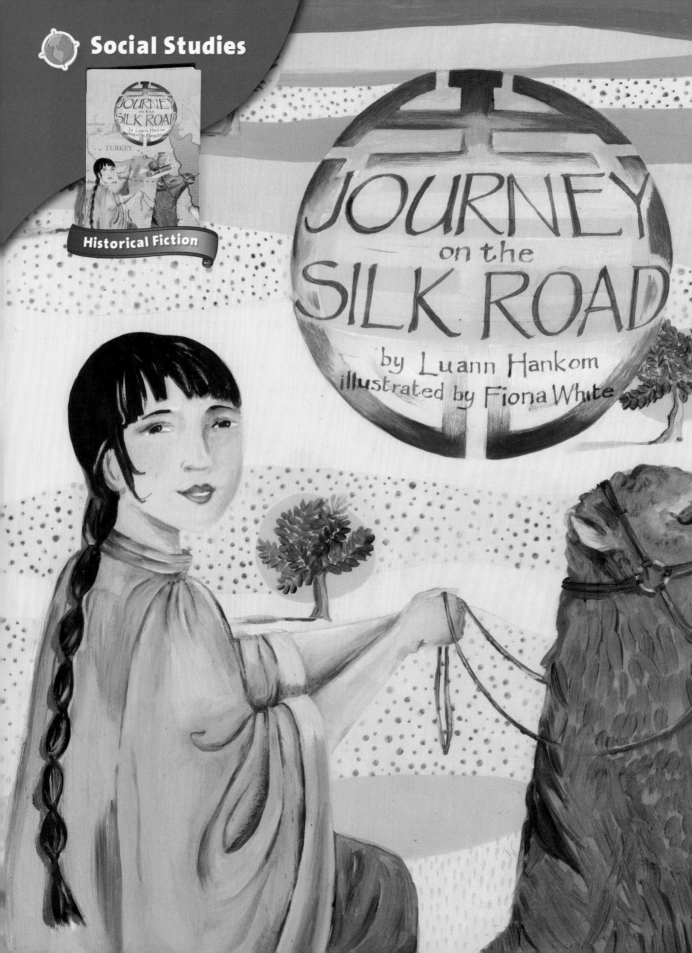

My name is Fa Zang. I am 12 years old, and the year is
A.D. 742. I am excited! I am joining my father on my first
caravan to a far-off city called Dunhuang (doon•hwahng).
My father has obtained porcelain, rhubarb, herbal medicine,
and silk cloth to trade. What treasures will we find on our
journey?

We begin our journey in Chang'an ('chahng•ahn), China,
where we live. Chang'an is a bustling city with two million
people. Our caravan includes private merchants such as my
father, Chinese government officials, and of course, camels.
Camels may be slow, but they are sturdy animals that can
carry our heavy loads.

Our prized trading item is silk, which comes from
silkworms. People in foreign lands use our silk cloth for
fancy clothes.

We leave Chang'an and travel through the Wei River
valley along the Imperial Highway. The landscape is green
and yellow—bright green fields and mulberry trees. The
ground is yellow with loess, a fine dust that blows in the
wind. If the wind is harsh, I will put a mask over my face,
so the dust doesn't get inside my mouth or eyes.

At night, my feet are sore from walking. Our caravan stops at a shelter, so we don't have to sleep out in the open. Other traders are at the shelter, too. They have dates, pistachio nuts, peaches, and pears. Someone tosses me a pear. Its sweet, slippery juice drips down my chin while I eat it.

The days and nights continue. We stop at farms for food along the way and meet caravans coming and going. We continue northwest through forests and hills and cross the Huang ('hwäng) River, sloshing through the water. We travel the foothills of the Nan Shan Mountains until we reach Dunhuang. I am tired and sore from the journey that has lasted many weeks. I am intrigued as my father starts exchanging goods with caravans from the West.

There are rare items such as green and white jade, fine-colored glass, and exotic perfumes. My father trades his silk for white jade and Persian metalwork. He trades the rhubarb for pistachio nuts and walnuts. He exchanges the herbal medicine for musical instruments. The government officials trade silk for horses. The officials are pleased—the horses will be for the emperor's army.

The men from the West describe unusual, foreign places on their journeys: Tyre and Byzantium. I have not heard of these cities before. They speak of the difficult journeys through the Taklamakan Desert and the Pamirs. Such adventures!

I can barely fall asleep, for thoughts of these exotic places and peoples fill my brain. I will travel to these cities someday! My father and I will travel back to Chang'an, so I must get my rest. It has been an exciting journey. I dream of travels yet to come.

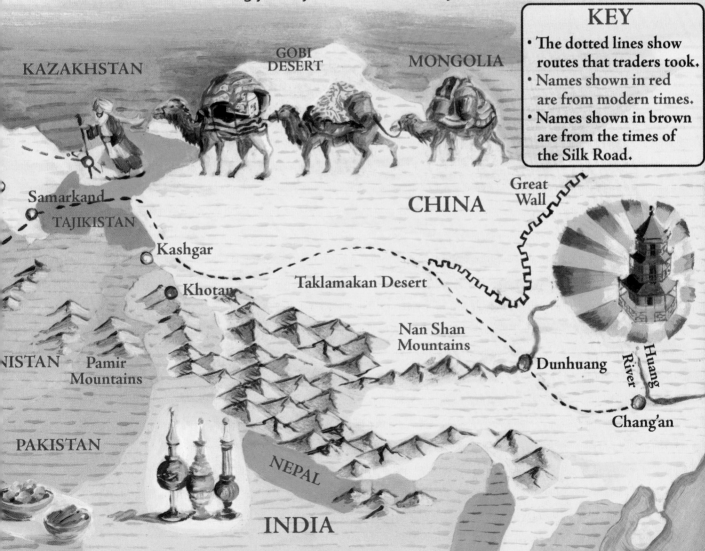

KEY
- The dotted lines show routes that traders took.
- Names shown in red are from modern times.
- Names shown in brown are from the times of the Silk Road.

KAZAKHSTAN

GOBI DESERT

MONGOLIA

Samarkand

TAJIKISTAN

CHINA

Great Wall

Kashgar

Khotan

Taklamakan Desert

NISTAN   Pamir Mountains

Nan Shan Mountains

Dunhuang   Huang River

Chang'an

PAKISTAN

NEPAL

INDIA

Connections

Comparing Texts

1. What kind of science project would you enjoy working on? What would you expect to learn from your project?

2. How are silk worms important to both Julia Song in "Project Mulberry" and Fa Zang in "Journey on the Silk Road"?

3. What lessons do you think Julia and Patrick learned from their science fair project? How could these lessons help them in the future?

Vocabulary Review

Word Webs

Work with a partner. Choose two Vocabulary Words. Create a web for each word. In the outer circles, write words and phrases that are related to the Vocabulary Word. Explain how each word or phrase is related to the Vocabulary Word.

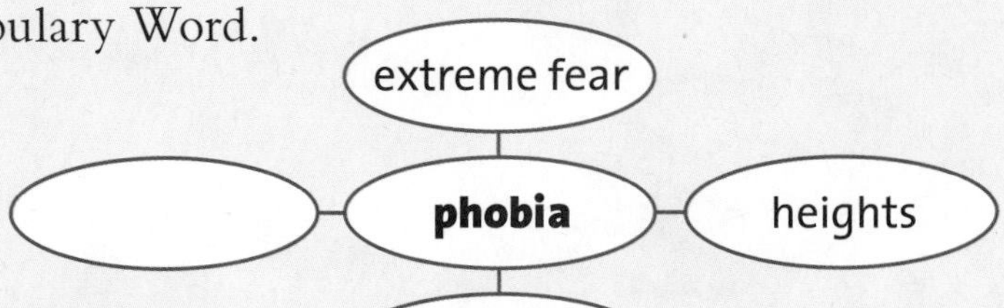

compartments

swayed

phobia

invasion

vetoed

wispy

extreme fear

phobia heights

Fluency Practice

Partner Reading

Work with a partner to choose a section of "Project Mulberry" to reread aloud. Read the text aloud as your partner listens and times you. Have your partner give you feedback on your reading rate. Read the section again, and try to increase your reading rate. Then switch roles and repeat the process.

Writing

Describe a Life Cycle

Think about an animal, such as a frog, that goes through many changes as it grows. Write a paragraph describing the life cycle of that animal.

Detail	Detail	Detail

Main Idea

My Writing Checklist

Writing Trait ➤ Voice

✔ I used a serious, informative tone in my writing.

✔ I used details to support my topic.

✔ I used a graphic organizer to organize my ideas.

Lesson 19 GEORGIA GPS Focus Wall

Big Idea
In nonfiction text such as biographies, the main idea can be stated or unstated.

Enduring Understanding
Readers collect related details to identify the stated or unstated main ideas.

Essential Question
How do readers identify the main idea?

Spelling Words

Homophones

steal	flare
steel	flair
waste	dual
waist	duel
weak	stationary
week	stationery
base	flower
bass	flour
pain	sight
pane	site

Challenge

alter	cymbals
altar	carrot
symbols	

Fluency
Reading Rate

Comprehension
- Focus Skill: Main Idea and Details
- Focus Strategy: Monitor Comprehension: Adjust Reading Rate

Robust Vocabulary
- tendency
- feat
- irrepressible
- prestigious
- device
- industry

Writing
- Letter to Request
- Word Choice

Lesson 19

NATIONAL GEOGRAPHIC

A PHOTOBIOGRAPHY OF
Thomas Alva
EDISON
Inventing the Future

BY MARFÉ FERGUSON DELANO

Letter from
Thomas Edison
to Henry Ford

Main Idea and Details

In a nonfiction selection, the **main idea** of a paragraph or section of text is not always stated in a topic sentence. When there is no topic sentence, look for **details** in the text. Think about how the details connect to each other.

- Sometimes the main idea is **stated** in a topic sentence.
- Sometimes the main idea is **unstated**. Summarizing and connecting the most important details will help you identify the unstated main idea of the text.

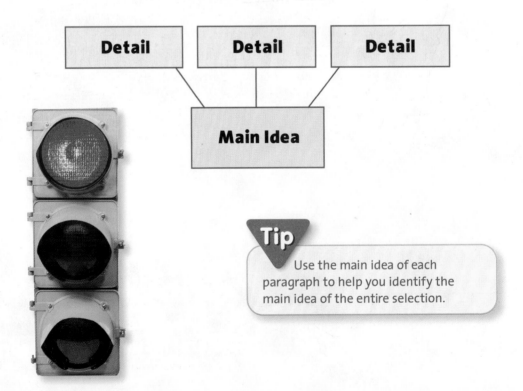

| Detail | Detail | Detail |

Main Idea

Tip
Use the main idea of each paragraph to help you identify the main idea of the entire selection.

Read the paragraph below. As you read, look for the details that are clues to the main idea. Then look at the graphic organizer below. It shows the three most important details from the paragraph. Think about how these details connect to each other.

In the early twentieth century, bicycles, automobiles, and horse-drawn carriages all shared the streets. Without traffic signals, accidents often happened. When Garrett Morgan witnessed a bad accident, he decided to do something about it. In 1923, he invented a traffic signal with three positions: stop, go, and all-direction stop. Operated by hand, it was used until the traffic lights of today were introduced.

Detail	**Detail**	**Detail**
Garrett Morgan wanted to prevent traffic accidents.	Garrett Morgan invented a traffic signal in 1923.	Garrett Morgan's invention directed traffic on the streets.

Main Idea
Garrett Morgan's invention made people's lives safer.

Try This!

Look back at the paragraph and the graphic organizer. Is the main idea stated or unstated? How can you tell?

www.harcourtschool.com/storytown

Vocabulary

Build Robust Vocabulary

irrepressible

feat

industry

tendency

device

prestigious

Inventor of Plastic

Leo Hendrik Baekeland was a scientist with an **irrepressible** desire to invent. His first successful **feat** was Velox, a new kind of photographic paper. Velox was a more convenient tool for people in the photographic **industry**. Before Velox, photographers couldn't develop their pictures on cloudy days because they needed sunlight for the process. With Velox, photographers could develop pictures indoors with artificial light.

Leo Hendrik Baekeland had a **tendency** to choose projects that brought him large profits.

In the early 1900s, Leo Baekeland changed the world by developing plastic. He invented a **device** called the Bakelizer, and used it to develop the first plastic that held its shape after it was heated. He called the plastic Bakelite. Manufacturers used Bakelite to make pens, telephones, cameras, radios, and much more. Leo Baekeland received many **prestigious** honors, including the Nichols Medal of the American Chemical Society.

 www.harcourtschool.com/storytown

Word Detective

 Your challenge this week is to find Vocabulary Words outside your classroom. For example, you might find the word irrepressible in a story about someone with a bubbly personality, and the word prestigious in a newspaper description of an important university. Look for words in magazines you have read, and listen for them on the radio or TV. Write the words you find in your vocabulary journal, and record where you found them.

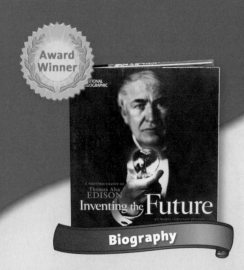

Biography

Genre Study

A biography is a written account of a person's life, told by someone else. As you read, look for

- events in the person's life in time order.

- details about why the person is important.

Comprehension Strategy

Monitor comprehension while you read by adjusting your reading rate. When you come to difficult sections of text, read them more slowly.

Inventing
the Future

A PHOTOBIOGRAPHY OF
THOMAS ALVA EDISON
by Marfé Ferguson Delano

Thomas Edison, age 4

Thomas Alva Edison never met a problem he didn't think he could solve. He was sure that if he worked hard enough and long enough at something, he would eventually discover a way to make it work. And he often did just that. In the process, he developed many inventions that would shape the way we live today.

Edison was born on February 11, 1847, in Milan, Ohio. His father, Samuel Edison, Jr., ran a shingle mill and grain business. His mother, Nancy Elliott Edison, was a schoolteacher before her marriage to Samuel. Thomas Alva was the last of their seven children, three of whom died in childhood. Called "Al" as a youngster, he was named for his great-uncle Thomas and for a family friend, Captain Alva Bradley.

When Edison was seven years old, his family moved to Port Huron, Michigan, a bustling port town on the southern tip of Lake Huron. Samuel ran a grocery store and worked in the grain and lumber businesses. He was always on the lookout for a way to make more money. Next to the family's house, he built a 100-foot-high wooden tower, which he promoted as a tourist attraction. Anyone willing to pay 25 cents could climb to its top and enjoy a bird's-eye view of the lake and surrounding countryside.

Edison was born in Milan, Ohio, in 1847, the same year this photograph of the town was taken.

When Edison was seven, his family moved to this house in Port Huron, Michigan. His father stands in the doorway.

Thomas Edison was the seventh and last child born to Nancy Elliott Edison and Samuel Edison, Jr.

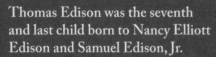

There was plenty to see in Port Huron. The town boasted lumber mills, shipyards, sawmills, and foundries, or iron factories. These industries used machinery that fascinated young Al, who by all accounts had a double dose of curiosity.

Like many children in 19th-century America, Al had little formal education. He attended an actual school for no more than a year or two. According to a story the inventor told later in life, one of his schoolmasters was angered by Al's tendency to daydream in class and one day called him "addled." When Al came home in tears about this, his mother acted swiftly. Edison later recalled, "I found out what a good thing a mother was, she brought me back to the school and angrily told the teacher that he didn't know what he was talking about. She was the most enthusiastic champion a boy ever had, and I determined right then that I would be worthy of her, and show her that her confidence had not been misplaced."

Nancy took her son out of the school and took charge of his education herself. Under her guidance, Edison developed a deep love of reading, which stayed with him for the rest of his life. One of the most important books Edison read in his youth was a science textbook called *A School Compendium of Natural and Experimental Philosophy*. Among the topics the book covered were mechanics, acoustics, optics, electricity, magnetism, and astronomy. It also featured a description of the electric telegraph, at the time the fastest form of communication ever invented.

Merely reading the book, however, was not enough for Al. He had to try the experiments for himself, so he could learn exactly how things worked. He even built his own telegraph set based on an illustration in the book. Like other electrical instruments of the time, it drew electricity from batteries attached to it. Al stretched a wire from his house to a friend's, half a mile away, so that they could practice sending each other the dots and dashes of the Morse code over the telegraph.

When a book on chemistry seized his imagination, Al set up a laboratory in the cellar of his house and gathered a large amount of chemicals to stock it. He spent many an hour mixing acids and other chemicals and alarming his parents with the occasional explosion.

Al was 12 years old when he talked his parents into letting him take a job aboard the Grand Trunk Railway, which had just opened a line in Port Huron. For the next four years, he sold newspapers including the *Detroit Free Press*, magazines, candy, peanuts, and other items to passengers on the daily round trip to Detroit. He also set up a stand at the Port Huron station to sell fruit and vegetables.

During the long layovers in Detroit, Al often passed the time in the library, reading all the books he could find on science and technology. His new job on the train didn't keep him from experimenting. He just performed his investigations in the baggage car. But when a chemical spilled and caught fire one day, the conductor put an end to his career as an onboard chemist.

When he was 14, Al set up a printing press in the baggage car and began publishing his own newspaper. It contained news of the day—which he picked up from telegraph operators at stations along the way—as well as train schedules, birth announcements, gossip, jokes, and market prices for butter, eggs, turkeys, and hogs. A subscription could be had for eight cents a month. One issue contained a headline that reflected his lifelong attitude toward work: "The more to do, the more done."

During the years he worked on the train, Edison noticed that his hearing was failing. Although never totally deaf, he gradually became very hard of hearing. Hearing loss seems to have run in his family. The condition might also have been caused by illness or injury. Whatever the cause, Edison did not look at his hearing loss as a disadvantage. On the contrary, he considered it an asset, saying that it helped him concentrate on his work and sleep without being disturbed by outside sounds.

At age 15, Edison dropped his childhood nickname of Al, preferring to be called Tom or Thomas. As he rode the rails, he saw firsthand the value of the telegraph—and one day he figured out how to use it to his advantage. People were always eager for news of the Civil War, which had broken out the previous year. When Edison arrived in Detroit on April 6, 1862, he went as usual to the offices of the *Detroit Free Press* to pick up the newspapers he would sell on the ride back home. Hot off the press was news of a bloody battle at Shiloh, Tennessee, where thousands of soldiers had been killed or wounded.

Radiating confidence, Edison poses for the camera at about age 14. By this time he had noticed that his hearing was failing. He later remarked, "I have not heard a bird sing since I was 12 years old."

Edison felt sure that if people knew about the battle, they would want to buy a newspaper to read the details. So he hatched a plan. First he persuaded the telegraph operator in Detroit to send news of the battle to the telegraph offices in the stations along the train's route. Then he bought 1,000 newspapers to sell, instead of the 100 he usually purchased. When the train pulled into the stations, people anxious to learn more about the battle crowded around to buy a paper. Not only did Edison sell all of the 1,000 copies, he also raised the price of the papers at each stop. By the time he got home to Port Huron, the few papers he had left sold for five times their usual price. Edison later recalled that not only did he make "what to me was an immense sum of money" that day, he also "started the next day to learn telegraphy."

Edison turned over some of his newsboy duties to his friends and began hanging around telegraph offices, watching the operators send and receive messages. He yearned to become a telegraph operator himself. One day, a twist of fate helped his dream come true. During a stop at a small station, Edison rescued a three-year-old boy playing on the tracks from an oncoming train. The child's father, a telegraph operator, offered to give Tom lessons in railroad telegraphy as a reward. Edison leaped at the opportunity, studied 18 hours a day, and soon landed a job as a telegraph operator in Port Huron.

Published many years after the actual event, a magazine illustration depicts the teenage Edison saving a child from being crushed by a train.

Pictured here during his "tramp telegrapher" days, Edison preferred to work night jobs, which he said gave him "more leisure to experiment."

Telegraph wires reached from coast to coast by this time. Invented by Samuel Morse in 1837, the telegraph was a sort of electric switch. Current passing through it could be turned on and off with the tap of a finger. Messages were created by sending long or short pulses of current through a telegraph at one end of a wire to another telegraph at the other end of the wire. At the receiving end of the wire, marks were indented on a roll of paper tape moving around a cylinder, a device called a Morse register. Long pulses made dashes, short pulses made dots. Morse created a code in which the dots and dashes represented the letters of the alphabet. Telegraph operators receiving a message translated the code into letters and wrote them down.

By the time Edison became a telegrapher in 1863, most telegraphs used a device called a sounder instead of a register. The sounder created Morse code by transforming the pulses into audible clicks, with short and long intervals between them. Operators had to mentally translate the clicks into letters and words and write down the message by hand—a feat that required fast thinking and faster handwriting.

Initially, the telegraph was used to send safety signals from train station to train station to prevent railway accidents. Soon, however, other kinds of information—including news reports and personal messages—crowded the lines. During the Civil War, the telegraph became a vital tool for military communications.

As the telegraph industry expanded, skilled operators were in great demand. At 16, Edison left Port Huron and set off on his own as a so-called "tramp telegrapher," taking jobs wherever a telegrapher was needed in cities throughout the Midwest and South. His skill and speed as an operator grew, which helped him land new jobs. Keeping them, however, was another matter.

Edison still had an irrepressible urge to experiment. It was part of a telegrapher's job to keep the equipment running, but that was too easily done for him to find it interesting. He couldn't resist tinkering with the machines to see how he might improve them. The chemicals used in the batteries that powered the telegraphs were also too tempting to pass up, so he conducted tests with them. Along the way, he learned a lot about how batteries and electricity worked. He also sometimes made a mess of the telegraph office and neglected his paid duties. Not surprisingly, his bosses frequently suggested that he move on. That was fine with Edison. He was eager to see more of the world and didn't want to settle down in one place for too long.

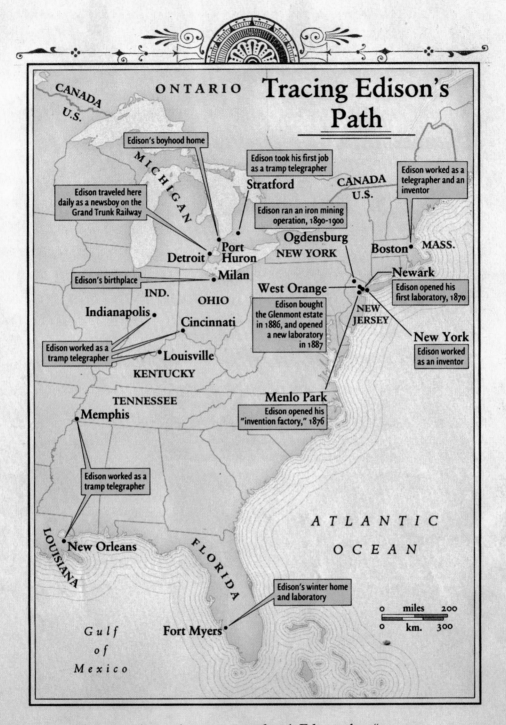

Tracing Edison's Path

CANADA
U.S.

ONTARIO

MICHIGAN

Edison's boyhood home

Edison took his first job as a tramp telegrapher

Stratford

CANADA
U.S.

Edison worked as a telegrapher and an inventor

Edison traveled here daily as a newsboy on the Grand Trunk Railway

Edison ran an iron mining operation, 1890-1900

Ogdensburg

Boston • MASS.

NEW YORK

Port
Huron

Detroit •

Edison's birthplace

• Milan

West Orange

Newark

Edison opened his first laboratory, 1870

IND.

OHIO

Indianapolis •

Cincinnati

Edison bought the Glenmont estate in 1886, and opened a new laboratory in 1887

NEW
JERSEY

New York

Edison worked as a tramp telegrapher

• Louisville

Edison worked as an inventor

KENTUCKY

TENNESSEE

Memphis

Menlo Park

Edison opened his "invention factory," 1876

Edison worked as a tramp telegrapher

ATLANTIC

OCEAN

LOUISIANA

FLORIDA

• New Orleans

Gulf
of
Mexico

Edison's winter home and laboratory

| 0 | miles | 200 |
| 0 | km. | 300 |

Fort Myers •

This map shows places associated with Edison. As a "tramp telegrapher," he worked in Stratford, Ontario, then followed jobs to Indianapolis, Cincinnati, Memphis, Louisville, and New Orleans. After working in Boston and New York, he opened his first laboratory in Newark, New Jersey.

Wherever he went, Edison continued to devour book after book. By now he was concentrating on volumes about electricity and telegraph technology. He preferred to work night jobs so that he could have the day to himself to read and experiment. This meant that he did not always get as much sleep as he needed. He started taking catnaps during the day, a practice he continued all his life.

In Indianapolis, Indiana, Edison set his sights on becoming a press operator, a highly paid and prestigious job. Press operators took down reports from news services and passed them along to newspaper publishers. Unfortunately, press copy came over the telegraph faster than he could write it down. Edison thought about this problem, then devised a solution. He figured that if he could receive the copy at a slower pace and get experience in writing it down, he could gradually increase the pace of the copy and thus his speed. So he devised a machine—considered his first true invention—to help him practice. Built with a pair of Morse registers, the instrument recorded a message at usual speed and then played it back at a slower speed.

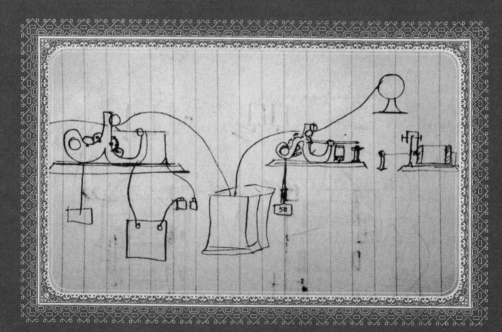

Edison drew this design for a telegraph practice instrument in 1867. Considered to be his first true invention, the device recorded a message at normal speed and then played it back at a slower pace.

In 1868, Edison took a job in the Western Union telegraph office in Boston. He found the city an exciting place. Not only did it have a large telegraphic community, it was filled with inventors. One of them was Alexander Graham Bell, who in 1876 would invent the telephone. Edison worked nights as a press operator and spent his days exploring the shops where telegraphs and other electrical devices were designed and made. Inspired by all the activity he found, Edison soon quit his job to focus full time on bringing out inventions. He met with people who had money to invest and persuaded them to provide the funds he needed to develop his ideas and have his inventions made. He specialized in telegraphic devices, but he also worked on other inventions.

When he was 22 years old, Edison received his first patent. It was for an electric vote recorder. A patent is an official document issued by the government that gives a person or company the sole right to make or sell an invention. Edison hoped the device would be used by state legislatures, but lawmakers were not interested in buying it. The experience taught him a valuable lesson: Never again would he invent something that people didn't want to buy.

Edison's electric vote recorder let lawmakers vote yes or no with the flip of a switch, then recorded and totaled the vote. But Edison could not sell the invention. Legislators preferred to cast their votes by voice.

In 1878, Edison demonstrated his phonograph at the National Academy of Sciences in Washington, D.C. While there, he posed with his invention for this photograph taken by famed Civil War photographer Mathew Brady.

Thomas Edison exhibits the first successful incandescent lamp.

Thomas Alva Edison never stopped doing. He was granted 1,093 patents for his inventions—more than any inventor ever. He filled more than 3,000 notebooks with ideas and sketches. He invented the first practical light bulb, the phonograph, and the kinetoscope. In so doing, he created the foundation for the modern power grid, the recording industry, and the motion picture industry.

Tireless Tom Edison
    invented the future.

THINK CRITICALLY

1 What was Thomas Edison's first job? How old was he when he began working? NOTE DETAILS

2 Read the third paragraph on page 500. What is the main idea of the paragraph? What details support it? MAIN IDEA AND DETAILS

3 Tell what type of person Thomas Edison was. Use details from the selection in your description. CHARACTER'S TRAITS

4 Thomas Edison's curiosity led him to invent devices that are still very important today. What are some things you are curious about? How do you think this curiosity will affect you? IDENTIFY WITH CHARACTERS

5 **WRITE** In "Inventing the Future," you read about many of Thomas Edison's inventions. Choose one of the inventions you read about. Describe the invention and tell how it was used. Use information and details from the selection in your answer. SHORT RESPONSE

MARFÉ FERGUSON DELANO

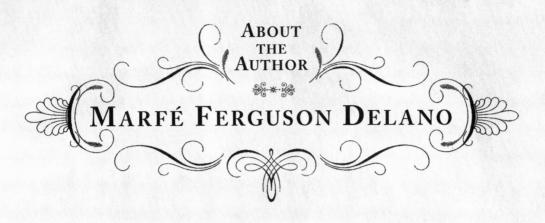

Marfé Ferguson Delano has written twelve books for children, mostly about scientific subjects, scientists, and inventors. She has chosen some of her subjects in unusual ways. For example, after learning that her husband was born on the day Albert Einstein died in the same hospital, she was inspired to write a book about Albert Einstein. The quality that impressed her most about Thomas Edison was his "stick-to-it-iveness." Marfé Ferguson Delano lives with her husband and two children in Alexandria, Virginia.

GO online www.harcourtschool.com/storytown

Social Studies

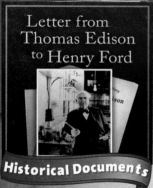

Letter from
Thomas Edison
to Henry Ford

Historical Documents

From the Laboratory
of
Thomas A. Edison

February 15, 1927

Dear Mr. Ford,

    The first phonograph in the world was made under my direction by one of the workmen at my laboratory at Menlo Park, New Jersey, in the early fall of 1877.

    I was the first person who spoke into the phonograph—and I recited the well-known verse:

> Mary had a little lamb.
> Its fleece was white as snow
> And everywhere that Mary went
> The lamb was sure to go.

    These were the first words ever recorded and reproduced in the phonograph.

Yours sincerely,

Thomas A. Edison

THE EDISON
NEW STANDARD
PHONOGRAPH.

PRICE $20 COMPLETE

EDISON NEW STANDARD, $20.00.
" Home Phonograph, 30.00.
" Spring Motor " 75.00.
" Electric " 75.00.

ALL GENUINE PHONOGRAPHS bear
this signature:

TRADE

Thomas A. Edison

MARK

Produces the same results as the other famous models of the GENUINE EDISON PHONOGRAPH, using the same records and the same reproducer. Simplest, most durable, and cheapest talking-machine.

Catalogue No. 3 free from the

NATIONAL PHONOGRAPH CO.,
New York.

St. James Building, Broadway & 26th St.,

Edison records 50 cents each, $5.00 per dozen.

Connections

Comparing Texts

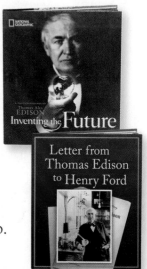

1. What device would you invent that could improve people's lives?

2. How is the information you get from reading the biography different from the information in the letter?

3. Explain how the world would be different if Thomas Edison had not invented a long-lasting electric light bulb.

Vocabulary Review

Rate a Situation

With a partner, read aloud each sentence below. Point to a spot on the line to show how happy you would be in each situation. Explain your choices.

Least Happy ——————————————————— Most Happy

- You developed a **tendency** to be shy.
- Someone said your curiosity was **irrepressible**.
- Someone called a reward you received **prestigious**.
- Your science fair project started an **industry**.

tendency

feat

irrepressible

prestigious

device

industry

Fluency Practice

Timed Reading

Read aloud the first two paragraphs on page 504. Then use a stopwatch to time your second reading of the paragraphs. Record your time. Set a goal to improve your reading rate. Practice reading the paragraphs until you have met your goal.

Writing

Write About an Invention

Choose an invention that interests you. Then write one paragraph to describe it.

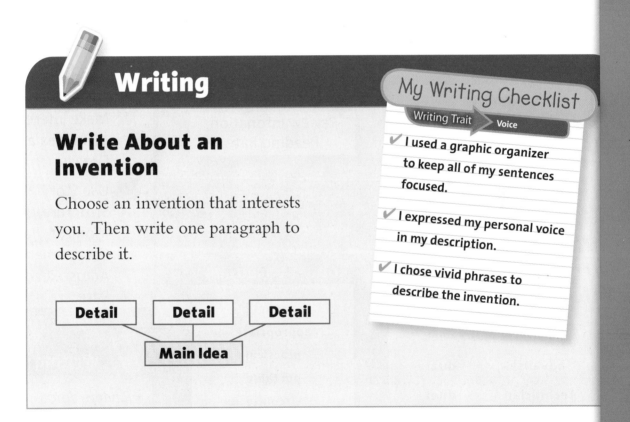

Detail	Detail	Detail

Main Idea

My Writing Checklist

Writing Trait ➤ Voice

✔ I used a graphic organizer to keep all of my sentences focused.

✔ I expressed my personal voice in my description.

✔ I chose vivid phrases to describe the invention.

Big Idea
Game show contestants demonstrate their motives through their actions and speech.

Enduring ! Understanding
In a dramatic performance, the audience uses details to identify and support the main idea, or focus, of each character.

Essential ? Question
What details in "The Invention Convention" support the main idea?

Spelling Words

Review

irreplaceable	cellist
immature	porous
indefinite	glorious
illiterate	spontaneous
independent	fictitious
applicant	mountainous
accountant	weak
insistent	week
novelist	dual
technician	duel

Fluency

Review Intonation, Reading Rate

Robust Vocabulary

scours
appropriate
practical
portable
circulate
protrude
boisterous
deduction
fickle
measly

Comprehension

Review

 Make Inferences, Main Idea and Details

 Use Story Structure, Monitor Comprehension: Adjust Reading Rate

Writing

- *Review* Voice, Word Choice
- Revise and Publish

Lesson 20

Theme Review and Vocabulary Builder

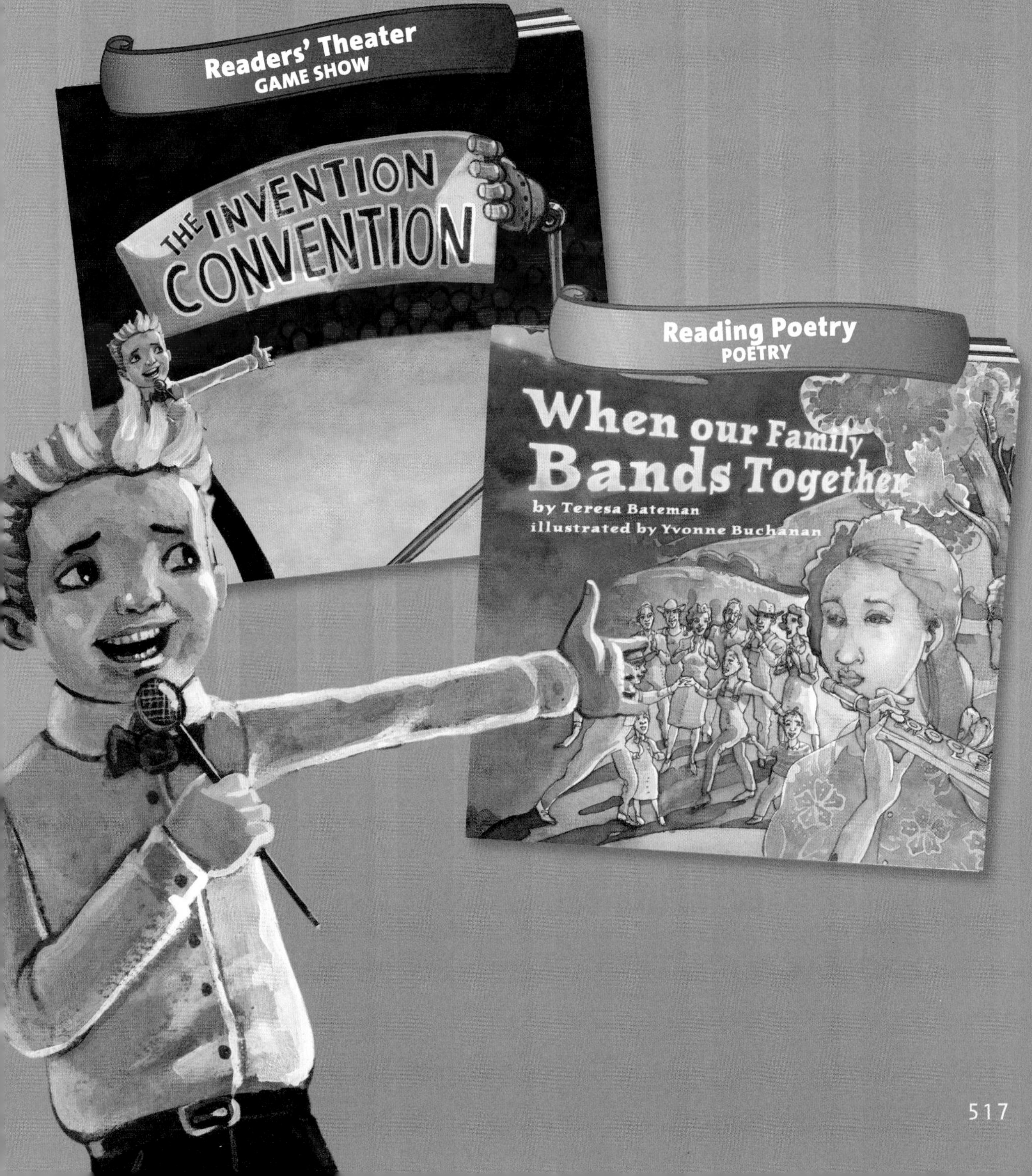
Readers' Theater
GAME SHOW
THE INVENTION CONVENTION
Reading Poetry
POETRY
When our Family Bands Together
by Teresa Bateman
illustrated by Yvonne Buchanan

scours

appropriate

practical

portable

circulate

protrude

boisterous

deduction

fickle

measly

Reading for Fluency

When reading a script aloud,

- Your reading rate should help your listeners understand your lines.

- Change your intonation to show the different feelings your character has.

THE INVENTION CONVENTION

illustrated by Aaron Jasinski

Characters

Elijah, co-host	Jeffrey
Malika, co-host	Carmela
Audience	Voice 1
Hope	Voice 2
Kai	Voice 3

Elijah: Good afternoon, everyone! I'm Elijah. Thanks for coming to *What Is That?* This is the most popular event at the Invention Convention.

Malika: What a throng of people we have here. It's like an invasion of inventors! I'm Malika, your co-host for this event. I promise that we'll show you some exciting new things. Are you ready to get started?

Audience: Yes, we're ready!

Elijah: For those of you who haven't been here before, let me explain how this game works. During the year, our research team scours the country in search of interesting and useful inventions. We've gathered a few of their most unusual discoveries here today.

Malika: Before we reveal those discoveries, we'll bring out several people selected from our audience to judge the inventions. They'll also choose one invention to receive the prestigious Invention of the Year Award. Elijah, can you bring out last year's award winner, the Choosy Box, to select our judges?

Elijah: This is very exciting. I've never used this device. Inside the Choosy Box are the cards you turned in at the entrance to the hall. I press this button here and . . .

Malika: Look! A little mechanical hand has emerged from the side of the box. It's reaching inside and pulling out a name.

Audience: That's amazing!

Elijah: Our four judges are Hope, Kai, Jeffrey, and Carmela. Please come up to the stage.

Audience: Welcome, judges!

Elijah: Please introduce yourselves and tell us how you became interested in inventions.

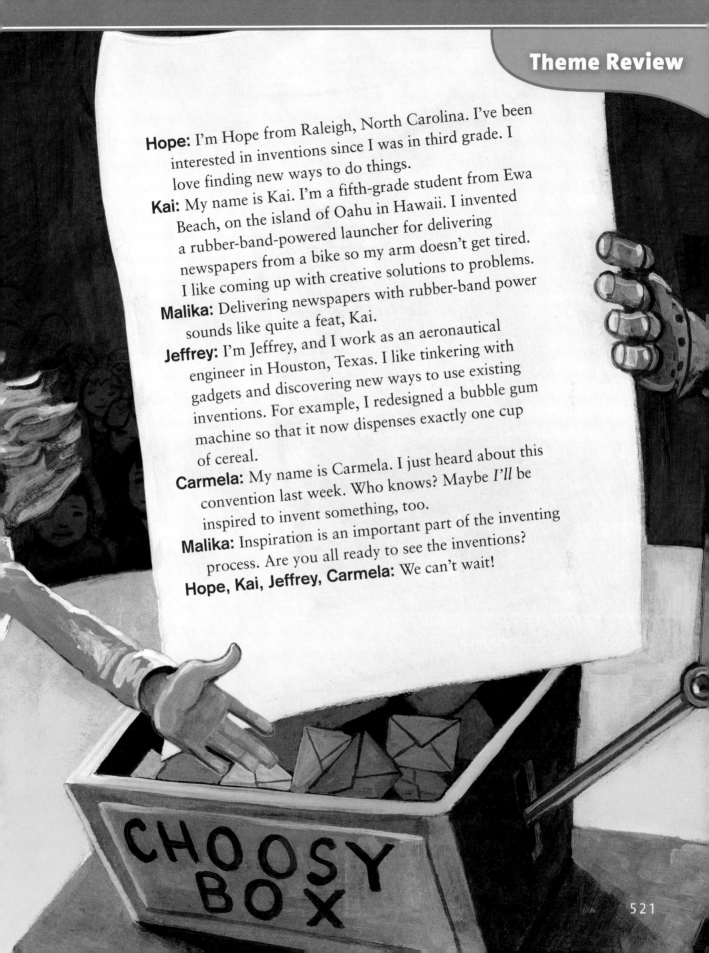

Hope: I'm Hope from Raleigh, North Carolina. I've been interested in inventions since I was in third grade. I love finding new ways to do things.

Kai: My name is Kai. I'm a fifth-grade student from Ewa Beach, on the island of Oahu in Hawaii. I invented a rubber-band-powered launcher for delivering newspapers from a bike so my arm doesn't get tired. I like coming up with creative solutions to problems.

Malika: Delivering newspapers with rubber-band power sounds like quite a feat, Kai.

Jeffrey: I'm Jeffrey, and I work as an aeronautical engineer in Houston, Texas. I like tinkering with gadgets and discovering new ways to use existing inventions. For example, I redesigned a bubble gum machine so that it now dispenses exactly one cup of cereal.

Carmela: My name is Carmela. I just heard about this convention last week. Who knows? Maybe *I'll* be inspired to invent something, too.

Malika: Inspiration is an important part of the inventing process. Are you all ready to see the inventions?

Hope, Kai, Jeffrey, Carmela: We can't wait!

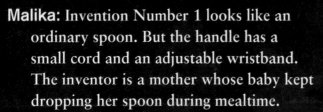

Malika: Invention Number 1 looks like an ordinary spoon. But the handle has a small cord and an adjustable wristband. The inventor is a mother whose baby kept dropping her spoon during mealtime.

Carmela: I wish I'd thought of that. It's really appropriate for people like me, who have children.

Jeffrey: I love to tinker, so I'd propose using a heat-resistant spoon instead of a metal one.

Malika: That's a practical suggestion, Jeffrey.

Hope: A fork with the same kind of attachment would be a good idea, too. I think the baby-product industry would want to sell these items.

Malika: Great insights, everyone.

Audience: Wow! A No Oops Spoon!
Elijah: Sounds like the No Oops Spoon
is a success with our judges.
Malika: Good inventions can be unusual,
but they should be useful and help
people do something better.

Malika: Invention Number 2 is perfect for busy people with a pet. You can program this alarm collar to sound at mealtime and at playtime so you don't forget to take good care of your pet.

Hope: A collar is certainly more portable than an alarm clock.

Elijah: Most pets circulate around the house rather than stay in one place. I wonder if the alarm is loud enough to be heard from another room.

Carmela: I heard "I'm hungry" and "Let's go outside" loud and clear.

Jeffrey: It's good that the alarm is inside the fabric of the collar and doesn't protrude. It won't get damaged by even the most boisterous, active pet.

Carmela: Does it come in different colors?

Kai: Do they make them for other animals?

Malika: Right now, the Rover Reminder is available only for dogs, but it does come in three colors.

Audience: Terrific!

Fluency Tip

Express the way your character reacts to a situation by using the appropriate intonation.

Malika: Invention Number 3 is no ordinary T-shirt. It's reversible and has the names and logos of two different football teams.

Hope: Perfect! If the team I cheer for loses, I can just turn my shirt inside out.

Elijah: Excellent deduction of the inventor's purpose for the Fickle Fan shirt.

Kai: I'm not a fickle fan, but I do like a lot of different sports teams. It would be nice to get two shirts for the price of one.

Malika: Yes, some of these inventions are very practical.

Fluency Tip

Knowing how to pronounce each word in your lines will help you improve your reading rate.

Elijah: And now it's time for our final invention.

Voice 1: I hear music, but Elijah is holding a toothbrush.

Voice 2: Is the music coming from the toothbrush?

Voice 3: I'm completely baffled.

Elijah: Invention Number 4 is the Tuneful Toothbrush

Carmela: That's not new. My nephew has one.

Malika: Not like this one. This toothbrush is programmed with two songs—

Jeffrey: That's a pretty measly selection.

Elijah: You didn't let Malika finish. You can also download new songs into it.

Malika: You can even record your own songs.

Kai: Really? That's awesome!

Hope: I'd love to brush my teeth to my own singing.

Malika: Audience, what do you think of this invention?

Audience: It's music to our ears!

Malika: This invention isn't just for fun, though.

Elijah: Dentists recommend that you brush your teeth for 2 to 3 minutes. The recorded songs are that long, so you know when to stop brushing.

Jeffrey: What a good invention!

Elijah: Now it's time to choose the Invention of the Year. Judges, which invention is the winner?

Kai: Anything that makes brushing my teeth more fun gets my vote.

Jeffrey: My instinct tells me the collar has the most possibilities.

Carmela: I have a baby at home, and I'd love to take that spoon home with me right now.

Hope: My two favorite teams are playing tomorrow, so I could really use that shirt.

Elijah: Audience, I guess you'll have to break the tie.

Audience: We choose . . . the Tuneful Toothbrush!

Elijah: Great choice, audience!

Malika: And that's the end of our program today. Thank you all for coming. Enjoy the rest of your stay at the convention. And keep thinking about inventions you can make yourself. See you next year!

COMPREHENSION STRATEGIES
Review

Reading Poetry

Bridge to Reading for Meaning Poetry is a type of writing told in verse that is rich in imagery and figurative language. Poetry's tone may be expressed in its rhythm and rhyme. The notes on page 529 point out some of the features of a poem. How can recognizing these features help you understand poems?

Review the Focus Strategies

You can also use the strategies you learned about in this theme to read poetry.

 Use Story Structure

As you read, identify story elements such as characters and setting. Think about how these elements add to the tone and meaning of the poem.

 Monitor Comprehension: Adjust Reading Rate

Monitor your comprehension as you read by adjusting your reading rate. Slow down or speed up to match the difficulty of the text.

As you read "When Our Family Bands Together" on pages 530–533, think about where and how to use the strategies.

STANZAS
Stanzas are sections of a poem. A stanza may focus on one main idea.

When Our Family Bands Together
by Teresa Bateman
illustrated by Yvonne Buchanan

On a soft-lit summer evening
when the mountain palmed the moon,
all the people in the valley
gathered in to hear a tune.

And their tippy-toes were tappin'
while their shoulders were a-sway,
and sore farming feet forgot
it was a plowing, plodding day.

Then an overall-clad fellow
grabbed his sweetheart by the hand,
and the two in matching denim
bowed and curtsied to the band.

Soon another couple joined them.
Everyone went *twirl* and *stomp*
as the valley folk commenced
to have a rippin', roarin' romp.

And the world was full of music
giving bounce to every boot,
as my father played the fiddle
and my mother played the flute.

IMAGERY
Poets may use vivid language to create mental images. Imagery often appeals to the senses.

RHYTHM
Rhythm is the poem's beat. Rhythm is produced when certain words or syllables are stressed more than others.

Apply the Strategies Read the following poem that describes a
family's musical celebration. As you read, use comprehension strategies,
such as recognizing story structure, to help you understand the poem.

When Our Family Bands Together

by Teresa Bateman
illustrated by Yvonne Buchanan

On a soft-lit summer evening
when the mountain palmed the moon,
all the people in the valley
gathered in to hear a tune.

And their tippy-toes were tappin'
while their shoulders were a-sway,
and sore farming feet forgot
it was a plowing, plodding day.

Then an overall-clad fellow
grabbed his sweetheart by the hand,
and the two in matching denim
bowed and curtsied to the band.

Soon another couple joined them.
Everyone went *twirl* and *stomp*
as the valley folk commenced
to have a rippin', roarin' romp.

And the world was full of music
giving bounce to every boot,
as my father played the fiddle
and my mother played the flute.

Stop and Think

Think about how the setting creates the mood for the poem.

USE STORY STRUCTURE

Even babies in their cradles
wagged their little toes in glee,
and they giggled and they gurgled
with the lilting melody.

Then the grandmas and the grandpas
showed us all some "heel and toe,"
weathered wrinkles catching lamplight
setting laughter lines aglow.

And the world was full of music
giving bounce to every boot,
as my father played the fiddle
and my mother played the flute.

Everyone was swinging someone.
Everybody held the hand
of the partner that they cherished,
then I looked up at the band.

And I saw my mother's shoulders droop
and heard my father sigh,
as his fiddle kept on fiddlin'
and her flute went low and high.

It's true the fiddle's perfect
when you're looking for romance,
but when married to the fiddler,
you don't often get to dance.

That evening, though, I had a plan.
My siblings all agreed.
And we raced across the dance floor
like a boy and girl stampede.

"Stop the music!" we all hollered.
"There's another band to play!
We think flute and fiddle players
need a dancing holiday!"

If the imagery is difficult to visualize, slow down your reading.
Then check your understanding. MONITOR COMPREHENSION: ADJUST READING RATE

My brothers took out pots and pans
and whacked them with a spoon.
My sisters buzzed waxed-paper combs
kazooing out a tune.

And I grabbed my father's fiddle
'cause he's teaching it to me,
and I pointed to the dance floor
just as stern as I could be.

Then my mother gave a kind of grin,
my father gave a shout,
as he swung her to the dance floor
and he spun her all about.

Then they danced as if their toes
had dancing stored up to their knees.
And I think I saw a kiss in there—
I know I saw a squeeze.

And the world is full of music
but it's fuller, still, of love,
and we whacked and buzzed and fiddled
while the moon glowed white above.

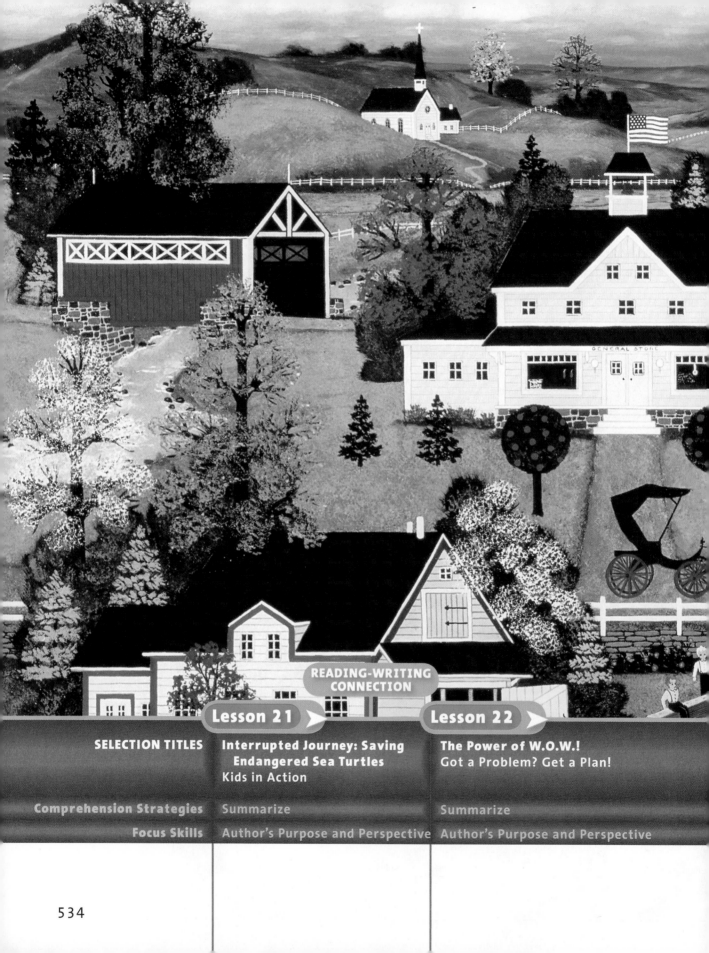

READING-WRITING
CONNECTION

Lesson 21 ➤

Lesson 22 ➤

SELECTION TITLES	**Interrupted Journey: Saving Endangered Sea Turtles** Kids in Action	**The Power of W.O.W.!** Got a Problem? Get a Plan!
Comprehension Strategies	Summarize	Summarize
Focus Skills	Author's Purpose and Perspective	Author's Purpose and Perspective

534

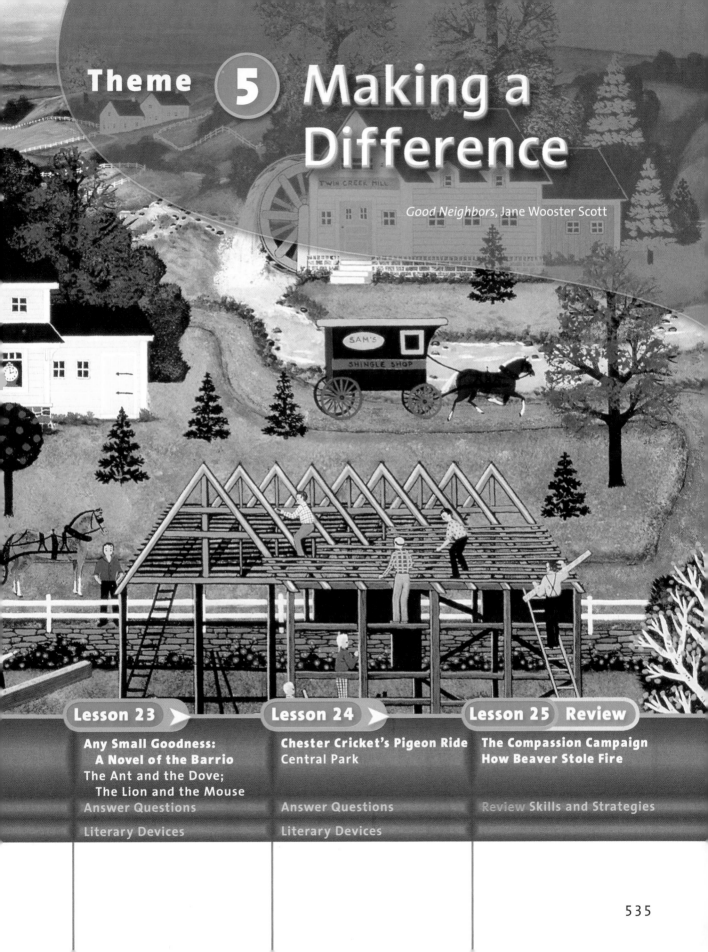

Theme (5) Making a Difference

Good Neighbors, Jane Wooster Scott

Big 💡 Idea
Authors of expository nonfiction write for a purpose and with a perspective.

Enduring ❗ Understanding
Readers establish if expository nonfiction is written to inform or persuade the reader about a topic to discover the author's perspective, or opinion.

Essential ❓ Question
How do readers determine an author's purpose and perspective?

Spelling Words

Words with Word Parts
in-, out-, down-, up-

incompetent	outpatient
uphold	outspoken
inconsiderate	outwit
indecisive	downbeat
outrank	downgrade
inhumane	downplay
inorganic	downtown
income	uplift
invertebrate	upstage
outgoing	uptight

Challenge

insensitive	downstage
outcry	insecure
upkeep	

Fluency

Expression

Comprehension

 Author's Purpose and Perspective

 Summarize

Robust Vocabulary

basking
sleek
vital
damage
analyzing
detect

Writing

• Persuasive Letter
• Sentence Fluency

Lesson 21

Genre: Expository Nonfiction

Interrupted Journey
Saving Endangered Sea Turtles

Kathryn Lasky • photographs by Christo

Kids in Action
by Elizabeth Schleichert

Genre: Magazine Article

Author's Purpose and Perspective

The reason an author writes is called the **author's purpose.** Authors of nonfiction write to **inform** or **persuade** readers. Authors of fiction usually write to **entertain** readers. An author's opinion about a subject is called the **author's perspective,** or viewpoint. Look for evidence, such as the author's choice of words and details, to help you determine the author's purpose and perspective.

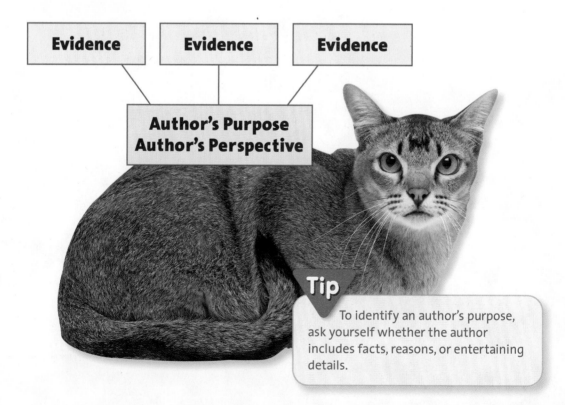

| Evidence | Evidence | Evidence |

**Author's Purpose
Author's Perspective**

Tip
To identify an author's purpose, ask yourself whether the author includes facts, reasons, or entertaining details.

Read the paragraph below. Then look at the graphic organizer. It shows evidence from the paragraph that helps you identify the author's purpose and perspective.

> When Hurricane Katrina struck the Gulf Coast of the United States in 2005, many people had to leave their pets behind. After the disaster, animal rescue organizations made a mighty effort to save the many cats and dogs stranded by the storm. When local shelters ran out of space, shelters in other areas stepped in. Charter flights flew animals to shelters as far away as California.

Evidence	**Evidence**	**Evidence**
gives information about pet rescues after a disaster	organizations worked to save stranded pets	shelters in various areas helped

Author's Purpose

to inform

Author's Perspective

People work together in times of need.

Try This!

Look back at the paragraph. How does the author feel about the subject? What words and details help you identify the author's perspective?

www.harcourtschool.com/storytown

Vocabulary

Build Robust Vocabulary

- vital
- sleek
- basking
- analyzing
- detect
- damage

Panther Protection

The Florida panther is one of the most endangered animals in the world. Long ago, the panther was a **vital** resident of Florida and parts of Louisiana and Tennessee. As people cleared land to farm and to build homes, there was less land left for the panthers. Panthers need large areas of forested land to survive. Today, only about 70 panthers are left, all in southwest Florida.

A **sleek** Florida panther lies **basking** in the early morning sunlight.

Loss of land isn't the panthers' only problem. By **analyzing** blood and tissue, researchers were able to **detect** that some Florida panthers were dying from metal poisoning. Air pollution from the mining of metals can **damage** the healthy growth of panthers.

However, the news is not all bad. People are working to extend the panthers' habitat and to make the air cleaner. With effort, we can help the Florida panther population grow so that these beautiful animals will be around for the future.

Male panthers need room to roam. An average male needs about 250 square miles of territory in order to thrive.

GO online www.harcourtschool.com/storytown

Word Champion

Your challenge this week is to use Vocabulary Words outside your classroom. Keep the list of words in a place at home where you can see it. Use as many of the words as you can. For example, you might ask a family member what can damage a plant's growth. At the end of each day, write in your vocabulary journal the ways in which you used the words.

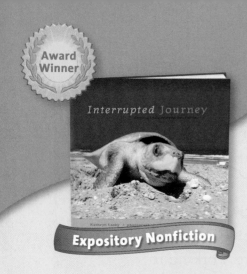

Interrupted Journey

Expository Nonfiction

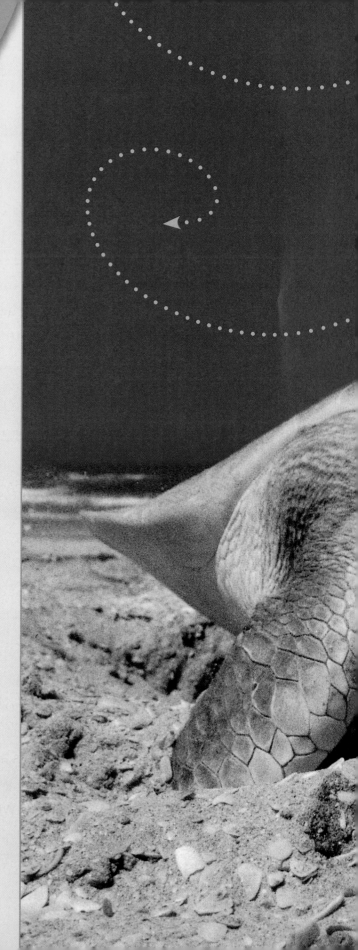

Genre Study

Expository nonfiction gives you facts and information about a topic. As you read, look for

• headings that begin sections of related information.

• the way the author organized ideas and information.

| Detail | Detail | Detail |

Main Idea

Comprehension Strategy

Summarize sections of text as you read to help you keep track of information.

INTERRUPTED *Journey*
Saving Endangered Sea Turtles

by Kathryn Lasky
photographs by Christopher G. Knight

STRANDED

The young turtle has been swimming for three months now in the same warm shallow bay, grazing on small crabs and plankton, basking in an endless dream of calm water and plentiful food. But as the days begin to shorten and the light drains out of the sky earlier and earlier, the water grows colder. It drops to fifty degrees Fahrenheit. The turtle is confused. Swimming is harder. Its heartbeat slows—and almost stops.

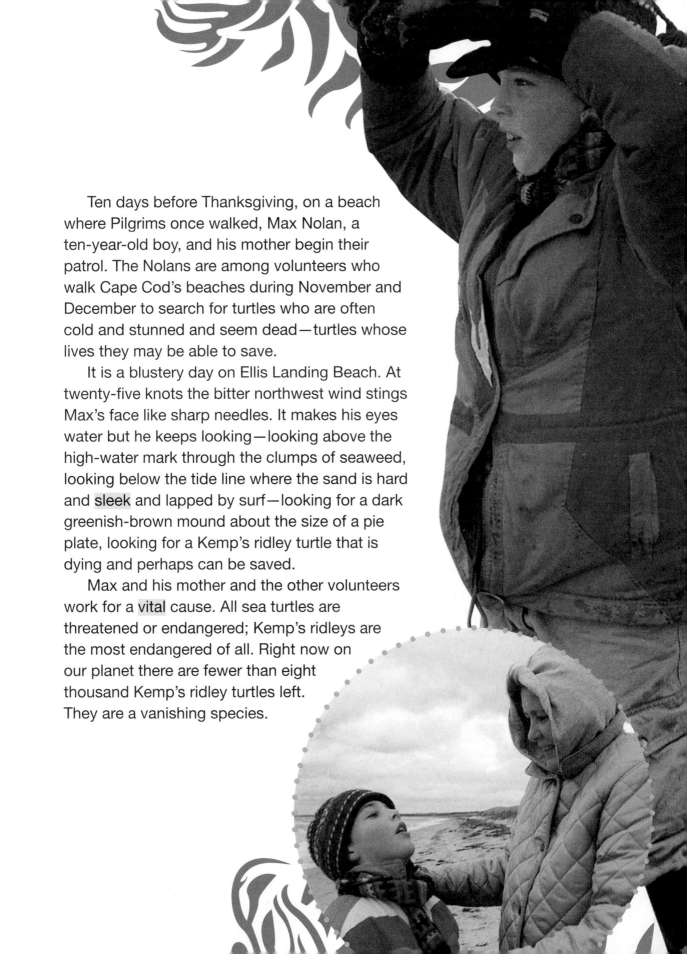

Ten days before Thanksgiving, on a beach where Pilgrims once walked, Max Nolan, a ten-year-old boy, and his mother begin their patrol. The Nolans are among volunteers who walk Cape Cod's beaches during November and December to search for turtles who are often cold and stunned and seem dead—turtles whose lives they may be able to save.

It is a blustery day on Ellis Landing Beach. At twenty-five knots the bitter northwest wind stings Max's face like sharp needles. It makes his eyes water but he keeps looking—looking above the high-water mark through the clumps of seaweed, looking below the tide line where the sand is hard and sleek and lapped by surf—looking for a dark greenish-brown mound about the size of a pie plate, looking for a Kemp's ridley turtle that is dying and perhaps can be saved.

Max and his mother and the other volunteers work for a vital cause. All sea turtles are threatened or endangered; Kemp's ridleys are the most endangered of all. Right now on our planet there are fewer than eight thousand Kemp's ridley turtles left. They are a vanishing species.

On Ellis Landing Beach, snow squalls begin to whirl down. The waves are building, and as they begin to break, the white froth whips across their steep faces. So far there is no sign of a turtle.

Max is far ahead of his mother when he sees the hump in the sand being washed by the surf. He runs up to it and shouts to his mom, "Got one!" The turtle is cold. Its flippers are floppy. Its eyes are open, but the turtle is not moving at all. It might be dead, but then again, it might not.

Max remembers the instructions given to all rescuers. He picks up the turtle, which weighs about five pounds, and moves it above the high-tide mark to keep it from washing out to sea. Then he runs to find seaweed to protect it from the wind. He finds a stick to mark the spot, and next, he and his mother go to the nearest telephone and call the sea-turtle rescue line of the Massachusetts Audubon Society.

Within an hour the turtle has been picked up and taken to the Wellfleet Bay Wildlife Sanctuary on Cape Cod. Robert Prescott, the director of the Sanctuary, examines the turtle. "It sure does look dead," he says softly. "But you never can tell." If the turtle is really alive, it must be brought out of its cold, stunned condition. That is a task for the New England Aquarium with its medical team who, over the years, have made a specialty of treating turtles.

Robert puts the new turtle in a plastic wading pool with another turtle that is quite lively. Max crouches by the edge and watches his turtle. It is as still as a stone. He gently touches a flipper. Nothing moves. Then after about twenty minutes, he thinks he might see a flicker in the turtle's left eyelid. He leans closer. "Hey, it's moving!" It wasn't just the eyelid. He saw the right rear flipper move a fraction of an inch. Over the next five minutes, he sees the turtle make three or four microscopically small motions with its right rear flipper. Soon, the rescue team from the New England Aquarium arrives.

EMERGENCY

Beth Chittick is a vet at the New England Aquarium. When the turtles arrive she is ready for them. The turtles are taken immediately into the examination room. Beth is joined by head veterinarian, Howard Crum. The temperature of the turtle Max found is fifty degrees Fahrenheit. Normal temperature for a turtle is usually about seventy-five degrees. Howard next tries to find a heartbeat. He listens intently. "I think I can hear a faint sound . . . " He holds the stiff turtle against his ear as one might hold a seashell. "Why, gee whiz, I can hear the ocean," he jokes.

Howard tries to find a heartbeat.

Howard is still not convinced that the turtle is dead. "With turtles," Howard says, "death is a relative term." Turtles can operate, can survive, even when their hearts slow down for periods of time. Events that might damage the larger, more complicated brains of other animals will not always prove fatal to turtles.

In fact, a turtle's heartbeat naturally slows down at times to just one or two beats per minute in order to conserve oxygen and keep vital organs like the brain working. So Howard won't give up on this turtle yet. The turtle does not seem dehydrated. The skin on its limbs is not wrinkled—a good sign.

An assistant swabs down an area on the turtle's neck, from which a blood sample will be taken. By analyzing the blood, Howard and Beth will be able to see how the turtle's kidneys and other organs are functioning.

Next the turtle is cleaned. The algae are washed and wiped from its shell. The doctors detect movement in its tail and then see some of the same movements that Max saw in its flippers. They are the motions a turtle makes when it swims. They do not necessarily mean that it is alive, though.

Nonetheless, the vets hook up the turtle to an intravenous needle through which fluids will be pumped very slowly at a temperature slightly higher than the turtle's body. Beth and Howard have learned much about the condition of this turtle but they are still not sure if it is really alive or dead.

Finally the turtle is tagged with a yellow-blue band. It will be known as Yellow-Blue. It is put in the Intensive Care Unit, a large temperature-controlled stainless steel box with a glass window. Inside, the turtle is placed on a soft pile of towels so its shell is supported and it will not have to rest on its ventrum, or bottom shell.

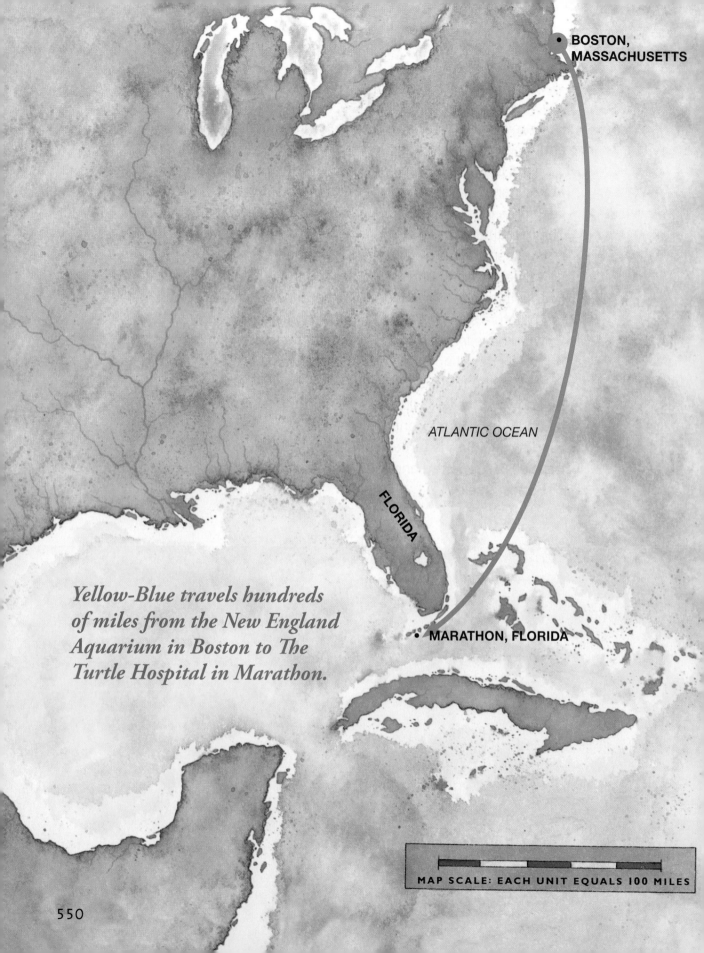

BOSTON, MASSACHUSETTS

ATLANTIC OCEAN

FLORIDA

MARATHON, FLORIDA

Yellow-Blue travels hundreds of miles from the New England Aquarium in Boston to The Turtle Hospital in Marathon.

MAP SCALE: EACH UNIT EQUALS 100 MILES

RELEASE

On a windy spring morning in April, five months after it was found, Yellow-Blue is taken from its small tank in the New England Aquarium and put into a plastic box with wet towels. Yellow-Blue has recovered from its ordeal. But for the first leg of its journey it will not swim—Yellow-Blue will fly. A small cargo jet will take the turtle to The Turtle Hospital in Marathon, in the Florida Keys.

Richie Moretti is the owner, director, and founder of the hospital. He is not a veterinarian. He is not a marine biologist. He is a man who loves turtles, and his calling in life is to help injured animals. In order to do this, Richie runs Hidden Harbor, a motel. With the money he makes from the motel, he runs the hospital.

The people who come to the motel can no longer swim in the motel pool. It is filled with injured sea turtles— loggerheads, green turtles, Kemp's ridleys, and hawksbills. Guests cannot even sunbathe or sit around the pool, for there are smaller tanks for baby and juvenile turtles not big enough, or too sick, to swim in the big pool. Veterinarians and volunteers come to the hospital to work with the turtles.

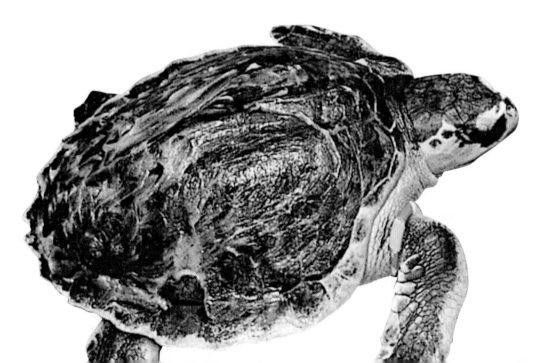

On the day of the release, Richie and his assistant remove Yellow-Blue from the tank and attach a permanent metal tag to its flipper so that the turtle can be tracked throughout its sea voyage. The turtle is feisty and flaps its flippers, perhaps sensing that something exciting is about to happen. Richie and his crew load Yellow-Blue and several larger turtles into his high-speed, shallow-bottomed boat. Before departing from the pier, Richie checks the charts of the waters around the southern keys. He wants to take Yellow-Blue to the quietest, calmest, and safest waters he knows—a place where there are no tourists racing around in speedboats or fishing boats or shrimp trawlers. He wants this turtle to have a fair chance of swimming out to the Sargasso Sea without getting hit by a boat, chopped by a propeller, or tangled in the deadly nets and lines of fishermen. They put Yellow-Blue in a box, cover its shell with wet towels, and then roar out into Florida Bay.

The boat goes fast, close to sixty miles an hour. Soon they are forty miles to the south and west. They are on the very most outlying keys of the Gulf side. The waters are shallow and calm. They cut the boat's engine and now the water is so shallow that Richie raises the outboard motor and poles in to what he considers the perfect place to release Yellow-Blue. It is in the still waters of a cove off a key named Content. Susan, a volunteer, lifts Yellow-Blue from its box and holds it half-in, half-out of the water. "Oh, you want to go! You want to go! Hang on, fella! Let's get used to things!"

Then she lowers Yellow-Blue so it is completely underwater. The flippers beat, and finally Susan's hands let go! Yellow-Blue streaks through the turquoise water, leaving a curling wake of bubbles. "So long, buddy," Richie calls.

THINK *Critically*

1 What is special about the Hidden Harbor motel? NOTE DETAILS

2 Why does Howard Crum refuse to give up on Yellow-Blue even though he has difficulty locating his heartbeat? MAIN IDEA

3 Do you think the author's feelings about endangered species affected the way she wrote the selection? Explain.
AUTHOR'S PURPOSE AND PERSPECTIVE

4 Why do you think it is important to help endangered animals?
EXPRESS PERSONAL OPINIONS

5 **WRITE** Imagine that you have found a cold, stunned turtle that has washed up onto a beach. Explain what you would do to help the turtle. Use information and details from the selection in your answer. SHORT RESPONSE

About the Photographer
Christopher G. Knight

About the Author
Kathryn Lasky

As a child, Kathryn Lasky often made up stories. One day, her mother told her that with her love of words, she should become a writer. For the first time, she gave the idea serious thought. Kathryn Lasky is equally comfortable writing fiction and nonfiction. She is married to Christopher Knight, a photographer who takes the pictures for many of her books, including this book.

When they were in college, Christopher Knight and his brother paddled a kayak from Alaska to Seattle, Washington. Christopher Knight photographed the entire voyage. Later, he photographed a canoe trip through seven European countries. These journeys marked the beginning of his career as a professional photographer. He and his wife, Kathryn Lasky, have traveled the world together, working on books. They have written and taken photographs for stories about the monarch butterfly, the birth of a new volcanic island near Iceland, and a fossil dig.

For *Interrupted Journey*, they traveled to the cold waters of Cape Cod, the warm waters of the Florida Keys, and the Kemp's ridley nesting site at Rancho Nuevo, Mexico.

GO online www.harcourtschool.com/storytown

Kids In Action
by Elizabeth Schleichert

Magazine Article

Kids

These kids are pitching in to help nature, and so can you! If you're like lots of other kids, you care about nature. And you want to do something to help wildlife and the environment. Check out what these kids have been up to.

Sea Savers

Some kids in the coastal town of Davenport, California, were worried. They noticed lots of trash piling up on the local beaches. They decided to find out where the trash was coming from—and to learn more about other problems facing the world's oceans.

They were shocked to learn that many people were dumping trash into the seas and all along the coasts too. Also, in places, fishermen have been catching too many fish. As a result, some kinds of fish have been nearly wiped out.

So, the students got busy! They grabbed some trash bags and headed out to clean up the nearby beaches. They talked to beachgoers too. The kids reminded them not to litter and to please carry their trash out. And they handed out guides to the best kinds of fish to buy—the kinds that aren't dying out. People agreed to do what the kids asked. So it was a great start toward helping the oceans!

in Action

by Elizabeth Schleichert

Flower Girl

How do city kids like Amani get to know and care for nature? Her Michigan hometown has few parks or wild places to explore. But Amani and some of her classmates at Salina Intermediate School are lucky. They are creating their own "park," turning a courtyard at their school into a flower garden. Some of the flowers the kids are planting will attract wildlife, including butterflies, and others will fill the air with sweet smells. Soon to come: a small pond, some bird feeders, and homes for toads. The kids can't wait for some wild visitors!

Super Star

At age 12, Illai wanted to do something special. Many kids she knew in her hometown in Georgia were having breathing problems because of the polluted air. Illai saw how people living in the poorer parts of the city suffered from the effects of pollution. And so she helped start Georgia Kids Against Pollution. KAP, as it's called, encourages people to work for clean air and water. Four years later, Illai is still speaking up for her cause.

Not long ago, Illai won a Brower Youth Award. It's given to a few outstanding young environmental heroes. Illai's proud mom was at the award ceremony—to give her daughter an even better award: a big hug!

557

Connections

Comparing Texts

1. Max Nolan likes to make a difference by helping turtles. What would you enjoy doing to make a difference?

2. How is the author's purpose for writing "Interrupted Journey" similar to the author's purpose for writing "Kids in Action"?

3. What are some ways your community can become a safer place for the people and animals that live there?

Vocabulary Review

Word Webs

Work with a partner. Choose three Vocabulary Words. Create a word web for each. In the outer circles of the web, write related words and phrases. Share your work with your classmates, explaining how the words in the webs are related.

basking

sleek

vital

damage

analyzing

detect

necessary — important — vital

Recorded Reading

Listen to "Interrupted Journey: Saving Endangered Sea Turtles" on *Audiotext 5*. Start at the beginning and follow along through page 546, where Max discovers the turtle. Listen carefully to the reader's expression. Replay the recording, and read aloud to match the reader's expression. Practice reading the section aloud until you are satisfied with your expression.

Writing

Write About an Endangered Species

Choose an endangered animal that lives in your state. Then write a paragraph describing the problems facing the animal and what you think should be done to keep the animal safe in the future.

Evidence	Evidence	Evidence

Author's Purpose Author's Perspective

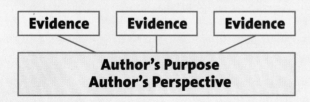

My Writing Checklist

Writing Trait ▸ Sentence Fluency

✔ I used complete sentences to describe the problem and solution.

✔ I used a graphic organizer to plan my writing.

✔ I included specific reasons and details to support my perspective.

Reading-Writing Connection

Analyze Writer's Craft: Persuasive Writing

The purpose of **persuasive writing** is to persuade readers to agree with the author's **opinion**. Authors give **reasons** and **examples** to support their arguments. They use powerful language to persuade the reader to take action. Read the paragraph below from "Interrupted Journey" by Kathryn Lasky. Look for ways the author tries to persuade readers to agree with her opinion.

Interrupted Journey

Kathryn Lasky • photographs by Christopher G. Knight

Writing Trait

WORD CHOICE
Carefully chosen words and phrases—*vital, threatened, most endangered of all,* and *vanishing*—give a sense of urgency about saving sea turtles.

   Max and his mother and the other volunteers work for a vital cause. All sea turtles are threatened or endangered; Kemp's ridleys are the most endangered of all. Right now on our planet there are fewer than eight thousand Kemp's ridley turtles left. They are a vanishing species.

Writing Trait

SENTENCE FLUENCY
The writer uses a variety of sentence lengths. Short sentences, such as *They are a vanishing species*, have a strong emotional impact.

Persuasive Composition

In a **persuasive composition**, a writer states an **opinion** and gives **reasons** that support the opinion. If a writer wants to persuade a reader to do something, the composition may end with a **call to action**. Read this persuasive composition written by a student named Daniel. Notice how Daniel's **word choices** appeal to the reader's emotions.

Student Writing Model

Protect Our Coasts
by Daniel K.

Everyone should help protect the coastlines of the United States. People depend on coastal areas for recreation and for many other things. Fish and other wildlife depend on these areas for food and shelter. Unfortunately, our shorelines are being destroyed.

How do people benefit from coastal areas? Numerous fishing grounds provide delicious foods such as fish, crab, shrimp, and lobster. In addition, some marine organisms are used to make medicines. These organisms need a clean environment to survive, but human activity is poisoning them. Sewage, fertilizers, and trash are killing marine life.

Writing Trait

SENTENCE FLUENCY Daniel begins the second paragraph with an **interrogative sentence** to interact with the reader.

561

Coastal habitats are important for animals, as well. Many mammals live on or near America's coasts. Migratory birds use the coastlines for food and shelter on their long journeys north and south. However, new homes and businesses are suffocating delicate marshes and wetlands as they take over these sites.

Daniel lists some **actions** that can be taken to solve the problem: *set aside land, limit construction, and stop littering.*

So what can we do to help? We should set aside more coastal land as nature and wildlife preserves. We should balance the amount of new construction with open space. Individuals can help in small ways, too. People should dispose of garbage properly instead of littering.

In his **conclusion,** Daniel restates his **opinion** and his **reasons,** and he states his **call to action.**

Our coasts are national treasures, and they need to be protected. Coasts and beaches are beneficial to humans and animals alike. Clean water and safe coastlines are very important to the survival of many living things. In order to protect our food sources and wildlife, we must begin to take care of our coasts—today.

Now look at how Daniel prepared to write his persuasive essay.

Brainstorm Ideas

First, Daniel used an idea web to brainstorm topics he is interested in. Then he chose the topic about which he has the strongest opinions—the beach. Next, Daniel listed his opinions about the beach. He chose *I think everyone should protect our coasts* because he had strong reasons to support this opinion.

Outline Ideas

Then Daniel created an outline to organize his supporting reasons and suggestions for solving the problem.

basketball

the beach

Topic Ideas

space shuttle

movies

My Opinions About the Beach
I think California has the best beaches.
* I think everyone should protect our coasts.
I think surfing is the best sport.

Title: Protect Our Coasts
I. Introduction
    A. Opinion
    B. Problem
II. Coasts Are Important to Humans
    A. Benefits
    B. Dangers
III. Coasts Are Important to Animals
    A. Benefits
    B. Dangers
IV. Actions to Solve Problem
    A. Create preserves
    B. Cut down on development
    C. Stop littering
V. Conclusion
    A. Summary
    B. Call to action

Big Idea

A play is an entertaining way to inform an audience about an author's perspective on a topic.

Enduring ! Understanding

The words and actions of the actors expose the author's purpose and perspective.

Essential ? Question

How is the author's purpose and perspective revealed in a play?

Spelling Words

Words with Word Parts
-ation, -ition, -sion, -ion

acceleration	repetition
accumulation	mansion
activation	pension
alteration	passion
authorization	tension
calculation	champion
cancellation	confusion
dedication	permission
organization	population
demolition	companion

Challenge

presentation	decision
fixation	diversion
modernization	

Fluency

Expression

Robust Vocabulary

- somberly
- stammers
- monopolize
- deflated
- enraptured
- enterprising
- cumbersome

Comprehension

 Author's Purpose and Perspective

 Summarize

Writing

- Persuasive Paragraph
- Sentence Fluency

Lesson 22

Genre: Play

The
Power
of
W.O.W.!

Got a Problem?
GET A PLAN!
by Karen Bledsoe • illustrated by Eric Sturdevant

SCHOOL BUS

Genre: Magazine Article

Focus Skill

Author's Purpose and Perspective

You have learned that an **author's purpose** is the author's reason for writing a text. An **author's perspective** is the author's opinion about a subject. You can often identify an author's perspective by thinking about the words the author uses. The details he or she has included in the text also provide clues.

Evidence	Evidence	Evidence

Author's Purpose
Author's Perspective

Tip

An author can have more than one purpose for writing something. For example, a story might entertain and teach about a topic.

Read the story below. Then look at the graphic organizer. It shows evidence in the text that can help you identify the author's perspective.

"It's a shame that this park is such a mess!" Tricia said. Every time she and Anita kicked the soccer ball, it hit a piece of trash.

"You're right," Anita agreed. "We should improve it. Let's do something. Let's organize a cleanup day."

Dozens of volunteers participated. The cleanup made the park cleaner and safer for everyone.

Evidence	**Evidence**	**Evidence**
entertaining story about cleaning up a park	the girls organize a cleanup day	dozens of volunteers participate

Author's Purpose
to entertain
Author's Perspective
People should work together to make their community better.

Try This!

What other purpose might the author have had for writing this story? How does the author's perspective affect the details and word choice in the text?

www.harcourtschool.com/storytown

Vocabulary

Build Robust Vocabulary

somberly

cumbersome

stammers

enterprising

deflated

monopolize

enraptured

Safe Swimming

Lina Joyce knocks on Mr. McLane's office door.

"Come in!"

Lina enters the room **somberly**. Mr. McLane frowns at her and nods at a chair in front of his desk. Lina pulls out the **cumbersome** chair and sits. She fiddles with the folder in her hand.

"I . . . you. . . I mean. . . ," Lina **stammers**. Then she takes a deep breath, and begins again. "I belong to an **enterprising** volunteer group that wants to make Silver Beach a safe public swimming spot. When we read about your plans for an oyster farm there, our hopes were **deflated**. We're afraid your farm will **monopolize** the beach. We believe Doan Beach is a better spot for your farm. We also think that location will save you money." Lina hands the folder to Mr. McLane.

Mr. McLane looks through the papers inside. Then he smiles at Lina. "Tell me more about your idea!" he exclaims, **enraptured**.

 www.harcourtschool.com/storytown

Word Detective

Your mission this week is to look for the Vocabulary Words outside your classroom. Be alert for them when you read novels, textbooks, magazines, and newspapers and as you watch television. Each time you see or hear a Vocabulary Word, write it in your vocabulary journal. Don't forget to record where or how you encountered the word.

The
Power
of
W.O.W!

Play

Genre Study

A play is a story that can be performed for an audience. As you read, look for

- plot events organized into acts and scenes.

- characters' actions and feelings shown through dialogue.

```
Characters        Setting
        ↓        ↓
        Conflict
           ↓
      Plot Events
           ↓
      Resolution
```

Comprehension Strategy

Summarize the main ideas and the most important details of the selection as you read.

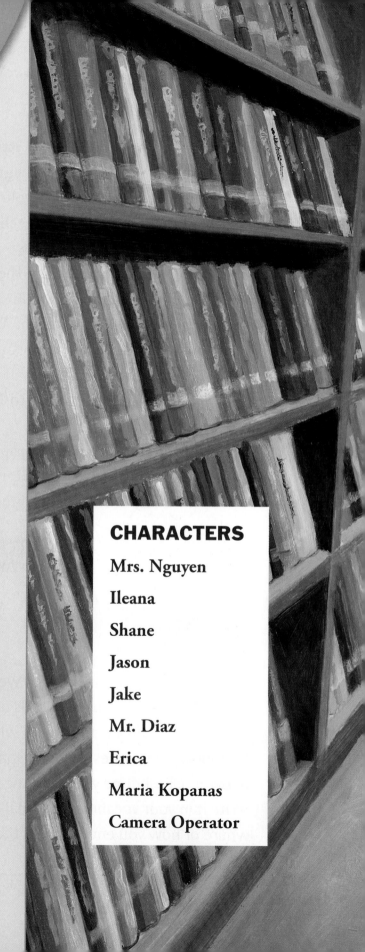

CHARACTERS

Mrs. Nguyen

Ileana

Shane

Jason

Jake

Mr. Diaz

Erica

Maria Kopanas

Camera Operator

The Power of W.O.W!

by Crystal Hubbard
illustrated by Eric Velasquez

ACT ONE

SCENE ONE

Time: *Present*

Setting: *Inside a bus that has been converted into a bookmobile—a traveling library. Mrs. Nguyen [WIN] sits at a narrow checkout counter. Ileana boards the bus and awkwardly sets a heavy stack of books on the checkout counter.*

Mrs. Nguyen: Hi, Ileana! Did you enjoy the books I recommended last week?

Ileana: (Displays top book) I didn't think I'd like Greek mythology, and I didn't. I loved it!

Mrs. Nguyen: Which myth was your favorite?

Ileana: The one about King Midas and how he wished that everything he touched would turn to gold. Boy, did that turn out to be a bad wish.

Mrs. Nguyen: (Speaks somberly) I don't think I'd mind having the golden touch, just for a minute.

Ileana: Is something wrong?

Mrs. Nguyen: (Forces herself to smile) Nothing you need to worry about. I'll just check your books in while you browse the shelves. We've got the latest book about Sam Thorne, Fifth-Grade Detective. It's called "The Case of the Missing Monkey's Paw."

Ileana: Now I know something's wrong. You're trying to distract me.

Mrs. Nguyen: (Sighs, and her shoulders slump) Words on Wheels won't be back after next week.

Ileana: Why not?

Mrs. Nguyen: Words On Wheels is just a pilot program. The library funded W.O.W. for one year, and the year's almost up. There's no more money to pay for gas and repairs, to pay the driver, or to buy new books. I'll have to go back to the library downtown.

Ileana: (Stammers in worry) B-but that's so far away! How will my neighborhood get books? The only time my grandmother can use a computer is when the W.O.W. bus comes. And I'll never get to see you, Mrs. Nguyen. Can't the library give you some more money?

Mrs. Nguyen: The library does the best it can, but the money it receives just doesn't go as far as we'd like. We rely on community support, and people just don't seem to be interested in contributing to W.O.W.

Ileana: I have some money saved. You can have it—all of it.

Mrs. Nguyen: That's very generous, Ileana, but I'm afraid you and I together wouldn't have nearly enough money to save W.O.W. It's an expensive program. I'm sorry.

SCENE TWO

Setting: *Shane's backyard. Ileana, Shane, and Jason are sitting at a picnic table, sipping juice and munching snacks.*

Shane: (Shaking his head) Wow. That's bad news about W.O.W.

Ileana: It's not funny, Shane.

Jason: What did Mrs. Nguyen mean when she said W.O.W. needs community support?

Ileana: Donations from people in the community pay for the library's special programs.

Jason: Well, we're the community, and if we want to save W.O.W., we have to find a way to make money to pay for it.

Ileana: I wish I had King Midas's golden touch. I could turn this picnic table into gold, and then we could sell it to pay for W.O.W.

Jason: Maybe we could sell something else.

Shane: I can't sell my bike. I need it to get to school.

Ileana: What if we sell our skills?

Jason: Our what?

Ileana: Our skills. Isn't there something we could do to raise money?

Shane: Let's ask Jake. He and his friends raised money for their school picnic last year. We could ask him how they did it.

Jake: (Calls to Shane from back door) Hey, Squirt. Mom wants to know if your little friends want to stay for dinner. We're having mutant chicken.

Ileana: (Exchanging a look of confusion with Jason) Mutant chicken?

Shane: Jake and I used to fight over the drumsticks, so my mom uses skewers to attach extra legs to a regular chicken. (To Jake) Could we ask you a question, Jake?

Jake: (Sits at picnic table) What's up?

Ileana: We need to make a lot of money really quickly. Mrs. Nguyen won't be coming to our neighborhood anymore because the W.O.W. program ran out of money.

Jake: (Thoughtfully) I never would have gotten an A on my science project if Mrs. Nguyen hadn't let me monopolize the W.O.W. computer. She showed me how to use a software program to create diagrams of the chemical compounds I wrote about in my report.

Shane: You're on your own for your next project if we can't figure out a way to save W.O.W. How did your class pay for last year's picnic?

Jake: We did a lot of things. (Picks up a handful of snacks and gobbles them) You could have a bake sale.

Jason: Is that what you and your friends did?

Jake: (Laughs) Bake sales are for kids. We held a car wash one Saturday morning, and we earned enough money to pay for the picnic.

Ileana: (Perking up) A car wash!

Shane: That's perfect!

Jason: That would be so much fun!

Jake: Hold on. You can't just stand on the street and yell "Car Wash." You have to organize it. You need a place to have it and supplies to wash the cars. You especially need a water source, and you have to advertise.

Shane: (Somewhat deflated) Wow. It's going to take a lot of work to save W.O.W.

Ileana: Shane, you're doing it again.

Shane: I'm sorry. I really don't mean to.

Jake: (To Ileana and Jason) If you guys stay for mutant chicken, we can discuss ways to save W.O.W.

575

ACT TWO

SCENE ONE

Setting: *Diaz Bakery. Mr. Diaz stands beside a counter next to a glass case filled with scrumptious-looking desserts. Ileana, Shane, and Jason enter the shop wearing hand-lettered buttons that read* P.O.W.W.O.W. *Each one carries a stack of papers of assorted colors.*

Mr. Diaz: *Hola, niños.*[1] (Reads buttons) What's "pow-wow"?

Shane: It stands for "Please Open Wallets for Words On Wheels." Ileana thought of it.

Ileana: (Clears her throat and speaks formally) We'd like to ask you for help, Uncle Carlos. Words on Wheels needs money to keep coming to our neighborhood.

Jason: W.O.W. brings the library to us when our parents can't take us to the library.

Ileana: We'd like to have a car wash this Saturday to raise money. Our parents donated all the cleaning supplies, and we used the W.O.W. computer and printer to make advertisements. (She hands Mr. Diaz a bright-blue flyer, which he reads.)

Jason: All we need now is a place to hold the car wash.

Mr. Diaz: (Chuckles softly) And that's where I come in, right?

Ileana: Well, you are a part of the community, Uncle Carlos. Mrs. Nguyen always stops the bookmobile right here in front of your shop so you can look up new cake recipes on the Internet.

Mr. Diaz: The orange chiffon cake recipe I found online last month has been one of my best sellers. And I always enjoy having coffee with Mrs. Nguyen. She loves my chocolate cake. (Thoughtfully strokes his chin) You can use my parking lot. You can hook up your hose right to the building.

Ileana: (Slaps high-fives with Shane, Jason, and Mr. Diaz) *Gracias,*[2] Uncle Carlos! Thank you!

Shane: *Gracias,* Señor Diaz. You won't be sorry. Just think of all the people who'll want to buy pies and cakes and cookies while we're washing their cars.

---

[1] *Hola, niños.*: Hi, kids.
[2] *gracias*: Thank you.

Jason: (Turns to Ileana and Shane) The next step is to get the word out.
We have to add the location to these flyers and hand them out. Let's
stick to the places that we know. I'll go to the Busy Bee Cleaners across
the street and to the Split Ends Barbershop and see if we can put flyers
there. Mr. Diaz, may I leave a stack of flyers for your customers?

Mr. Diaz: Of course, and I'll give a free coffee to anyone who lets you
wash their car.

Jason: *Muchas gracias,*[3] Mr. Diaz.

Mr. Diaz: *De nada,*[4] Jason.

Shane: I'll go to the Sweet Delights Candy Shop and the Clickety-Clack
Toy Store.

Ileana: And I'll take my flyers to Mrs. Romero's market, the Twinkle Time
Bead Shop, and Flora's Glorious Florals.

Mr. Diaz: (Impressed) You're very organized.

Ileana: The bookmobile has a lot of information on fund-raising.

Shane: That's the power of W.O.W.

Mr. Diaz: After you finish handing out your flyers, meet back here and I'll
show you the power of orange chiffon cake!

---

3 *muchas gracias*: Thank you very much.
4 *de nada*: You're welcome.

SCENE TWO

Setting: *Parking lot of Diaz Bakery. Jake uses a water hose to rinse his father's car. Shane and Jason towel-dry a car they have just finished washing. Erica accepts a few bills from the driver and hurries the money over to Ileana, who holds the cash jar.*

Erica: (Excitedly) That man gave us five whole dollars extra! How much
    do we have so far?

Ileana: We've washed Uncle Carlos's car and all of our parents' cars, and with
    that last customer, we have a whopping sixty-five dollars.

Erica: We've been out here for three hours, and that's it?

Ileana: I thought for sure we'd have tons of cars. I guess. . .
    (Voice trails off as she stares over Erica's shoulder.)

Erica: (Turns to see what has Ileana enraptured) There's a van coming. We should charge extra to wash that big silver pole on top.

Jake: (Jogs over to Ileana and Erica, with Shane and Jason on his heels) That's a television van! (Shoves the cash from his father into the money jar) I've seen that lady on the news.

Maria Kopanas: (Holding a microphone, she exits the passenger side of the van. She uses her index finger to polish her teeth in the side-view mirror while the driver retrieves a heavy camera from the back of the van. The two approach the children.) Hello, my name is Maria Kopanas, and I'm a roving reporter for Channel 7. My aunt owns the Busy Bee Cleaners, and she told me about the car wash today to raise money for the Words on Wheels bookmobile. May I speak to the organizer of today's event?

Ileana: (Reluctantly allows Shane, Jason, Jake, and Erica to push her forward; reporter holds microphone toward her.)

Maria: You're the organizer of . . . (Checks flyer in her pocket) . . . Please Open Wallets for Words on Wheels?

Shane: (Leans toward microphone) Co-organizer.

Camera Operator: (Stands back and aims camera toward Maria and the group of children, who crowd close together) We're on the air in five . . . four . . . three . . . (Raises two fingers and then one; then points to Maria)

Maria: (Smiles widely and speaks loudly and clearly) I'm Maria Kopanas reporting live from the parking lot of Diaz Bakery. I'm with some enterprising young people who decided to do something when they learned that their beloved bookmobile, Words on Wheels, no longer had the money to operate. I'll let the children introduce themselves. (Holds microphone to each)

Ileana: Hi. I'm Ileana, and this is my sister Erica. (Puts an arm around her shoulders)

Erica: (Shrugs off Ileana's arm) I can say my own name! (Sweetly, to camera) I'm Erica. And Diaz Bakery makes the best orange chiffon cake in town!

Shane: I'm Shane. (Waves) Hi, Mom!

Jason: I'm Jason.

Jake: I'm Jake.

Shane: (Pulling microphone from Jake's face to his own) He's my brother. He wants to be a veterinarian.

Maria: (Speaking into microphone) How have you done so far?

Ileana: (Uncomfortably) Not too well, actually. There haven't been that many cars.

Maria: Why's the bookmobile so important to you?

Ileana: It's the only way the kids in my neighborhood can get library books and use a computer. The library downtown is too far away, so it's nice to have a library that comes to us. P.O.W. stands for Please Open Wallets, but it could also stand for Power of Words. A book isn't just a bunch of pages. A book can give you an adventure.

Shane: Or make you laugh.

Erica: Or make you scared, but in a good way.

Jason: Or teach you something.

Jake: Books mean a lot of different things to different people, and we want to make sure that books keep coming to us.

Maria: (Speaks directly into camera) It's a beautiful day for a car wash, folks, and I hope to see you and your dirty cars down here to help the power of words remain in this dedicated community.

Camera Operator: (Shuts off camera) And we're out, Maria. Good job, kids.

Maria: (Hands him her microphone) Before we head back to the station, I think the news van could use a good wash.

Shane: Wow! A reporter's going to help out W.O.W.!

Ileana: Shane!

SCENE THREE

Setting: *Parking lot of Diaz Bakery. Shane, Jason, Jake, their parents, and the camera operator are washing a long line of cars. Erica ferries the money to Ileana, who has to mash the cash down in the overfilled money jar. The W.O.W. bus lumbers into the parking lot. Drivers honk their horns as Mrs. Nguyen exits the bookmobile.*

Ileana: (Ecstatic) Look, Mrs. Nguyen! (Meets her halfway with the money jar hugged to her body) This is for W.O.W.

Mrs. Nguyen: (Accepts jar) Ileana, this is unbelievable!

Ileana: We started out really slowly, but after Maria Kopanas put us on the news, all of a sudden tons of cars showed up. We had to call our families to help us. I don't know if there's enough money here to save W.O.W., but it looks like a good start, doesn't it?

Mrs. Nguyen: That's what I came to tell you, Ileana. Many people in the community picked up your flyers and saw you on television, and they've promised to do something to help. (Sets cumbersome jar on the asphalt and pulls envelopes from her pocket) All of these contain checks! They're from Busy Bee Cleaners, Split Ends Barbershop, Sweet Delights, Clickety-Clack Toy Store, Twinkle Time Bead Shop, Flora's Glorious Florals, Mrs. Romero's market, Channel 7, your parents, and so many other people in the neighborhood. Oh, Ileana! W.O.W. can keep running for a long time to come!

Ileana: (Jumps for joy and shouts to her friends) Wow! We saved W.O.W.!

Think Critically

1 In what ways is the W.O.W. program important to Ileana and her friends?
NOTE DETAILS

2 Is it believable that people change their minds quickly about supporting the W.O.W. program? Explain. MAKE JUDGMENTS

3 What are some community programs that help people in your city or town? Why is each important? EXPRESS PERSONAL OPINIONS

4 What is the author's opinion about the role of the public library in a community? How do you know? AUTHOR'S PURPOSE AND PERSPECTIVE

5 **WRITE** Write a brief news story about the P.O.W.W.O.W. car wash for the next morning's newspaper. Tell why the car wash was held and what the outcome was. SHORT RESPONSE

About the Author
Crystal Hubbard

As a child growing up in St. Louis, Missouri, Crystal Hubbard dreamed of being a writer. She worked toward that dream when she wrote for her college newspaper and, later, for Boston-area newspapers. She lives in Wakefield, Massachusetts, with her husband, their children, and two goldfish named Eyeballs and Rocks.

About the Illustrator
Eric Velasquez

Eric Velasquez inherited a love of drawing from his mom, a love of film from his dad, and an appreciation of music from his grandmother. He said, "Becoming an artist was a natural choice for me. I have never thought of being anything else." He has illustrated more than 300 book jackets, and several of his own picture books have been published. He lives in Hartsdale, New York.

 www.harcourtschool.com/storytown

APPLESEEDS
A Cobblestone Publication

GREAT STORIES ABOUT KIDS WHO HAVE DONE IT!

KIDS CAN Change the World

HOW YOU CAN DO IT TOO!

Magazine Article

Got a Problem?
GET A PLAN!

by Karen Bledsoe • illustrated by Eric Sturdevant

Your school's jogging path is worn out, there's litter in the park, and the animal shelter needs new doghouses. Someone should do something! That someone could be you.

You, your family, or your class can carry out service projects to solve problems in your community. But before you begin, you need a good action plan.

An action plan is a detailed plan of your project from beginning to end. A good plan helps you decide exactly what needs to be done and how to do it, so there won't be any unpleasant surprises.

Follow these steps to create your action plan:

1. Brainstorm ideas for your project. Decide on something that you want to do.
2. Find out whom to call to get permission to carry out the project.
3. Write down exactly what needs to be done. Make sure everyone understands.
4. Decide how many people you will need. Recruit volunteers to help.
5. List any materials you will need. Find out where to get them and how much they will cost. (Don't forget tools, drinks, snacks, and a first-aid kit.)
6. Figure out how long your project will take. Choose a starting date.
7. List the things your helpers will need to bring, such as work gloves and lunch.
8. Give your helpers a reminder call one or two days before the starting date of the project.
9. On the day you begin, make sure you're the first one there. That way, you can answer any questions people have about what you are doing, and you can help volunteers get started as soon as they arrive.
10. When the project is over, celebrate! And remember to give a big "thanks" to all your helpers. You couldn't have done it without them!

Connections

Comparing Texts

1. The young people in "The Power of W.O.W.!" raise money for something they believe in. Describe a group activity you would like to participate in for a good cause.

2. What is the theme of both "The Power of W.O.W.!" and "Got a Problem? Get a Plan!"?

3. What are some ways to get people interested in a cause?

Vocabulary Review

The enterprising student enraptured everyone with her plan.

Word Pairs

Work with a partner. Write the Vocabulary Words on index cards. Place the cards face down. Take turns flipping over two cards and writing a sentence using both words. Read the sentences aloud to your partner. You must use both words correctly to keep the cards. The player with the most cards wins.

somberly

stammers

monopolize

deflated

enraptured

enterprising

cumbersome

Fluency Practice

Partner Reading

Work with a partner. Choose a section of the play that has two to four speaking roles, and decide which roles each of you will take. Discuss how the characters you have chosen might feel at that point in the play and what they might sound like. Read aloud the text you have chosen, focusing on expression. Repeat the process until you are satisfied with your expression.

Writing

Write a Radio Ad

Think about someone who makes a difference in your community. Write a radio ad to help people in your community become aware of the work this person does.

Who?	
What?	
When?	
Where?	
Why?	
How?	

My Writing Checklist

Writing Trait → Sentence Fluency

✔ I used a variety of sentences to make my ad more interesting.

✔ I used a graphic organizer to plan my writing.

✔ I used persuasive language in my ad.

Big Idea
A writer uses imagery in realistic fiction to create a mental picture of people, places, things, and ideas for the reader.

Enduring Understanding
Readers use the writer's vivid descriptions to understand the characters, settings, and events.

Essential Question
How do readers use a text's sensory-based images?

Spelling Words

Words with Silent Letters

assign	knowledge
autumn	lightning
column	resign
crumb	rhyme
debris	solemn
delight	thorough
design	scenery
glisten	whirl
hasten	wreath
knead	wrestled

Challenge

scenic	rhythm
yacht	handkerchief
aisle	

Fluency

Pace

Comprehension

 Literary Devices

 Answer Questions

Robust Vocabulary

- gouges
- desolate
- bustles
- fervor
- immaculate
- assuage

Writing

- Poem
- Organization

Lesson 23

TONY JOHNSTON

Any Small Goodness

a novel of the barrio

APPLE *Classics*

retold by Ann McGovern

Aesop's Fables

Focus Skill

 ## Literary Devices

Authors use many kinds of literary devices to make their writing vivid and interesting. **Imagery** is a literary device that uses vivid language to describe people, places, things, and ideas. Imagery appeals to the senses of sight, hearing, smell, taste, and touch.

Text Example	Sense It Appeals To

Tip

Literary devices, such as imagery, help readers create images in their minds.

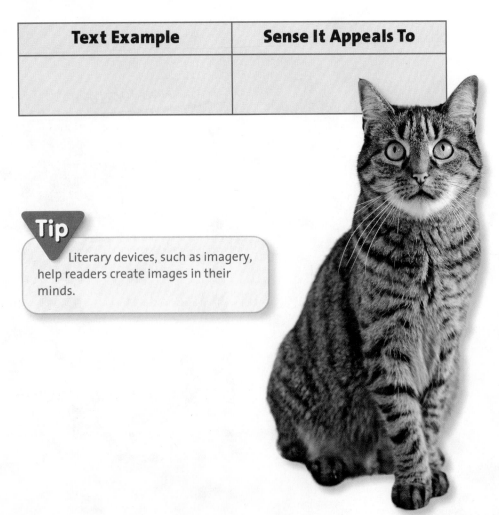

Read the paragraph below. The graphic organizer lists examples of imagery and the senses they appeal to.

Val watched her cat, Mr. Meow, hunt stray beams of sunlight that cut across the yard. Finally, bored or tired, he headed to where Val sat. His soft, silent walk didn't make a single leaf rustle. He hopped onto her lap and licked her hand with his sandpaper-rough tongue. Val giggled and petted him. Mr. Meow purred loudly at first and then softly as he settled into a catnap.

Text Example	Sense It Appeals To
stray beams of sunlight	sight
didn't make a leaf rustle	sound

Try This!

Reread the paragraph. Look for an example of imagery that appeals to the sense of touch.

 www.harcourtschool.com/storytown

591

Vocabulary

Build Robust Vocabulary

- bustles
- gouges
- desolate
- assuage
- immaculate
- fervor

Curious Cat Sets Sail

Delilah the cat normally **bustles** around her Wisconsin home and neighborhood each day. She **gouges** claw marks into a fence post as she makes her way through her hometown.

One day, though, Delilah sneaked into a warehouse full of cargo containers. Little did she know that she was about to take a three-week ocean voyage. Delilah hopped inside one of the huge containers. Before she could get out, it was loaded onto a ship on its way to France!

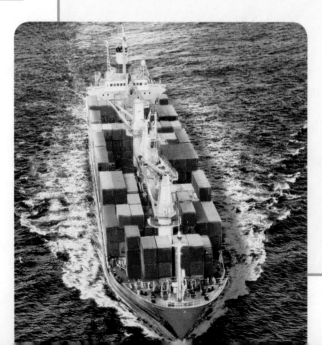

Newscasters around the world spoke about Delilah's amazing sea adventure.

Back home, Delilah's family felt lonely and **desolate**. Nothing could **assuage** their sorrow at Delilah's disappearance.

When the ship landed in France, dockworkers were shocked to find Delilah aboard. Fortunately, she was wearing identification tags. The workers quickly called her family in the United States. Imagine how surprised they were!

Delilah's family is glad the ship was not in **immaculate** condition. They suspect Delilah survived the voyage by catching mice. Delilah is probably one of the few cats to have traveled internationally on her own.

 www.harcourtschool.com/storytown

Delilah devours a snack with **fervor** before flying home.

Word Champion

 Your challenge this week is to use Vocabulary Words outside your classroom. Keep the list of words in a place at home where you can see it. Use as many of the Vocabulary Words as you can when you speak with family members and friends. For example, you might tell your brother that you think his room is immaculate. Write in your vocabulary journal the words you used, and tell how you used them.

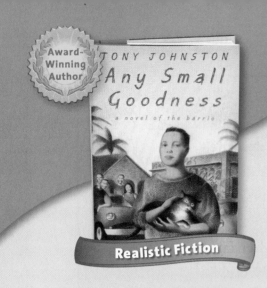

Realistic Fiction

Genre Study

Realistic fiction has characters and events that are like people and events in real life. As you read, look for

- challenges and problems that might happen in real life.

- characters with realistic traits.

Character

Comprehension Strategy

Answer questions you have by looking in the story and thinking about what you already know.

Any Small Goodness

A Novel of the Barrio

by Tony Johnston • • • • illustrated by Raúl Colón

It has been three years since Arturo Rodriguez and his family moved from Mexico to Los Angeles, California, and they are slowly adjusting to life in the United States. Arturo's older brother, Luis, has formed a band that practices in the garage. No one notices the cat, Huitla (WEET•lah), napping in the garage until she flies out, scared by the band's first blast of song. Arturo forgets about Huitla's wild escape until that night.

Mami's stirring the various pots that will become dinner. "Where's Huitla?" she asks. Because that cat has always twined around her legs when food's available, nearly tripping her sometimes. Mami doesn't mind. She always stops cooking, stoops her dove-shaped body down, giving Huitla a little pat. "*Ay,*[1] Huitla, old black lump," she croons gently. "One day you will simply break Mami's old neck. Then what will those greedy ones do for a cook?" She chuckles a lot, she finds herself so humorous.

"That Huitla," Mami repeats. "*¿Dónde está?*"[2]

Luis gouges a taste of refried beans from a saucepan. "*No sé.*"[3] He grunts.

"She took off," I say, in explanation of everything.

Things are pretty quiet at dinner. Except for cat questions. We're all wondering where Huitla's gone. Rosa wanders from room to room. "Huitla!" She calls over and over. "*Ven,*[4] kitty! Come!"

But she doesn't. Not tonight. Not any night.

From the start we search everywhere. All of Huitla's favorite spots. Like beside the scarecrow in the corn plot, where she loves to plop her lazy self down, in the fullest sun. The neighbors help. They love our little cat for her sweetness. And for her funky stuck-out tongue.

With crayons, Rosa makes a sign. Just the face of a little black cat, poking out the tip of its tongue. MY KITTY IS LOST, she writes, with our help, and gives the number of our telephone.

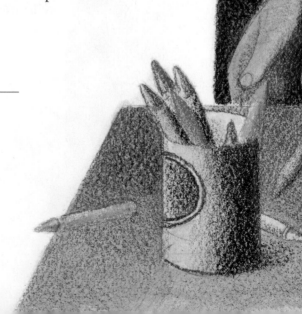

----

1   *ay:* oh

2   *¿Dónde está?:* Where is she?

3   *No sé.:* I don't know.

4   *ven:* come

It's two weeks since we've seen her. Now a little silence moves through the house, as if filling Huitla's space. Nobody ever says so, but maybe we guess she's dead. Or at least that she won't return.

Abuelita has her words of comfort to say. "We will find her."

Rosa's the one most desolate. She sometimes crawls into my lap and says nothing, just sucks her thumb.

· · · · · ·

It's a typical night at home. Rosa's blabbling into a big plastic bottle, squeaking like Alvin the Chipmunk. Luis's blazing out "*Chango*" on the radio.

"Turn it down, I'm trying to study!" I shout.

"Well, try harder!"

Above the blare, the phone rings.

"¡*Zafo*!" Luis yells, which means "dibs not answering."

"¡*Zafo*!" Rosa echoes.

Though she's sitting close, Abuelita also refuses to answer. *Or speak face-to-face, or don't speak at all*, is her thought on the subject of telephones. Given the chance, she'd throw it off a cliff.

I dash up and take the call. At first, there's only breathing on the line.

"Hello?"

At last a voice comes. "Hello. This is Leo Love speaking."

This is Leo Love breathing, I think.

Leo Love! It's got to be one of those crank romantic calls you hear about sometimes! I don't want to become involved in anything weird, so I nearly hang up.

"I've got Hoo—Hoo—" The voice makes frustrated-owl calls, then just blurts, "I've got your cat."

"Huitlacoche!" I shout into the receiver.

"Yes, Hootlecooch," the man agrees.

Over a series of explosions of joy in the room, I take the guy's *datos*[5] down. Name, address, telephone. I say, "We're on our way."

And we are, all of us piling into Papi's car, Valentín. Laughing, all ecstatic. And crying.

Valentín goes jittering down the streets, slowing, speeding up, sometimes stopping in full so we can check the directions. We're all so anxious. When we reach the given address, it seems like we've been driving forever. Actually, it's not many blocks.

Mr. Leo Love doesn't need to hear his doorbell. We arrive in such an excitement, he can't miss us. He opens the door.

He's an old white guy, wire-bearded and small. No Mr. Universe, but more with the build of a sparrow. Pants creased sharp enough to slice *chorizo*.[6] Dressed in tweed, so he looks like he's wrapped in tree bark. He talks stiff as bark, too. Like every word makes a difference to his life.

Then, suddenly, he nearly blasts his bark off with a sneeze. A chorus of *saluds*[7] follows.

Quickly, Abuelita holds out a lime from her lumpy purse. She never travels without limes.

Leo Love looks surprised.

---

5   *datos*: information

6   *chorizo:* a type of sausage

7   *salud:* bless you

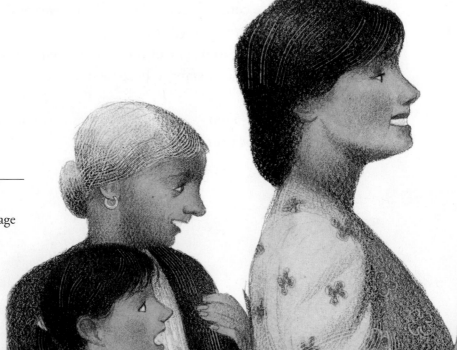

"You take this," she orders him. "Good for all things."

He lamely takes the lime.

"I am allergic to cats," he says, embarrassed, holding out Huitla.

"*Limones*[8] good also for that," says Abuelita.

By now, Rosa's popcorning up and down so much that for safety, Leo Love hands the cat to Mami.

Squashed-in face. Tip of pink tongue flagging out. It's our cat, all right.

"Hey, Fish Breath," Luis greets her. Words of love, for him.

What's the next step? Everyone's in confusion. Everyone except Abuelita. She bustles up and embraces this stranger. Plants kisses on his tortilla-white cheeks.

"*Estimado*[9] Señor Mister Leo Love," she says with fervor, "you are a most very good hero."

Señor Mister Leo Love seems amazed by that. And touched. In confusion, he invites us into his immaculate house. Everyone sits in a perched position, the furnishings are so clean. Mami's eyes survey the room. They say that she loves his housekeeping.

8   *limones:* limes
9   *estimado:* esteemed

Leo Love offers coffee. We all accept. In her excitement, even Rosa. This is a happy time. I guess that's why Mami allows it. Anyway, when Rosa's done, it's not coffee. Just some pale gunk, mainly sugar, so thick it could hold bricks together.

While Rosa glugs this down, she never lets go of Huitla. (Now that she's semi-settled down, Mami allows Rosa to hold the cat.)

On her chair, Abuelita leans forward. Like a small and eager bird. We await the prize words that are surely coming.

"Now, Señor Mister Leo Love," she says with respect and careful words, like taking careful steps on stairs, "how arrived our sweet little *gatita*[10] to your door?"

Somehow Leo Love has followed this thick braid of conversation. He sips his coffee and says, "Actually, she did not arrive at the door. I discovered her near my avocado tree."

"I do not wish to seem rude," says Papi, who has never seemed rude in his whole life. "But two weeks—"

Leo Love nods his head. "Yes. It is certainly a long time not to communicate. However, there was nothing to identify her."

Huitla has tags. From the vet. He even had to make them two times, because of problems of spelling.

"She had no tags," he continues. "And I have allergies. But, what could I do? I decided that at my age, I had earned the right to throw caution away. I decided to keep the little creature. I hadn't much else to offer, so I fed her trout."

A shadow skims Mami's face. It seems to mean, *I cannot compete with trout.* Leo Love goes on.

"However, all the trout in the world could not assuage my guilt. Someone must miss her terribly. A child, most probably. Today, I searched the rescue site again, and by good fortune found the cat's collar. Broken. It was precisely then that I dialed your number."

At that, Abuelita perks up. She puts two and two together fast. "You believe in God?" She bores into him, all energized.

Leo Love looks at her as if seeing a blink of new light about his situation. He says, "It is something always worth considering."

For the moment, that satisfies Abuelita.

---

10 *gatita:* kitty

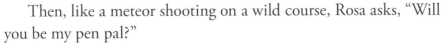

Then, like a meteor shooting on a wild course, Rosa asks, "Will you be my pen pal?"

Even though he lives so close she could spit about as far as his house, he agrees.

When we leave, Leo Love asks, "Hootlecooch, what sort of name is that?"

Abuelita explains, "It's Mexico—for corn fungus."

Leo Love looks stunned.

"Soon I bring you some."

And she will. And she'll see that he eats it, too.

We've thanked Leo Love so much, he's retreated. We're outside the house, standing under the avocado tree. A slight breeze breathes by. The rustle of leaves sounds like I'm inside a flight of birds.

The newspaper boy wheels up in a gravelly crunch.

"That your cat?" he asks, eyeing Huitla.

"Yeah."

"What a pain!"

We all ask what he means.

"Mr. Love spent a whole night in that tree," he says, pointing to where we are. "Baby-sitting the cat. He's kinda old. And a handful of cat—plus fear of falling—kept him up there."

"How do you know this?" Papi asks.

"I found him. Next morning. Firemen got 'em down."

The day flames out in a smog-sunset, a wild gift of L.A.

On the way home Papi says, "This Leo Love is a brave man. In spite of fear he saved Huitla. When no eyes are upon him, that is a person's true test."

I file this inside of myself. Maybe one day when no eyes are on me, I'll have a true test, too.

· · · · · ·

Now Huitla's home. Sleeping on the sofa in a happy sprawl of fur. I sit beside her, totally sunken down. Our sofa's so soft, sitting on it's like being swallowed by a clam. I think about old Leo Love, who Abuelita now calls *El Estimado*, The Esteemed One. Going against allergies and dizziness and possible broken bones to save our cat.

You could do worse than be like such a person.

Think Critically

1 How do Rosa's actions reveal her feelings when Huitla is missing?
CHARACTER'S EMOTIONS

2 On page 604, the author describes the newspaper boy "wheeling up in a gravely crunch." Which sense helps you visualize this scene, and how?
 LITERARY DEVICES

3 Do you agree with Papi that Leo Love is brave? Why or why not?
MAKE JUDGMENTS

4 What would you do if you found a lost animal? Explain your actions.
MAKE CONNECTIONS

5 **WRITE** How might meeting Leo Love change Arturo's definition of a hero? Use information and details from the selection to explain.
SHORT RESPONSE

About the Author

Tony Johnston

When Tony Johnston was growing up, she wanted to be a "bugologist" because she was fascinated by every insect that flew or crawled. Instead, she became a writer who has now written more than one hundred books. Many of her stories have been published in Spanish. Tony Johnston grew up in Los Angeles. Later she lived in Mexico for fifteen years. In Mexico, her passion was collecting hand-woven sashes and recording the history of the craftspeople who made them. Her advice to young readers is, "Read your brains loose!"

About the Illustrator

Raúl Colón

As a young boy, Raúl Colón was often ill with asthma and had to stay indoors for days at a time. He spent that time filling notebook after notebook with his drawings. Raúl Colón knew early on that he wanted to be an artist. Now that he's accomplished that goal, he hopes that one of his other childhood dreams will come true—traveling to the moon.

AESOP'S

Aesop lived in Greece about 3,000 years ago. He became famous for the clever animal fables through which he showed the wise and foolish behavior of people. Today, there are many versions of the tales that Aesop told so long ago.

Fable

THE ANT AND THE DOVE

A thirsty Ant went to the river to drink. To reach the river he had to climb down the steep bank on a blade of grass. Halfway down he slipped and fell into the swirling waters.

A Dove, perched in a nearby tree, saw the Ant's desperate plight. Quickly she plucked a leaf from the tree and dropped it into the river, close to the Ant. The Ant was able to climb up on the leaf and float safely to shore.

As soon as he was on dry land, the Ant saw a hunter of birds hiding behind a tree with a net in his hand. Seeing that the Dove was in danger, he crawled up to the hunter and bit him on his heel. The startled hunter dropped his net, and the Dove flew off.

The Dove, perched safely in the tree, called down to the Ant, "Thank you, my little friend."

"Not at all," said the Ant. *"One good turn deserves another."*

FABLES

retold by Ann McGovern
illustrated by Todd Kale

THE LION AND THE MOUSE

A Lion was awakened from sleep by a Mouse running across his face. With a terrible roar, the Lion seized the Mouse with his paw and was about to kill him.

"Oh please," the Mouse begged. "Spare my life! I will be sure to repay your kindness."

The King of Beasts was so amused at the thought of a Mouse being able to help *him* that he let the frightened creature go.

Shortly afterward the Lion fell into a trap set by some hunters and was hopelessly caught in strong ropes. In his misery the Lion roared so loudly that all the beasts in the forest heard him.

The Mouse recognized the roar of his former captor and ran to the place where the Lion lay trapped. At once the Mouse began to gnaw the ropes with his teeth. He gnawed rope after rope until at last the Lion was free.

"Thank you," said the grateful Lion. "I know now that *in time of need the weak may help the strong.*"

Connections

Comparing Texts

1. The members of Arturo's family share a love for Huitla. Describe something that you have in common with your friends or family members.

2. "Any Small Goodness" and the two fables by Aesop all have similar themes. What are the themes, and how are they alike?

3. Leo Love and Arturo's family might never have met if Huitla hadn't gotten stuck in Leo Love's tree. How can difficult situations sometimes bring people closer together?

Vocabulary Review

Word Sort

Work in a group. Sort the Vocabulary Words into categories. Discuss your sorted words with the group, explaining your choices. Then choose at least one Vocabulary Word from each category. Write a sentence for each word.

gouges

desolate

bustles

fervor

immaculate

assuage

Feelings	Actions	Appearance

Fluency Practice

Partner Reading

Work with a partner. Choose a section of "Any Small Goodness" to read aloud. Focus on your pace as you read. Ask your partner to tell you if you are reading too quickly or too slowly to match the mood and the action. Then switch roles with your partner and repeat the procedure.

Writing

Write a Descriptive Paragraph

Write a descriptive paragraph about an everyday event. Use imagery that appeals to the senses to help the reader picture what you are describing.

My Writing Checklist

Writing Trait ▸ Organization

✓ I organized the details of my topic.

✓ I used a graphic organizer to develop sensory language.

✓ I chose words that appealed to the senses.

Example	Sense It Appeals To

Big 💡 Idea

Authors of fantasy use figurative language to engage the reader's interest.

Enduring ❗ Understanding

Readers recognize the use of *like* and *as* plus descriptive words in figurative language.

Essential ❓ Question

How do readers use word clues to identify similes, metaphors, and personification?

Spelling Words

Words with Unusual Plurals

addresses	radios
armies	halves
calves	hooves
countries	knives
leaves	taxes
buses	tomatoes
videos	opportunities
echoes	volcanoes
shelves	stitches
studios	wolves

Challenge

tornadoes	vetoes
patios	crises
quizzes	

Fluency

Pace

Comprehension

 Literary Devices

 Answer Questions

Robust Vocabulary

- excursions
- giddy
- pinnacle
- gleeful
- panic
- turbulent
- precious

Writing

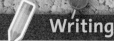

- Narrative
- Organization

Lesson 24

Genre: Fantasy

Chester Cricket's
Pigeon Ride

by George Selden

Pictures by Garth Williams

Central
Park
by John J. Bonk   illustrated by Cheryl Cooper

Genre: Poetry

Literary Devices

You have learned that imagery is one kind of literary device. Authors use it to appeal to the senses. **Figurative language** expressions are another type of literary device. These expressions have meanings that are different from the literal meanings of the words that make them up. The following are three kinds of figurative language.

- A **simile** compares two things by using the word *like* or *as*.
- A **metaphor** compares two things by saying that one thing is the other. Metaphors do not use the words *like* or *as*.
- **Personification** gives human traits to animals or objects.

Text Example	Type of Figurative Language	Meaning

Tip

Look for the word *like* or *as* to identify a *simile*.

614

Read the paragraph below. The graphic organizer shows examples of personification and simile from the paragraph and tells what they mean.

When I stay at Aunt Judy's farm, the night keeps me awake with all of its noises. Frogs sing a chorus of croaks, and crickets join in with their chirps. Cats screech and fight. Not even a pillow over my head blocks out the noise! Then, even before the sun rises, the rooster starts crowing. He sounds like a car alarm, yelling at the day to make it wake up!

Text Example	Type of Figurative Language	Meaning
Frogs sing a chorus	personification	The frogs croak as if singing a song.
He sounds like a car alarm	simile	The rooster is loud and annyoying, like a car alarm.

Try This!

How is "the night keeps me awake with all of its noises" an example of personification?

 www.harcourtschool.com/storytown

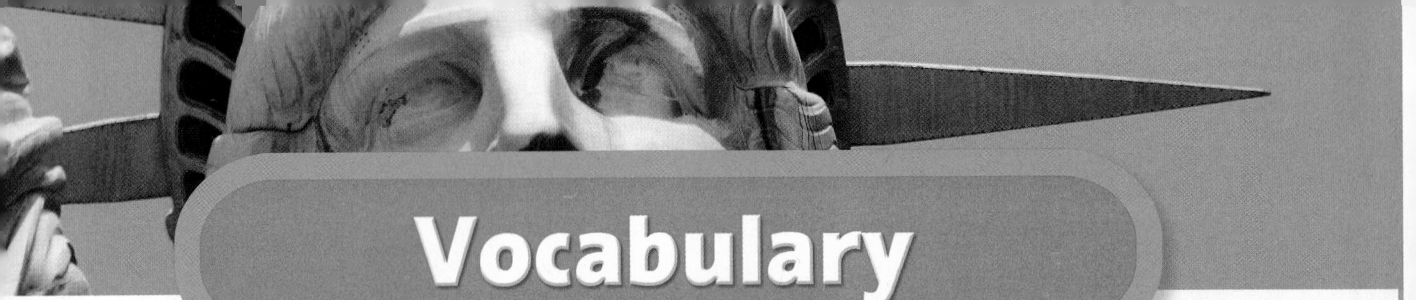

Vocabulary

Build Robust Vocabulary

- excursions
- giddy
- turbulent
- gleeful
- panic
- pinnacle
- precious

Nights on the Prowl

Frida and I are an unlikely pair. She is a plump, noisy cat who spends the darkest parts of the night outdoors. I am a shy spider who minds my own business.

One night, Frida invited me to join her on one of her nighttime **excursions**. I spun a line of silk around her left ear and hung on tight. I felt **giddy**! It was a **turbulent**, thrilling ride. After I got over feeling dizzy, I was **gleeful**! I'd never had so much fun.

Another night, Frida offered to introduce me to the cats who go trash-tasting with her. **Panic** set in. I worried her friends wouldn't like me and might hurt me.

Unlike Frida, I usually spend my nights indoors.

We crossed the bridge that arched over the river. From the **pinnacle** of the bridge, Frida spotted a new trash can. We raced to it. I crawled up the can and peeked inside, discovering the remains of a tasty meal. The cats knocked over the can and dined. During the rest of the night I quickly crawled up and looked inside each can, saving the cats **precious** time. They were so pleased that they invited me to their next trash-tasting!

www.harcourtschool.com/storytown

Word Scribe

This week, your task is to use the Vocabulary Words in your writing. In your vocabulary journal, write sentences to show the meanings of the words. For example, you could write about excursions you went on, or you could tell about something that makes you feel gleeful. Use as many of the Vocabulary Words as you can. Share your writing with your classmates.

Chester Cricket's Pigeon Ride

by George Selden

Pictures by Garth Williams

Fantasy

Genre Study

A fantasy is an imaginative story that may have unrealistic characters and events. As you read, look for

- story events or settings that could not happen in real life.

- characters that behave in an unrealistic way.

```
┌──────────────┐   ┌──────────────┐
│  Characters  │   │   Setting    │
└──────┬───────┘   └──────┬───────┘
       └──────┐    ┌──────┘
          ┌───▼────▼───┐
          │  Conflict  │
          └─────┬──────┘
                ▼
          ┌────────────┐
          │ Plot Events │
          └─────┬──────┘
                ▼
          ┌────────────┐
          │ Resolution │
          └────────────┘
```

Comprehension Strategy

Answer questions about a story by looking in the text and thinking about what you already know.

Chester Cricket's Pigeon Ride

by George Selden
illustrated by Garth Williams

*Chester Cricket finds life in New York City thrilling. Mario, the
boy who found Chester his first night in the city, has taken him to
many places, but Chester is homesick. He longs for the fields and
trees of his Connecticut home. In Times Square, Chester meets
a new friend, Lulu Pigeon. She takes him on a wild ride, and he
finds a little bit of the country he's been missing.*

"You don't know where Central *Park* is?" said Lulu.
"Big beautiful Central Park!—the best place in the city—"

"I guess I don't," Chester apologized. He explained that Mario
had taken him on several excursions, but not, as yet, to Central Park.

"Say!" exclaimed Lulu. "How would you like a real tooor of
Nooo York? One that only a pigeon could give."

"Well, I'd love one," said Chester, "but—"

"Hop on my back, just behind my neck. Nope—" Lulu bobbed
her head jerkily, trying to think. "—Yooo couldn't see down through
my wings too well." Then she gave a big scratch and exclaimed,
"I got it! You sit on my claw—take the left one there—and wrap
a couple of feelers around." Chester hesitated a minute or two.
He was quite sure no cricket had ever done *this* before.

"Go on! Get on!" Lulu ordered. "You're in for a thrill."

"All right—" Chester mounted the pigeon's claw, with a
feeling that was partly excitement, partly fear, and held on tight.

"First I gotta rev up." Lulu flapped her wings a few times. And then—before Chester could gasp with delight—*they were flying*!

To fly—oh, be flying!

"Sorry for the bumpy takeoff," said Lulu.

But it hadn't seemed bumpy to Chester at all.

"It'll be better when I gain altitooode."

Back in Connecticut, in the Old Meadow, when Chester made one of his mightiest leaps—usually showing off in front of a friend like Joe Skunk—he sometimes reached as high as six feet. But in seconds Lulu had passed that height, and in less than a minute she was gliding along at the level of the tops of the sycamore trees.

"Okay down there?" she called into the rush of air they sped through.

"Oh—oh, sure—I mean, I guess—" There are times when you don't know whether you feel terror or pleasure—or perhaps you feel both all at once, all jumbled together wonderfully! "I'm fine!" the cricket decided, and held on to Lulu's leg even tighter. Because now they were far above even the tops of the trees, and Chester could see whole blocks of buildings below him. He suddenly felt all giddy and free.

"How about a spin up to Central Park first?"

"Great, Lulu! I want to see *everything*!"

The pigeon flew east, to Fifth Avenue, and then due north. High though they were flying, Chester could see how beautiful the store windows were in the street beneath. The finest shops in all the world are on Fifth Avenue, and the cricket would have liked to fly a bit lower, to get a closer look. But he thought better of it and decided to leave all the navigating to Lulu. Besides, there was something strange up ahead. A huge rectangle of dark was sliding toward them—close, then closer, then under them.

"Here's Central Park," Lulu screeched against the wind.

And now Chester had another thrill. For there weren't only sycamore trees in the park. The cricket could smell birches, beeches, and maples—elms, oaks—almost as many kinds of trees as Connecticut itself had to offer. And there was the moon!—the crescent moon—reflected in a little lake. Sounds, too, rose up to him: the shooshing of leaves, the nighttime countryside whispering of insects and little animals, and—best of all—a brook that was arguing with itself, as it splashed over rocks. The miracle of Central Park, a sheltered wilderness in the midst of the city, pierced Chester Cricket's heart with joy.

"Oh, can we go down?" he shouted up. "Lulu?—please!"

"'Course, Chester C." The pigeon slowed and tilted her wings. "Anything you want. But let's not call on my relatives. They're a drag, and they're all asleep by now anyway."

"I don't want to *visit* anybody!" said Chester, as Lulu Pigeon coasted down through the air, as swiftly and neatly and accurately as a little boy's paper airplane, and landed beside the lake. "All I want is—is—" He didn't know how to say it exactly, but all Chester wanted was to sit beside that shimmering lake—a breeze ruffled its surface—and look at the jiggling reflection of the moon, and enjoy the sweet moisture and the tree-smelling night all around him.

And chirp. Above all, Chester wanted to chirp. Which he did, to his heart's content. And to Lulu Pigeon's heart's content, too.

But even the loveliest intervals end.

Song done—one moment more of silent delight—and then Lulu said, "Come on, Chester C., let me show you some more of my town"—by which she meant New York.

"Okay," said Chester, and climbed on her claw again.

"I want you to see it *all* now!" said Lulu. Her wings were beating strongly, rhythmically. "And the best place for that is the Empire State Building."

They rose higher and higher. And the higher they went, the more scared Chester got. Flying up Fifth Avenue had been fun as well as frightening, but now they were heading straight for the top of one of the tallest buildings in all the world.

Chester looked down—the world swirled beneath him—and felt as if his stomach turned over. Or maybe his brain turned around. But something in him felt queasy and dizzy. "Lulu—" he began anxiously, "—I think—"

"Just hold on tight!" Lulu shouted down. "And trust in your feathered friend!"

What Chester had meant to say was that he was afraid he was suffering from a touch of acrophobia—fear of heights. (And perched on a pigeon's claw, on your way to the top of the Empire State, is not the best place to find that you are afraid of great heights.) But even if Lulu hadn't interrupted, the cricket couldn't have finished his sentence. His words were forced back into his throat. For the wind, which had been just a breeze beside the lake, was turning into a raging gale as they spiraled upward, around the building, floor past floor, and approached their final destination: the television antenna tower on the very top.

And they made it! Lulu gripped the pinnacle of the TV antenna with both her claws, accidentally pinching one of Chester's legs as she did so. The whole of New York glowed and sparkled below them.

Now it is strange, but it is true, that although there are many mountains higher than even the tallest buildings, and airplanes can fly much higher than mountains, *nothing* ever seems quite so high as a big building that's been built by men. It suggests our own height to ourselves, I guess.

Chester felt as if not only a city but the entire world was down there where he could look at it. He almost couldn't see the people. 'My gosh!' he thought. 'They look just like bugs.' And he had to laugh at that: like bugs—perhaps crickets—moving up and down the sidewalks. And the cars, the buses, the yellow taxis, all jittered along like miniatures. He felt that kind of spinning sensation inside his head that had made him dizzy on the way up. But he refused to close his eyes. It was too much of an adventure for that.

"Lulu, my foot," said Chester, "you're stepping on it. Could you please—"

"Ooo, I'm sorry," the pigeon apologized. She lifted her claw.

And just at that moment two bad things happened. The first was, Chester caught sight of an airplane swooping low to land at LaGuardia Airport across the East River. The dip of it made his dizziness worse. And the second—worse yet—a sudden gust of wind sprang up, as if a hand gave them both a push. Lulu almost fell off the Empire State.

Lulu *almost* fell off—but Chester *did*! In an instant his legs and feelers were torn away from the pigeon's leg, and before he could say, 'Old Meadow, farewell!' he was tumbling down through the air. One moment the city appeared above him—that meant that he was upside down; then under him—he was right side up; then everything slid from side to side.

He worked his wings, tried to hold them stiff to steady himself—no use, no use! The gleeful wind was playing with him. It was rolling him, throwing him back and forth, up and down, as a cork is tossed in the surf of a storm. And minute by minute, when he faced that way, the cricket caught glimpses of the floors of the Empire State Building plunging upward as he plunged down.

Despite his panic, his mind took a wink of time off to think: 'Well, *this* is something that can't have happened to many crickets before!' (He was right, too—it hadn't. And just at that moment Chester wished that it wasn't happening to *him*.)

He guessed, when New York was in the right place again,
that he was almost halfway down. The people were looking more
and more like people—he heard the cars' engines—and the street
and the sidewalk looked *awfully* hard! Then—

Whump! He landed on something both hard and soft. It was
hard inside, all muscles and bones, but soft on the surface—feathers!

"Grab on!" a familiar voice shouted. "Tight! Tighter! That's it."
Chester gladly did as he was told.

"*Whooooey!*" Lulu breathed a sigh of relief. "Thought I'd never
find you. Been around this building at least ten times."

Chester wanted to say, 'Thank you, Lulu,' but he was
so thankful he couldn't get one word out till they'd reached
a level where the air was friendly and gently buoyed them up.

But before he could even open his mouth, the pigeon—
all ready for another adventure—asked eagerly, "Where now,
Chester C.?"

"I guess I better go back to the drainpipe, Lulu. I'm kind of tired."

"Aw, no—!" complained Lulu, who'd been having fun.

"You know, I'm really not all that used to getting blown off the Empire State Building—"

"Oh, all right," said the pigeon. "But first there's one thing you *gotta* see!"

Flying just below the level of turbulent air—good pilot that she was—Lulu headed south, with Chester clinging to the back of her neck. He felt much safer up there, and her wings didn't block out as much of the view as they'd thought. He wanted to ask where they were going, but he sensed from the strength and regularity of her wingbeats that it was to be a rather long flight. And the wind was against them too, which made the flying more difficult. Chester held his peace, and watched the city slip beneath them.

They reached the Battery, which is that part of lower New York where a cluster of skyscrapers rise up like a grove of steel trees. But Lulu didn't stop there.

With a gasp and an even tighter hold on her feathers, Chester realized that they'd flown right over the end of Manhattan. There was dark churning water below them. And this was no tame little lake, like the one in Central Park. It was the great deep wide bay that made New York such a mighty harbor. But Lulu showed no sign whatsoever of slowing. Her wings, like beautiful trustworthy machines, pumped on and on and on and on.

At last, Chester saw where the pigeon was heading. On a little island, off to the right, Chester made out the form of a very big lady. Her right hand was holding something up. Of course it was the Statue of Liberty, but Chester had no way of knowing that. In the Old Meadow in Connecticut he never had gone to school—at least not to a school where the pupils use books. His teacher back there had been Nature herself.

Lulu landed at the base of the statue, puffing and panting to get back her breath. She told him a little bit about the lady—a gift from the country of France, it was, and very precious to America—but she hadn't flown him all that way just to give him a history lesson.

"Hop on again, Chester C.!" she commanded—and up they flew to the torch that the lady was holding. Lulu found a perch on the north side of it, so the wind from the south wouldn't bother them.

"Now, just look around!" said Lulu proudly, as if all of New York belonged to her. "And don't anybody ever tell *this* pigeon that there's a more beautiful sight in the world."

Chester did as he was told. He first peered behind. There was Staten Island. And off to the left, New Jersey. To the right, quite a long way away, was Brooklyn. And back across the black water, with a dome of light glowing over it, the heart of the city—Manhattan.

Think Critically

1. Why does Chester Cricket decide to go for a ride with Lulu? CHARACTER'S MOTIVES

2. The author writes that in Central Park there is *a brook that was arguing with itself*. What kind of figurative language is this, and what does it mean? LITERARY DEVICES

3. How does Lulu feel about New York City? How do you know? CHARACTER'S EMOTIONS

4. Lulu is very outgoing, and Chester is quiet and timid. Which character are you more like? Explain. PERSONAL RESPONSE

5. **WRITE** How does Chester feel about each of the places where Lulu takes him? Use information from the story to support your answer. EXTENDED RESPONSE

About the Author

George Selden

Like Chester Cricket, George Selden came from Connecticut. In New York City, he heard a cricket chirp in the subway, and immediately had an idea. "The story formed in my mind within minutes," he said. "An author is very thankful for minutes like those, although they happen all too infrequently." George Selden wanted his readers to be able to connect with the animal characters he created. To make this possible, he gave his characters emotions and feelings similar to those of real people.

About the Illustrator

Garth Williams

Garth Williams grew up in a family of artists. "Everybody in my house was always either painting or drawing," he said. "So I thought there was nothing else to do in life but make pictures."

Garth Williams spent a lot of time studying the animals he drew in his books. He said, "I start with the real animal, working over and over until I can get the effect of human qualities and expression and poses."

 www.harcourtschool.com/storytown

COBBLESTONE
New York City

Poetry

Central Park

by John J. Bonk   illustrated by Cheryl Cooper

Whisk me away to a tree-covered world
 and surround me with nothing but
  green.
Squawking ducks in a lake, and long walks
 we could take,
Where the air is all dewy and clean.

Pack up a lunch and we'll picnic till dusk
 on a hill overlooking a stream.
In the distance the sound of a merry-go-
  round.
Faces covered with smiles and ice cream.

Kick off your shoes and we'll tickle our toes
   as we frolic through crispy tall grass.
Then we'll rest for a bit, find a nice bench
    and sit,
As we watch all the passersby pass.

Horses clop by pulling tourist-filled carriages
   driven by men in top hats.
Sweethearts stroll hand in hand toward the
   souvenir stand.
Muddy kids lug their baseballs and bats.

People on skateboards, and babies in
   buggies,
   and grandmothers having long talks.
Joggers jog, hikers hike, skaters skate, bikers
    bike,
Barking dogs take their owners for walks.

Artists at easels are capturing scenery,
   sunbathers soak up the sun.
Little children aglow at a free puppet show,
Crowds are cheering a marathon run.

People applaud for a man with a saxophone
    playing a medley of tunes.
Toss some coins in his case, watch it light
    up his face,
And we'll spend all the rest on balloons.

Faraway skyscrapers seem to be stretching
    their necks
    for a peek in the park.
They pop over the trees just as if to say,
    "Please,
Hurry home now before it gets dark!"

Riders on horseback head back to the stables,
    and bird watchers call it a day.
Games of chess disappear as the evening
    grows near.
Hot dog vendors are rolling away.

Wait, not so fast! There are still things to see
    like an outdoor Shakespearean play.
There are concerts at night under stars and
    moonlight,
Ending under a fireworks display.

Shaking the ground comes a rumbling of
    thunder
    and lightning is piercing the sky.
Grab your stuff! Better run! We've had
    nothing but fun.
But for now, Central Park, it's good-bye!

Connections

Comparing Texts

1. On Chester's first flight, he feels the thrill of excitement and fear "all jumbled together wonderfully." Describe a time when you felt that way.

2. Compare how George Selden and John J. Bonk use figurative language to describe Central Park.

3. Why might someone who is moving to a new place feel at ease after meeting a friend like Lulu?

Vocabulary Review

Rate a Situation

With a partner, read aloud each sentence below. Point to a spot on the line to show how happy you would feel in each situation. Explain your choices.

Least
Happy ————————————————— Most
Happy

- Your airplane ride is **turbulent**.
- The swim meet is the **pinnacle** of your summer.
- You must stop your **excursions** to the park.
- You feel **giddy** after winning a contest.

excursions

giddy

pinnacle

gleeful

panic

turbulent

precious

Fluency Practice

Repeated Reading

Read the passage on page 629 that
begins, "Lulu landed at the base of the
statue." Pay careful attention to your
pace, matching it to the action of the
story. Read the passage several times
until you feel you have the correct pace.
Then read the passage aloud to a partner.

Writing

Write a Journal Entry

Imagine that Chester Cricket is flying over
your city or town for the first time. Write
a journal entry that describes Chester's
experience of flying over your city.

```
    First Event
        ↓
    Next Event
        ↓
    Next Event
        ↓
    Last Event
```

My Writing Checklist

Writing Trait → Organization

✔ I organized the information
sequentially.

✔ I used a graphic organizer to
plan my journal entry.

✔ I used the correct format for
a journal entry.

Big 💡 Idea

A dramatic presentation of a news report provides the audience with factual information about real-life topics.

Enduring ❗ Understanding

News reporters use vivid language to help the audience get a mental image of the characters, settings, and events.

Essential ❓ Question

How do reporters create the scene while delivering the news?

Spelling Words

Review

indecisive	autumn
outpatient	knowledge
downgrade	rhyme
uptight	scenery
acceleration	wrestled
demolition	armies
pension	shelves
champion	radios
authorization	tomatoes
cancellation	videos

Fluency

Review Expression, Pace

Comprehension

Review

 Author's Purpose and Perspective, Literary Devices

 Summarize, Answer Questions

Robust Vocabulary

- loathe
- bland
- mentor
- dilapidated
- coordination
- altruism
- sensibility
- advocacy
- mistreated
- compassionate

Writing

- *Review* Sentence Fluency, Organization
- Revise and Publish

Lesson 25
Theme Review and Vocabulary Builder

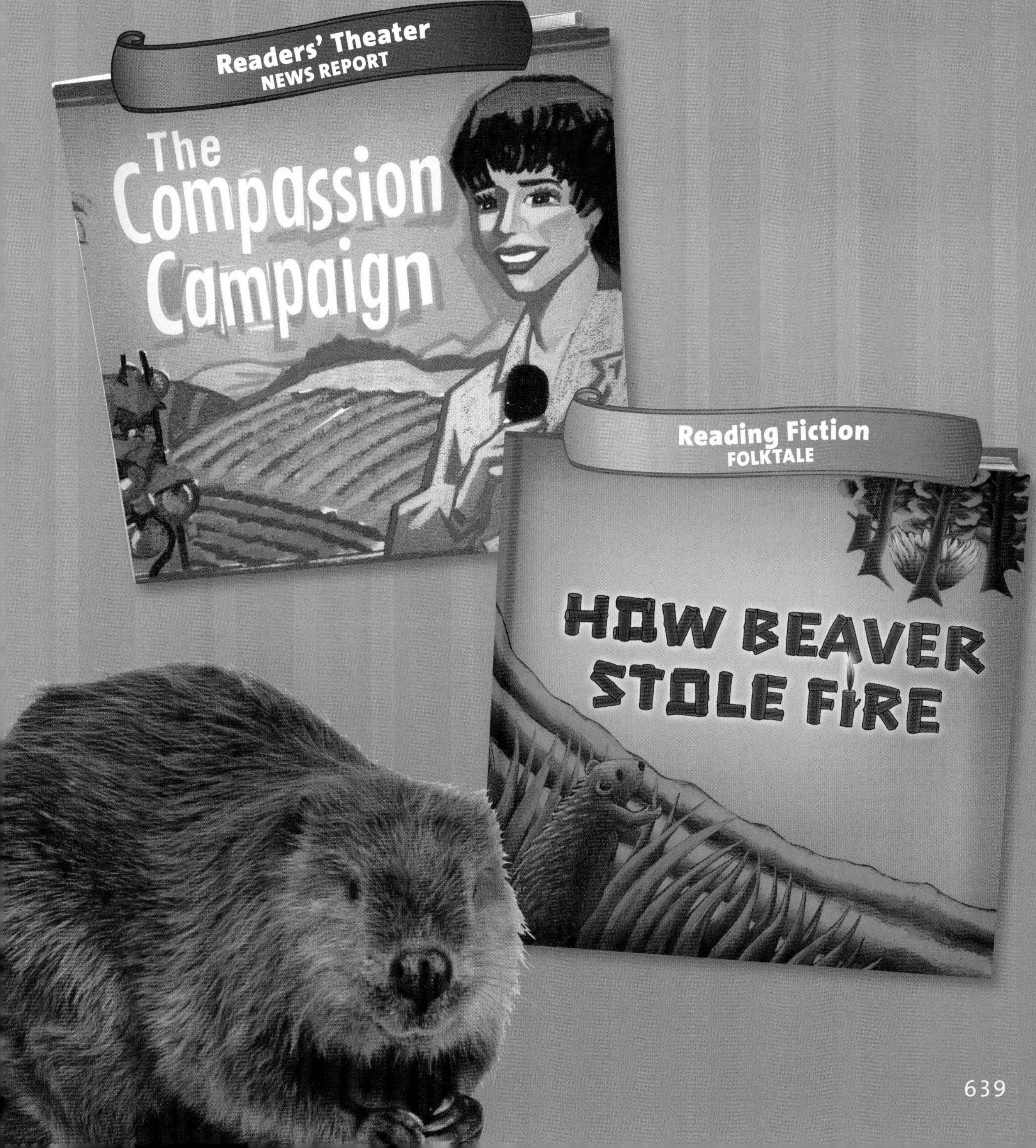
Readers' Theater
NEWS REPORT
The Compassion Campaign
Reading Fiction
FOLKTALE
HOW BEAVER STOLE FIRE

loathe

bland

mentor

dilapidated

coordination

altruism

sensibility

advocacy

mistreated

compassionate

Reading for Fluency

When reading a script aloud,

- Read with expression to match your character's emotions.

- Adjust your pace to match the action in the text.

The Compassion Campaign

illustrated by Sally Wern Comport

Characters

Penny Baldwin	Brent	Sheila
Eva Soto	Jacob Stein	Randy Vasquez
Kiyoshi	Kavi	Felix
Friends	Family	
T. J. Mark	Addison Base	

Penny Baldwin: Good afternoon, I'm Penny Baldwin, and you've tuned in to television's most inspiring program, "The Compassion Campaign." Each month, we profile five kids who make their communities better places to live. Reporter Eva Soto joins us now from California.

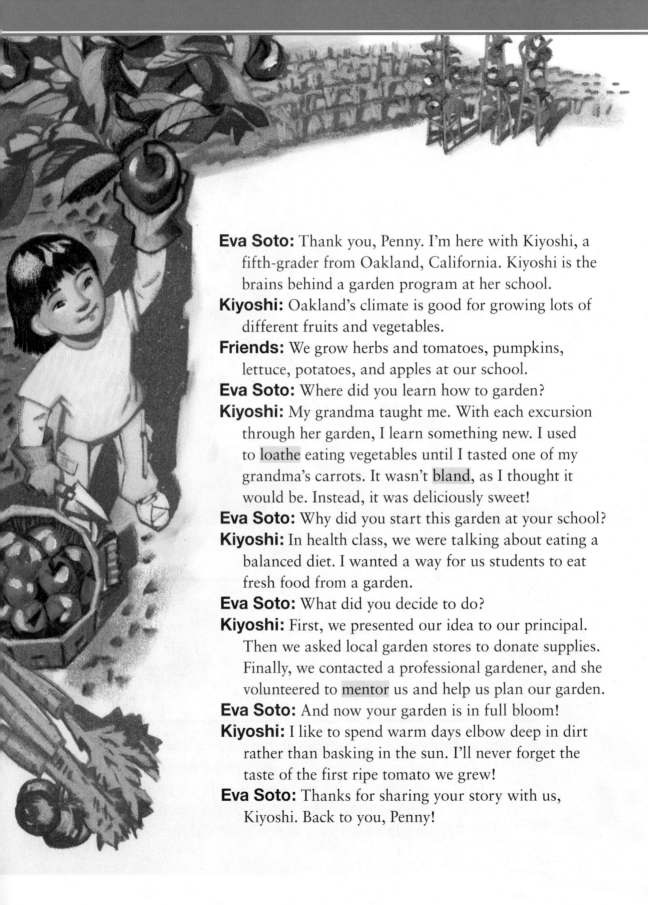

Eva Soto: Thank you, Penny. I'm here with Kiyoshi, a fifth-grader from Oakland, California. Kiyoshi is the brains behind a garden program at her school.

Kiyoshi: Oakland's climate is good for growing lots of different fruits and vegetables.

Friends: We grow herbs and tomatoes, pumpkins, lettuce, potatoes, and apples at our school.

Eva Soto: Where did you learn how to garden?

Kiyoshi: My grandma taught me. With each excursion through her garden, I learn something new. I used to loathe eating vegetables until I tasted one of my grandma's carrots. It wasn't bland, as I thought it would be. Instead, it was deliciously sweet!

Eva Soto: Why did you start this garden at your school?

Kiyoshi: In health class, we were talking about eating a balanced diet. I wanted a way for us students to eat fresh food from a garden.

Eva Soto: What did you decide to do?

Kiyoshi: First, we presented our idea to our principal. Then we asked local garden stores to donate supplies. Finally, we contacted a professional gardener, and she volunteered to mentor us and help us plan our garden.

Eva Soto: And now your garden is in full bloom!

Kiyoshi: I like to spend warm days elbow deep in dirt rather than basking in the sun. I'll never forget the taste of the first ripe tomato we grew!

Eva Soto: Thanks for sharing your story with us, Kiyoshi. Back to you, Penny!

Fluency Tip

Think about how a reporter tells the news. Match your expression to that of a reporter's.

Penny Baldwin: Thank you, Eva. Now we turn our attention to Houston, Texas, and reporter T. J. Mark.

T. J. Mark: Many music legends began their careers by playing in the family garage. Let's meet one young man who started the same way. Brent, how did you form your band?

Brent: I've always enjoyed playing the guitar. A couple of my friends play other instruments. One day we started practicing in my parents' garage.

T. J. Mark: I hear you've taken your show on the road.

Brent: Yes. My grandfather lives in Larson Manor, a place for senior citizens. The residents miss going out for entertainment. A nurse suggested our band bring some entertainment to the residents.

Friends: We loved the idea!

Brent: I was afraid they might not like our music. But their enjoyment wasn't hard to detect. They cheered!

Friends: One man even asked if he could join in on the drums!

Brent: You should come with us the next time we play. We have a gig there next week.

T. J. Mark: I'll be there! Back to you, Penny.

Penny Baldwin: Our next stop is sunny Florida, where Jacob Stein is reporting on how one fifth-grader's fervor moved people to action.

Jacob Stein: I'm on the Gulf Coast of Florida with Kavi, who took it upon herself to brighten the lives of some hurricane survivors.

Kavi: Florida's hurricane season runs from June through November. Not long ago, this area was hit by a terrible hurricane.

Family: We boarded up our house and got out before the storm hit land. Not everyone was as lucky.

Kavi: The hurricane left many people homeless, without vital medicines and other things they needed for living. Some of those people were our neighbors.

Family: Kavi had an idea.

Fluency Tip

Use a pace that best reflects the mood and tone of the text.

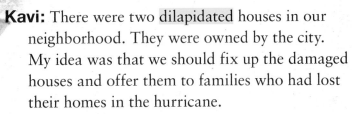

Kavi: There were two dilapidated houses in our neighborhood. They were owned by the city. My idea was that we should fix up the damaged houses and offer them to families who had lost their homes in the hurricane.

Jacob Stein: That must have taken a lot of coordination.

Kavi: Yes. I bustled around, visiting city officials, plumbers, electricians, and house painters. I asked city officials for permission to fix the houses, and I asked the tradespeople to donate their services.

Jacob Stein: With great results.

Kavi: Thanks! Because of the community's efforts, we provided new homes for two families who had nothing left.

Jacob Stein: As you can see, Penny, Kavi's altruism created a fresh start for people who needed some help.

645

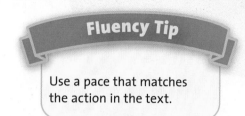

Penny Baldwin: What a moving story. Next, let's go to Ohio and Addison Base, our reporter who's talking with Sheila.

Addison Base: Sheila used her artistic sensibility and her passion for the environment to connect people from Columbus, Ohio, with people around the world. Sheila, please tell us about it.

Sheila: Last summer, I was the giddiest girl in all of Ohio! My uncle invited me to go with him on an ecological research trip to Costa Rica.

Addison Base: How was the trip?

Sheila: It was a great adventure! The rain forest is an amazing place that everyone *should* be able to enjoy. But soon people may not be able to, because the rain forests there are in big trouble.

Addison Base: So you decided to take action.

Sheila: I thought people might be more interested in preserving these precious forests if they could see how beautiful they are. I asked twelve of my friends to each draw a rain forest scene based on the photographs my uncle had taken. We put our illustrations together to make calendars.

Addison Base: That must have been fun.

Sheila: It was! We sold copies of the calendars at a craft fair and donated all the money to an advocacy group that works to protect rain forests.

Addison Base: Sheila's enterprising effort really paid off! Back to you, Penny.

646

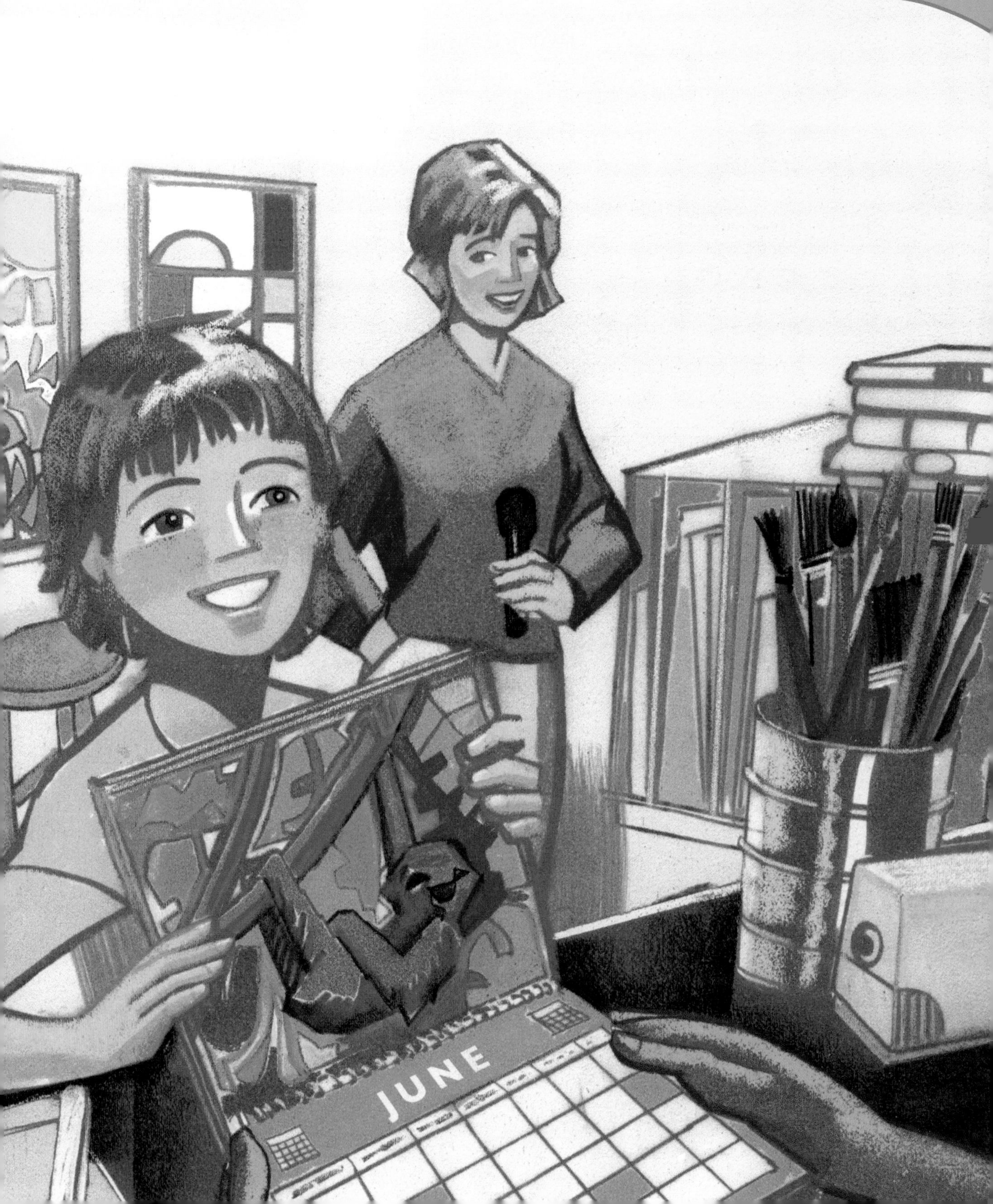
JUNE

Penny Baldwin: For our last story, we go to Atlanta, Georgia, where Randy Vasquez talks to Felix and his furry friends.

Randy Vasquez: Felix, you have a greyhound, a golden retriever, and a poodle—all wanting to be petted.

Felix: These dogs can't get enough attention. That's the main reason I spend so much time at the animal shelter. Animals get lonely, too.

Randy Vasquez: The shelter director told me that you come here every Saturday with a group of friends.

Felix: For my birthday, my dad took me to the shelter to pick out a puppy. I ended up getting a clumsy mutt named Rascal. He's my pal, and he goes with me everywhere. Visiting the shelter made me feel bad for all of the other animals, though.

Randy Vasquez: So you organized a program?

Felix: Right. We take the dogs on walks. They love to stretch their legs and enjoy the fresh air. We use old socks and string to make toy mice for the cats. They love to chase them around.

Randy Vasquez: What is the most unusual animal you've seen in the shelter?

Felix: Once, a pig was brought to the shelter. We named him Mr. Oink. Mr. Oink had been mistreated. We helped build his trust again by being gentle and patient with him.

Randy Vasquez: What other kinds of animals are in the shelter?

Felix: Sometimes birds are brought in. When birds are under stress, they can lose their feathers. You know they're feeling safe again when their feathers grow back.

Randy Vasquez: Maybe you'll grow up to be a veterinarian one day or have a shelter of your own! Keep up the good work, Felix. Penny, back to you.

Penny Baldwin: All five stories today show that good things happen when kids turn compassionate feelings into compassionate actions. Tune in next month, when we travel to New York to check out murals in the making. Good-bye for now!

COMPREHENSION STRATEGIES
Review

Reading Fiction

Bridge to Reading for Meaning Folktales reflect the values and customs of the culture from which they come. They are passed down from one generation to the next and often teach a lesson. The notes on page 651 point out characteristics of folktales, including story elements and explanations for things in nature. Understanding these characteristics can help you better understand the lesson the folktale is teaching.

Review the Focus Strategies

You can use the strategies you learned about in this theme to help you better understand the literature you read.

 Summarize

Stop now and then to summarize the most important events. That will help you understand and remember what you have read.

 Answer Questions

Use your prior knowledge and the information in the text to answer questions about what you are reading.

As you read "How Beaver Stole Fire" on pages 652–655, think about where and how to use comprehension strategies.

CHARACTERS
The characters in folktales often have a specific characteristic, such as bravery.

HOW BEAVER STOLE FIRE

a Nez Perce folktale
by Nancy Van Laan
illustrated by Lisa Desimini

One icy cold day, Beaver was fishing in the Grande Ronde River in Idaho. Near the banks, he saw a great circle of pine trees. He watched as some of the pines made their way down to the icy water, jumped in to bathe, then quickly ran back to the center of the circle.

Sneaking closer, Beaver saw a huge fire. The pines were standing around it, warm and dry.

When Beaver saw that the tallest pines were guarding the fire, he understood. Those unfriendly pines wanted to keep this great magic all for themselves! He crawled under the banks and hid.

Suddenly the fire crackled. The fire popped. A live coal burst out of the flames and rolled down the riverbank right in front of Beaver's hiding place.

At once, Beaver grabbed it and tucked the hot coal inside his thick fur. *Oph!* It was burning! He ran off as quickly and quietly as he could.

But a guard saw Beaver and cried out, "Stop, thief!" Immediately, all of the other pines took off after him.

At first, Beaver was able to run in a straight line. But as the pines got closer, he began to zigzag this way and that to escape them. The Grande Ronde River, who disliked secrets of any kind, wanted to teach the pine trees a lesson. To help Beaver, the river followed his roundabout path and blocked the pine trees. And that is the way it still flows today.

CONFLICT
The conflict, or problem, comes up early in a story.

EXPLANATIONS
Folktales often include explanations for things that happen in nature.

Apply the Strategies Read this folktale about how the secret of fire became known. As you read, use different comprehension strategies, such as summarizing, to help you understand the text.

HOW BEAVER STOLE FIRE

a Nez Perce folktale
by Nancy Van Laan
illustrated by Lisa Desimini

One icy cold day, Beaver was fishing in the Grande Ronde River in Idaho. Near the banks, he saw a great circle of pine trees. He watched as some of the pines made their way down to the icy water, jumped in to bathe, then quickly ran back to the center of the circle.

Sneaking closer, Beaver saw a huge fire. The pines were standing around it, warm and dry.

When Beaver saw that the tallest pines were guarding the fire, he understood. Those unfriendly pines wanted to keep this great magic all for themselves! He crawled under the banks and hid.

Suddenly the fire crackled. The fire popped. A live coal burst out of the flames and rolled down the riverbank right in front of Beaver's hiding place.

652

Stop and Think

As you read, summarize the steps Beaver takes to steal fire. SUMMARIZE

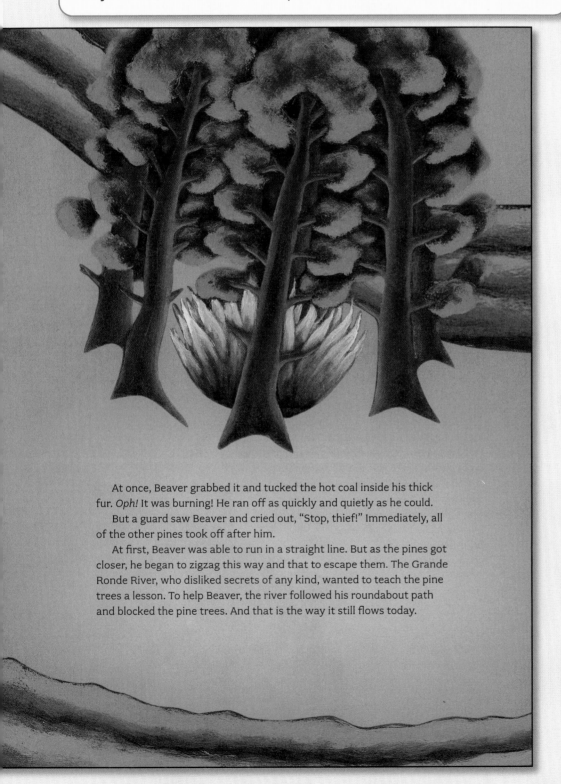

At once, Beaver grabbed it and tucked the hot coal inside his thick fur. *Oph!* It was burning! He ran off as quickly and quietly as he could.

But a guard saw Beaver and cried out, "Stop, thief!" Immediately, all of the other pines took off after him.

At first, Beaver was able to run in a straight line. But as the pines got closer, he began to zigzag this way and that to escape them. The Grande Ronde River, who disliked secrets of any kind, wanted to teach the pine trees a lesson. To help Beaver, the river followed his roundabout path and blocked the pine trees. And that is the way it still flows today.

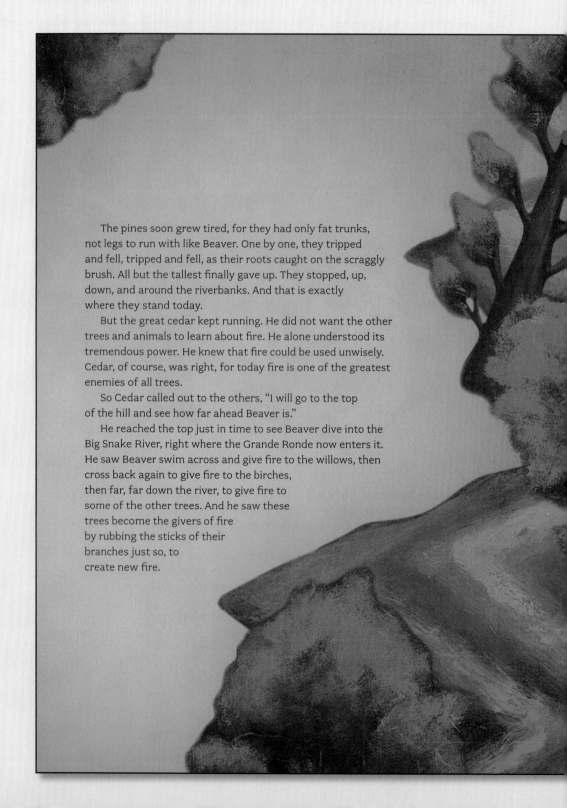

The pines soon grew tired, for they had only fat trunks, not legs to run with like Beaver. One by one, they tripped and fell, tripped and fell, as their roots caught on the scraggly brush. All but the tallest finally gave up. They stopped, up, down, and around the riverbanks. And that is exactly where they stand today.

But the great cedar kept running. He did not want the other trees and animals to learn about fire. He alone understood its tremendous power. He knew that fire could be used unwisely. Cedar, of course, was right, for today fire is one of the greatest enemies of all trees.

So Cedar called out to the others, "I will go to the top of the hill and see how far ahead Beaver is."

He reached the top just in time to see Beaver dive into the Big Snake River, right where the Grande Ronde now enters it. He saw Beaver swim across and give fire to the willows, then cross back again to give fire to the birches, then far, far down the river, to give fire to some of the other trees. And he saw these trees become the givers of fire by rubbing the sticks of their branches just so, to create new fire.

The great cedar also saw that there was nothing more he could do. Beaver had stolen fire. Every animal and tree would soon know this secret. Now all who wanted fire would be told how to rub willow and birch or other sticks together in a special way. They would be able to create a fire of their own.

So the tallest pine tree finally gave up too. Today that great old cedar, his top now dead, still stands all alone on the hill where the Big Snake River meets the Grande Ronde. There are no other cedars within a hundred miles upstream from where he stands. Every animal who passes by points at that tree and remembers Beaver.

READING-WRITING
CONNECTION

Theme 6 Feats of Daring

Tulip Reconnaissance, Jack Gunter

Big Idea
Readers summarize and paraphrase narrative nonfiction to gain its meaning.

Enduring Understanding
Readers include only the most important information when they summarize, but they paraphrase when they retell the story.

Essential Question
How do readers summarize and paraphrase text?

Spelling Words

Words with Prefix + Base Word + Suffix

unsuccessful	impassible
undoubtedly	encouragement
impossibly	unbelievable
disloyalty	unselfishly
deactivation	rearrangement
unlikable	discoverable
replacement	dishonestly
unsafely	unbreakable
uncollectible	reappearance
immeasurable	reassurance

Challenge

indestructible	unhelpful
unmistakable	unnoticeable
irretrievable	

Fluency

Accuracy

Comprehension

 Summarize and Paraphrase

 Monitor Comprehension: Read Ahead

Robust Vocabulary

- asset
- intently
- profusely
- ordeal
- terrain
- dismal
- peril
- esteem

Writing

- Paragraph of Explanation
- Ideas

Lesson 26

Cornerstones of Freedom

Lewis and Clark

R. Conrad Stein

Hupa and Yurok Baskets

by Gerald Hausman

Focus Skill

Summarize and Paraphrase

When you are reading a text, it is important to be able to **summarize** and **paraphrase** the ideas in it. When you summarize, you tell in one or two sentences the most important information. When you paraphrase, you retell a text in your own words without changing its meaning.

Summary	
Paraphrase	

Tip

Include only the most important ideas in a summary.

Read the paragraph below. Then look at the graphic organizer to see how summarizing and paraphrasing are different.

Sacagawea traveled with Lewis and Clark on part of their journey to the Pacific Ocean. Thanks to the journals the explorers kept, we know that Sacagawea helped them in many ways. She pointed out landmarks, obtained horses, and found edible plants. But there are many things we don't know about her. Did her name mean "Bird Woman" or "Boat Pusher"? Did she die at the age of 25, or live to be 96? No one knows for certain.

Summary	We know much about Sacagawea because of the journals Lewis and Clark kept. However, some things about her are still unknown.
Paraphrase	Because of the journals kept by Lewis and Clark, we know that Sacagawea helped them during their journey to the Pacific Ocean. She pointed out landmarks, obtained horses, and found edible plants. However, the meaning of her name and how long she lived are mysteries.

Try This!

Look back at the graphic organizer. Compare the summary and the paraphrase. How are they similar? How are they different?

 www.harcourtschool.com/storytown

Vocabulary

Build Robust Vocabulary

peril

terrain

dismal

esteem

intently

ordeal

profusely

asset

Pike's Purposes

Zebulon Pike was an explorer who faced **peril** willingly. He led expeditions to two parts of the Louisiana Purchase. The first expedition, in 1805-1806, was to find the source of the Mississippi River and establish American authority in the area. Pike and his group traveled nearly 5,000 miles over rugged **terrain** in **dismal** weather. Despite their efforts, they did not achieve their goals.

Pike's second expedition, in 1806-1807, was to explore the Arkansas and Red Rivers. Pike was also directed to enter Spanish territory and estimate troop numbers.

American leaders came to **esteem** Zebulon Pike's leadership abilities. They promoted him to general during the War of 1812.

In mid-November of 1806, Pike and his men found themselves in Colorado at the base of the Rockies. Pike gazed **intently** at a mountain he called Grand Peak. It was later named for him—Pikes Peak. The mountain winter was a terrible **ordeal**. It snowed **profusely**. Then, in February, Pike and his men were captured by the Spanish and led into Mexico. While a captive, Pike observed Spanish troop movements. After he was set free, he reported his findings to his superiors. His information was an **asset** to American leaders.

Pikes Peak in Colorado

 GO online www.harcourtschool.com/storytown

Word Scribe

 This week your task is to use the Vocabulary Words in your writing. Write sentences in your vocabulary journal that show the meanings of the words. For example, did you read your social studies book intently before your last test? Was your studying an asset? Use as many of the Vocabulary Words as you can. Share your writing with your classmates.

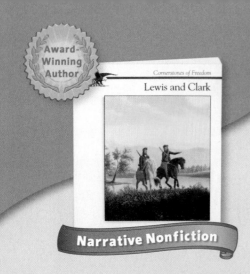

Cornerstones of Freedom
Lewis and Clark

Narrative Nonfiction

Genre Study

Narrative nonfiction tells about people, things, events, or places that are real. As you read, look for

- text features such as photographs and captions.

- facts and important ideas about history.

Summary	
Paraphrase	

Comprehension Strategy

Monitor comprehension when you do not understand a text by **reading ahead** to find an explanation.

LEWIS AND CLARK

by R. Conrad Stein

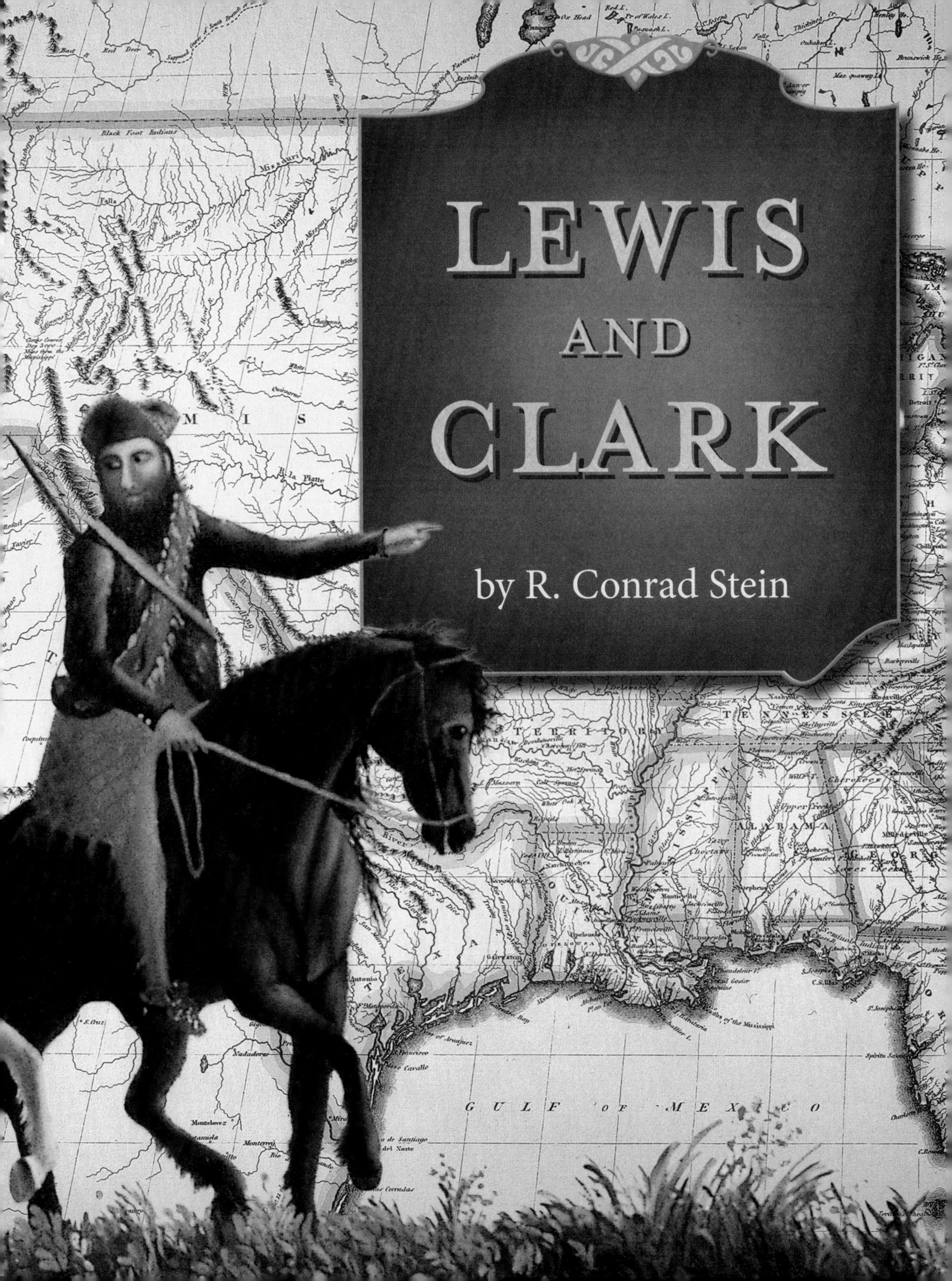

In 1803, President Thomas Jefferson doubled the size of the United States through an agreement known as the Louisiana Purchase. Then Jefferson decided that American explorers should make a journey through the Louisiana Territory, which stretched from St. Louis, Missouri, to the Pacific. He enlisted Meriwether Lewis to lead a group called the Corps of Discovery. Lewis then selected William Clark to help lead the expedition. In 1804, Lewis and Clark began their journey from St. Louis. They traveled through the Great Plains and then stopped for the winter season. A trader and his wife, a Native American named Sacagawea (sak•uh•juh•WEE•uh), decided to travel with the expedition when it resumed its journey in April 1805 into territory never before seen by outsiders.

Lewis considered the Mandan (MAN•duhn) Indians' stories about huge bears to be fanciful tales until one of the explorers was chased by a grizzly bear.

William Clark had perhaps the best eyesight of any crew member. On May 26, he saw the outline of a great mountain range to the west. In the next few days, all of the explorers could see the snow-covered Rocky Mountains on the horizon. The sight was inspiring as well as troubling. The explorers knew that they would have to find a way to cross the incredible barrier.

Before they could cross the Rockies, the Corps of Discovery faced the Great Falls of the Missouri River in present-day Montana. Here the river tumbled down a bluff that was as high as a modern

The Great Falls of the Missouri River were a beautiful sight, but also were difficult to travel around.

six-story building. The roar of the water was deafening. Lewis called it, "the grandest sight I ever beheld." But the waterfall meant that the explorers had to carry their boats and supplies up steep cliffs before they could set out again on quieter waters upstream. Traveling around the falls took the party twenty-four days, and left everyone exhausted.

Carrying her baby boy on her back, Sacagawea won the admiration of the crew. She carefully scanned the riverbank to find edible roots and fruit. These foods provided a welcome relief from the customary diet of meat and water. And in the mountain country, the Missouri River became a crooked stream that split into many small tributaries. Sacagawea pointed out landmarks that she remembered from a journey as a slave child, and she helped the captains choose the correct river branches on which to travel.

Soon the members of the party began to wonder why they had not yet seen any Shoshone (shoh·SHOH·nee) or other American Indians. They had seen signs of Indian settlement—hunters' trails and abandoned campsites—but since they left the Mandan and Hidatsa (hee·DAHT·suh) villages, the Corps of Discovery had not encountered any other people at all.

In mid-August, Meriwether Lewis, hiking ahead of the party with a few other explorers, came upon three Shoshone women and several children. Lewis had carried an American flag in his pack for just such a meeting.

Sacagawea quickly proved to be a valuable asset to the expedition

He waved the banner and walked slowly toward the group. One of the children fled. The women sat very still as if frozen with fear. Lewis explained that he was an explorer, and the women led him to their village.

The Shoshone were a small tribe who were almost always at war with their powerful neighbors, the Blackfeet. They had never seen white people, but constant warfare made the Shoshone suspicious of all outsiders. Lewis hoped to buy horses from the tribe. Now that the rivers had all but disappeared, he needed horses to cross the peaks of the Rocky Mountains. But the chief, Cameahwait (kuh•MEE•uh•wayt), would not part with any of the animals. Lewis did persuade Cameahwait to send a few Shoshone to find Clark and the rest of the party and bring them to the village.

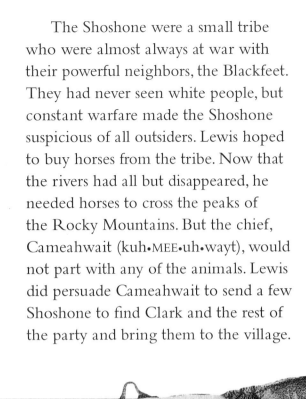

The journals kept by Captains Lewis, Clark, and several members of their expedition have been compiled into many published accounts since the journey ended in 1806.

The next morning, Clark and the others arrived at the village, and a meeting was held with Chief Cameahwait. Sacagawea prepared to serve as the translator. When the meeting began, Sacagawea stared intently at the chief. Then she broke into tears of joy. Lewis wrote, "She jumped up, ran, and embraced him, and threw her blanket over him, and cried profusely." Sacagawea recognized Cameahwait as her brother, whom she had not seen in six years. Cheers and laughter rose from the village. The Shoshone hailed Sacagawea as a lost daughter who had come home.

On September 1, 1805, the Corps of Discovery left the Shoshone territory. Chief Cameahwait not only provided the party with horses, he also gave them a guide to show them the best route through the mountains. Crossing the Rockies proved to be a difficult ordeal. The trails were too rugged to ride on, so the party walked and used the horses as pack animals.

The expedition crossed the Rockies on foot, using the horses to carry their equipment and supplies.

In mid-September, a blinding snowstorm struck. Even the Shoshone guide got lost. Worst of all, the once-abundant wild game could not be found on the high mountain peaks. The explorers were forced to kill some of their pack animals for meat. The explorers' journals report that the men laughed out loud when they finally crossed the mountains and reached grasslands on level terrain.

The Lewis and Clark expedition emerged from the Rocky Mountains into the lovely valley of the Clearwater River in present-day Idaho. The waters

Upon reaching the Clearwater River Valley, the expedition built new canoes to continue their journey west.

were so clear that the river bottom and schools of fish were visible despite the river's depth. In the Clearwater country, Lewis and Clark abandoned their pack horses and built new canoes. They reasoned that the streams on this side of the Rockies would all eventually flow into the Columbia River, the major river of the Pacific Northwest. American Indians called the Columbia River the *Ouragon* or *Origan*. The land around it was later called the Oregon Territory.

Traveling the rivers, the voyagers met the Nez Perce (NES PURS) Indians, who taught them valuable techniques for building and sailing log canoes. Less friendly were the Chinook (shih•NOOK) who drove hard bargains when trading for goods. But encountering the Chinook meant that the Pacific Ocean was not far away. One of the Chinook wore a black navy coat that he may have bought from a North American or European sailor.

The explorers experienced some difficulty in dealing with the Chinook Indians, but their encounter brought signs that the Pacific Ocean was near.

A dismal rain pelted the travelers in early November as they sailed down the Columbia River. They made a camp near an Indian village and spent a restless night. On the morning of November 7, 1805, the rain stopped and the fog cleared. A chorus of shouts suddenly went up from the camp. William Clark scribbled in his notes, "Ocean in view! O! the joy." On the horizon, still many miles to the west, lay the great Pacific Ocean. Upon seeing the ocean, some of the explorers wept, and others said prayers of thanksgiving.

But arriving at the Pacific Ocean did not end the Lewis and Clark expedition. The party still had to return home to St. Louis. President Jefferson had provided Meriwether Lewis with a letter of credit guaranteeing payment to any ship captain who would take the explorers to the eastern coast. The party made a winter camp at the mouth of the Columbia River near present-day Astoria, Oregon, and kept a watch for ships. No vessels were spotted. Finally, on March 23, 1806, the crew broke camp and began the long trek east toward St. Louis.

To the explorers, the six-month return journey seemed to be easier than their first journey because they knew what to expect in the river and mountain country. When the crew reached the Mandan village, they said good-bye to Sacagawea and her husband and continued back to St. Louis.

On September 23, 1806, the Lewis and Clark expedition arrived safely back in St. Louis, Missouri, where their journey had begun more than two years earlier. The travelers had gone a distance of just less than 4,000 miles (6,400 km) from St. Louis to the mouth of the Columbia River and back. But the twisting rivers and mountain trails meant that the Corps of Discovery had actually covered about 8,000 miles (13,000 km) on the history-making trip. Throughout the explorers' travels, they encountered more than fifty American-Indian tribes.

Sacagawea is remembered as a vital reason for the success of the Lewis and Clark expedition. This statue of Sacagawea stands in Bismarck, North Dakota.

The explorers saw the Pacific Ocean for the first time near present-day Astoria, Oregon.

Washington. U.S. of America. July 4. 1803.

Dear Sir

In the journey which you are about to undertake for the discovery of the course and source of the Missisipi, and of the most convenient water communication from thence to the Pacific ocean, your party being small, it is to be expected that you will encounter considerable dangers from the Indian inhabitants. should you escape those dangers and reach the Pacific ocean, you may find it imprudent to hazard a return the same way, and be forced to seek a passage round by sea, in such vessels as you may find on the Western coast. but you will be without money, without clothes, & other necessaries; as a sufficient supply cannot be carried with you from hence. your resource in that case can only be in the credit of the U.S. for which purpose I hereby authorise you to draw on the Secretaries of State, of the Treasury, of War & of the Navy of the U.S. according as you may find your draughts will be most negociable, for the purpose of obtaining money or necessaries for yourself & your men: and I solemnly pledge the faith of the United States that these draughts shall be paid punctually at the date they are made payable. I also ask of the Consuls, agents, merchants & citizens of any nation with which we have intercourse or amity, to furnish you with those supplies which your necessities may call for, assuring them of honorable and prompt retribution. and our own Consuls in foreign parts where you may happen to be, are hereby instructed & required to be aiding & assisting to you in whatsoever may be necessary for procuring your return back to the United States. And to give more entire satisfaction & confidence to those who may be disposed to aid you, I Thomas Jefferson, President of the United States of America, have written this letter of general credit for you with my own hand, and signed it with my name.

Th. Jefferson

To Capt. Meriwether Lewis.

Jefferson's letter of credit survived the journey west, but it was never used because the explorers returned home overland, instead of by ship.

The expedition returned with numerous samples of plant and animal life that had never before been seen by American scientists. Before the expedition, President Jefferson had hoped that the explorers would find a broad river that ships could use to sail directly to the Pacific Ocean. Lewis and Clark failed to find such a river, and the expedition was final proof that an inland waterway in North America did not exist.

From St. Louis, Lewis and Clark traveled to Washington, D.C. Almost every town they passed through brought out bands to welcome them as heroes. In Washington, D.C., the explorers delighted President Jefferson with tales of grizzly bears and high mountain passes. The president said, "Lewis and Clark have entirely fulfilled my expectations . . .

The world will find that those travelers have well earned its favor."

To Meriwether Lewis and William Clark, the mission itself was their greatest reward. Traveling through virtually unexplored lands was an exhilarating experience that they would cherish for the rest of their lives. Although they faced many dangers, the thrill—not the peril—of the expedition bursts from the pages of the journals they kept. As Lewis wrote the day he left the Indian village to enter the Western wilderness, "I could but esteem this moment of my departure as among the most happy of my life."

The Lewis and Clark expedition is commemorated by many historic sites along the route the explorers traveled.

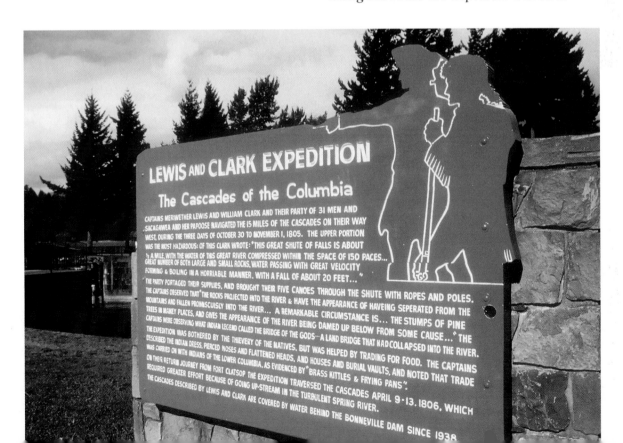

THINK
CRITICALLY

1 What did President Thomas Jefferson hope Lewis and Clark would find on their expedition? What discovery did they make instead? NOTE DETAILS

2 How was crossing the Rockies a challenge for the Corps of Discovery? SUMMARIZE AND PARAPHRASE

3 Why do you think the author quoted Lewis and Clark directly in different parts of the selection? AUTHOR'S PURPOSE

4 What would be a worthwhile expedition for a group of skilled people to go on today? Would you be willing to be a part of this expedition? Explain. EXPRESS PERSONAL OPINIONS

5 **WRITE** Write a newspaper article about the Corps of Discovery as if you were a journalist writing on the day the expedition returned to St. Louis, Missouri. In your article, use details and information from the selection. SHORT RESPONSE

ABOUT THE AUTHOR
R. CONRAD STEIN

R. Conrad Stein has published more than eighty books for young readers. Many of them are biographies or focus on history. Mr. Stein believes that his job as a writer is to express the drama of historical events. Born and raised in Chicago, he knew from the time he was twelve years old that he wanted to be a writer. After serving as a Marine, he studied history at the University of Illinois. A few years after he graduated, his background in history helped him get assignments writing history books for young readers.

GO online www.harcourtschool.com/storytown

HUPA AND YUROK ◆BASKETS◆

by Gerald Hausman

Imagine living in a time and place when you could not go to the store to buy the things you need. Look around you. What could you use to make everyday things, such as plates, bowls, and pans? The Hupa and Yurok American Indians, who live in the mountains of northern California, are very good at using the trees, plants, and grasses around them to make useful and beautiful baskets.

Long ago, basket makers spent much of the year collecting materials. In April and May, they collected hazelnut sticks to make the bases of their baskets. All year, weavers gathered roots to make the horizontal weave of the baskets. During the summer, weavers gathered materials to decorate their baskets. They might use bear grass to make light-colored patterns or maidenhair ferns to make dark patterns. Bark, roots, and rotten acorns were all used to make dyes for the baskets. The most talented weavers even wove porcupine quills into their designs.

N

HOOPA VALLEY

★
SACRAMENTO

CALIFORNIA

The Hoopa Valley, in California

LOS ANGELES

Weavers followed simple steps to make a basket. First, they wet their materials to make them flexible. Then, they used hazelnut sticks to make the base of the basket. Next, they built the basket by twisting together strands of grasses, ferns, and twigs. They continued to weave until the basket was as wide or as tall as they wanted. Many of these techniques are still followed today.

Sometimes basket makers combined strands of dyed grasses with natural ones. The weavers created patterns by using the different colors. The patterns often represented nature or values, such as friendship. Weavers today still use many of these patterns in their baskets.

▲ bear grass

Besides being beautiful, the baskets were also useful. Skilled basket makers could weave so tightly that their baskets could hold water. Weavers made baskets for storing acorns, serving food, and drying fish. They also made basket hats, cradles, and baby carriers.

Today, the Hupa and Yurok people continue to make baskets. People around the world collect the baskets, and weavers are well paid for their work. More importantly, making baskets is a way for the Hupa and Yurok to remember their heritage and keep their traditions alive.

Traditional Native Basket Patterns of Northwest California

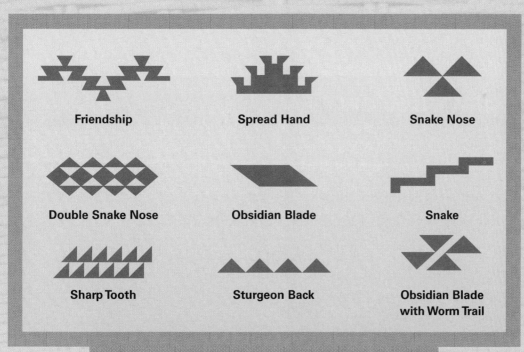

Basket patterns often reflected values or a love of the natural world. Can you tell why these patterns are named as they are?

Connections

Comparing Texts

1. Would you have been a good member of Lewis and Clark's expedition? Why or why not?

2. How are the genres of "Lewis and Clark" and "Hupa and Yurok Baskets" alike? How are they different?

3. What did you know about the Lewis and Clark expedition before you read this selection? What did you learn from the selection?

Vocabulary Review

Word Sort

Work in a group. Sort the Vocabulary Words into categories. Compare your sorted words with the group, explaining your choices. Then choose at least one Vocabulary Word from each category. Write a sentence for each word.

Positive Words	Neutral Words	Negative Words

asset

intently

profusely

ordeal

terrain

dismal

peril

esteem

Fluency Practice

Repeated Reading

Remember that when you read with accuracy, you automatically recognize the letter patterns in words and read them correctly. Look back at page 670 of "Lewis and Clark." Read the page aloud three times or until you can read it with accuracy.

Writing

Write Captions

Imagine that you are helping to write captions for a map showing the westward route of Lewis and Clark. Select two places where the expedition set up camp. Write a caption to go with each location that tells what the explorers did there.

My Writing Checklist

Writing Trait → Ideas

✓ I used a graphic organizer to organize information for the captions.

✓ My captions are focused on the most important information.

✓ My captions are accurate paraphrases of the information.

Summary	
Paraphrase	

Reading-Writing Connection

Analyze Writer's Craft: Narrative Nonfiction

Narrative nonfiction gives facts and information about a topic. It may include headings, diagrams, photographs, and captions. When you write narrative nonfiction, you can use the work of authors such as R. Conrad Stein as writing models. Read the paragraph below from "Lewis and Clark," and notice how the author organized his **ideas**.

Cornerstones of Freedom
Lewis and Clark

R. Conrad Stein

Writing Trait

IDEAS
The **topic** of this paragraph is how Sacagawea won the respect of the crew. **Facts** and **details** support the topic.

Carrying her baby boy on her back, Sacagawea (sak•uh•juh•WEE•uh) won the admiration of the crew. She carefully scanned the riverbank to find edible roots and fruit. These foods provided a welcome relief from the customary diet of meat and water. And in the mountain country, the Missouri River became a crooked stream that split into many small tributaries. Sacagawea pointed out landmarks that she remembered from a journey as a slave child, and she helped the captains choose the correct river branches on which to travel.

Writing Trait

CONVENTIONS
To help the reader pronounce a difficult word, the author may include a **phonetic spelling**; for example, (sak•uh•juh•WEE•uh).

Research Report

A **research report** is a type of **expository nonfiction**. It gives facts and information about a topic. A research report includes a list of the books, articles, and online sources in which the writer found the information. As you read this research report written by a student named José, notice the text features and text **organization** José used.

Student Writing Model

Spanish Missions in Texas
by José M.

Writing Trait

IDEAS
In his introduction, José gives general information about the **topic**. Then he mentions his three **main ideas** for the report.

José uses a **heading** to begin each section of related information.

The first Spanish mission in Texas was built in 1682, near present-day El Paso. The missions were built by Spanish priests called missionaries. Missions were designed to be self-sufficient communities. Daily life was difficult, but the people of the missions helped shape modern-day Texas.

Design and Structure

Each mission was designed like a small town with a church at its center. Around the church the missionaries built houses, workplaces, and a school. The buildings were surrounded by a large walled quadrangle called a *presidio*. The walls and buildings were built of stone or of *adobe*, a kind of brick made from mud and chopped straw. Mission farms and ranches were built nearby so that the settlers could grow food and raise livestock.

Daily Life

Life in a mission was focused on religion and hard work. Each morning, the missionaries called everyone together for prayers, religious classes, and breakfast. During the workday, the men did carpentry, ironworking, and other jobs. The women made candles, soap, and weavings. Other settlers worked on the nearby farms and ranches. In time, the mission community was able to make everything it needed.

Effect on Modern Texas

Spanish missions formed the bases of many modern Texas cities, such as San Antonio. Today, the Mission at San Antonio de Valero, better known as the Alamo, is one of the most popular tourist destinations in the United States. Many other missions are still standing. Most are historical sites or state parks.

The Alamo, San Antonio, Texas

Writing Trait

ORGANIZATION
In his **conclusion** José sums up the supporting ideas of his report. Then he tells why his topic is important.

The strong walls of the Spanish missions have lasted for hundreds of years, and the hard work of the people who lived in them is still remembered. The missions shaped modern Texas, and they will always be an important part of Texas history.

Writing Trait

CONVENTIONS
Titles of magazine articles, online articles, and book chapters are enclosed in quotation marks. Book titles are typed in italics or underlined if written by hand.

List of Sources

Kalman, Bobbie and Greg Nickles. *Spanish Missions*. New York, NY: Crabtree, 1996.

Currie, Stephen. "The First Mexican Americans." *Cobblestone Magazine*. May 2004: 3–5.

San Antonio Missions National Historical Park. "History." Feb. 3, 2006.
<http://www.nps.gov/saan/visit/History.htm>

Now look at what José did to prepare to write his research report.

Notes

José used note cards to write down information from a variety of sources. He made a new notecard for each important idea and included the source for each note.

Design and Structure
- like a small town, with church at center
- surrounded by a presidio
- built of adobe

Kalman, Bobbie and Greg Nickles. <u>Spanish Missons</u>. New York, NY: Crabtree, 1996.

Men's Daily Life
- carpentry
- ironworking
- farm work

San Antonio Missions National Historical Park. "History." Feb. 3, 2006.
<http://www.nps.gov/saan/visit/History.htm>

Outline

Then José created an outline to show the order of ideas he would follow as he wrote his report.

Title: Spanish Missions in Texas

I. Introduction

    A. History and background

    B. Main ideas

II. Design and Structure

    A. Design

    B. Building materials

III. Daily Life

    A. Religion

    B. Hard work

IV. Effect on Modern Texas

    A. Formed modern towns

    B. Many still standing

V. Conclusion

    A. Summary of main ideas

    B. Importance of missions

Big Idea

Readers summarize and paraphrase information from biographies to gain meaning from text.

Enduring Understanding

To summarize, a reader briefly identifies important information and paraphrases when they retell the information in their own words.

Essential Question

How are summarizations and paraphrases different?

Spelling Words

Words with Greek Word Parts

astronomy	cyclical
disaster	bicyclist
asterisk	cyclone
astronaut	encyclopedia
asteroid	hydrogen
chronic	hydrant
chronicle	hydrate
chronology	optic
chronological	optician
synchronize	optical

Challenge

polygraph	hydroplane
asthma	biohazard
astrodome	

Fluency

Accuracy

Robust Vocabulary

- remote
- laden
- appalled
- invest
- floundered
- grueling
- isolated

Comprehension

 Summarize and Paraphrase

 Monitor Comprehension: Read Ahead

Writing

- Paragraph of Historical Information
- Ideas

Lesson 27

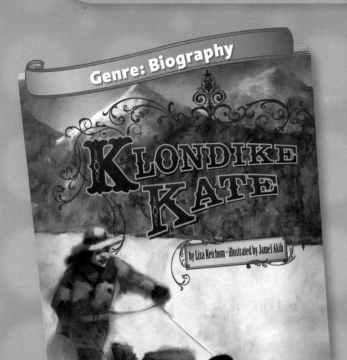

Genre: Biography

KLONDIKE KATE

by Liza Ketchum · illustrated by Jamel Akib

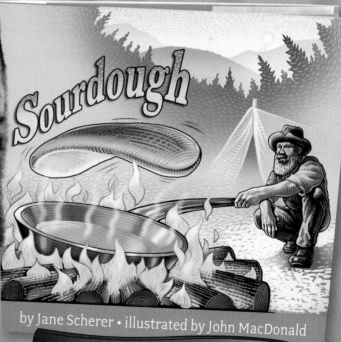

Sourdough

by Jane Scherer · illustrated by John MacDonald

Genre: Magazine Article

Focus Skill

Summarize and Paraphrase

You have learned that when you **summarize** a text, you tell the most important information. Your summary should only be a sentence or two.

A **paraphrase** should be longer because you are retelling part of a text in your own words. Here are some tips for paraphrasing:

- Replace some words with synonyms.
- Change the order of words in sentences.
- Leave out unimportant words and phrases.
- Combine sentences that are related.

Summary	
Paraphrase	

Tip
When you paraphrase, make sure you do not change the meaning of what the author wrote.

Read the paragraph below. Then look at the graphic organizer. The summary shows the main idea of the paragraph. In the paraphrase, all of the important information is restated.

In July 1897, American newspapers announced the discovery of gold in Canada's Yukon Territory. More than 100,000 gold seekers stampeded north. However, only about 30,000 made it all the way. By the time the stampeders reached the goldfields, local people had claimed all the richest creeks. Very few stampeders became rich. Some stayed to work in the area, but most headed home.

Summary	The discovery of gold in Canada's Yukon Territory was announced in 1897.
Paraphrase	The discovery of gold in Canada's Yukon Territory was published in American newspapers in July 1897. Many people went north, but fewer than one-third of them made it to the Yukon Territory. Once they arrived, they found that the richest creeks were already taken.

Try This!

Look back at the paragraph. What other important ideas would you add to the paraphrase?

www.harcourtschool.com/storytown

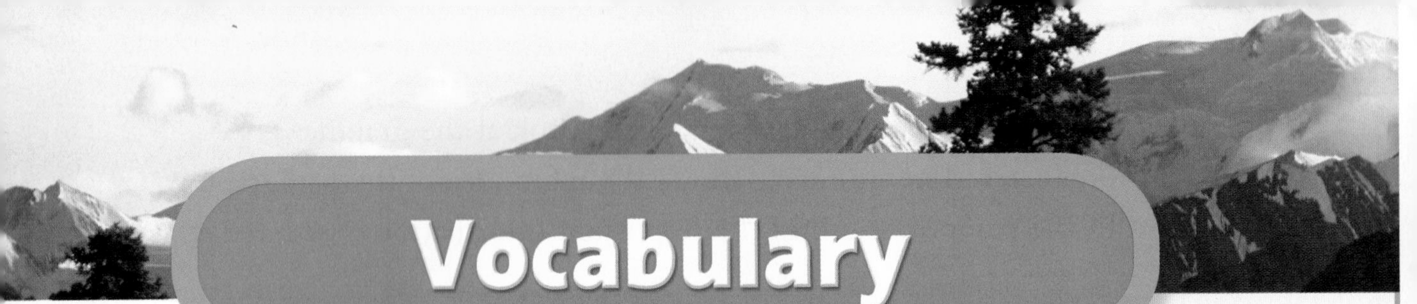

Vocabulary

Build Robust Vocabulary

remote

appalled

laden

grueling

invest

isolated

floundered

Stagecoach Mary

Mary Fields was an unlikely pioneer. Born into slavery in Tennessee in 1832, she did not become free until the end of the Civil War. She then moved to Ohio and worked for a nun, Mother Amadeus, in a convent.

Mother Amadeus later left the convent for a **remote** part of Montana. **Appalled** at the conditions faced by women there, she set up a school for women and girls of the Blackfoot Indian tribe. When Mother Amadeus became ill, Mary Fields moved west to care for her friend. She took a job driving a freight wagon, often heavily **laden** with goods for the school.

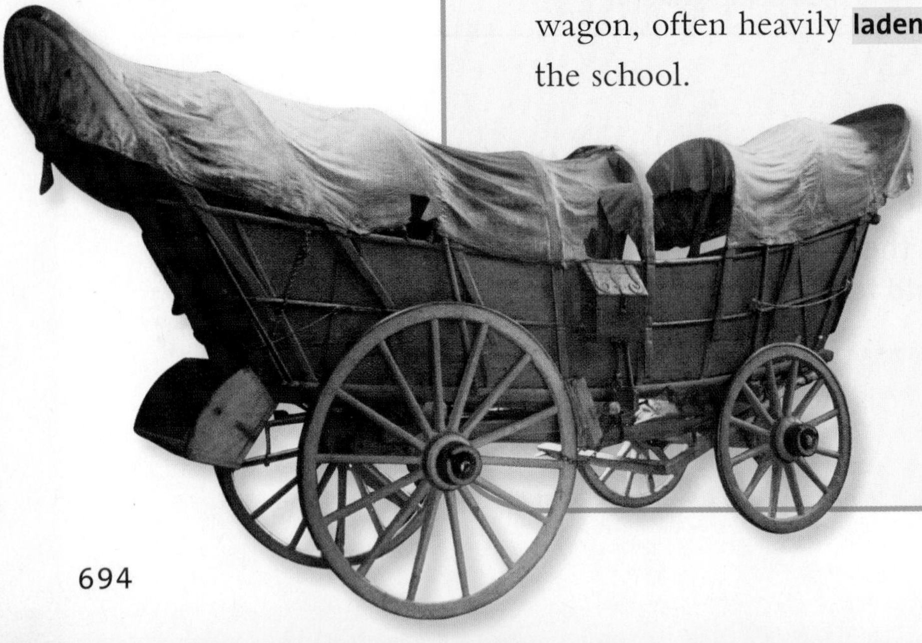

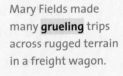

Mary Fields made many **grueling** trips across rugged terrain in a freight wagon.

Some years later, Mary Fields left that job after a dispute with a haughty worker. Mother Amadeus then offered to **invest** in a café in nearby Cascade, Montana, if Mary Fields would run it. Mary Fields did so, but the café was not a success.

At the age of 63, Mary Fields took the job that would make her locally famous. She drove a U.S. Mail stagecoach to **isolated** outposts. While other drivers **floundered** in deep snow, Mary Fields managed to get the mail through. In her eight years on this job, Stagecoach Mary reportedly never missed a day of work!

Mary Fields did not retire when she stopped driving the stagecoach. She opened a laundry in Cascade.

 www.harcourtschool.com/storytown

Word Detective

 Your challenge this week is to find Vocabulary Words outside your classroom. You might find them in a newspaper, a magazine, on television, or on the radio. Write the words you find in your vocabulary journal, and record where you found them.

Biography

Genre Study

A biography is a written account of a person's life, told by someone else. As you read, look for

- information about the person's life.
- events presented in time-order.

Event	Summary	Paraphrase

Comprehension Strategy

Monitor comprehension when you do not understand a text by **reading ahead** to find an explanation.

KLONDIKE KATE

by Liza Ketchum · illustrated by Jamel Akib

"Gold! They've found gold!" The paperboy waved a copy of the *Vancouver Sun*. "Gold in the Yukon!"

It was a hot morning in July, 1898. Kate Ryan, a twenty-eight-year-old nurse, was on her way to the hospital in Vancouver, Canada. She hurried to join the crowd around the newsboy. According to the story, a Tagish Indian named Skookum Jim was guzzling water from his hat when he looked down and discovered chunks of gold as "big as beans" floating inside. Skookum Jim and his partners quickly grabbed a frying pan and began finding "nuggets everywhere."

This news was almost a year old when it reached Kate Ryan. Rabbit Creek, where the gold was discovered, was a tributary of the Klondike River. It flowed through a remote region of northern Canada, far from telegraph lines. Once ice locked up the rivers, boat travel stopped and letters took months to reach the outside world. Now that word of the discovery was finally out, it spread up and down the coast like a raging brushfire.

In Seattle, Washington, five thousand people who had heard the news waited for the steamer *Portland* to pull into the harbor. A rough band of miners straggled down the gangway, their suitcases, boxes, and trunks laden with gold weighing more than a ton. One passenger, Ethel Berry, had left California with sixty dollars in her pocket. Now she stood on the deck in a torn dress, waiting for help with her bedroll, which was too heavy to lift alone. It held $100,000 in gold.

Newspaper reporters rushed to interview Berry. What would she tell other women who wanted to go north?

"Why, to stay away, of course," she said.

If Kate Ryan knew about Ethel Berry's advice, she ignored it. Kate had grown up in the wilderness of Johnville, New Brunswick, and she didn't like city life. Besides, times were hard all over the country, and she was restless in her job. Always eager for adventure, Kate said later she was lured by "the call of the wild. That, and nothing else." And so, she said, "I joined the procession."

Her friends were appalled. Had she lost her mind? Women shouldn't travel alone to that part of the world—and how would she get there? Boats could only navigate the Yukon River in summer, and there were no roads or trains. Other warnings appeared in the papers. A woman reporter for the *Skaguay News* warned that "delicate women have no right attempting the trip. . . . Those who love luxury, comfort, and ease would better remain at home. It takes strong, healthy, courageous women to stand the terrible hardships."

At six feet tall, Kate Ryan *was* strong and healthy. As a teenager, she had developed perfect posture by walking on the roof beams of her family's barn. And she had never known much comfort. Her parents, Patrick and Ellen Ryan, had migrated to Canada to escape Ireland's potato famine and had cleared land in the thick forest of New Brunswick. They struggled to feed their family of seven children on the small earnings from their farm and a shop attached to their house. Kate, the youngest, had worked hard since she was little, picking potatoes until her hands were raw, chopping wood, helping her father mind the store and the animals.

Now a fortune beckoned from rivers whose veins of gold, some said, lay as thick as cheese in a sandwich. Kate just needed to figure out which route to take.

There were two ways to reach the remote Klondike. The coastal route, which took passengers up the Yukon River, was only passable in the summer and was very expensive. Kate chose the cheaper, but more dangerous, "All Canada Route," crossing the Alaskan panhandle into Canada. Most of the trip was overland, which was fine with Kate—boats made her seasick.

After a few months, Kate had saved enough money to buy
her ticket and supplies. The Canadian government had passed
a law requiring Klondike adventurers to bring enough food,
tools, and warm clothes to last a year. The *Skaguay News*
published a recommended clothing list for women which
advised them to bring practical items such as tall "bicycle
shoes" (lace-up boots) and a mattress ticking which could
be "filled with dried moss."

Kate brought her list to the Hudson Bay Company,
where a clerk helped her pick out warm clothes, as
well as a heavy waterproof mackinaw (a heavy cloth
of wool or wool and other fibers), a sleeping bag,
and an ax. The clerk presented her with a gift: a
small black leather bag with a secret pocket. "Any
lady with the courage to head out to the Yukon
on her own deserves the support of the Hudson
Bay Company," he told her.

Kate's food supplies were enormous. She bought fifty pounds of flour, one hundred and fifty pounds each of bacon and split peas, as well as canned milk and fruit. Finally, she purchased her ticket for the steamer *Tees*, scheduled to leave in February. The boat would only take her as far as Wrangell Island, Alaska. How would she get from there to the northern goldfields?

She first thought of pack horses. Kate had ridden horses since she was young, and her father had taught her how to pick out a good animal. But she couldn't find horses sturdy enough to carry heavy loads through deep snow. So Kate spent $100 on a team of huskies and a sled—even though she knew nothing about driving a dog team.

At last, on February 28, 1898, Kate climbed on board the *Tees*. In addition to her dogs, sled, and other equipment, she carried her Bible, a rosary, and a five-dollar gold piece from her friends in Vancouver. They wanted her to invest it for them in the Klondike. When Kate waved good-bye to her friends at the dock, she didn't know if she'd ever see them again. Kate was setting off for one of the most remote stretches of wilderness left on the continent.

Rough seas battered the *Tees* as she headed north with a cargo of men, a few women, and many animals. The horses, sled dogs, cows, chickens, and even a few goats made for a noisy, smelly ride. The steamer passed boats full of disappointed gold seekers headed south, warning of the dangers ahead. But Kate was too seasick to notice.

After four days at sea, the ship dumped its passengers and their cargo on the muddy beach at Wrangell Island. Kate gathered her supplies, untangled her dogs, and hurried to find a ride to the mainland. She needed to mush her team up the frozen Stikine River before the spring thaw melted the ice.

While on the island, Kate visited a troop of Northwest Mounted Police, who were waiting for a ferry. A friendly Mountie named George Chalmers offered her a cup of bitter coffee and told her his sad story. The camp's cook had left, and Chalmers had been ordered to take his place. The Mounties were complaining about his terrible meals. Could Kate advise him on cooking dinner?

Fortunately, Kate had grown up in a big family and knew how to cook for a crowd. They set up the stove, then fried pork and baked biscuits. The Mounties wolfed down the food. When their chief officer, Inspector Primrose, praised her cooking, Kate made him an offer: She would cook for his unit until they reached the Canadian border if he would put her name on his list of ferry passengers.

Primrose agreed immediately. The next morning, Kate visited Wrangell's baker. He gave Kate a fistful of sourdough "starter" and taught her how to turn the mix of flour and water into bread, biscuits, and pancakes. Kate didn't realize how much this gift would help her as she began her adventures in the North.

When Kate and the Mounties finally crossed to the mainland, Kate loaded her sled, hitched up her huskies, and buttoned her mackinaw. Kate and her dogs floundered through deep snow and slush as they followed the Mounties up the Stikine River to the town of Dewdney, where it began to rain. Water poured through Kate's tent, soaking her clothes and supplies. The Mounties set up a permanent camp to patrol the border and urged Kate to stay. She had become their friend as well as their cook. But Kate had to push on before the ice melted. Besides, she told a reporter years later, "I wasn't built for going backwards. When I once step forward, I must go ahead." Kate continued north alone.

The Stikine River cut through deep canyons, with rocky walls rising steeply on each side. It was almost unheard of for a woman to travel this route, known as the most treacherous path to the Klondike. Yet it could be done. One brave African American woman named Lucille Hunter had made the journey with her husband the year before—while she was nine months pregnant!

Trudging behind her dogs, Kate traveled eight to ten grueling miles a day. When she finally pulled into the tiny settlement of Glenora, eighty miles up the river, the news spread fast: A white woman was in town! Not only that—she was as tall and strong as the men who were packing supplies into the North, and she wore a broad-brimmed cow driver's hat over her auburn curls. Jim Callbreath, a local resident who became Kate's friend, said, "Any woman who could make it up the Stikine River on the ice should be treated as an equal to any packer in the territory."

Kate told Callbreath that thousands of people with "gold fever" would be arriving by boat as soon as the ice broke up. When Callbreath decided to build a hotel, Kate took the five-dollar gold piece from her secret pocket and offered Callbreath a deal: If she invested in his project, could she open a restaurant in his building? He agreed, and soon an old packing shed and warehouse were converted into the Glenora Hotel and Restaurant. Kate's restaurant became a popular meeting spot for customers who enjoyed her stews and her sourdough bread and biscuits, which rose thanks to her original fistful of starter.

At the end of April, the river ice began to groan and crack like pistol shots. Huge chunks of ice swept down the river. Before long, boats full of prospectors pulled into town. Passengers who expected a railroad were shocked to find a sleepy village of less than a hundred people, with no transportation further north. Houses and tents sprang up overnight. Callbreath went away for two weeks and, when he returned, he found someone had added onto his store (without his permission), an army unit was camped in his potato field, and Kate had so many customers she didn't have time to talk. The town also had a brand-new newspaper, which boasted that Glenora was "the town that was built in a day."

Kate spent most of the next year in Glenora, living in her tent. As winter cut off supplies of fresh food, she hired young boys to catch fish and learned to cook with dried eggs, potatoes, and onions. The restaurant was wildly successful. When spring came, Kate could call herself a true "sourdough," the label given to an outsider who had survived a northern winter. She had also saved up plenty of gold without ever going into the diggings. But Kate was restless. When she heard rumors about even bigger strikes in the Klondike, she sold her restaurant and headed north again.

Kate rode out of town alone, leading a string of pack horses. She wore a short, split skirt, which allowed her to ride astride. Traveling through swamps thick with mosquitoes and heavy forests where she could hardly find the trail, Kate finally reached Teslin Lake. There, she planned to catch a boat to Dawson.

But a thin skim of ice already covered the lake. There were no boats in sight and it was too late to go back. Kate didn't have enough supplies to start another restaurant. Fortunately, Kate's friend Inspector Primrose heard she was in the area. The Mounties at his new camp needed a nurse. Primrose remembered that Kate had once worked in a hospital and sent her a message, asking her to come for the winter.

Although she never had any formal training as a nurse, Kate had cared for a woman in Seattle who was dying of tuberculosis before she worked at the Vancouver hospital. She accepted the inspector's offer right away, covering the sixty miles in five days. She had to cross a mountain pass in temperatures that started at minus 40 degrees and fell to minus 60 degrees.

Kate arrived safely and was soon living in her tent again. All winter, she took care of sick Mounties and did their washing, one of the worst jobs in the North. She melted snow for wash water, scrubbed the dirty clothes on a washboard, then wrung them out by hand and dried them near the stove. The Mounties were so happy to have clean shirts that they paid high prices for her labor.

The winter was incredibly difficult. The isolated settlement ran low on food. With no fresh fruit or vegetables, many people suffered from scurvy. Others developed frostbite. At Christmas, Kate added her tiny supply of six potatoes—sent by her family in New Brunswick—to make the meager dinner more festive. On the coldest nights, her loyal Mountie friends took turns loading her stove, to make sure her fire never went out.

Kate was relieved when spring came and she could walk along the rough trail to the town of Whitehorse. As soon as she arrived, she set up her tent, poked her stovepipe through the roof, and was in business again. This time, at a friend's suggestion, she posted a sign outside that read "Klondike Kate's Café." The name stuck, and she was soon known to all as "Klondike Kate."

Kate took out a free miner's license, which allowed her to pan for gold herself. She also loaned miners money to help them get started with their claims. In northern Canada and Alaska, the ground stays frozen all year, so prospectors needed extra cash to support themselves through the winter months while they built fires to melt the permafrost, then dug out the "paydirt." In the spring, they washed out the gold and Kate got her money back—along with a share of their earnings. She also invested in copper mines, continued to take in washing, and sometimes helped people who were sick, although she never charged for her nursing services.

After six months, Kate had earned enough money to build her own cabin. For the first time since she'd left Vancouver, she had walls, a floor, and curtains over the windows. At the same time, she moved her restaurant into a hotel. No more cooking or sleeping in a tent!

As the town grew, so did the crime rate. Usually, men got in trouble, but occasionally, the Northwest Mounted Police took a woman into custody. They wished they had a policewoman on the force to deal with female prisoners. When the Canadian Parliament passed a law allowing the Mounties to hire women, the Yukon detachment asked Kate Ryan to be their first "Woman Special."

Kate knew nothing about being a police officer. But then, she'd mushed a team of dogs up a river, opened restaurants, panned for gold, and performed minor surgery—all without much training. She became a Woman Special in February, 1900, exactly two years after she'd left Vancouver.

Kate stayed on in Whitehorse for many years. Like many women who left a more civilized life to follow the "call of the wild," Kate never sought fame—yet she was celebrated all over the North for her courage and her great heart. Her great-niece described Kate as "very straitlaced," yet generous to the rough miners who lived around her. According to one prospector, "Kate was known everywhere as the miner's friend. Whenever she heard that some poor man was lying sick and alone on the trail she'd get to him. . . . I've known her in the wintertime to mush in with a dog team for a hundred miles and bring a sick fellow out."

In spite of all the hardships she faced, Kate always preferred life in the wilderness. She could never be happy in cities or towns. "I love the North," she said. "It is a glorious country, and has a wonderful future." Like other unsung western heroines, Kate Ryan left her own permanent mark on the frontier.

THINK CRITICALLY

1 How did Klondike Kate become a "sourdough"? NOTE DETAILS

2 How might you have handled the hardships of Klondike Kate's journey? EXPRESS PERSONAL OPINIONS

3 Klondike Kate said about herself, "I wasn't built for going backwards. When I once step forward, I must go ahead." Did Klondike Kate describe herself accurately? Give an example to support your answer. MAKE JUDGMENTS

4 Summarize what caused Klondike Kate to become celebrated all over the north. SUMMARIZE AND PARAPHRASE

5 WRITE Write a letter from Klondike Kate to her friends in Vancouver, telling them why she wanted to stay in the north, at Whitehorse. In your letter, include details from the selection. SHORT RESPONSE

ABOUT THE AUTHOR

LIZA KETCHUM

Liza Ketchum is the author of fourteen books for young readers. She grew up in the Vermont countryside where she had few friends nearby and no television. For entertainment, she made up stories about her stuffed animals, giving each a name and personality. Her parents read many books to her, and by the time she was in second grade, she was stapling together her own books of stories and pictures. As an adult, she became fascinated by stories of pioneers. She wondered what it had been like for women and children pioneers who had traveled on the Oregon Trail or had lived during the California Gold Rush. Today, Liza Ketchum lives with her husband in Massachusetts and shares a cabin in Vermont with her two grown sons.

 www.harcourtschool.com/storytown

THE CALIFORNIA GOLD RUSH

Sourdough

by Jane Scherer illustrated by John MacDonald

Sourdough breadmakers use a portion of their starter to begin each batch of bread. They then add flour and water to replace what has been removed, and store the starter in a warm place to keep the yeast alive.

714

About five thousand years ago, in one of those lucky accidents of history, a baker left his batter out in the open air. Wild (found in the air) yeasts fell in, and when he baked his bread, the baker had a light, tender loaf. Centuries later, in California, this "sourdough" became as much a part of the gold rush as the gold itself.

No baking powder or yeast was available to the miners. People had to depend on wild yeasts, but it took time to capture them. Sometimes the yeasts were bad, and the batter had to be thrown away. Thus, every prospector took pains to save his sourdough *starter*. A miner who lost his starter might have had to walk miles to borrow some.

To keep his starter alive, a miner carried it under his shirt or in a pot strapped to his pack. On cold nights, he even took it to bed with him to keep it warm.

Traveling through the West with the miners, sourdough found its way to San Francisco. Some of the breads made there today use starters that have been kept going since the gold rush days.

To make your own sourdough starter, combine 1 tablespoon dry yeast, 2 cups unbleached white flour, and 2 cups warm water (80° F to 85° F) in a large glass jar or bowl. The mixture will be lumpy. Cover the jar and leave it on a countertop or table where it is warm. Label the jar with the date and time. Leave it alone for 3 to 4 days, then use it to make bread or some sourdough pancakes.

Connections

Comparing Texts

1. Kate Ryan learned skills that helped her earn money. What practical skills would you like to develop?

2. In "Sourdough," the discovery of sourdough is described as a lucky accident. How was sourdough a lucky accident for Kate Ryan?

3. Kate Ryan never gave up. Do you think her attitude is a good one to have? Explain.

Vocabulary Review

Word Webs

Work with a partner. Choose two Vocabulary Words. Create a web for each word. In the outer circles, write words and phrases that are related to the Vocabulary Word. Explain how each word or phrase is related to the Vocabulary Word.

shocked — dismayed

appalled

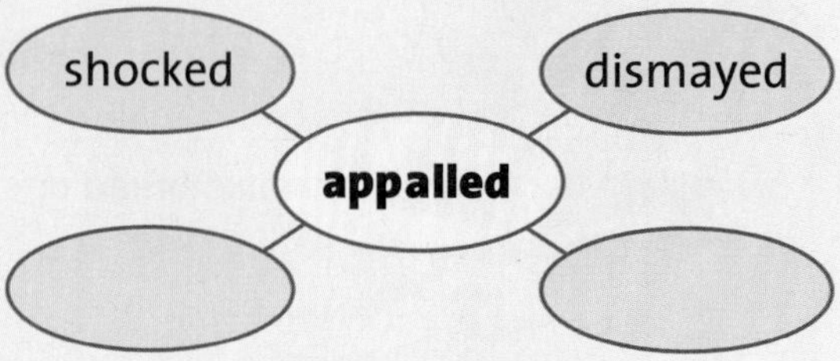

remote

laden

appalled

invest

floundered

grueling

isolated

Fluency Practice

Recorded Reading

Play "Klondike Kate" on Audiotext 6 from the beginning, on page 702 through page 703. As you listen, follow the print silently. Play the recording again. This time, practice your accuracy by reading along in a quiet voice. Keep rereading the text until you can read it with accuracy.

Writing

Write a Character Sketch

Write a character sketch of Kate Ryan. Summarize information from "Klondike Kate" and add your own interpretation of Kate Ryan.

Summary	
Paraphrase	

My Writing Checklist

Writing Trait ▶ Ideas

✔ I used a graphic organizer to summarize and paraphrase descriptions from "Klondike Kate."

✔ My writing is focused on Kate Ryan's traits.

✔ I chose specific words to help readers picture the character.

Big 💡 Idea

Authors use both facts and opinions in expository nonfiction.

Enduring ❗ Understanding

Word clues offer the evidence that supports facts and identifies opinions.

Essential ❓ Question

Why are word clues important when identifying facts and opinions?

Spelling Words

Words with Latin Word Parts

tractor	rupture
distract	audio
traction	audible
contract	audience
attract	auditorium
subtract	audition
erupt	verdict
bankrupt	diction
interrupt	dictate
abrupt	predict

Challenge

dictator	dictionary
auditor	corruption
tractable	

Fluency

Phrasing

Comprehension

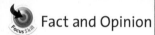

🔶 Fact and Opinion

🔶 Summarize

Robust Vocabulary

summit

accustomed

streamlined

essential

secure

acclimate

Writing

- How-to Paragraph
- Conventions

Lesson 28

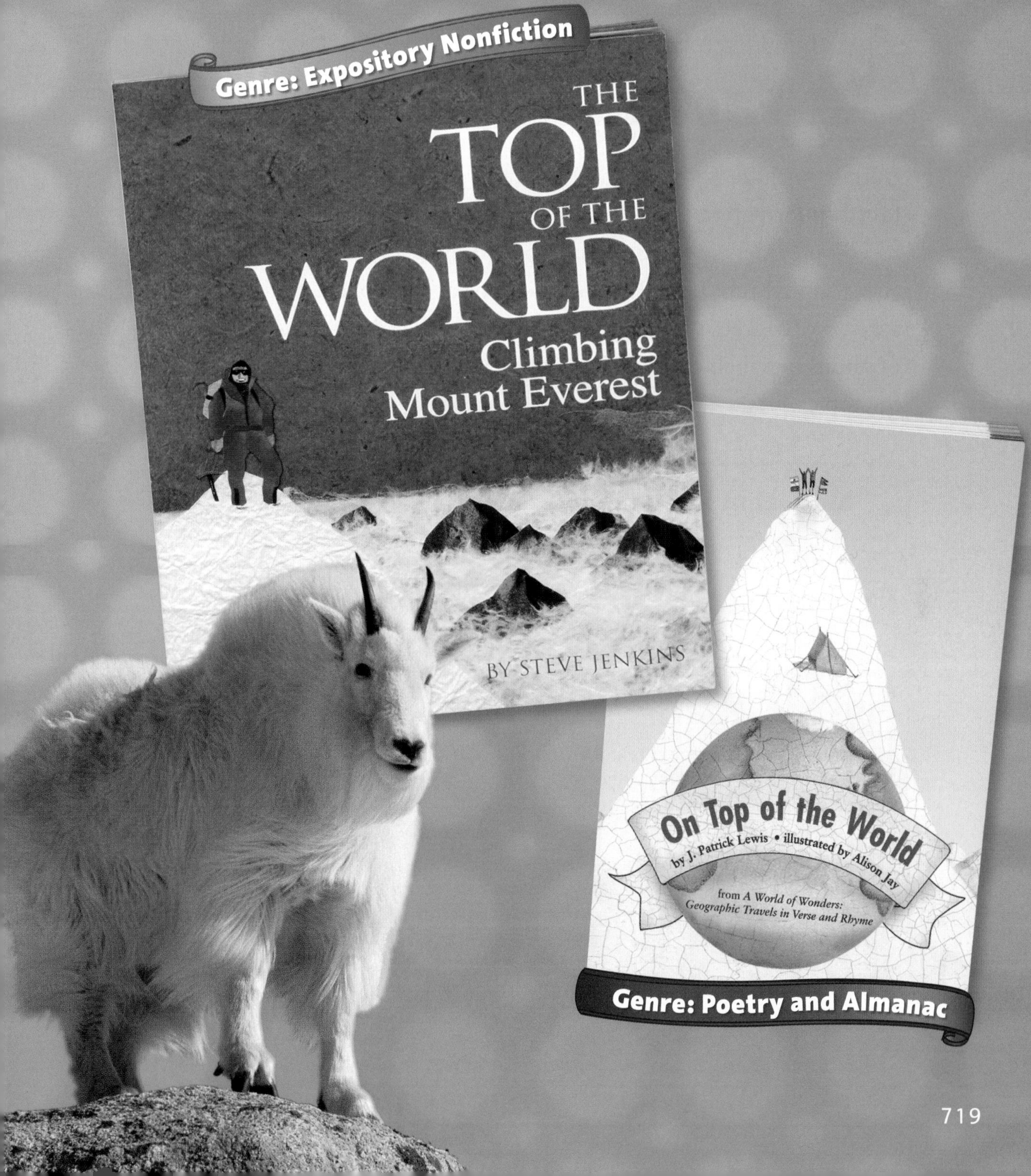
Genre: Expository Nonfiction
THE TOP OF THE WORLD
Climbing Mount Everest
BY STEVE JENKINS
On Top of the World
by J. Patrick Lewis • illustrated by Alison Jay
from A World of Wonders: Geographic Travels in Verse and Rhyme
Genre: Poetry and Almanac

Fact and Opinion

Authors include both facts and opinions in their writing. A **fact** is information that can be proved to be true. Facts are based on evidence. An **opinion** is a thought, feeling, or belief about something. Usually, opinions cannot be proved. You may agree or disagree with an author's opinion. Reading an author's opinions may help you understand the author's feelings about the topic.

Statement	Fact or Opinion?	Evidence

Tip
You can often prove the truth of a statement by checking a reliable source, such as an encyclopedia, a textbook, or a map.

Read the paragraph below. Then look at the graphic organizer. It lists statements from the paragraph, identifies them as facts or opinions, and gives evidence to support why the statement is a fact or opinion.

> Junko Tabei is the best role model young female athletes could ever have. On May 16, 1975, Tabei, who is from Japan, became the first woman to climb Mount Everest. I think Tabei's expedition was the most dangerous journey ever attempted on any mountain. An avalanche struck Tabei's camp and buried her under snow. A guide saved her life. Instead of quitting, though, Tabei continued to climb.

Statement	Fact or Opinion?	Evidence
Junko Tabei is the best role model young female athletes could ever have.	opinion	can't be proved; others may consider another athlete a better role model
Junko Tabei became the first woman to climb Mount Everest.	fact	can be proved by checking information in an encyclopedia

Try This!

How do you think the author feels about Junko Tabei? List the words and phrases that support your opinion.

GO online www.harcourtschool.com/storytown

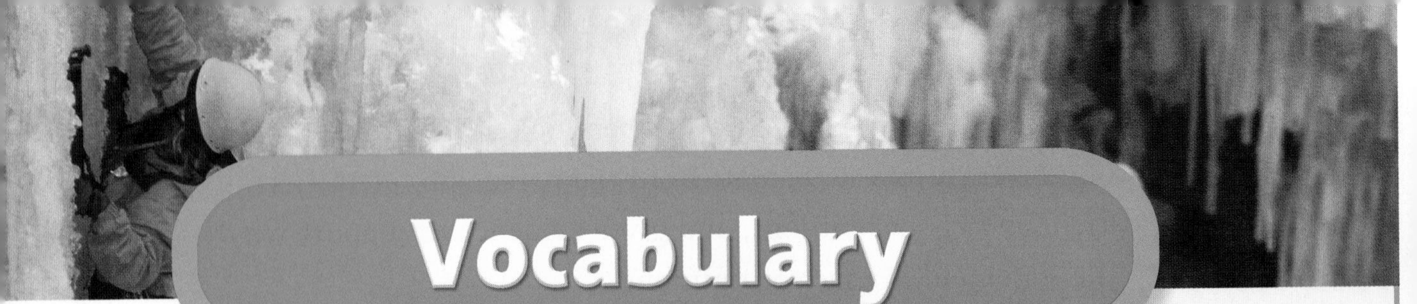

Vocabulary

Build Robust Vocabulary

- summit
- accustomed
- acclimate
- streamlined
- essential
- secure

A Mountain Mystery

There are many Mount Everest legends, but one mystery will always intrigue climbers. In 1924, two British explorers, George Mallory and Andrew Irvine, set out to climb Mount Everest. Were they the first climbers to reach the **summit**? We will never know. When George Mallory and Andrew Irvine were last seen, they were just two blurry figures climbing the mountain. No one ever saw them again. Unlike George Mallory, who was **accustomed** to the harsh conditions, Andrew Irvine had never climbed that high. Perhaps he was not able to **acclimate** to the altitude.

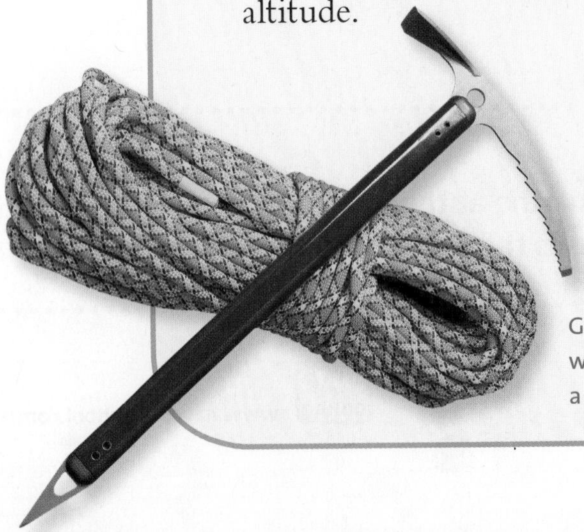

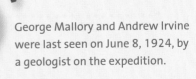

George Mallory and Andrew Irvine were last seen on June 8, 1924, by a geologist on the expedition.

Were the men lost before or after they reached the summit? Researchers have offered various explanations for the tragedy. The climbers did not have the equipment—ropes, oxygen, a tent with a **streamlined** shape—that are now considered **essential** to climbing Mount Everest. Without this equipment, the men would have been less **secure** scaling the mountain than climbers are today. They may have been trapped by an avalanche of rocks or snow. So far, though, no one can prove what happened to George Mallory and Andrew Irvine.

Mount Everest

 www.harcourtschool.com/storytown

Word Detective

Your challenge this week is to search for Vocabulary Words outside your classroom. You may hear them on television, see them in an advertisement, or read them in an adventure story. When you find a word, write it in your vocabulary journal. Remember to write where you saw it.

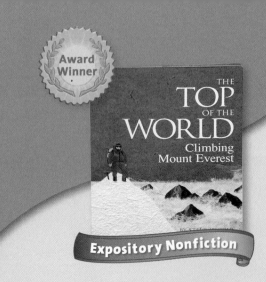

Expository Nonfiction

Genre Study

Expository nonfiction tells about real people, places, or events. As you read, look for

- vivid words and details describing a place.

- facts and information about people's experiences.

What I Know	What I Want to Know	What I Learned

Comprehension Strategy

Pause to **summarize** sections of text as you read to keep track of important ideas.

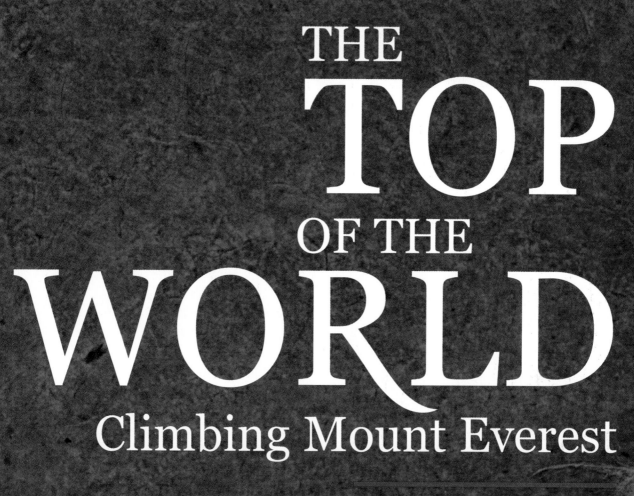

THE
TOP
OF THE
WORLD
Climbing Mount Everest

by Steve Jenkins

726

Mount Everest

Its summit is the highest point on earth, $5\frac{1}{2}$ miles above sea level. For thousands of years, the mountain has been a sacred place for those who live in its shadow. The rest of the world, however, wasn't really aware of the mountain until about 180 years ago. Ever since that time, climbers, scientists, and adventurers have been fascinated by this peak. Many have tried to climb it. Some have succeeded, but many more have failed. Some have died trying.

Mount Everest is a place of great beauty, adventure, and danger. If you ever want to climb it, here are a few things to think about.

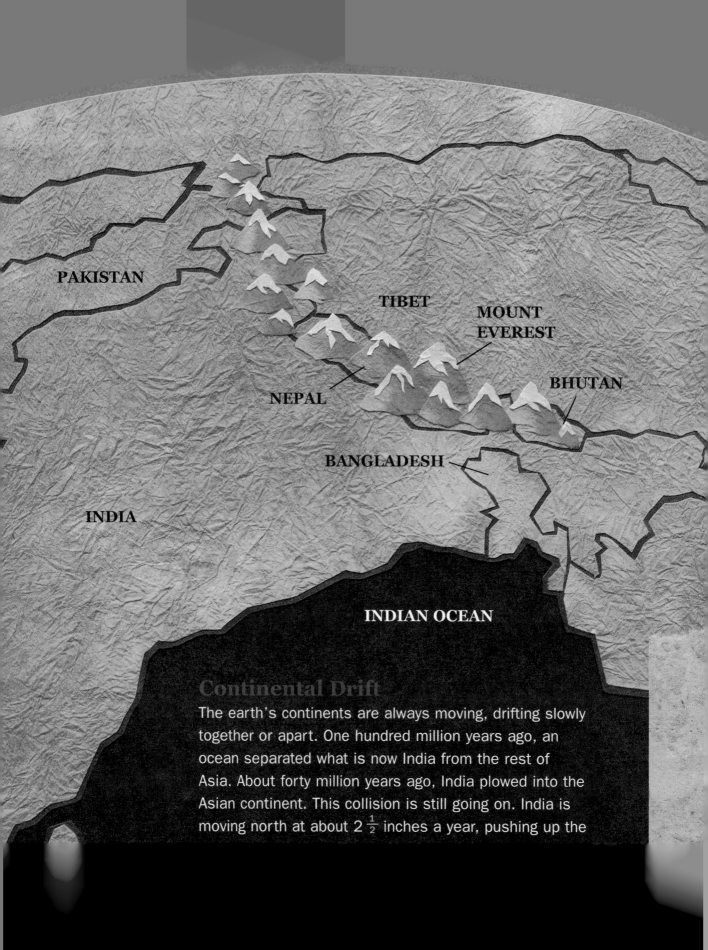

PAKISTAN

TIBET

MOUNT
EVEREST

NEPAL

BHUTAN

BANGLADESH

INDIA

INDIAN OCEAN

Continental Drift

The earth's continents are always moving, drifting slowly together or apart. One hundred million years ago, an ocean separated what is now India from the rest of Asia. About forty million years ago, India plowed into the Asian continent. This collision is still going on. India is moving north at about $2\frac{1}{2}$ inches a year, pushing up the

The Roof of the World

Rising between India and China, the Himalayas are the highest mountain range on earth. More than 1,500 miles long, the range includes many of the world's tallest peaks. The highest of them all, Mount Everest, stands on the border of Nepal and Tibet. Its summit is 29,028 feet above sea level.

Nepal, a small country that borders India, is the home of the Sherpa people. Tibet is an ancient country that is now part of China. People in Nepal and Tibet think of Mount Everest as a holy place, full of power and mystery.

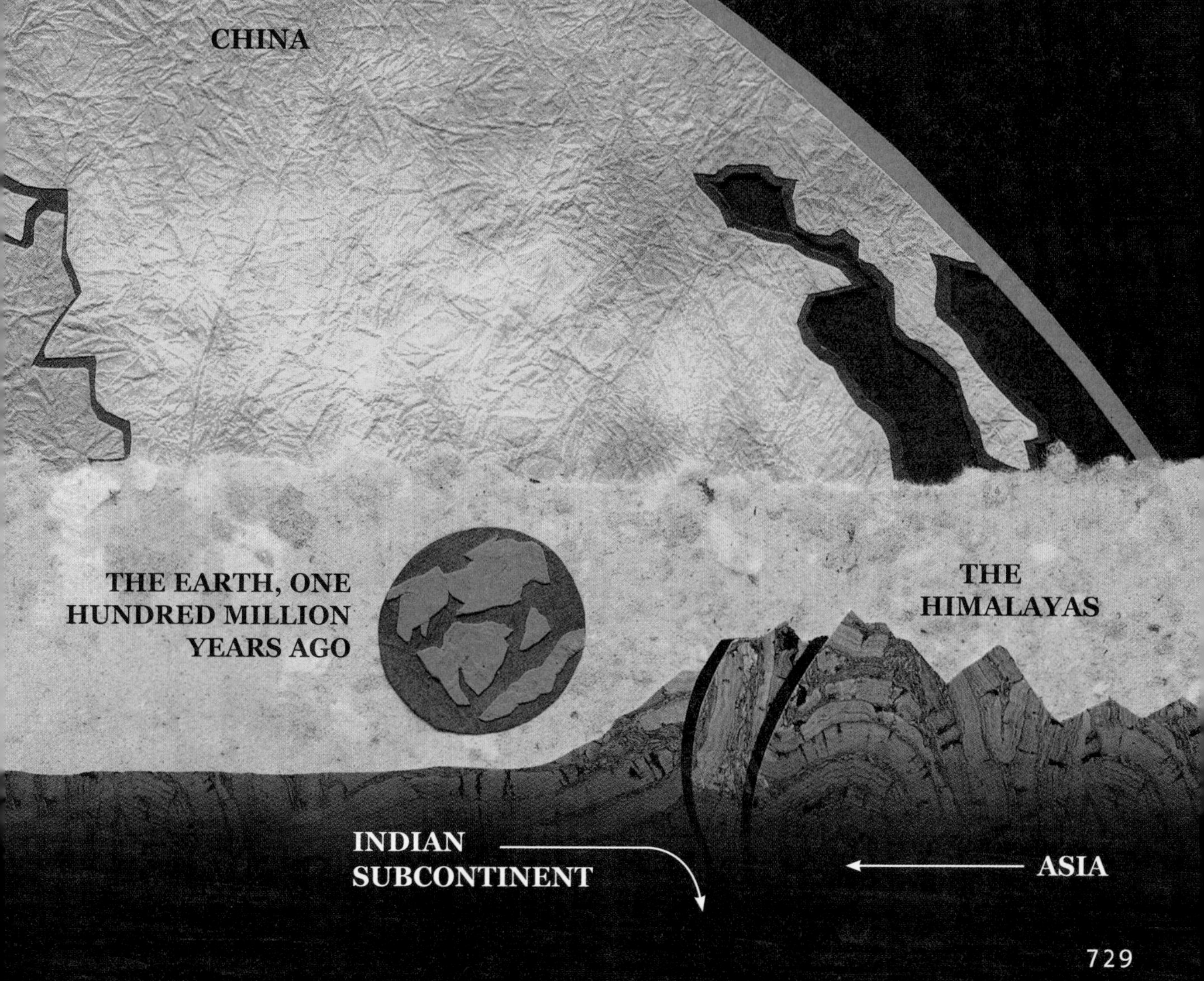

CHINA

THE EARTH, ONE HUNDRED MILLION YEARS AGO

THE HIMALAYAS

INDIAN SUBCONTINENT ⟶

ASIA ⟵

Flying In

Most expeditions to the Himalayas begin with a plane flight to Kathmandu, the capital of Nepal. Passenger jets cruise at about the same altitude as Everest's summit.

The Sherpas

Since the first British adventurers came to Nepal,
a group of native people known as Sherpas have worked
with climbers as guides and partners. They are famous
for their strength, climbing skill, and honesty.
Sherpas are born and raised in the mountains,
so they are accustomed to the altitude and
can work well high on the mountain.

Land of the Yak

Many Sherpas live by raising
yaks, animals that are closely
related to cattle. Yaks can
withstand the harsh cold of the
mountains and are often used
to help carry expedition supplies
to base camp.

731

Packing for the Trip

It takes a lot of special gear to climb Mount Everest. Here is some of the equipment you'll need.

Jumar
A device used in climbing a rope; a jumar slips easily up but cannot slide down.

Tent
It's important to take a strongly built tent with a streamlined shape that can withstand the gale-force winds and shed the heavy snow you'll probably experience on the mountain.

Ropes
On Everest, the guides or lead climbers anchor the rope above steep and dangerous sections of the route. Climbers attach themselves to the rope for safety.

Oxygen Mask and Tank
All but the strongest and most experienced climbers must use extra oxygen at the mountain's higher altitudes.

Sleeping Bag
Down-filled and warm enough for the bitter cold of the mountain, a good sleeping bag is essential for surviving the nights on Everest.

Crampons
These sets of sharp metal spikes attach to your boots to give you secure footing on icy surfaces.

Mountaineering Boots
These boots have a plastic outer shell and several layers of insulation to keep your feet warm and dry.

Radio

The members of a climbing party use radios to stay in contact with each other and to call for help in an emergency.

Stove

A reliable stove melts snow into drinking water and allows climbers to make hot tea.

Trekking Poles

Used for balance, the poles can be adjusted in length for different kinds of terrain.

Ice Ax

This multipurpose tool can be held like a walking stick for balance, used like a pick to cut footholds in the ice, or driven into the snow to keep you from sliding down the mountain after a fall. Stopping a slide in this way is called a "self-arrest."

Mittens

The inner and outer layers keep your hands warm and dry. The mittens must be extremely warm but flexible enough for you to use an ice ax and other tools.

Backpack

You'll need a good backpack to carry food, climbing equipment, and extra clothes. Since it's dangerous to remove your mittens for even a moment in the extreme cold, the zippers and storage compartments must be easy to operate.

Glacier Glasses

The sun is dangerously bright at high altitudes, especially when reflected by snow. Even a few minutes without eye protection can result in painful eye burns and make you temporarily snow-blind.

Shovel

The shovel acts as an anchor in deep snow, and is used to clear tents after snowstorms and to dig out climbers buried by avalanches.

Climbing Suit

Worn as the outermost of several layers, this down-filled one-piece suit can keep you warm at temperatures of −100°F.

Mountain Life

The temperature drops about $3\frac{1}{2}$°F for every 1,000 feet climbed, so a journey from Kathmandu to base camp is a bit like traveling from the tropics to the Arctic. Along the way, you'll see how plants and animals change with the increasing altitude.

The snow line—snow always covers the ground above this point (17,000 ft., 32°F).

Moss and lichens (13,000 ft.–17,000 ft., 39°F)

The snow leopard, the rarest of the big cats, lives on the slopes of the Himalayas.

The ibex, a Himalayan mountain goat

Small shrubs and grasses (11,000 ft.–13,000 ft., 48°F)

The tree line, the point above which it is too cold and windy for trees to grow (11,000 ft., 54°F)

Forests of rhododendron, birch, and evergreens (5,000 ft.–8,000 ft., 70°F)

(Temperatures are average summertime highs)

The Trek

It's a 100-mile trek, or hike, from Kathmandu to the base of Mount Everest. The trail leads through lush forests, over roaring rivers, and finally into a cold, rugged landscape above the tree line. During the journey, the elevation rises from 5,000 feet to over 17,000. Because there's a lot less oxygen in the air at high altitudes, many people begin to feel weak or ill as they get higher. The three-week-long trek allows your body to adjust slowly to the lack of oxygen.

Home Away from Home

Mount Everest's severe cold, high winds, and heavy snowfall make the climb possible only during a few weeks in the spring and late summer. During those times, as many as several hundred climbers, guides, doctors, Sherpas, cooks, and others live in base camp, a tent city at the foot of the mountain. Waiting here for your chance to climb the mountain helps your body to acclimate, or get used to the lack of oxygen in the air.

The Icefall

The most popular climbing route from base camp to the top of Everest, the South Summit route, passes through the Khumbu icefall. The icefall is created by the Khumbu glacier as it flows over a steep section of the mountain. Because the glacier moves two or three feet each day, the icefall is one of the most dangerous and frightening parts of the climb. Deep cracks, or crevasses, are constantly opening and closing. Huge towers of ice, called séracs, can topple over without warning. You have to cross many sections of the icefall on shaky aluminum ladders placed by the Sherpas.

Gasping for Breath

Less oxygen in each breath means you have to breathe much faster. Everyone at very high altitudes feels tired, dizzy, and weak. Some people may have more serious problems: their lungs or brain stop working properly. If this happens, they must descend to a lower altitude immediately, or they may die.

Brrr!

The constant cold adds to the challenge of high-altitude mountain climbing. At the top of Everest, typical high temperatures in summer are around –20°F. Nighttime temperatures of –100°F are common.

To make matters worse, when there's less oxygen available, it's much harder to stay warm. Well-insulated clothes are a matter of life or death on the mountain.

Summit
29,028 feet

MOUNT
EVEREST

THE
SOUTH COL
ROUTE

Up and Down

At 29,000 feet, there is only one third as much oxygen as at sea level. In fact, if someone at sea level were suddenly transported to the top of Everest, he or she would die within a few minutes from the lack of oxygen. To prepare for the extremely thin air, you must make several round trips from base camp to higher and higher points on the mountain, sometimes spending the night before starting back down. Staying for increasing periods of time high on the mountain helps keep you from getting altitude sickness on summit day.

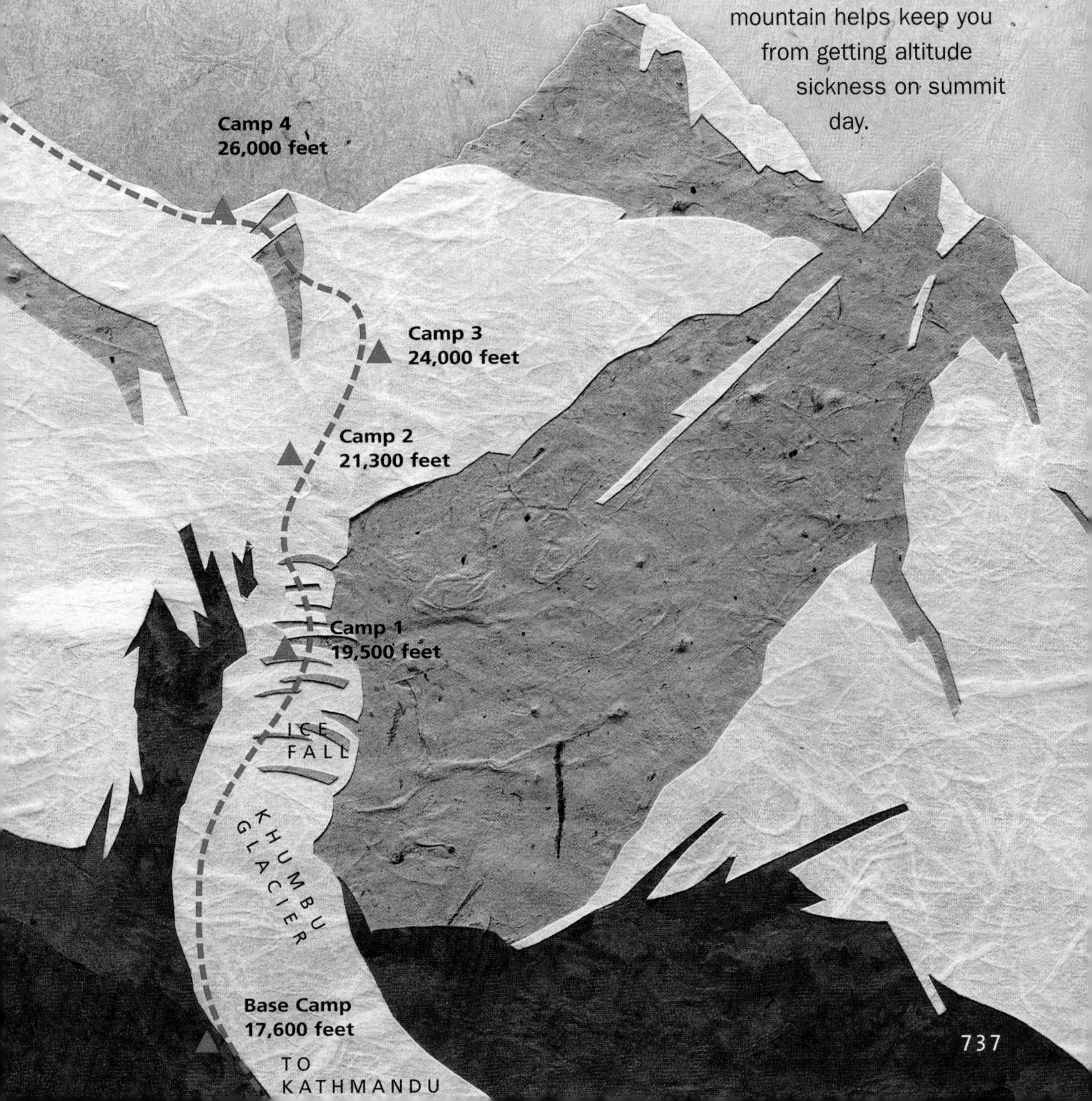

Camp 4
26,000 feet

Camp 3
24,000 feet

Camp 2
21,300 feet

Camp 1
19,500 feet

ICE
FALL

K H U M B U
G L A C I E R

Base Camp
17,600 feet

TO
KATHMANDU

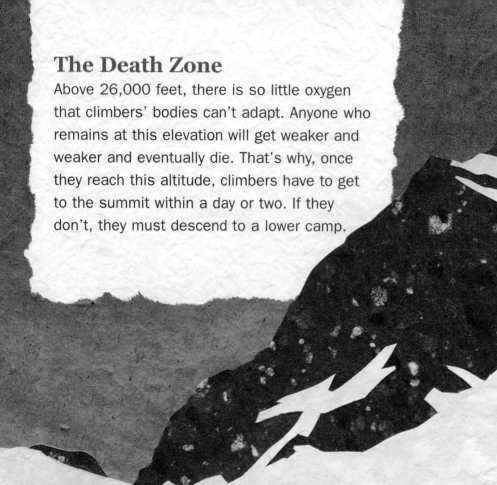

The Death Zone

Above 26,000 feet, there is so little oxygen that climbers' bodies can't adapt. Anyone who remains at this elevation will get weaker and weaker and eventually die. That's why, once they reach this altitude, climbers have to get to the summit within a day or two. If they don't, they must descend to a lower camp.

Summit Day

It can take more than twelve hours to climb to the top from Camp 4. Since it's critical to make it back to camp before dark, climbers usually set out before midnight, and climb through the night by the light of a headlamp. With luck, these climbers will be on top the following noon.

The Summit

When you stand on top of Mount Everest, you are the highest thing on earth. For most people, reaching this point is the reward for years of hard work and planning. You can't stay long, though. Your body needs oxygen, which means getting back to a lower altitude quickly. Because you're so exhausted, the descent is one of the most dangerous parts of the climb, so you'll have to be very careful on the way down.

Think Critically

1 What causes people to feel weak as they climb Mount Everest? NOTE DETAILS

2 Is the statement "Mount Everest is a place of great beauty, adventure, and danger" a fact or an opinion? How do you know? FACT AND OPINION

3 How do the diagrams and illustrations that the author includes help you better understand the text? GRAPHIC AIDS

4 The author describes the special gear a climber needs when trekking on Mount Everest. What is another situation in which you need special equipment or tools? PRIOR KNOWLEDGE

5 **WRITE** Summarize some of the changes you would witness or experience as you trekked from Kathmandu to the top of Mount Everest. Use details from the text and diagrams to support your answer. SHORT RESPONSE

About the Author and Illustrator
Steve Jenkins

Steve Jenkins's father encouraged him to explore the natural world. When he was young, Steve Jenkins thought he would be a scientist. Instead, he became a graphic designer. He says he feels "incredibly lucky to have found a way to unite my early interest in science and my chosen career of creating art." Steve Jenkins has a strong interest in the Himalayas. He considers himself an "armchair adventurer," meaning that he reads many adventure books. He says, "*Everest* allowed me to introduce climate, geology, geography, continental drift, altitude, and history in a book that is both an adventure and a survival story."

GO online www.harcourtschool.com/storytown

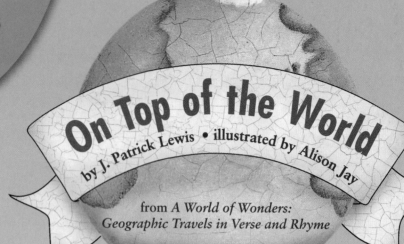

On Top of the World
by J. Patrick Lewis • illustrated by Alison Jay

from A World of Wonders:
Geographic Travels in Verse and Rhyme

Five miles from earth, they set up camp.
A vicious wind tore at their tent.
They ate sardines, drank melted snow
Before they made the last ascent.

Exhausted, short of breath, the men
Climbed up the final razor wall.
On top now, looking down, they saw

India,

Tibet,

Sikkim,

Nepal!

And Tenzing raised four flags

for they had conquered

Everest

after all.

Edmund Hillary and Tenzing Norgay
First men to climb Mount Everest
The Himalayas
29,028 feet May 29, 1953

Top 5 Highest U.S. Mountains
(by elevation)

Mt. McKinley
Alaska
20,320 ft
(6,194 m)

Mt. St. Elias
Alaska-Yukon
18,008 ft
(5,489 m)

Mt. Foraker
Alaska
17,400 ft
(5,304 m)

Mt. Bond
Alaska
16,550 ft
(5,044 m)

Mt. Blackburn
Alaska
16,390 ft
(4,996 m)

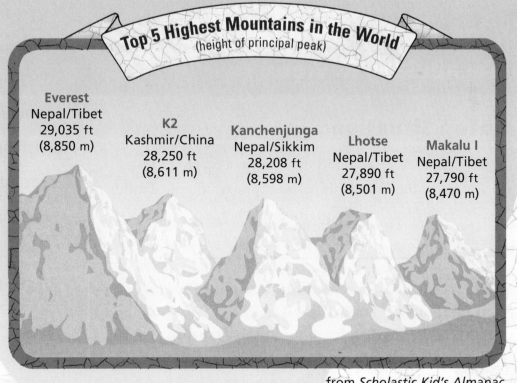

Top 5 Highest Mountains in the World
(height of principal peak)

Everest
Nepal/Tibet
29,035 ft
(8,850 m)

K2
Kashmir/China
28,250 ft
(8,611 m)

Kanchenjunga
Nepal/Sikkim
28,208 ft
(8,598 m)

Lhotse
Nepal/Tibet
27,890 ft
(8,501 m)

Makalu I
Nepal/Tibet
27,790 ft
(8,470 m)

from *Scholastic Kid's Almanac*

Connections

Comparing Texts

1. Do you agree that only expert climbers should be allowed to climb Mount Everest? Why or why not?

2. How do the poem, the almanac entries, and the main selection each express people's interest in Earth's mountains?

3. Which lessons from "The Top of the World: Climbing Mount Everest" could be useful in other kinds of situations?

Vocabulary Review

Rate a Situation

With a partner, read aloud each sentence below. Point to a spot on the line to show how prepared you would feel in each situation. Explain your choices.

Least
Prepared ———————————————— Most
Prepared

- You had a checklist of **essential** equipment.
- You forgot your **streamlined** tent.
- You lost the map of the route to the **summit**.
- You were **accustomed** to the harsh conditions you faced.

summit

accustomed

secure

streamlined

essential

acclimate

Fluency Practice

Repeated Reading

Choose a page from the selection. Look at the punctuation marks for clues that tell you when to pause between groups of words. Read the passage aloud several times until you are satisfied with your phrasing.

Writing

Write an Expository Paragraph

Write a paragraph explaining how the Himalayas formed. Use information from reference sources and the main selection in your writing.

What I Know	What I Want to Know	What I Learned

My Writing Checklist

Writing Trait → Conventions

✓ I used a chart to plan my writing.

✓ I used information from the main selection and reference sources in my writing.

✓ I used correct spelling and grammar in my paragraph.

Big Idea

A biography contains both facts and opinions about a person.

Enduring Understanding

Readers use prior knowledge and word clues to distinguish between the facts and the opinions of authors.

Essential Question

How do readers determine if a text is based on fact or opinion?

Spelling Words

Borrowed Words

banana	chlorine
chimpanzee	kayak
yogurt	parka
almanac	balcony
syrup	replica
cousin	anchor
stomach	urban
language	coyote
foyer	chocolate
acronym	vanilla

Challenge

bronco	plaza
éclair	petite
alligator	

Fluency

Phrasing

Comprehension

 Fact and Opinion

 Summarize

Robust Vocabulary

- ignited
- squinting
- jettisoned
- tranquility
- cramped
- potentially

Writing

- Essay of Explanation
- Conventions

Lesson 29

Genre: Biography

By Bea Uusma Schyffert

the man who went to the far side of the moon

The Story of Apollo 11 Astronaut Michael Collins

THE SPACE RACE

Genre: Time Line

Focus Skill

Fact and Opinion

You have learned that a **fact** is a piece of information that can be proved. An **opinion** is a thought, feeling, or belief about something. Remember that authors may include opinions in nonfiction text. When you read nonfiction, be careful not to mistake opinions for facts.

Statement	Fact or Opinion?	Evidence

Tip

Adjectives such as *greatest* often signal an opinion.

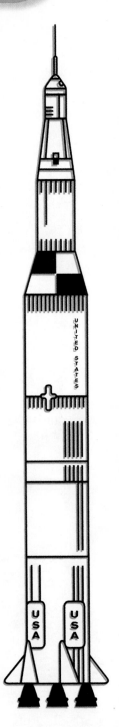

Read the paragraph below. The graphic organizer shows a fact and an opinion found in the paragraph. It points out that the opinion cannot be proved. It also shows how the fact can be proved.

> Robert Goddard was the greatest scientist who ever lived. When he said that a rocket would someday reach the moon, many people laughed at him. They did not realize how important his work would turn out to be. In 1926, he invented and tested the first successful liquid-fuel rocket. If it hadn't been for Goddard, people never would have landed on the moon.

Statement	Fact or Opinion?	Evidence
Goddard was the greatest scientist who ever lived.	opinion	This statement cannot be proved.
Goddard created the first liquid-fuel rocket in 1926.	fact	This statement can be checked by looking in a science book.

Try This!

Find another opinion statement in the paragraph. What phrase helped you know that the statement is an opinion?

www.harcourtschool.com/storytown

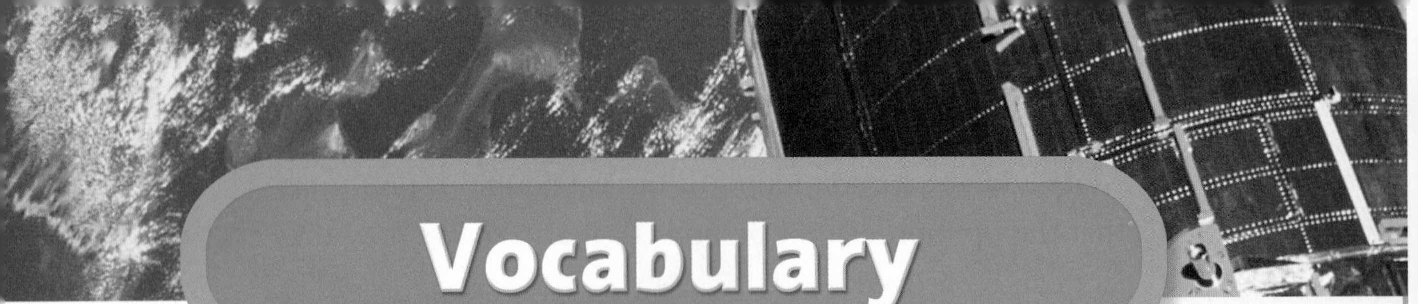

Vocabulary

Build Robust Vocabulary

- ignited
- potentially
- squinting
- tranquility
- cramped
- jettisoned

Dining in Space

Almost Like Home

From the time their rocket's fuel is **ignited** until the moment their spacecraft returns to Earth, today's astronauts **potentially** enjoy the same kinds of meals they dine on at home. They may eat steaming scrambled eggs for breakfast, or gooey macaroni and cheese for lunch.

Squinting into the darkness, astronauts can enjoy the **tranquility** of space and a cup of hot tea.

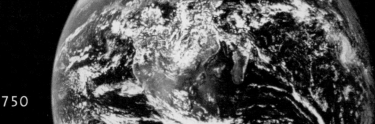

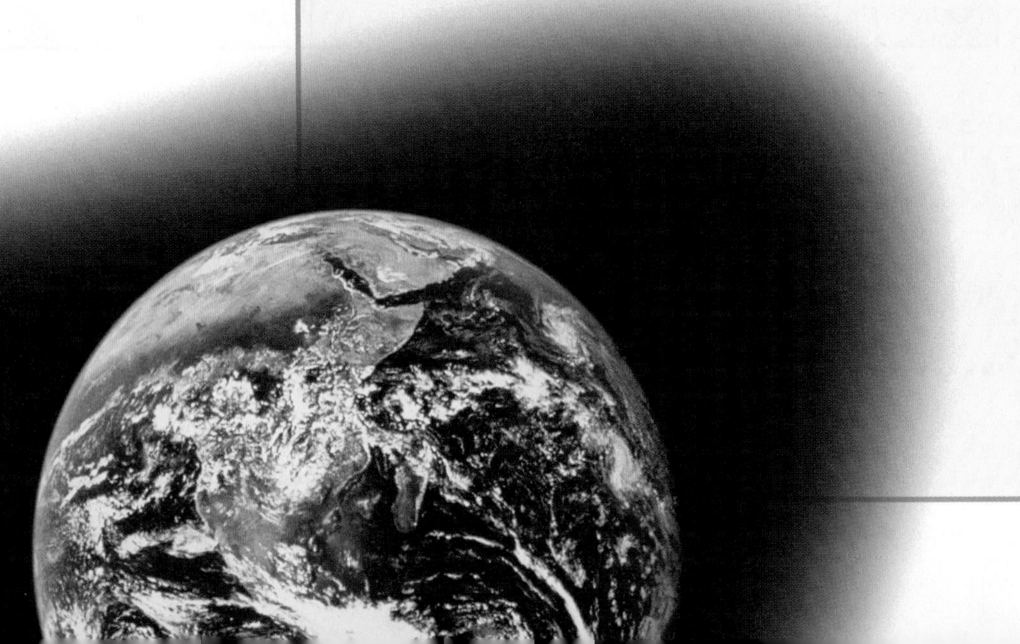

Dining In

On the space shuttles, room is limited. Astronauts eat in **cramped** spaces with food trays strapped to their legs. In contrast, the interior of the International Space Station is large and can even accommodate a dining table. Footholds beneath the table allow astronauts to sit down to a meal and not float away! When they have finished eating, some trash is **jettisoned** into outer space. However, in the future, full recycling may be possible.

The International Space Station has enough room to allow astronauts to eat comfortably.

 www.harcourtschool.com/storytown

Word Champion

 Your challenge this week is to use Vocabulary Words outside your classroom. Keep the list of words in a place at home where you can see it. Use as many of the Vocabulary Words as you can when you speak with family members and friends. For example, you might ask you mother to describe a place where she finds tranquility. Write in your vocabulary journal the words you used, and tell how you used them.

Award Winner

the man
who went to
the far side
of the moon
The Story of Apollo 11 Astronaut Michael Collins

By Bea Uusma Schyffert

Biography

Genre Study

A biography is a written account of a person's life, told by someone else. As you read, look for

- opinions and personal judgments based on facts.

- events presented in time order.

What I Know	What I Want to Know	What I Learned

Comprehension Strategy

Pause to **summarize** sections of text as you read to keep track of important ideas.

752

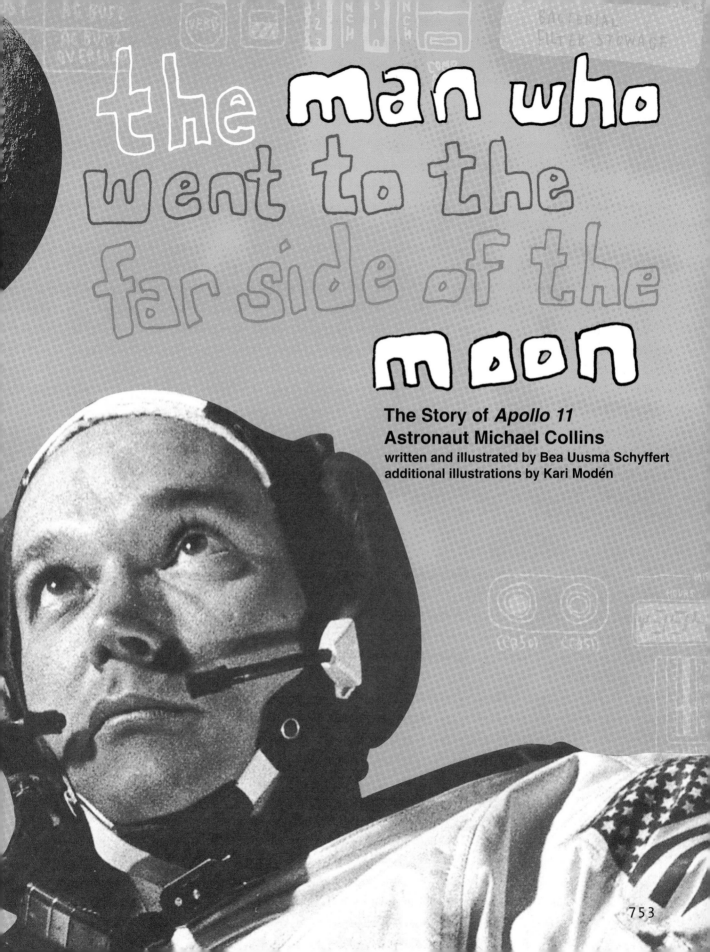

the man who went to the far side of the moon

moon

The Story of *Apollo 11*
Astronaut Michael Collins
written and illustrated by Bea Uusma Schyffert
additional illustrations by Kari Modén

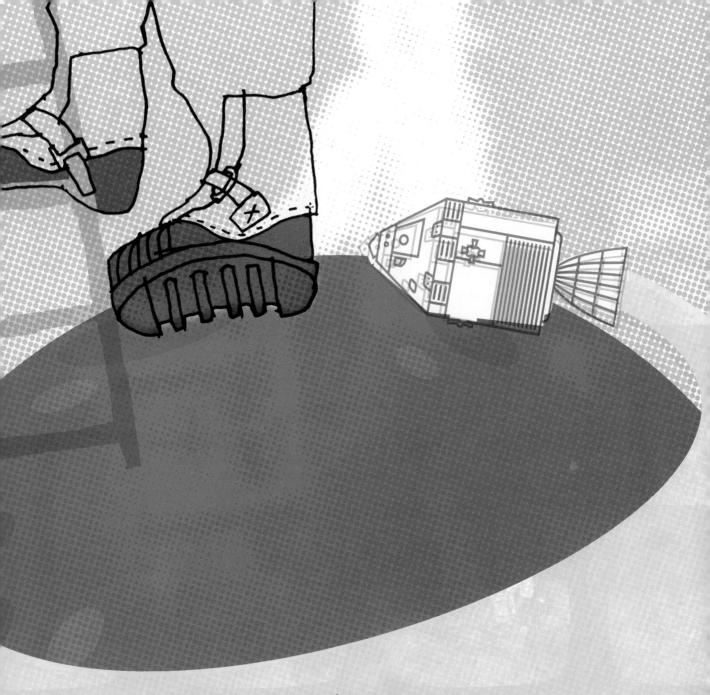

ASTRONAUT Neil Armstrong's heart is beating 156 times per minute as he lands the lunar module on the moon with only 45 seconds left of fuel. He opens the hatch. He climbs down the ladder, slowly. One-fifth of the Earth's population are sitting in front of their TV sets, holding their breath, as Neil Armstrong carefully sets the first footprint in the lunar dust.

Meanwhile—on the other side of the moon—a small spacecraft, named *Columbia*, orbits in the darkness. Inside the silvery craft sits Michael Collins. He will never walk on the moon. His task is to maneuver the capsule and wait while Neil Armstrong and Buzz Aldrin land the lunar module. He can't even hear Neil and Buzz over the radio. No one is farther away from Earth than he is. For 14 lonely turns, Michael Collins circles the moon. Each time he reaches the far side of the moon he spends 48 minutes without radio communication. The only thing between him and outer space is some insulation and a thin sheet of metal.

As he disappears into the shadow of the far side of the moon, Michael Collins thinks to himself that he sees a new color. The darkness outside the windows of the capsule can't be described by any earthly name. "Black" is not enough. Because there is no light, he can no longer see the surface of the moon, but he knows it's there because in that part of the sky there are no stars. They are blocked by the moon.

Circling the moon, turn after turn, he waits for Neil and Buzz to finish up down there. The windows of the capsule have misted over. The walls are squeaking a little. He has brought a camera. He takes pictures of his stubbled face. He talks into a tape recorder. He thinks about his family. He says his children's names aloud, slowly. Kate. Ann. Michael.

Before Neil and Buzz can take off from the moon and return to the capsule, Michael has to make 850 computer commands. Surrounding him on the walls of the capsule are more than 700 switches, levers, alarm buttons, gauges, warning lights, and computer keys. There are sensors that should never, *ever*, point to red. There are yellow-and-black-striped buttons with functions so important that they are covered with plastic lids to prevent a tired, lonely astronaut from pushing them by mistake.

The president calls Neil and Buzz on the moon. No one calls Michael. When he is on the far side of the moon, radio transmission from Earth is not even possible.

BLAST OFF!

It is July 16, 1969. A Wednesday. Although it is only half past nine in the morning, it is already 86°F (30°C) outside. One million people have gathered at Kennedy Space Center in Florida. There are people as far as the eye can see, sitting beside their campers and tents, scattered among the dunes, on picnic blankets and folding chairs. Many are still stuck in traffic on the highway.

The rocket *Saturn 5* is standing on Launch Pad 39A. It is the largest rocket ever built. It is larger than a football field set on end. In the very top of the rocket, inside the spacecraft, three astronauts are securely fastened in their seats. So far, 23 American astronauts and 17 Soviet cosmonauts have been sent into space, but this is the first time anyone will try to land on the moon. For more than 10 years, the United States and the Soviet Union have been racing to see who will get there first.

Michael Collins, Buzz Aldrin, and Neil Armstrong have written farewell letters to their wives and children. The envelopes will be opened only if the astronauts do not return.

The air is still at Launch Pad 39A.

At 09:31:51 the engines are ignited.

At 09:32:00 the rocket takes off from the ground.

Space is 11 minutes and 42 seconds away. That is the time it takes before Earth releases its grip on the rocket, propelling it into weightlessness.

Down on the ground, one million people are squinting at the spacecraft, now just a spot in the sky, watching it get smaller and smaller. Within moments it is lost from sight. Then it is gone altogether. People get up, fold their blankets, and head for their cars, going home or back to work. Everything is back to normal again. For everyone, except for three people.

apollo 11
round-trip to the moon

1 LIFTOFF: THE ROCKET TAKES OFF WITH *APOLLO 11*. THE FIRST AND SECOND ROCKET STAGES ARE IGNITED AND SEPARATED. THE THIRD ROCKET STAGE IS IGNITED. *APOLLO 11* GOES INTO EARTH ORBIT PHASE.

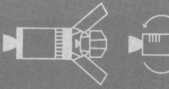
2 THE THIRD ROCKET STAGE IS REIGNITED TO PROPEL *APOLLO 11* TOWARD THE MOON. THE ROCKET STAGE IS THEN SEPARATED. THE COMMAND AND SERVICE MODULE TURNS AROUND BY FIRING SMALL ROCKET THRUSTERS . . .

3 . . . AND DOCKS WITH THE LUNAR MODULE.

4 THE COMMAND AND SERVICE MODULE TRAVELS THE ENTIRE WAY TO THE MOON WITH THE LUNAR MODULE CONNECTED TO ITS FRONT.

5 ALMOST THERE: NEIL AND BUZZ CLIMB INTO THE LUNAR MODULE, WHICH THEN UNDOCKS FROM THE COMMAND AND SERVICE MODULE. MICHAEL STAYS IN LUNAR ORBIT IN THE COMMAND MODULE AS THE LUNAR MODULE DESCENDS TO THE MOON.

6 THE LUNAR MODULE ASCENDS FROM THE MOON AND DOCKS WITH THE COMMAND AND SERVICE MODULE. NEIL AND BUZZ CLIMB BACK INTO THE SPACECRAFT. THE LUNAR MODULE IS JETTISONED AND CRASHES ON THE MOON.

7 THE SPACECRAFT RETURNS TO EARTH. RIGHT BEFORE REENTRY INTO EARTH'S ATMOS-PHERE, THE SERVICE MODULE IS SEPARATED. THE COMMAND MODULE TURNS AROUND AND TRAVELS THROUGH THE ATMOSPHERE FOR 14 MINUTES.

8 THE COMMAND MODULE SPLASHES DOWN IN THE OCEAN WITH PARACHUTES.

The interior of the spacecraft *Columbia* is as small as the inside of an ordinary car. The capsule is the astronauts' living room, office, kitchen, bedroom, and bathroom. It is equipped with 15 miles (24 kilometers) of power cables. It is made of two million pieces. This means that even if 99.9 percent of all the components were working, there would still be 2,000 broken pieces.

Despite the fact that the capsule is so small, it is easy to lose things due to weightlessness. Since everything floats away as soon as it is put down, the astronauts have attached hundreds of Velcro pieces to the walls of the capsule to hold lists, pens, sunglasses, star maps, and packs of gum.

Maximum speed of the spacecraft between Earth and moon:
    25,000 miles (40,000 kilometers) per hour
At splashdown in the ocean: 25 miles (40 kilometers) per hour
Travel time to the moon: 3 days, 4 hours
Travel time from the moon: 2 days, 12 hours
    (homebound travel is quicker due to Earth's gravity)

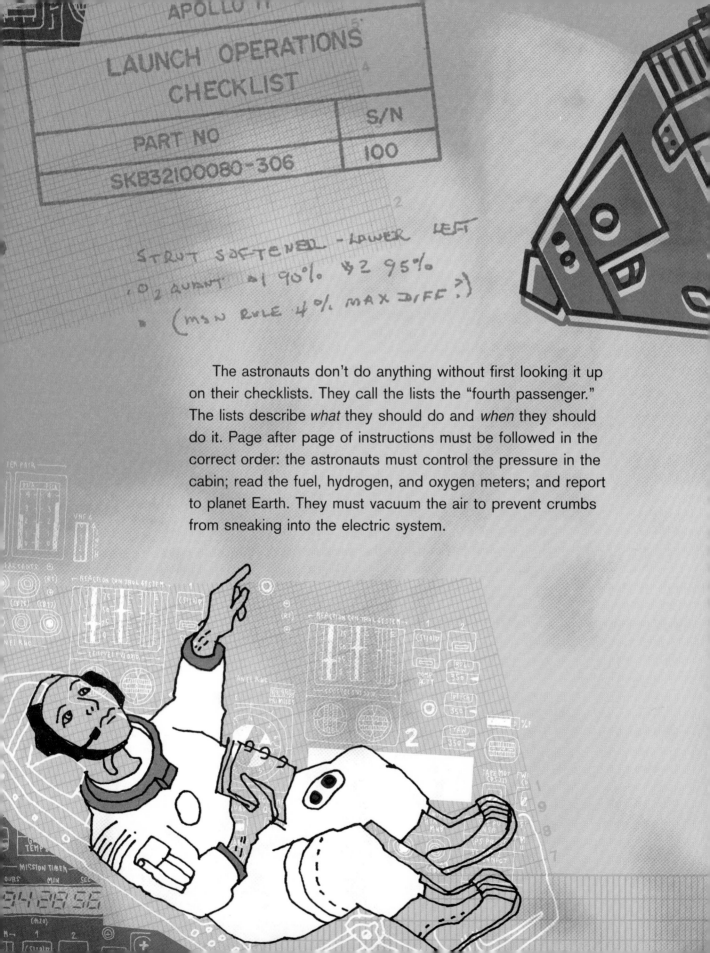

APOLLO 11
LAUNCH OPERATIONS
CHECKLIST

PART NO	S/N
SKB32100080-306	100

STRUT SOFTENER - LOWER LEFT
O₂ QUANT. 1 90% #2 95%
(MSN RULE 4% MAX DIFF ?)

The astronauts don't do anything without first looking it up on their checklists. They call the lists the "fourth passenger." The lists describe *what* they should do and *when* they should do it. Page after page of instructions must be followed in the correct order: the astronauts must control the pressure in the cabin; read the fuel, hydrogen, and oxygen meters; and report to planet Earth. They must vacuum the air to prevent crumbs from sneaking into the electric system.

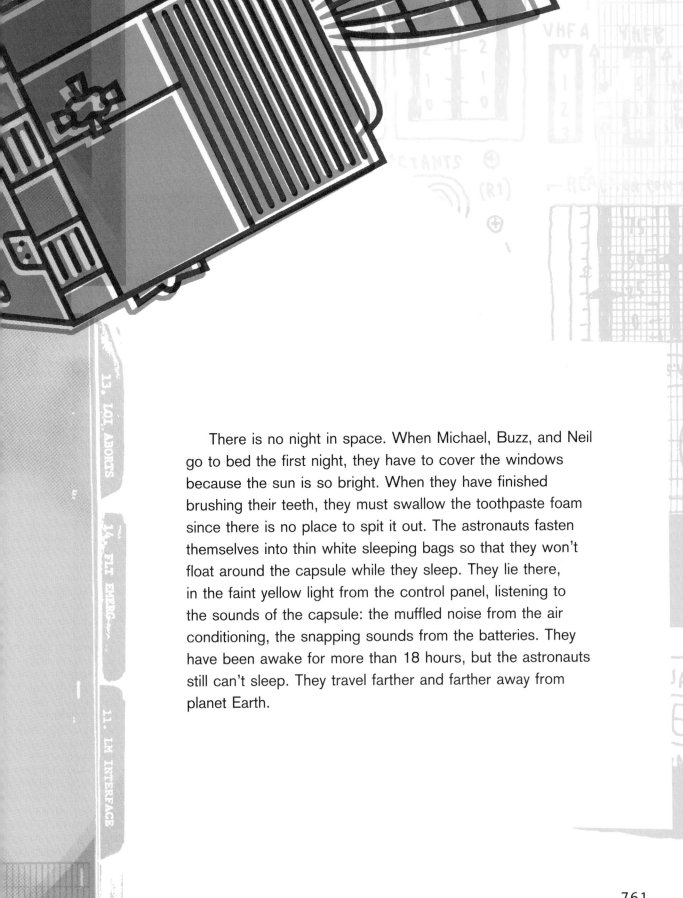

There is no night in space. When Michael, Buzz, and Neil go to bed the first night, they have to cover the windows because the sun is so bright. When they have finished brushing their teeth, they must swallow the toothpaste foam since there is no place to spit it out. The astronauts fasten themselves into thin white sleeping bags so that they won't float around the capsule while they sleep. They lie there, in the faint yellow light from the control panel, listening to the sounds of the capsule: the muffled noise from the air conditioning, the snapping sounds from the batteries. They have been awake for more than 18 hours, but the astronauts still can't sleep. They travel farther and farther away from planet Earth.

On the moon

It is July 20, 1969. A Sunday. It's four minutes to ten in the morning. It is -250°F (-180°C) in the shade and +250°F (+120°C) in the sun at the Sea of Tranquility, where Neil and Buzz have landed the *Eagle*. They are 242,000 miles (390,000 kilometers) from Launch Pad 39A at Kennedy Space Center in Florida.

In the earliest versions of the checklists, Buzz Aldrin would be the first man to step down onto the moon. But the lunar module hatch opens inward to the right, and Buzz, who stood right behind it, had difficulty climbing out. When the astronauts tried to switch places during practice, they damaged the cramped cabin. A few months before the launch, it was decided that Neil should go first. He crawls backward through a tiny hatch near the floor. As he looks toward the horizon, he can see that they have landed on a sphere: the horizon is a little bent since the moon is so small. His arms are covered with goose bumps. There is no air. No sound. No life. No footprints.

Wait: now there is one.

Neil Armstrong is the first man on the moon.

Neil and Buzz stay on the moon for 21 hours and 36 minutes, but only a little more than 2 hours of that time is spent outside the lunar module. They perform three minor experiments and load two aluminum suitcases with 48 pounds (22 kilograms) of moon dust and rocks.

When they have climbed back into the lunar module and shut the hatch, they take their helmets off. They look at each other because they both sense a strong smell. Neil thinks it smells like wet ashes. Buzz says it smells like spent gunpowder. It is the moon. The moon has a smell.

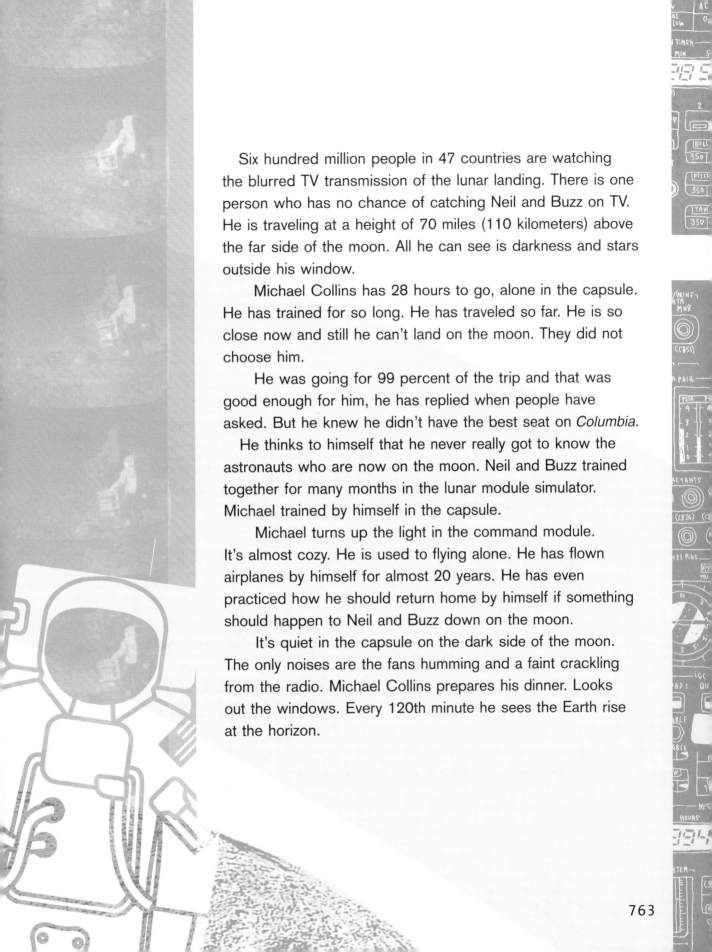

Six hundred million people in 47 countries are watching the blurred TV transmission of the lunar landing. There is one person who has no chance of catching Neil and Buzz on TV. He is traveling at a height of 70 miles (110 kilometers) above the far side of the moon. All he can see is darkness and stars outside his window.

Michael Collins has 28 hours to go, alone in the capsule. He has trained for so long. He has traveled so far. He is so close now and still he can't land on the moon. They did not choose him.

He was going for 99 percent of the trip and that was good enough for him, he has replied when people have asked. But he knew he didn't have the best seat on *Columbia*.

He thinks to himself that he never really got to know the astronauts who are now on the moon. Neil and Buzz trained together for many months in the lunar module simulator. Michael trained by himself in the capsule.

Michael turns up the light in the command module. It's almost cozy. He is used to flying alone. He has flown airplanes by himself for almost 20 years. He has even practiced how he should return home by himself if something should happen to Neil and Buzz down on the moon.

It's quiet in the capsule on the dark side of the moon. The only noises are the fans humming and a faint crackling from the radio. Michael Collins prepares his dinner. Looks out the windows. Every 120th minute he sees the Earth rise at the horizon.

It is July 24, 1969. A Thursday. Ever since they left the moon, the astronauts have been eager to get back home. After 8 days, 3 hours, and 18 minutes in *Columbia* without washing, the entire body itches. It is hard to breathe in the spacecraft now. It smells like wet dogs and rotten swamp. Michael Collins has flown *Columbia* during reentry into the Earth's atmosphere. For 14 minutes, the astronauts have been pushed down into their seats. They have weighed seven times their weight on Earth. Now the capsule has splashed down in the ocean near Hawaii.

No one knows if the astronauts have been exposed to dangerous lunar germs that could potentially wipe out the human race. Because of this they are sent straight to a quarantine facility: a silver-colored mobile home. Inside, the astronauts write reports about their trip. Michael beats Neil in cards. As they sit there, bored as can be, they begin to understand just what they have experienced. During the trip itself they were so focused on their job that they didn't have time to think about what they have actually done. Everyone on Earth gathered together because of the moon landing. But the astronauts themselves have been far, far away.

As they watch a taped recording of the moon landing, Buzz suddenly turns to Neil and says: "Neil, we missed the whole thing!"

In the past, Michael Collins never really cared about the machines he has flown, but this time it's different. On the second night of quarantine, he climbs back into *Columbia* and takes a seat. Then he leans over and scribbles a message in ballpoint pen on the capsule wall, in the tiniest handwriting imaginable:

SPACECRAFT 107— ALIAS APOLLO 11— ALIAS COLUMBIA
THE BEST SHIP TO COME DOWN THE LINE
GOD BLESS HER
MICHAEL COLLINS, CMP

To find out if the astronauts are carrying deadly germs, mice are let into the quarantine trailer. The mice have grown up in a germ-free laboratory. After 17 days the astronauts are let out. For the first time in a month they breathe fresh air. If the mice had died, Michael Collins, Buzz Aldrin, and Neil Armstrong might still be quarantined.

When Michael Collins returned from the moon, he made a decision to never travel again. He wanted to spend the rest of his life fishing, bringing up his children, taking care of his dogs, and sitting on the porch with his wife.

Sometimes, when he's talking to other people, the thought strikes him: I have been to places and done things that no one can ever imagine. I will never be able to explain what it was like. I carry it inside, like a treasure.

At night, Michael Collins tends to the roses in his garden at the back of his house. The soil smells good. The wind feels warm and humid against his face. He looks up at the yellow disk in the sky and thinks to himself: I have been there. It was beautiful, but compared to Earth it was nothing.

He never wants to go back to the moon.

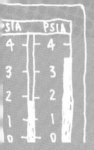

think critically

1 Look at the chart on page 758. What happened right after Neil Armstrong and Buzz Aldrin climbed back into the spacecraft? SEQUENCE

2 Does Michael Collins prefer Earth or the moon? How do you know? NOTE DETAILS

3 While Collins was alone on the far side of the moon, he thought about his family and the darkness around him, and he took pictures of himself. If you had been in that situation, how would you have spent your time? MAKE CONNECTIONS

4 At the beginning of the selection, the author tells readers that one-fifth of the world watched the moon landing on television. Is this statement a fact or an opinion? What was the author's purpose for including it? FACT AND OPINION

5 **WRITE** Compare and contrast Michael Collins's experience in going to the moon with the experiences of Neil Armstrong and Buzz Aldrin. Use information and details from the story to explain
- how the experiences of the three astronauts were SIMILAR.
- how their experiences were DIFFERENT. EXTENDED RESPONSE

About the Author/Illustrator

Bea Uusma Schyffert

Bea Uusma Schyffert became a writer and an illustrator so that she could learn more about any topic that interested her. She spent several years researching and drawing space topics before writing *The Man Who Went to the Far Side of the Moon.* She also went with a polar expedition to prepare for a book about polar explorers and the Arctic.

About the Illustrator

Kari Modén

Kari Modén is a Swedish illustrator who loved drawing horses as a child. As she grew older, she never stopped drawing and now she works as an illustrator for many Swedish and international companies. She has a simple graphic style and loves working with both black and white and with strong colors.

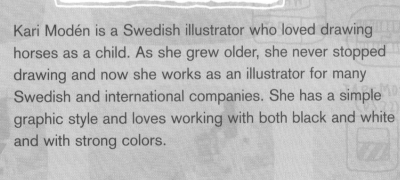

 www.harcourtschool.com/storytown

Science

Time Line

The first human-made object in space was *Sputnik 1*. When the Russian satellite made its debut on October 4, 1957, its steady "beep, beep" sent the United States into a tizzy. Until that day, Americans assumed that they had the technological edge in the Cold War with Russia (then the Soviet Union). *Sputnik 1* launched a "space race" between the two countries, taking humans to the moon and making the U.S. a leader in space.

November 3, 1957

Russia follows up on *Sputnik 1* with *Sputnik 2*, in which a small dog named Laika becomes the first live animal in orbit. These advances prompt U.S. fears that Russia will conquer space. Within one year, the U.S. creates the National Aeronautics and Space Administration (NASA) and begins spending more money on science and math education.

May 5, 1961

Alan B. Shepard becomes the first American in space, with a flight of 15 minutes and 28 seconds. Shortly after, President John F. Kennedy challenges the U.S. to put a person on the moon before the decade is out.

1950s   1960s

April 12, 1961

Russian Yuri Gagarin becomes the first human in space, with a flight of one hour and 48 minutes.

February 20, 1962

John Glenn is the first American to orbit Earth.

768

THE SPACE RACE

June 16, 1963
Russian Valentina Tereshkova becomes the first woman in space.

April 12, 1981
The U.S. space shuttle *Columbia*, the world's first reusable spacecraft, makes its first flight.

1970s

1980s

July 20, 1969
Apollo 11 astronauts Neil Armstrong (left) and Buzz Aldrin (right), helped by crewmate Michael Collins (middle), become the first humans to walk on the moon.

May 14, 1973
Skylab, the first U.S. space station, is launched. Astronauts do experiments in the station for 171 days.

June 18, 1983
Sally Ride becomes the first American woman in space.

April 24, 1990
The Hubble Space Telescope is put in orbit. After its blurry vision is corrected in 1993, it peers deeper into space than any other telescope.

1980s   1990s   2000s

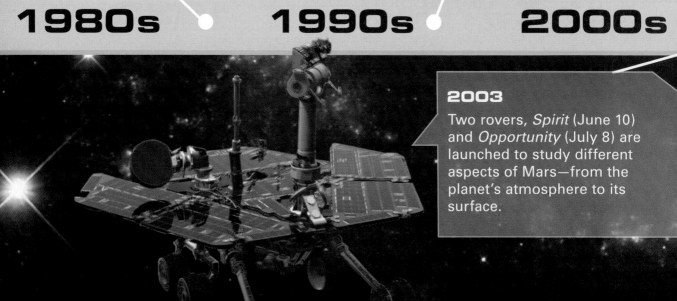

2003
Two rovers, *Spirit* (June 10) and *Opportunity* (July 8) are launched to study different aspects of Mars—from the planet's atmosphere to its surface.

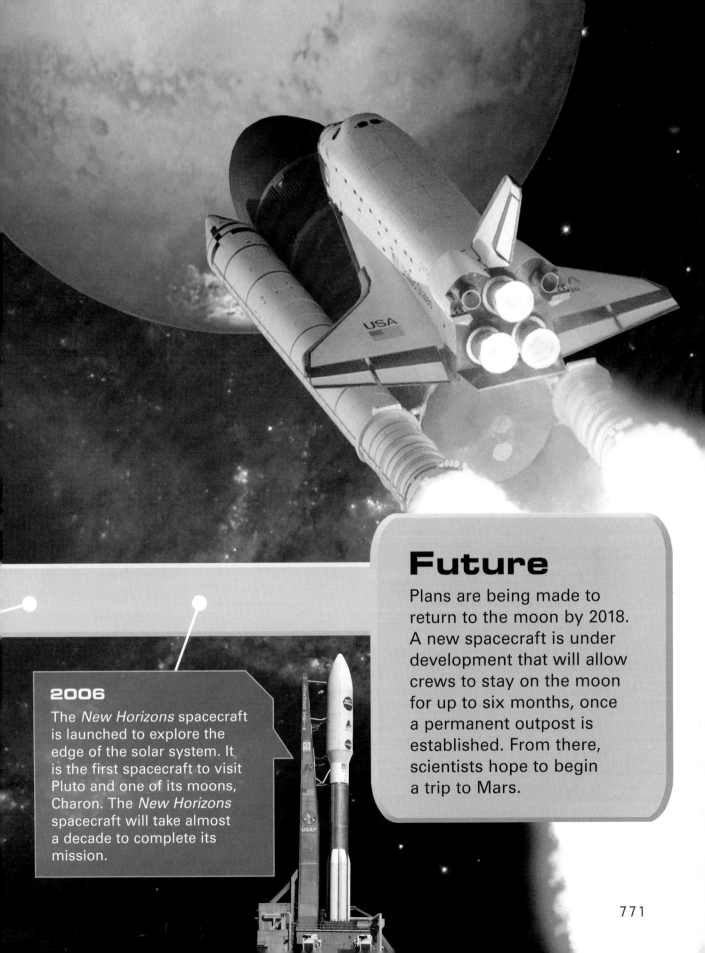

Future

Plans are being made to return to the moon by 2018. A new spacecraft is under development that will allow crews to stay on the moon for up to six months, once a permanent outpost is established. From there, scientists hope to begin a trip to Mars.

2006

The *New Horizons* spacecraft is launched to explore the edge of the solar system. It is the first spacecraft to visit Pluto and one of its moons, Charon. The *New Horizons* spacecraft will take almost a decade to complete its mission.

Connections

Comparing Texts

1. If you could be part of a space exploration team, what job would you want? Explain.

2. Compare the ways the authors of "The Man Who Went to the Far Side of the Moon" and "The Space Race" organized their information.

3. People were fascinated with the first moon landing. Describe another important event you know about.

Vocabulary Review

Word Pairs

After they jettisoned some belongings, the boat was less cramped.

Work with a partner. Write the Vocabulary Words on separate index cards. Place the cards face down. Take turns flipping over two cards and writing a sentence that uses both words. Read your sentence aloud to your partner. You must use both words correctly to keep the cards. The player with more cards wins.

ignited

squinting

jettisoned

tranquility

cramped

potentially

Fluency Practice

Partner Reading

With a partner, choose a paragraph from the main selection. While you read the paragraph aloud, your partner should listen carefully for the pauses between phrases and mark those places with self-stick notes. Reread the paragraph together to make sure each mark appears after a phrase. Then take turns rereading the paragraph aloud, pausing at the marked places.

Writing

Write a Want Ad

Write a want ad seeking candidates for the job of astronaut. List the skills and qualities needed for this position.

Who?	
What?	
Where?	
When?	
Why?	
How?	

My Writing Checklist

Writing Trait ▶ Ideas

✔ I used persuasive language to capture readers' attention.

✔ I used a graphic organizer to focus the information in my want ad.

✔ I clearly identified the most important skills and qualities needed for the job.

Big 💡 Idea

Actors' dialogue portrays opinions and provides evidence to support facts.

Enduring ❗ Understanding

The actors use different word clues, facial expressions, and gestures when stating facts or expressing opinions.

Essential ❓ Question

How does the audience determine the difference between facts and opinions in a dramatic presentation?

Spelling Words

Review

impossibly	contract
deactivation	bankrupt
immeasurable	audible
unbreakable	diction
reappearance	almanac
asteroid	language
chronology	balcony
cyclone	chlorine
hydrate	cousin
optical	urban

Fluency

Review Accuracy, Phrasing

Comprehension

Review

 Summarize and Paraphrase, Fact and Opinion

 Monitor Comprehension: Read Ahead, Summarize

Robust Vocabulary

- poised
- earnestly
- insufficient
- exceptional
- achievement
- bickering
- equivalent
- regal
- customary
- provoke

Writing

- *Review* Ideas, Conventions
- Revise and Publish

Readers' Theater
EXPEDITION

Exploring the Gulf Coast

illustrated by Chris Buzelli

Content-Area Reading
SOCIAL STUDIES TEXTBOOK

YOUR
Social Studies
TEXTBOOK

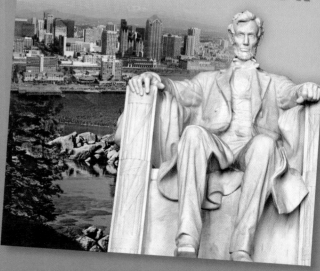

poised

earnestly

insufficient

exceptional

achievement

bickering

equivalent

regal

customary

provoke

Reading for Fluency

When reading a script aloud,

- Read with accuracy, pronouncing every word correctly.

- Pay attention to phrasing by pausing between groups of words that go together.

Exploring the Gulf

Coast

illustrated by Chris Buzelli

FLORIDA

CHARACTERS
Narrator
Captain Carolyn
Sammy
Amir
Lynda
Dominic
William
Chorus

Narrator: Four explorers, a boat captain, and a photographer
from the nature magazine *Big Wild World* are in a small boat
along Florida's Gulf Coast. It's a sunny day, and the Gulf is calm.

Captain Carolyn: Welcome, explorers! I'm Captain Carolyn, and
today we will be adventuring along Florida's Gulf Coast. This is
Sammy, an award-winning nature photographer.

Sammy: Thanks, Captain Carolyn! When *Big Wild World* magazine
sent me on assignment to take photographs of Florida's Gulf
Coast, I knew I needed some help. I'm not accustomed to
exploring coastal terrain.

Amir: Then you are in for a treat!

Fluency Tip

Read words in groups to make your phrasing sound natural.

Lynda: Exactly what are you looking for as we explore the Gulf Coast?

Sammy: My editor asked me to take photographs of a green turtle, a cottonmouth snake, and a red wolf—nothing special.

Amir: Nothing special? This is a potentially impossible task!

Sammy: What do you mean?

Dominic: Green turtles are an endangered species, and they're very hard to find. As far as I know, they make their nests on the Atlantic coast, not here on the Gulf Coast.

Lynda: The cottonmouth snake is a dangerous, poisonous snake. It's also difficult to find.

William: And how do you expect us to find wolves while traveling in a boat?

Amir: This may be a grueling experience.

Chorus: You've got a challenge ahead of you, crew!

Captain Carolyn: Fellow explorers, we're poised for a great challenge. I'm up for it—are you?

Dominic: Yes!

Lynda: You bet!

Amir and William: Count us in.

Narrator: Captain Carolyn starts the boat. The explorers hold their binoculars ready, and Sammy checks his camera.

Sammy: While we're looking for the animals, can anyone give me some facts about Florida's Gulf Coast? They might come in handy for the article.

Amir: I earnestly believe the best parts of the coast are the areas that are most isolated. I'm appalled at how the development of cities and towns has destroyed much of the wildlife on the coast.

Lynda: I believe that the variety of wildlife is what makes Florida's Gulf Coast so special!

Sammy: Thank you for your opinions, but opinions are insufficient. I need information I can prove. For example, exactly how long is the coastline?

Amir: Long.

Lynda: Very long.

Chorus: Facts can be proven—remember that, crew! Tell us something we can find to be true.

Dominic: The coast is more than 700 miles long.

Lynda: Here's another fact. The tree that looks as if it's standing on many legs in the water is a red mangrove. It's the most common mangrove species in Florida.

William: Mangrove forests protect the high land from storm winds. They also protect the land from erosion.

Lynda: Mangroves are truly remarkable!

William: Remember, Sammy asked us for facts. Do you have any facts to support your opinion?

Lynda: You bet! Mangroves can live in salt water, because they've adapted so that they can extract fresh water from salt water. Some use their roots to block salt, and others "sweat" salt through their leaves.

Captain Carolyn: We're about to pass an estuary on our right.

Sammy: What's an estuary?

Lynda: Only one of nature's most exceptional environments.

Amir: An estuary is the place where fresh water meets salt water.

Dominic: The Calusa Indians relied on the estuaries as sources of shellfish and other food. The Calusa lived on the Gulf Coast long before European settlers. They constructed impressive canals across Florida.

Fluency Tip

Practice reading unfamiliar words aloud several times to improve your accuracy.

Amir: Experts say that the Calusa's canals were the greatest architectural wonder in North America!

Lynda: The canals are great, but not as great as the cliff dwellings in the Southwest.

Amir: I disagree! The canals are greater!

Dominic: There's no way to prove which is the greatest early architectural achievement on this continent. You could go back and forth with your opinions all day!

Captain Carolyn: No more bickering. Let's get down to business. We still haven't seen a green turtle or any of the other animals Sammy is looking for.

Dominic: A green turtle can weigh the equivalent of the weight of two adult humans!

William: The green turtle has a heart-shaped shell and a small head. It also has single-clawed flippers.

Lynda: It's the most regal creature to roam the sea.

Chorus: Facts can be proven, of course, of course.
You won't find that in a reference source!

William: The green turtle breeds on the beaches along
Florida's Atlantic Coast.

Amir: Then it comes to feed in the Gulf.

Dominic: Sadly, many things can harm the green turtle.
For example, sometimes green turtles eat debris in the
water, such as balloons, plastic bags, and plastic foam.

Sammy: What's its customary food?

William: Green turtles like to eat turtle grass, the largest sea grass in
Florida. Its leaves look like ribbons. The grass grows near estuaries.

Lynda: Let's get up close to an estuary and see if we can find a
green turtle.

Captain Carolyn: I'll turn off my engine. Silence is essential—
otherwise, the turtles will dive out of sight.

> ### Fluency Tip
>
> Commas can be clues that
> tell you where to pause
> and naturally break text
> into phrases.

Lynda: Look! Near the clumps of sea grass.

Amir: Do you see what I see?

Sammy: I sure do. It's a green turtle. Wow, what a shot I got!

Chorus: Good job, crew. You found the green turtle.

Captain Carolyn: Next, let's try to find a cottonmouth.

Dominic: The cottonmouth has a thick head that's conspicuously broader than its neck. When you look at it from above, you can't see its eyes.

Amir: Cottonmouths are scary.

Chorus: Facts can be proven—remember that, crew! Tell us something we can find to be true!

William: The cottonmouth got its name because the interior of its mouth is white. The cottonmouth is also called a water moccasin.

Dominic: It feeds on fish and frogs.

Chorus: The cottonmouth snake is a dangerous snake! Leave it alone! Just let it be! That's a fact that we guarantee!

Amir: Never provoke a snake. You can't always tell if it's dangerous.

Lynda: Look above us on that tree limb. That's the fiercest snake I've ever seen!

Amir: Look out! It's flinging itself at us.

Narrator: Captain Carolyn quickly maneuvers the boat away. The snake lands in the water, narrowly missing the boat's deck.

Chorus: Good job, Captain Carolyn!

Sammy: I got a couple of incredible shots of the cottonmouth.

William: I'm sorry to disappoint you, but that wasn't a cottonmouth.

Chorus: Then what was it?

William: A harmless brown water snake. They like to bask in the sun on tree limbs.

Dominic: When boats rush toward them, they get frightened and try to escape by throwing themselves into the water.

William: Many people confuse the water snake and the cottonmouth.

Sammy: You mean we weren't in peril after all?

Amir: No, but you would be if you stepped on that log over there. That brown coil is the snake you're looking for.

Narrator: Sammy snaps several photos of the cottonmouth on the log.

Captain Carolyn: Onward! We still need to find a red wolf.

Lynda: Let's head to the adjacent St. Vincent National Wildlife Refuge.

Sammy: Why?

Lynda: St. Vincent is an island with no human habitation. The absence of people allows wildlife to flourish.

Dominic: The refuge was supposed to be a sanctuary for wood ducks and the blue-winged teal.

William: We may find red wolves there. They look a little like coyotes, but they have red coloring around the face, neck, and legs.

Captain Carolyn: That's St. Vincent ahead of us. I'll slowly circle the island.

Narrator: Everyone leans forward, squinting at the island before them.

Amir: There! On that little hill! Are those wolves?

Narrator: Captain Carolyn steers the boat closer for a better look.

Amir: They are! They're red wolves!

Sammy: This is going to be my best photo yet.

William: I enjoy the tranquility of sailing along the coast, but this is an explorer's dream day.

Chorus: You found all the animals! Now take a picture to celebrate!

Sammy: Everyone huddle together.

Chorus: One, two, three . . .

Captain Carolyn, Amir, Lynda, Dominic, and William: Cheese!

Fluency Tip

To read with accuracy, look for familiar word parts in words you don't know.

COMPREHENSION STRATEGIES
Review

Reading a Social Studies Textbook

Bridge to Content-Area Reading Textbooks give facts and information about many topics. The notes on page 787 point out text features of social studies textbooks, including headings, time lines, and maps. These features provide information that can help you better understand the information in a textbook.

Review the Focus Strategies

If you do not understand what you are reading, use the strategies you learned about in this theme.

 Monitor Comprehension: Read Ahead

It is important to monitor your comprehension as you read. If you don't understand something, read ahead to find an explanation.

 Summarize

Summarize main ideas and important details to help you remember what you read.

As you read the social studies lesson on pages 788–791, think about where and how to use comprehension strategies.

> **TIME LINES**
> A time line visually represents the sequence of events.

· LESSON ·

1

DRAW CONCLUSIONS
As you read, draw conclusions about why the Louisiana Purchase was important to the growth of the United States.

BIG IDEA
The United States grew west of the Mississippi River.

VOCABULARY

inauguration
pathfinder
trespass

After the Louisiana Purchase, soldiers at the fort at New Orleans replaced the French flag with the United States flag. The French artist, who mistakenly added hills and cactus to the area, had probably never been to New Orleans.

The Louisiana Purchase

1800–1806

By 1800 Vermont, Kentucky, and Tennessee were added to the original 13 states, and the Northwest Territory was divided into the territories of Ohio and Indiana. Americans were moving west in greater numbers. Some Americans even began to look beyond the Mississippi to the land the French had named Louisiana. France had given Spain this huge region after France lost the French and Indian War in 1763. At this time Spain also controlled all the lands along the Gulf coast.

The Louisiana Purchase

On March 4, 1801, Thomas Jefferson became the third President of the United States. At his **inauguration** (ih•naw•gyuh•RAY•shuhn), or taking office, Jefferson spoke of his hopes for the young nation. He called the United States "a rising nation, spread over a wide and fruitful land." He knew, however, that the nation faced some serious problems.

The United States had no ports of its own on the Gulf of Mexico. Farmers who lived in Kentucky, Tennessee, and the Northwest Territory had to ship their goods down the Mississippi River to New Orleans. From there they could sell the goods to ships sailing for ports in Europe or along the Atlantic coast of the United States.

The Louisiana Purchase

Place **The Louisiana Purchase doubled the size of the United States.**
What natural features of the territory made it easy to explore?

Spain once had allowed American farmers to load and unload their goods free of charge at New Orleans. That changed, however, and it became more costly for farmers to sell their products. Jefferson worried that people in the western United States might not stay loyal to the government if they had no way to ship their products to market.

Soon after Jefferson became President, he learned that Spain had given Louisiana back to France. The French leader, Napoleon Bonaparte (nuh•POH•lee•uhn BOH•nuh•part), hoped to once again establish French power in North America. However, Jefferson knew that having the French in control of Louisiana could prevent the United States frontier from moving farther west.

Jefferson sent representatives to France to ask Bonaparte to sell the land along the

east bank of the Mississippi River, including New Orleans, to the United States. With this land, the United States would have a port on the Gulf of Mexico.

At this time France was getting ready for war with Britain. People in the French colony of St. Domingue (SAN daw•MANG) in the Caribbean had also rebelled against French rule. Bonaparte needed money to fight two wars. He offered to sell *all* of Louisiana—more than 800,000 square miles (2,071,840 sq km)—to the United States for about $15 million.

The agreement to buy Louisiana was made on April 30, 1803. The sale of this huge territory became known as the Louisiana Purchase.

REVIEW Why did Jefferson want to buy the land along the east bank of the Mississippi?

DRAW CONCLUSIONS

> **HEADINGS**
> Headings tell the main idea of a section of text.

> **MAPS**
> Maps show the locations of places discussed in the text.

Apply the Strategies Read this textbook lesson about the Louisiana Purchase. As you read, use comprehension strategies such as reading ahead to help you understand the text.

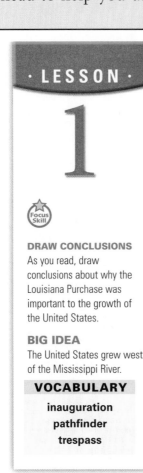

(Focus Skill)

DRAW CONCLUSIONS
As you read, draw conclusions about why the Louisiana Purchase was important to the growth of the United States.

BIG IDEA
The United States grew west of the Mississippi River.

VOCABULARY

inauguration
pathfinder
trespass

After the Louisiana Purchase, soldiers at the fort at New Orleans replaced the French flag with the United States flag. The French artist, who mistakenly added hills and cactus to the area, had probably never been to New Orleans.

The Louisiana Purchase

1800–1806

By 1800 Vermont, Kentucky, and Tennessee were added to the original 13 states, and the Northwest Territory was divided into the territories of Ohio and Indiana. Americans were moving west in greater numbers. Some Americans even began to look beyond the Mississippi to the land the French had named Louisiana. France had given Spain this huge region after France lost the French and Indian War in 1763. At this time Spain also controlled all the lands along the Gulf coast.

The Louisiana Purchase

On March 4, 1801, Thomas Jefferson became the third President of the United States. At his **inauguration** (ih•naw•gyuh•RAY•shuhn), or taking office, Jefferson spoke of his hopes for the young nation. He called the United States "a rising nation, spread over a wide and fruitful land." He knew, however, that the nation faced some serious problems.

The United States had no ports of its own on the Gulf of Mexico. Farmers who lived in Kentucky, Tennessee, and the Northwest Territory had to ship their goods down the Mississippi River to New Orleans. From there they could sell the goods to ships sailing for ports in Europe or along the Atlantic coast of the United States.

Stop and Think

Use headings and the information in graphic aids, such as maps, to help you summarize the most important ideas. SUMMARIZE

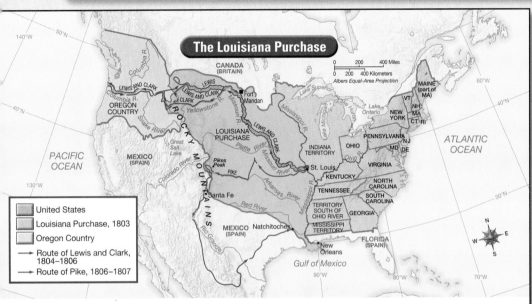

The Louisiana Purchase

140°W · 50°N

CANADA (BRITAIN)

0 200 400 Miles
0 200 400 Kilometers
Albers Equal-Area Projection

MAINE (part of MA)

60°W

OREGON COUNTRY

Columbia R.
LEWIS AND CLARK
LEWIS
J. CLARK
Fort Mandan

Columbia R.
Yellowstone R.
Snake River

40°N

Lake Superior

VT
NH
MA
CT RI

NEW YORK

40°N

PACIFIC OCEAN

LOUISIANA PURCHASE

MEXICO (SPAIN)

Great Salt Lake

Platte River

Missouri R.

Mississippi R.

INDIANA TERRITORY

OHIO

PENNSYLVANIA

NJ
MD DE

ATLANTIC OCEAN

130°W

Pikes Peak
PIKE

St. Louis

VIRGINIA

KENTUCKY

Santa Fe

Arkansas River

Red River

Colorado River

Rio Grande

MEXICO (SPAIN)

Natchitoches

TENNESSEE

TERRITORY SOUTH OF OHIO RIVER

MISSISSIPPI TERRITORY

New Orleans

Gulf of Mexico

NORTH CAROLINA

SOUTH CAROLINA

GEORGIA

FLORIDA (SPAIN)

30°N

90°W

80°W

70°W

N
W E
S

☐ United States
☐ Louisiana Purchase, 1803
☐ Oregon Country
→ Route of Lewis and Clark, 1804–1806
→ Route of Pike, 1806–1807

GEOGRAPHY THEME

Place The Louisiana Purchase doubled the size of the United States.

❖ What natural features of the territory made it easy to explore?

Spain once had allowed American farmers to load and unload their goods free of charge at New Orleans. That changed, however, and it became more costly for farmers to sell their products. Jefferson worried that people in the western United States might not stay loyal to the government if they had no way to ship their products to market.

Soon after Jefferson became President, he learned that Spain had given Louisiana back to France. The French leader, Napoleon Bonaparte (nuh•POH•lee•uhn BOH•nuh•part), hoped to once again establish French power in North America. However, Jefferson knew that having the French in control of Louisiana could prevent the United States frontier from moving farther west.

Jefferson sent representatives to France to ask Bonaparte to sell the land along the east bank of the Mississippi River, including New Orleans, to the United States. With this land, the United States would have a port on the Gulf of Mexico.

At this time France was getting ready for war with Britain. People in the French colony of St. Domingue (SAN daw•MANG) in the Caribbean had also rebelled against French rule. Bonaparte needed money to fight two wars. He offered to sell *all* of Louisiana—more than 800,000 square miles (2,071,840 sq km)—to the United States for about $15 million.

The agreement to buy Louisiana was made on April 30, 1803. The sale of this huge territory became known as the Louisiana Purchase.

REVIEW Why did Jefferson want to buy the land along the east bank of the Mississippi?

DRAW CONCLUSIONS

Lewis and Clark

Few people in the United States knew much about the Louisiana Purchase. It was a huge region, reaching from the Mississippi River to the Rocky Mountains and from New Orleans north to Canada. Americans had never explored it, so President Jefferson asked Congress for money to pay for an expedition to find out more about it.

Jefferson then chose Meriwether Lewis to lead the expedition. Lewis had been an army officer and had served in the Northwest Territory. Jefferson also chose William Clark, a good friend of Lewis and brother of the Revolutionary War hero George Rogers Clark, to help lead the expedition.

William Clark used this compass in the expedition to the Louisiana Purchase.

Lewis and Clark put together a group of about 30 soldiers. They called their group the Corps of Discovery. One member of the Corps of Discovery was York, William Clark's African American slave who was skilled in hunting and fishing.

In May 1804 the group left its camp near present-day St. Louis and traveled up the Missouri River by boat. By October the expedition had reached present-day North Dakota. With winter coming on, they built a small camp near a Mandan Indian village. They named their camp Fort Mandan.

Meriwether Lewis (far right) and William Clark (right) led the Corps of Discovery through the Louisiana Purchase. The painting shows Sacagawea using sign language to communicate with the Chinooks during the expedition.

If you come to a part of the text that confuses you, read ahead to find information that gives an explanation. **MONITOR COMPREHENSION: READ AHEAD**

At Fort Mandan, Lewis and Clark hired a French fur trader to interpret some Indian languages for them. The fur trader was married to a Shoshone (shoh•SHOH•nee) Indian woman named Sacagawea (sa•kuh•juh•WEE•uh). Sacagawea agreed to guide the expedition when it reached the land of the Shoshones.

In the spring of 1805, the Lewis and Clark expedition set out again. They moved farther up the Missouri River toward the Rocky Mountains. With Sacagawea's help, the expedition got horses from the Shoshones and continued their journey through the mountain passes of the Rockies. Once over the mountains, the explorers built boats and rowed down the Clearwater, Snake, and Columbia Rivers toward the Pacific coast.

In November 1805, after traveling for more than a year and covering more than 3,000 miles (about 4,800 km), the Lewis and Clark expedition reached the Pacific Ocean. Clark wrote in his journal,

❝Great joy in camp. We are in view of the . . . great Pacific Octean [Ocean], which we have been so long anxious to see, and the roreing [roaring] or noise made by the waves brakeing [breaking] on the rockey [rocky] shores (as I may suppose) may be heard distinctly. ❞

In March the Corps of Discovery began the long journey back to St. Louis. They reached the settlement in September 1806. The expedition had collected many facts about the Louisiana Purchase. They brought back seeds, plants, and even living animals. They could tell what the people and the land were like, and they had drawn maps to show where mountain passes and major rivers were. In later years the work of these pathfinders helped American settlers find their way to the Pacific coast. A **pathfinder** is someone who finds a way through an unknown region.

REVIEW Who led the first expedition to the Louisiana Purchase?

Using the Glossary

Like a dictionary, this glossary lists words in alphabetical order. To find a word, look it up by its first letter or letters.

To save time, use the **guide words** at the top of each page. These show you the first and last words on the page. Look at the guide words to see if your word falls between them alphabetically.

Here is an example of a glossary entry:

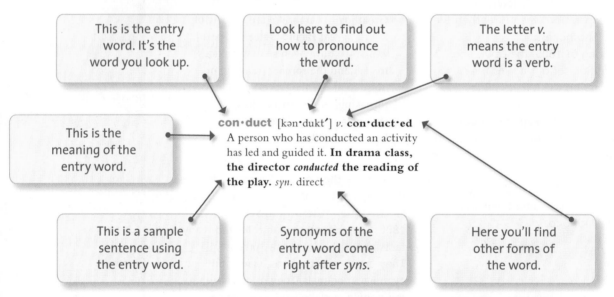

This is the entry word. It's the word you look up.

Look here to find out how to pronounce the word.

The letter *v.* means the entry word is a verb.

This is the meaning of the entry word.

con·duct [kən·dukt′] *v.* **con·duct·ed** A person who has conducted an activity has led and guided it. **In drama class, the director** *conducted* **the reading of the play.** *syn.* direct

This is a sample sentence using the entry word.

Synonyms of the entry word come right after *syns.*

Here you'll find other forms of the word.

Word Origins

Throughout the glossary, you will find notes about word origins, or how words came into use and have changed over time. Words often have interesting backgrounds that can help you remember what they mean. Here is an example of a word origin note:

> **— Word Origins —**
> **charity** The origin of *charity* is the Latin word *carus*, which means "dear" and "love." In the Middle Ages, *carus* became *cherite* and *charite*, meaning "love of other people" and "kindness."

Pronunciation

The pronunciation in brackets is a respelling that shows how the word is pronounced. The **pronunciation key** explains what the symbols in a respelling mean. A shortened pronunciation key appears on every other page of the glossary.

PRONUNCIATION KEY

a	add, map	m	move, seem	u	up, done
ā	ace, rate	n	nice, tin	û(r)	burn, term
â(r)	care, air	ng	ring, song	yo͞o	fuse, few
ä	palm, father	o	odd, hot	v	vain, eve
b	bat, rub	ō	open, so	w	win, away
ch	check, catch	ô	order, jaw	y	yet, yearn
d	dog, rod	oi	oil, boy	z	zest, muse
e	end, pet	ou	pout, now	zh	vision, pleasure
ē	equal, tree	o͝o	took, full	ə	the schwa, an
f	fit, half	o͞o	pool, food		unstressed vowel
g	go, log	p	pit, stop		representing the
h	hope, hate	r	run, poor		sound spelled
i	it, give	s	see, pass		*a* in *above*
ī	ice, write	sh	sure, rush		*e* in *sicken*
j	joy, ledge	t	talk, sit		*i* in *possible*
k	cool, take	th	thin, both		*o* in *melon*
l	look, rule	t͟h	this, bathe		*u* in *circus*

Other symbols:
- · separates words into syllables
- ′ indicates heavier stress on a syllable
- ′ indicates lighter stress on a syllable

Abbreviations: *adj.* adjective, *adv.* adverb, *conj.* conjunction, *interj.* interjection, *n.* noun, *prep.* preposition, *pron.* pronoun, *syn.* synonym, *v.* verb

ab·sent·mind·ed [ab'sənt·mīn'did] *adj.* Someone who is absentminded forgets things easily. **Naomi thought Pedro was *absentminded* because he forgot to order food for the party.** *syn.* forgetful

ac·cli·mate [ak'lə·māt] *v.* If you acclimate to something, you adjust to a new condition or environment. **The goldfish had to *acclimate* to the larger tank.** *syns.* adapt, adjust

acclimate

ac·cu·mu·late [ə·kyoom'yə·lāt] *v.* When things accumulate, they collect over time. **When I noticed the newspapers *accumulate* in front of Mr. Smith's house, I realized he was probably out of town again.** *syn.* pile up

---

FACT FILE

accumulate Literally, *accumulate* means "to heap up." This meaning is reflected in the name *cumulus* clouds for the big, fluffy clouds that heap up in the sky.

ACADEMIC LANGUAGE

accuracy When you read with *accuracy*, you read without making mistakes.

---

ac·cus·tomed [ə·kus'təmd] *adj.* If you are accustomed to something, you are used to it because it has been a regular part of your life. **Charlie became *accustomed* to eating cereal for a snack.** *syn.* acclimated

a·chieve·ment [ə·chēv'mənt] *n.* An achievement is the result of a successful effort. **Janice was proud of her *achievement* as winner of the spelling bee.** *syns.* accomplishment, success

ad·just [ə·just'] *v.* When you adjust, you change your behavior to fit a new situation. **When the cat moved from the shelter to a home with three small children, it had to *adjust* to its new environment.** *syn.* modify

ad·vo·ca·cy [ad'və·kə·sē] *n.* Advocacy is giving support to a person, idea, or cause. **Amar showed his *advocacy* for stray animals by asking his parents if he could adopt a dog from the Humane Society.** *syns.* support, backing

a·ghast [ə·gast'] *adj.* If you are aghast, you feel shocked and disgusted about something. **Keisha was *aghast* at her friend's rude behavior.** *syn.* appalled

al·tru·ism [al'troo·iz·əm] *n.* Altruism is being concerned about others before worrying about oneself. **David showed that *altruism* was part of his nature when he volunteered to read to children at the day-care center.** *syn.* kindness

a·mend [ə·mend'] *v.* **a·mends** When you amend something, you make positive changes, such as amending a shopping list or a recipe. **After forgetting to invite Xenia to her party, Aylana *amends* her mistake by inviting Xenia to a sleepover.** *syn.* correct

an·a·lyze [an'ə·līz] *v.* **an·a·lyz·ing** A scientist who is analyzing something is studying it closely to figure out how it works or what it is made of. **The scientist in the laboratory is *analyzing* the water to make sure it is safe to drink.** *syn.* examine

ap·pall [ə·pôl'] *v.* **ap·palled** Someone who is appalled is shocked and horrified at something. **After the storm, Mercedes was *appalled* to find that a tree had fallen on the roof of her house.** *syn.* dismay

---

— Word Origins —

appall The word *appall* traces its roots back to the French word *apallir,* which means "to become or make pale." It was not used to mean "shock and dismay" until the nineteenth century.

---

ap·peal [ə·pēl'] *v.* **ap·pealed** If you have appealed to someone, you have made a request with a lot of feeling. **Alejandro *appealed* to Ramona's good nature when he begged her to help him study for the math test.** *syn.* plead

ap·pro·pri·ate [ə·prō'prē·it] *adj.* If you wear appropriate clothing, you choose an outfit that is right for the situation. **Dwayne felt that a suit and tie would be the *appropriate* attire for the award ceremony.** *syn.* suitable

as·set [as′et] *n.* An asset is a resource, person, or object that is valuable to have. **My mother says her most valuable *asset* is her family.** *syn.* resource

as·suage [ə·swāj′] *v.* To assuage guilt is to make it less painful and troubling. **To *assuage* his bad feelings about spilling ketchup on his father's best shirt, Dan mowed the lawn.** *syn.* pacify

as·sure [ə·shoor′] *v.* **as·sured** If someone has assured you of something, he or she has said words to make you feel positive that things will be all right. **My older brother *assured* me that he had changed the flat tire and that it was safe to continue our trip.** *syn.* guarantee

> ### ACADEMIC LANGUAGE
> **autobiography** An *autobiography* is the story of a real person's life written by that person.

— B —

baf·fled [baf′əld] *adj.* Someone who is baffled by something cannot understand or explain it. **Emiko was *baffled* when she saw that her mother had sent cookies and candy, instead of the usual sandwich, for lunch.** *syn.* puzzled

bask [bask] *v.* **bask·ing** If an animal is basking, it is exposing itself to warmth in the sun. **Miguel was *basking* in the backyard on the lawn chair.** *syn.* sunbathe

bel·low·ing [bel′ō·ing] *adj.* A bellowing sound is a loud, low-pitched sound, usually made to show distress. **My dog makes *bellowing* sounds when he goes to the veterinarian.** *syn.* crying

be·tray [bi·trā′] *v.* **be·trayed** If you betrayed someone who trusted you, you gave away his or her plans, ideas, or secrets to others. **Megan said I had *betrayed* her when I told Stephanie her secret.** *syn.* double-cross

bick·er [bik′ər] *v.* **bick·er·ing** People who are bickering are arguing about something unimportant. **Jeff and Hilda are *bickering* about who gets the window seat on the plane ride.** *syn.* argue

> ### ACADEMIC LANGUAGE
> **biography** A *biography* is the story of a real person's life written by another person.

bland [bland] *adj.* Something that is bland is dull and unexciting. **Aunt Elena's chicken casserole was *bland* because she had forgotten to add salt and pepper.** *syn.* flavorless

bois·ter·ous [bois′tər·əs *or* bois′trəs] *adj.* A boisterous person or animal is noisy and has lots of energy. **The *boisterous* new puppy was constantly jumping on the furniture.** *syn.* rowdy

brim [brim] *v.* **brim·ming** Something that is brimming is filled to the very top. **Liang was thirsty, so he filled his cup until it was *brimming* with juice.** *syn.* full

brimming

broach [brōch] *v.* **broached** A ship that has broached is in danger of sinking because it has veered so that the waves strike its side. **I saw a movie in which a ship *broached* and objects were falling overboard.** *syn.* capsize

bus·tle [bus′əl] *v.* **bus·tles** When someone bustles, he or she moves in a busy, energetic way. **When my mother has guests for dinner, she *bustles* about the kitchen making sure the food is correctly prepared.** *syn.* dart

— C —

char·i·ty [char′ə·tē] *n.* Charity is showing kindness by giving money or gifts to organizations that need them. **She shows *charity* by giving some of her allowance to the Animal Rescue League.** *syn.* goodwill

> **— Word Origins —**
> **charity** The origin of *charity* is the Latin word *carus*, which means "dear" and "love." In the Middle Ages, *carus* became *cherité* and *charité*, meaning "love of other people" and "kindness."

a	add	e	end	o	odd	o͞o	pool	oi	oil	th	this		*a* in *above*
ā	ace	ē	equal	ō	open	u	up	ou	pout	zh	vision		*e* in *sicken*
â	care	i	it	ô	order	û	burn	ng	ring			ə =	*i* in *possible*
ä	palm	ī	ice	o͝o	took	yo͞o	fuse	th	thin				*o* in *melon*
													u in *circus*

cir·cu·late [sûr′kyə·lāt] *v.* When you circulate, you move freely around an area. **When the doorbell rang, Susan had just begun to *circulate* among the guests at her party.** *syn.* wander

coax [kōks] *v.* **coaxed** If you are coaxed into doing something, you are gently talked into it by someone else. **Akedo *coaxed* Aretha into jogging with him, even though she doesn't like outdoor exercise.** *syn.* persuade

com·part·ment [kəm·pärt′mənt] *n.* **com·part·ments** An item that has compartments has separate sections for keeping things. **My craft box has many *compartments,* in which I store items such as crayons, markers, and brushes.** *syn.* section

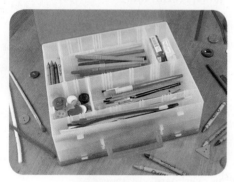

compartment

com·pas·sion·ate [kəm·pash′ən·it] *adj.* A compassionate person is kindhearted and understanding. **Isabel showed that she was *compassionate* by inviting the new girl to eat lunch with her.** *syn.* kind

con·ceit·ed [kən·sē′tid] *adj.* A conceited person thinks too highly of herself or himself. **Michael's announcement that he is the most well-liked student in the school shows how *conceited* he is.** *syn.* arrogant

con·coc·tion [kən·kok′shən] *n.* A concoction is a mix of different things, often one put together without much planning. **In science class, we put together a *concoction* of white glue, food coloring, and rock salt to make objects that represented precious stones.** *syn.* mixture

con·duct [kən·dukt′] *v.* **con·duct·ed** A person who has conducted an activity has led and guided it. **In drama class, the director *conducted* the reading of the play.** *syn.* direct

ACADEMIC LANGUAGE

conventions A *convention* is an agreement about what is correct in usage or custom. Conventions of the English language include the rules of grammar, spelling, punctuation, and capitalization.

co·or·di·na·tion [kō·ôr′də·nā′shən] *n.* Coordination involves organizing the different parts of something so that they work well together. **The sports award assembly was successful thanks to the *coordination* by Marshall.** *syn.* management

cramped [krampt] *adj.* A place that is cramped is uncomfortable because there is very little free space. **Sitting around the dinner table gets especially *cramped* when Aunt Sylvia and Uncle Harry bring their children to visit.** *syn.* crowded

cri·sis [krī′səs] *n.* A crisis is a situation that suddenly becomes very dangerous or difficult. **Chita smelled smoke and immediately knew a *crisis* existed in her apartment building.** *syn.* emergency

cru·cial [krōō′shəl] *adj.* If something is crucial, it is extremely important. **Manuel's mother and father made a *crucial* decision to move to another state.** *syn.* important

cru·sade [krōō·sād′] *v.* **cru·sad·ed** A person who has crusaded has worked hard to make a change based on his or her beliefs. **Pam's parents *crusaded* for her school to include an art program and a music program as part of the curriculum.** *syn.* campaign

cum·ber·some [kum′bər·səm] *adj.* Something that is cumbersome is large, heavy, and difficult to handle. **My suitcase was too *cumbersome* to lift into the overhead compartment, so I put it under my seat.** *syn.* unwieldy

cus·tom·ar·y [kus′tə·mâr′ē] *adj.* Something that is customary is what is usual or normal. **In the spring, it is *customary* for Sergio and his friends to play baseball in the park.** *syn.* usual

D

dam·age [dam′ij] *v.* If you damage something, you harm or injure it. **A hurricane can *damage* the electrical system of an entire region.** *syn.* harm

de·bris [də·brē′] *n.* Debris is scattered pieces of something that has been destroyed. **The tornado turned our storage shed into a trail of** *debris.* *syn.* rubble

> **FACT FILE**
>
> **debris** The word *debris* comes from the French word *débriser,* which means "to break down or crush." Nearly thirty percent of the words in the English language have a French origin.

de·duc·tion [di·duk′shən] *n.* A deduction is a conclusion you reach, based on the information you have been given. **Tomás read the buyer's guide and made the *deduction* that the more expensive bicycle was the better choice.** *syn.* conclusion

de·flate [di·flāt′] *v.* **de·flat·ed** If someone feels deflated, he or she has lost confidence about something. **Janice felt *deflated* and unsure of her baking abilities after she lost the cookie–baking contest.** *syn.* drain

des·ig·nat·ed [dez′ig·nāt·ed] *adj.* If a place is designated, it is chosen for a special purpose. **The bookstore was the *designated* meeting place for Guillermo and George.** *syn.* assigned

des·o·late [des′ə·lit] *adj.* A person who feels desolate feels lonely and sad. **Jenny felt *desolate* after all her friends went out of town for the summer.** *syn.* lonely

des·per·ate·ly [des′pər·it·lē] *adv.* Wanting something desperately means wanting it so much that you'll do almost anything to get it. **Darnel *desperately* wants to become a famous writer and the author of best-selling books.** *syn.* greatly

des·ti·ny [des′tə·nē] *n.* To believe in destiny is to feel that certain things will happen because they were meant to be. **When Toshi found a violin in the attic, he felt it was his *destiny* to enter music school.** *syn.* fate

de·tect [di·tekt′] *v.* When you detect something, you notice or discover it. **She would be a good computer technician because she can *detect* and repair problems in computer hardware.** *syns.* discover, notice

de·vice [di·vīs′] *n.* A device is an object that has been made for a special purpose. **Tony's aunt wears a hearing aid, a *device* that helps people with hearing loss.** *syn.* tool

dig·ni·fied [dig′nə·fīd] *adj.* To act in a dignified way means to behave in a calm, serious, and respectful manner. **Everyone behaved in a *dignified* manner during the meeting.** *syn.* respectful

dignified

di·lap·i·dat·ed [di·lap′ə·dā·təd] *adj.* A dilapidated building looks worn out and run down. **After the neighbors complained that the *dilapidated* house was dangerous, the owner made repairs to make the place safe.** *syns.* run down, decayed

dis·grun·tled [dis·grun′təld] *adj.* If you are disgruntled, you are unhappy because things have not turned out the way you wanted. **The worker was *disgruntled* and wanted a better job.** *syn.* unhappy

dis·heart·ened [dis·här′tənd] *adj.* If you are disheartened, you feel disappointed and less hopeful. **Lisa wants to be an actor, so she was *disheartened* that she didn't get a part in the movie.** *syn.* disappointed

dis·mal [diz′məl] *adj.* Something that is dismal is bleak and depressing. **The constant rain made April a *dismal* month.** *syn.* gloomy

> ── **Word Origins** ──
>
> **dismal** In medieval times, certain days were thought to be unlucky. These days were said to be *dies mali,* which in Latin means "bad days." Over the years, *dies mali* came into English as *dismal* and means "gloomy."

a add	e end	o odd	o͞o pool	oi oil	th this	a in *above*
ā ace	ē equal	ō open	u up	ou pout	zh vision	e in *sicken*
â care	i it	ô order	û burn	ng ring		ə = { i in *possible*
ä palm	ī ice	o͝o took	yo͞o fuse	th thin		o in *melon*
						u in *circus*

dis·may [dis·mā′] *v.* **dis·mayed** When you are dismayed, you are upset about something and unsure of how to deal with it. **Eduardo's sisters were *dismayed* when he refused to let them ride on his new bike.** *syn.* upset

dra·mat·i·cal·ly [drə·mat′i·klē] *adv.* If something is done dramatically, it is done in a striking or impressive way. **Connie *dramatically* and excitedly told about seeing a bear while camping with her family in a national park.** *syns.* vividly, spectacularly

dwell [dwel] *v.* The place where you dwell is where you live. **I think it might be hard to *dwell* in an igloo for a long time.** *syns.* reside, inhabit

E

ear·nest·ly [ûr′nist·lē] *adv.* Someone who speaks earnestly says things in an especially serious and honest way. **In his report about the environment, Terrel *earnestly* expressed his views.** *syn.* candidly

ec·cen·tric [ik·sen′trik] *adj.* An eccentric person has habits or opinions that seem odd to other people. **Everyone thinks Akemi is *eccentric* because she walks backward up flights of stairs.** *syns.* odd, unusual

---
Word Origins

eccentric The word *eccentric* comes from the Greek word *ékkentros,* which means "out of the center." It wasn't until the early 1800s that the term *eccentric* was used to describe a person who seemed odd or unusual.

---

e·las·tic [i·las′tik] *adj.* Something that is elastic stretches easily. **These shorts have an *elastic* waistband.** *syn.* flexible

---
FACT FILE

elastic If something is *elastic*, it might be made of rubber. Natural rubber comes from the juice of fig-like trees that grow in areas near the equator.

---

e·lon·gate [i·lông′gāt] *v.* **e·lon·gates** Something that elongates stretches to a longer length. **Mark *elongates* the clay pieces he uses for the hair of his sculpture.** *syns.* lengthen, extend

em·bark [im·bärk′] *v.* **em·barked** If you have embarked on a journey, you have begun a new adventure. **After Lana packed her gear, she *embarked* on her trip to the mountains.** *syn.* start

em·i·nent [em′ə·nənt] *adj.* An eminent person is well known and important. **The *eminent* doctor developed a number of procedures for saving lives.** *syns.* renowned, famous

en·coun·ter [in·koun′tər] *v.* **en·coun·tered** If you encountered someone, you met that person unexpectedly. **Shuko was very surprised when he *encountered* his father in the fast-food restaurant.** *syn.* meet

en·deav·or [in·dev′ər] *n.* An endeavor is an activity or task you take on in an effort to accomplish it. **In her *endeavor* to raise money for band uniforms, Rosario organized a car wash.** *syn.* effort

en·rap·ture [in·rap′chər] *v.* **en·rap·tured** A person who is enraptured is delighted and thrilled with something. **The students planted a garden and were *enraptured* when they saw the flowers bloom.** *syn.* enchant

en·ter·pris·ing [en′tər·prīz·ing] *adj.* People who are enterprising do new and difficult things in order to achieve their goals. **Andrew took the *enterprising* step of opening an art gallery at the school.** *syn.* adventurous

en·vi·sion [in·vizh′ən] *v.* **en·vi·sioned** If you have pictured something in your mind, you have envisioned it. **Reneé *envisioned* herself arriving at a castle on a winged horse.** *syn.* visualize

e·quiv·a·lent [i·kwiv′ə·lənt] *adj.* Things that are equivalent are equal. **My twin sister and I received *equivalent* gifts at our birthday party.** *syn.* alike

es·ca·pade [es′kə·pād] *n.* **es·ca·pades** Escapades are carefree, mischievous, or reckless adventures. **Carmen and Gabriella play board games for fun and never go on *escapades*.** *syn.* adventure

es·sence [es′əns] *n.* The essence of something is its most basic, important quality. **The *essence* of being a mathematician is being able to work well with numbers.** *syn.* core

es·sen·tial [i·sen′shəl] *adj.* Something that is essential is absolutely necessary. **Jerome knew that it was *essential* to study in order to pass the test.** *syns.* necessary, crucial

es·teem [i·stēm′] *v.* To esteem something means to judge it to be of value. **I *esteem* it an honor to be elected to student council.** *syns.* regard, value

ex·cep·tion·al [ik·sep′shən·əl] *adj.* Something that is exceptional is special, and it stands above others like it. **Ramón's *exceptional* character showed when he decided to volunteer at the senior citizen center.** *syn.* extraordinary

ex·cur·sion [ik·skûr′zhən] *n.* **ex·cur·sions** An excursion is a short journey or outing. **Melanie's family went on an *excursion* down the river.** *syn.* outing

excursion

ex·hil·a·rate [ig·zil′ə·rāt′e] *v.* **ex·hil·a·rat·ed** If you feel exhilarated, you feel very excited and energetic. **Ryan was *exhilarated* to learn that he placed first in the swimming competition.** *syns.* excite, thrill

ex·pec·ta·tion [ek·spek·tā′shən] *n.* **ex·pec·ta·tions** Expectations are hopes about how well others will do or about how they should behave. **Wilma's parents have *expectations* that she will be on her best behavior at summer camp.** *syns.* hope, belief

---

ACADEMIC LANGUAGE

expository nonfiction *Expository nonfiction* presents and explains facts about a topic. Photographs, captions, and headings are commonly found in these texts.

expression Reading aloud with *expression* means using your voice to match the action of the story and the characters' feelings.

---

ex·trav·a·gant [ik·strav′ə·gənt] *adj.* Something extravagant is much more costly or elaborate than what is really needed. **Nina thought the *extravagant* ring was beautiful.** *syn.* excessive

extravagant

--- F ---

ACADEMIC LANGUAGE

fable A *fable* is a short story that teaches a lesson or moral about life. Fables often include animals as characters.

fantasy A *fantasy* is an imaginative story that may have unrealistic characters and events.

---

faze [fāz] *v.* If things faze you, they bother or confuse you. **Even though Steve wanted to make the chess team, it didn't *faze* him that the tryouts were cancelled.** *syn.* daunt

feat [fēt] *n.* A feat is a difficult act that impresses people. **Climbing the highest mountain in the world is a *feat* not many people in the world can claim.** *syn.* accomplishment

fer·vor [fûr′vər] *n.* A person who speaks with fervor speaks with great emotion and strong belief. **Frances spoke to the students with *fervor* in her speech at the graduation ceremony.** *syn.* enthusiasm

fe·ver·ish·ly [fē′vər·ish·lē] *adv.* If you are working feverishly, you are working quickly and excitedly. **As the thunderstorm became more threatening, Gibran worked *feverishly* to bring the lawn furniture inside.** *syn.* busily

fick·le [fik′əl] *adj.* Fickle people keep changing their minds about what they like or want. **Shantell is *fickle* about her clothes because she wears her outfits a couple of times but then wants to give them away and get new ones.** *syn.* indecisive

flop [flop] *n.* A flop is a failure. **Jorge's ant farm was a *flop* at the science fair because all the ants died.** *syn.* failure

---

a add	e end	o odd	o͞o pool	oi oil	t͟h this	ə =	a in *above*
ā ace	ē equal	ō open	u up	ou pout	zh vision		e in *sicken*
â care	i it	ô order	û burn	ng ring			i in *possible*
ä palm	ī ice	o͝o took	yo͞o fuse	th thin			o in *melon*
							u in *circus*

floun·der [floun′dər] *v.* **floun·dered** People or animals that have floundered have made wild movements trying to get something done. **Otis *floundered* about on the dance floor as he tried to learn the new dance step.** *syn.* blunder

fret [fret] *v.* When you fret about something, you keep thinking and worrying about it. **Brad tried not to *fret* about giving his book report in front of the class.** *syn.* worry

fringe [frinj] *n.* **fring·es** The fringes of a place are areas along its edges, far away from the center of action. **In the cattle drives of the late 1800s, cattle were herded to the railroads from the *fringes* of the territory.** *syns.* border, outskirts

gen·ial [jēn′yəl] *adj.* A genial person is warm and friendly. **Nora welcomed her cousins in a *genial* way and invited them to stay for dinner.** *syns.* friendly, hospitable

ges·ture [jes′chər] *n.* A gesture is something you say or do in order to express a feeling to someone. **Elliot gave Sierra a new set of drumsticks as a *gesture* of welcoming her to the band.** *syn.* token

gid·dy [gid′ē] *adj.* If you feel giddy, you feel happy in a silly, dizzy way. **Tamika felt *giddy* when she got on her new bike for the first time.** *syn.* excited

glee·ful [glē′fəl] *adj.* A person who is gleeful is excited and happy, sometimes as a result of someone else's mistake. **When Abby spelled her third word correctly, she had the *gleeful* feeling that she could win the spelling bee.** *syn.* joyful

gouge [gouj] *v.* **goug·es** If someone gouges something, he or she makes a deep cut or dent in it. **Using a sharp tool, Tito's dad *gouges* a design in the wood frame.** *syn.* cut

gour·met [gŏŏr·mā′] *adj.* Gourmet food is food that is expensive, rare, or carefully prepared. **My father always makes a *gourmet* meal to celebrate my birthday.**

grate·ful [grāt′fəl] *adj.* To be grateful is to feel thankful for someone or something. **Reggie is *grateful* that his grandparents let him spend every summer on their farm because he wants to be a farmer, too.** *syn.* appreciative

grim [grim] *adj.* If something looks grim, it appears serious and forbidding. **With their frowns and crossed arms, Joann and Debbie looked *grim*.** *syn.* dour

grim

grudg·ing·ly [gruj′ing·lē] *adv.* If you say something grudgingly, you say it without really wanting to. **Bob *grudgingly* told Frank that he could use his computer.** *syn.* reluctantly

gru·el·ing [grōō′əl·ing] *adj.* A grueling experience is extremely difficult and exhausting. **The jogger chose to run in the morning because working out in the afternoon heat was too *grueling*.** *syns.* demanding, exhausting

H

hes·i·tate [hez′ə·tāt] *v.* **hes·i·tat·ing** If you are hesitating, you are pausing before doing something because you are feeling unsure. **Hector is *hesitating* before entering the music contest because he is not sure he will have enough time to practice.** *syn.* vacillate

hi·a·tus [hī·ā′təs] *n.* A hiatus is a break for a period of time between events. **Miya had an unexpected *hiatus* from the basketball team when she sprained her ankle.** *syns.* break, pause

ACADEMIC LANGUAGE

historical documents *Historical documents* are papers written in the past.

historical fiction *Historical fiction* stories are set in the past and portray people, places, and events that did happen or could have happened.

hu·mil·i·a·tion [hyōō·mil′ē·ā′shən] *n.* Humiliation is a feeling of shame or embarrassment. **Julio guided the new student to the right classroom to spare her the *humiliation* of arriving in class late.** *syn.* embarrassment

I

ig·nite [ig·nīt′] *v.* **ig·nit·ed** When something is ignited, it is lit or made to burn. **The workers who *ignited* the Fourth of July fireworks were trained in a special safety course.** *syn.* inflame

im·mac·u·late [i·mak′yə·lət] *adj.* Something that is immaculate is extremely clean and tidy. **Liana's house is ready for guests at any moment because she keeps it in *immaculate* shape.** *syn.* clean

im·pass·a·ble [im·pas′ə·bəl] *adj.* A road or path that is impassable is impossible to travel on. **In the winter, certain roads through the Sierra Nevada are *impassable* because of heavy snows.** *syn.* blocked

in·ad·e·quate [in·ad′ə·kwit] *adj.* Something that is inadequate is not as good or as large as it needs to be. **The number of pancakes the chef had prepared was *inadequate* for the huge breakfast crowd.** *syn.* insufficient

Word Origins

inadequate The word *inadequate* is made up of the Latin prefix *in*, which means "not" and the Latin word *adaequātus*, which means "equalized."

in·di·ca·tion [in·də·kā′shən] *n.* An indication is a sign that something exists or might happen. **The baby's crying all night was an *indication* that he was sick.** *syn.* sign

in·dig·nant·ly [in·dig′nənt·lē] *adv.* When you say something indignantly, you show irritation because you feel you have been insulted or treated unfairly. **Ira declared *indignantly* that if he couldn't sit in the front seat, he didn't want to go on the trip.** *syn.* resentfully

in·dus·try [in′dəs·trē] *n.* An industry is all the people and companies that make a certain type of product or provide a certain type of service. **The automobile *industry* puts on shows every year to introduce the new models.** *syn.* business

Word Origins

industry The origin of the word *industry* can be traced back to the Latin word *indostruus*, whose root, *struere*, means "to build." The Latin word part *indu* means "in." The word came to have its present usage in the mid-sixteenth century.

in·flam·ma·ble [in·flam′ə·bəl] *adj.* Something that is inflammable can catch fire easily and burn rapidly. **Parents should be careful not to dress their babies in pajamas that are *inflammable*.** *syn.* combustible

ACADEMIC LANGUAGE

informational narrative An *informational narrative* is a story that presents information and facts.

informational text *Informational text* presents information and facts.

a add	e end	o odd	ōō pool	oi oil	th this		*a* in *above*
ā ace	ē equal	ō open	u up	ou pout	zh vision		*e* in *sicken*
â care	i it	ô order	û burn	ng ring		ə =	*i* in *possible*
ä palm	ī ice	ōō took	yōō fuse	th thin			*o* in *melon*
							u in *circus*

in·fu·ri·ate [in·fyŏŏr′ē·āte] *v.* **in·fu·ri·at·ed** Something that infuriated you made you feel extremely angry. **Jay was *infuriated* when his brother ate the last piece of Jay's birthday cake.** *syn.* enrage

in·sight [in′sīt] *n.* **in·sights** If you have insights, you notice or understand important things that other people may not see. **The teacher seemed to have special *insights* about which of her students would make good leaders.** *syn.* perception

in·stinct [in′stingkt] *n.* An instinct is a natural, almost automatic way that people or animals react to things. **The mother bear's *instinct* was to protect her cub from other animals.** *syn.* intuition

in·suf·fi·cient [in·sə·fi′shənt] *adj.* If something is insufficient, there is not enough of it or it is not good enough to meet the need. **The two cans of paint Pat bought were an *insufficient* amount to paint the entire house.** *syn.* inadequate

in·tent·ly [in·tent′lē] *adv.* When you do something intently, you do it with great concentration. **I enjoy learning about the oceans, so I watched and listened *intently* to the documentary about global currents.** *syn.* attentively

in·ter·nal [in·tûr′nəl] *adj.* Something that is internal is inside a person, an object, or a place. **Sharing with others and caring for people are some of Zena's *internal* qualities.** *syn.* inner

---

ACADEMIC LANGUAGE

interview An *interview* is a series of questions and answers that give information about a topic or about the person being interviewed.

intonation *Intonation* is the rise and fall of your voice as you read aloud.

---

in·tri·cate [in′tri·kit] *adj.* If something is intricate, it is complicated or involved and has many small parts or details. **Psychologists try to understand the *intricate* reasons for certain behavior.** *syn.* complicated

in·va·sion [in·vā′zhən] *n.* An invasion happens when someone interrupts or disturbs you in an unwelcome way. **Elizabeth felt it was an *invasion* when her little brother eavesdropped on her phone conversation.** *syn.* intrusion

in·vest [in·vest′] *v.* To invest money in a project means that you put your funds into it, with the hope that in the future, it will earn more money. **Lester decided to *invest* in his uncle's successful business so that he, too, could earn a profit.** *syn.* finance

ir·re·pres·si·ble [ir·i·pres′ə·bəl] *adj.* A feeling or action that is irrepressible cannot be controlled or held back. **The scientist's *irrepressible* desire to explore nature led to his discovering a new species of ant.** *syns.* unmanageable, uncontainable

ir·re·sis·ti·ble [ir·i·zis′tə·bəl] *adj.* Something that is irresistible is difficult to turn away from. **Mother found the sparkling bracelet *irresistible*, so she bought it right away.** *syns.* appealing, desirable

i·so·lat·ed [ī′sə·lāt′əd] *adj.* A place that is isolated is a long way from large towns and is difficult to reach. **Sofia lives out in the countryside on an *isolated* farm.** *syn.* secluded

isolated

jet·ti·son [jet′ə·sən] *v.* **jet·ti·soned** Something that is jettisoned is deliberately cast away from a moving object, sometimes to make the object lighter. **Before the boat sank, we *jettisoned* the extra cargo and paddled to shore.** *syn.* discard

---

Word Origins

jettison The word *jettison* can be traced to the Latin word *jectáre,* meaning "to toss about." Later, the French changed *jectáre* to *getaison* and used it to mean "the act of throwing (goods overboard)."

---

lad·en [lād′ən] *v.* If something is laden, it is weighed down with a heavy load. **Sandra was *laden* with stacks of books to use for her research report.** *syn.* overloaded

loathe [lōth] *v.* If you loathe something, you hate it. **My friends *loathe* being asked to wear formal clothing to parties.** *syns.* dislike, detest

ma·neu·ver [mə·n(y)o͞o′vər] *v.* **ma·neu·vered** To have maneuvered something is to have moved it or guided it very carefully. **The captain *maneuvered* the boat into its slip near the dock.** *syns.* manipulate, manage

ma·ven [mā′vən] *n.* A maven is someone with special knowledge about a particular subject. **My science teacher is a *maven* on the subject of migrating birds.** *syn.* expert

meas·ly [mēz′lē] *adj.* A measly amount of something is a very small amount. **Sherwin got a *measly* half-cup of soup with his sandwich.** *syns.* scanty, insufficient

men·tor [men′tər] *n.* A mentor is a trusted person who gives a person helpful advice. **Trina's volleyball *mentor* teaches excellent playing strategies that she learned while playing on a professional team.** *syn.* teacher

FACT FILE

mentor In Greek mythology, Mentor was a friend of Odysseus, the hero of Homer's epic poem *The Odyssey*. Mentor was the helper and teacher of Odysseus' son, Telemachus. After Odysseus went away to battle, Mentor often helped Telemachus choose the right course of action.

mis·treat [mis·trēt′] *v.* **mis·treat·ed** If something is mistreated, it is used in a way that harms or hurts it. **Sam thought his younger sister *mistreated* her bicycle by leaving it outside on the wet grass every evening.** *syn.* harm

mod·est [mod′əst] *adj.* A modest person does not brag or show off. **Hardly anyone knew that Sally had shown her paintings in several art galleries because she was *modest* about her talent.** *syn.* humble

mo·nop·o·lize [mə·nop′ə·līz] *v.* People who monopolize something control it and prevent others from using it. **Marcos tries not to *monopolize* the remote control when he watches TV with his friends.** *syn.* dominate

FACT FILE

monopolize *Monopolize* can be traced back to the Greek word *monopolion*. The word part *mono* means "single," and *polein* means "to sell." The popular board game *Monopoly,* in which players buy and sell property, appeared in 1935.

mo·not·o·nous [mə·not′ə·nəs] *adj.* If something is monotonous, it is repetitive and boring. **Juanita says that practicing the musical scales over and over on the piano is *monotonous*.** *syns.* boring, tedious

mor·ti·fy [môr′tə·fī] *v.* **mor·ti·fied** If you feel mortified, you feel extremely embarrassed or ashamed. **Shawna was *mortified* during the play when she couldn't remember her most important lines.** *syns.* humiliate, embarrass

a add	e end	o odd	o͞o pool	oi oil	th this		a in *above*
ā ace	ē equal	ō open	u up	ou pout	zh vision	ə =	e in *sicken*
â care	i it	ô order	û burn	ng ring			i in *possible*
ä palm	ī ice	o͝o took	yo͞o fuse	th thin			o in *melon*
							u in *circus*

N

ACADEMIC LANGUAGE

narrative nonfiction *Narrative nonfiction* is a story that tells about people, things, events, or places that are real.

nudge [nuj] *v.* **nudged** If you nudged a person or thing, you pushed it or poked it gently. **I forgot to set my alarm clock last night, so it's a good thing my dog *nudged* me when it was time to get up.** *syn.* push

O

or·deal [ôr·dēl´ *or* ôr·dē´əl] *n.* An ordeal is a very difficult experience that is unpleasant to go through. **Living through the flood was an *ordeal*, but rebuilding our community was just as difficult.** *syn.* challenge

ACADEMIC LANGUAGE

organization Writers create *organization* by ordering ideas in ways that make sense, such as in a time-order sequence. Stories, poems, essays, and other genres are organized according to rules and patterns specific to each writing form.

out·cast [out´kast] *n.* An outcast is someone who has been rejected or driven out by others. **After Hannah became a theater star, she was an *outcast* among her old friends because she went for weeks without calling them.** *syn.* outsider

out·land·ish [out·lan´dish] *adj.* If something is outlandish, it is bizarre, strange, and unusual. **The clowns wore *outlandish* outfits, making everyone smile.** *syn.* peculiar

outlandish

o·ver·come [ō·vər·kum´] *v.* When you are overcome by something, you are overpowered by it. **Derek was *overcome* by a sudden fear of speaking in front of the group.** *syn.* overwhelm

P

ACADEMIC LANGUAGE

pace Reading aloud at an appropriate *pace* means reading with smoothness and consistency, not too fast or too slow.

pan·ic [pan´ik] *n.* Panic is a strong feeling of fear and anxiety that makes a person act unreasonably or without thinking carefully. **When the burglar alarm sounded, Jocelyn went into a state of *panic* and started to scream.** *syn.* fear

FACT FILE

panic The word *panic* comes from *Pānikós*, the Greek word that means "of Pan." In Greek mythology, Pan is the god of the woods. The Greek people believed that Pan startled animals in the woods and caused them to run or fly away.

parched [pärcht] *adj.* Something that is parched is dried out from lack of water. **The farmer hoped the rain clouds in the distance would bring much-needed water to his *parched* fields of corn.** *syn.* dehydrated

per·il [per´əl] *n.* Peril is great danger. **Claire visited the library during the day because walking alone at night would put her in *peril*.** *syns.* danger, risk

per·se·ver·ance [pûr·sə·vir´əns] *n.* If you try hard and don't give up, you are showing perseverance. **Margaret's many hours of practicing her gymnastics routine showed her *perseverance*.** *syn.* determination

ACADEMIC LANGUAGE

personal narrative In *personal narratives*, authors reveal thoughts and feelings about their experiences. Personal narratives are told in first-person point of view.

per·suade [pər·swād′] *v.* **per·suad·ing** Persuading someone means trying to get him or her to agree with your plan or opinion. **Richard was intent on *persuading* Fernando to play tennis with him.** *syn.* convince

ACADEMIC LANGUAGE

persuasive text *Persuasive text* is written to persuade readers to take action or to convince them of the author's viewpoint on a topic. Editorials, reviews, and advertisements are examples of persuasive text.

pes·ky [pes′kē] *adj.* Something that is pesky is annoying but not important. **Picnics are a lot of fun until those *pesky* ants show up!** *syns.* annoying, irritating

pho·bi·a [fō′bē·ə] *n.* To have a phobia is to be terrified of something without having a good reason for the fear. **Tyrell's *phobia* of flying kept him from traveling to faraway places.** *syn.* fear

ACADEMIC LANGUAGE

photo essay A *photo essay* gives information through photographs and captions.

phrasing *Phrasing* is grouping words into meaningful "chunks," or phrases, when you read aloud.

pin·na·cle [pin′ə·kəl] *n.* The pinnacle of a building is a tall, pointed piece at its top. **The *pinnacle* of the Empire State Building lights up at night.** *syns.* peak, top

pinnacle

ACADEMIC LANGUAGE

play A *play* is a story that is meant to be performed for an audience. Plays often include stage directions that tell the characters how to act and may be divided into acts and scenes.

poetry *Poetry* is a form of expressive writing that uses verse.

poised [poizd] *adj.* When you are poised, you are calm and ready to get started. **The ballerina stood *poised* in the wings, waiting for her cue.** *syn.* composed

port·a·ble [pôr′tə·bəl] *adj.* Something that is portable can be moved or carried by hand. **We laughed because Dad brought a *portable* TV and his cell phone on the camping trip.** *syn.* movable

po·ten·tial·ly [pə·ten′chə·lē] *adv.* Something that could potentially happen could possibly happen. **If Ken studies more, he *potentially* could get all *A*'s.** *syn.* probably

prac·ti·cal [prak′ti·kəl] *adj.* Something that is practical is useful. **Even though the winter coat was on sale, Erin didn't think it would be *practical* for her summer vacation in Arizona.** *syns.* useful, realistic

— **Word Origins** —

practical The word *practical* came from the Greek word *praktikos,* which means "fit for action." It was used later in Middle English as *practicale.*

pre·car·i·ous [pri·kâr′ē·əs] *adj.* In a precarious situation, things are uncertain and can suddenly become dangerous. **Cheng didn't hear the lifeguard's warning and found himself in the *precarious* state of swimming in rough water.** *syns.* risky, uncertain

pre·cious [presh′əs] *adj.* If something is precious to you, it has value and special meaning to you. **Martha never misses appointments for her dog's check-ups because he is *precious* to her.** *syn.* valued

a	add	e	end	o	odd	$\overline{oo}$	pool	oi	oil	th	this
ā	ace	ē	equal	ō	open	u	up	ou	pout	zh	vision
â	care	i	it	ô	order	û	burn	ng	ring		
ä	palm	ī	ice	$\overline{oo}$	took	y$\overline{oo}$	fuse	th	thin		

ə = {
a in *above*
e in *sicken*
i in *possible*
o in *melon*
u in *circus*
}

pres·ti·gious [pres·tē′jəs] *adj.* Something that is prestigious is highly respected and admired. **The principal of a school has a *prestigious* job.** *syns.* impressive, noteworthy

pro·claim [prō·klām′] *v.* **pro·claimed** If you have announced something to a group of people, you have proclaimed it. **The referee *proclaimed* to the crowd that the hometown team was the district winner.** *syns.* announce, declare

pro·fuse·ly [prō·fyoōs′lē] *adv.* Something done profusely is done in great quantity. **Clifton apologized *profusely* after insulting his good friend.** *syns.* lavishly, exuberantly

prog·nos·ti·ca·tion [prog·nos′tə·kā′shən] *n.* A prognostication is a forecast or prediction. **After watching the football team of every school, the sports writer made a *prognostication* about which team would be the best that year.** *syn.* prediction

pro·por·tion [prə·pôr′shən] *n.* If something is in proportion, none of its parts are too large or too small. **The class's diorama of New York City showed the figures and automobiles in the correct *proportion* to the tall buildings.** *syns.* ratio, size

pro·pose [prə·pōz′] *v.* **pro·posed** A person who proposed something put forth the ideas to do it. **The best ideas for the fund-raiser were *proposed* by the new girl because she had ideas we had never thought of.** *syns.* suggest, recommend

pro·test [prō′test] *n.* A protest is a way of demonstrating that you are against something. **The parents held a *protest* about having too many soda machines and not enough water fountains in the school building.** *syn.* objection

pro·trude [prō·troōd′] *v.* To protrude is to stick out. **If the lumber will *protrude* from the back of the truck, you should tie a red cloth to the end of it so that other drivers can see it.** *syns.* jut, obtrude

pro·voke [prə·vōk′] *v.* When you provoke someone, you do something to make him or her feel angry. **Kathryn didn't mean to *provoke* Sol when she didn't return the CD she had borrowed.** *syns.* aggravate, irritate

pry [prī] *v.* **pried** If you have pried something off, you have forced it away from a surface. **A nail can usually be *pried* from a board by using the right tool.** *syn.* extract

pry

R

rasp·y [ras′pē] *adj.* A raspy noise sounds rough and harsh, like sandpaper scraping wood. **Leon's voice sounded *raspy* because he had a chest cold.** *syns.* gruff, harsh

ACADEMIC LANGUAGE

reading rate Your *reading rate* is how quickly you can read a text correctly and still understand what you are reading.

realistic fiction *Realistic fiction* stories have characters, settings, and plot events that are like people, places, and events in real life. The characters face problems that could really happen.

re·coil [ri·koil′] *v.* To recoil means to jerk back suddenly. **The dog's loud barking made the cat *recoil* and run away.** *syn.* withdraw

re·count [ri·kount′] *v.* If you recount a story, you tell what happened. **Glendina's reading assignment was to *recount* the story in a summary.** *syn.* tell

re·gal [rē′gəl] *adj.* If something is regal, it is fit for a king or queen. **The German hotel looked *regal,* and we found out later that it had once been a real palace.** *syn.* majestic

reign [rān] *v.* **reigned** If someone has reigned, he or she has been very important in a particular place. **Principal Jones *reigned* over Southeast Middle School until he retired last June.** *syn.* preside

re·lent [ri·lent′] *v.* **re·lent·ed** Someone who has relented has agreed to something he or she once refused. **The students cheered when the school principal** *relented* **and allowed them to have a "bring-your-pet-to-school" day.** *syn.* yield

re·mote [ri·mōt′] *adj.* A remote place is far away from cities and towns. **Kyle's grandparents live in such a** *remote* **area that the only things they hear outside are the wind, the birds, and the insects.** *syns.* faraway, secluded

re·plen·ish [ri·plen′ish] *v.* **re·plen·ish·ing** Replenishing something means refilling it or making it complete again. **Next weekend, my parents will be going to the market and** *replenishing* **our refrigerator with food.** *syns.* refill, restock

rep·u·ta·tion [rep′yə·tā′shən] *n.* A person's reputation is what he or she is known for. **The senator has a** *reputation* **for being honest and fair, so many people in the government trust him.**

res·i·dent [rez′ə·dənt] *n.* **res·i·dents** Residents are the people or animals that live in a place. **Alligators and snakes are** *residents* **of many swamps.** *syns.* inhabitant, dweller

re·sist [ri·zist′] *v.* **re·sist·ed** If a person or an object has resisted, that person or object was very difficult or impossible to change. **The painting** *resisted* **all of Barry's attempts to restore it to its original condition.** *syn.* oppose

re·strain [ri·strān′] *v.* If you restrain something, you hold it back or limit it. **To** *restrain* **the sheep from wandering too far, the rancher put up a fence.** *syn.* control

rev·el·er [rev′əl·ər] *n.* **rev·el·ers** Revelers are people who are having fun at a lively party or celebration. **Cinco de Mayo is a Mexican holiday in which** *revelers* **enjoy parades and parties.** *syn.* partygoer

rig·id [rij′id] *adj.* An object that is rigid is stiff and does not change shape easily. **When the clay hardens, the sculpture becomes** *rigid.* *syn.* firm

> **Word Origins**
>
> **rigid** The word *rigid* is based on the Latin word *rigere,* which means "to be stiff."

row·dy [rou′dē] *adj.* People who are rowdy are noisy, rough, and out of control. **Guards monitored the crowd of** *rowdy* **fans as they exited the rugby stadium.** *syn.* disorderly

ruck·us [ruk′əs] *n.* To raise a ruckus is to make a lot of noise and fuss about something. **The dog alerted its sleeping owner of danger by making a** *ruckus.* *syn.* disturbance

schol·ar [skol′ər] *n.* **schol·ars** Scholars are people who have studied certain topics and know a lot about them. **Many English professors are** *scholars* **in the literature of a particular time period.** *syn.* intellectual

scour [skour] *v.* **scours** If someone scours a place for something, he or she searches thoroughly for it. **Penelope** *scours* **the yard in hopes of finding her necklace.** *syn.* search

se·cure [si·kyŏŏr′] *adj.* Something that is secure is safe and not likely to give way. **Evelyn uses a** *secure* **lock on her door to keep out intruders.** *syns.* safe, protected

secure

> **Word Origins**
>
> **secure** The word *secure* came from the Latin phrase *se cura,* which means "free from care." The word was first used in English with its current meaning in about 1533.

sel·dom [sel′dəm] *adv.* If something seldom happens, it hardly ever happens. **Rainbows are** *seldom* **seen in desert areas.** *syns.* rarely, infrequently

a add	e end	o odd	ōō pool	oi oil	th this		a in *above*
ā ace	ē equal	ō open	u up	ou pout	zh vision		e in *sicken*
â care	i it	ô order	û burn	ng ring		ə =	i in *possible*
ä palm	ī ice	ŏŏ took	yōō fuse	th thin			o in *melon*
							u in *circus*

sen·si·bil·i·ty [sen'sə·bil'ə·tē] *n.* A sensibility is a special awareness in a certain area; for example, a person can have an artistic sensibility or a musical sensibility. **The interior designer has a *sensibility* for creating a mood through the use of color.** *syn.* feeling

shat·ter [shat'ər] *v.* When things shatter, they break suddenly and violently into small pieces. **If the puppies knock over the vase, it will *shatter* into a hundred pieces.** *syns.* break, destroy

sin·cere [sin·sir'] *adj.* If you are being sincere, you are being honest, and you mean what you say. **Joyce was *sincere* when she told the teacher she liked doing science experiments.** *syns.* honest, genuine

FACT FILE

sincere Most experts trace the word *sincere* to the Latin word *sincerus,* meaning "clean, pure, or sound." However, other experts say the word has its roots in the marble quarries of the sixteenth century, in which workers would rub wax on marble blocks to hide flaws. In time, the government declared that all marble had to be *sine cera,* or "without wax."

sleek [slēk] *adj.* Something that is sleek is smooth. **A seal's wet fur looks *sleek*.** *syns.* shiny, glossy

sleek

smirk [smûrk] *n.* A smirk is an unkind smile. **The producer had a *smirk* on his face as he talked about the famous actor having trouble finding work.** *syn.* simper

sneer [snir] *v.* **sneered** If you sneered at someone, you showed with your words and expression that you had little respect for that person. **The arrogant hotel guest *sneered* at the desk clerk when he couldn't find her reservation.** *syn.* scoff

som·ber·ly [som'bər·lē] *adv.* When you act somberly, you speak and act in a serious way. **The news anchor *somberly* reported the details of the train accident.** *syns.* seriously, sadly

sor·row·ful [sor'ə·fəl] *adj.* If you feel sorrowful, you are sad. **The listeners were *sorrowful* as they heard about the victims of the fire.** *syns.* distressed, unhappy

spe·cial·ize [spesh'əl·īz] *v.* **spe·cial·ized** Someone who has specialized in something has given it most of his or her time and attention. **The doctor *specialized* in heart surgery.** *syns.* concentrate, focus

spec·i·men [spes'ə·mən] *n.* **spec·i·mens** Specimens are examples of things scientists collect in order to study. **Entomologists collect *specimens* of insects.** *syn.* sample

spec·tac·u·lar [spek·tak'yə·lər] *adj.* Something that is spectacular is very impressive and draws a lot of attention. **Lei's room faces west, giving her views of the region's *spectacular* sunsets.** *syn.* amazing

squint [skwint] *v.* **squint·ing** Someone who is squinting is squeezing his or her eyes partly shut in order to see. **It's hard to have a picture taken on a bright, sunny day without *squinting*.** *syn.* peer

stam·mer [stam'ər] *v.* **stam·mers** A person who stammers speaks with difficulty, often stopping or repeating himself or herself. **Because she is nervous, Ines *stammers* as she gives her speech.** *syn.* stutter

stream·lined [strēm'līnd] *adj.* A streamlined design is efficient and has no unneeded parts. **The car salesperson boasted about the *streamlined* design of the new, faster sports model.** *syn.* sleek

strick·en [strik'ən] *v.* If you are stricken, you are suddenly and badly affected by something, such as illness or fear. **When Stanley heard that the tornado had demolished all of the houses in his community, he was *stricken* with grief.** *syn.* afflict

sum·mit [sum′it] *n.* A mountain's summit is its very top. **While touring Tanzania, Janeka climbed to the** *summit* **of Mount Kilimanjaro.** *syns.* top, peak

---
Word Origins

summit The word *summit* has its origins in the Latin word *summus,* meaning "highest." When the French adopted the word *summus,* they changed it to *sommette,* meaning "the highest part or top of a hill."

---

sus·tain [sə·stān′] *v.* When you sustain something, you keep it going by giving it what it needs. **In order to** *sustain* **the school library, the parents donated money and books.** *syns.* maintain, continue

swarm [swôrm] *v.* **swarmed** If animals have swarmed, they have moved quickly and gathered in large numbers. **In the spring, honeybees** *swarmed* **around the nest to protect the queen bee.** *syns.* group, cluster

sway [swā] *v.* **swayed** Something that swayed was moving back and forth. **The audience** *swayed* **to the music of the orchestra.** *syn.* rock

T

ACADEMIC LANGUAGE

tall tale A *tall tale* is a humorous story about impossible or exaggerated happenings.

---

teem [tēm] *v.* **teem·ing** Something that is teeming is overflowing with life or energy. **The stadium was** *teeming* **with fans for the championship soccer game.** *syn.* abound

tempt [tempt] *v.* **tempt·ed** If you are tempted to do something, you really want to do it, even though you know you shouldn't. **Natalia is** *tempted* **to listen to her new CD instead of writing her book report.** *syn.* entice

ten·den·cy [ten′dən·sē] *n.* To have a tendency is to have a habit of doing something in a certain way. **Because Arup has a** *tendency* **to wait until the last minute to do his assignments, he often turns in his work late.** *syn.* inclination

ter·rain [tə·rān′] *n.* Terrain is the kind of land that is found in a place; for example, terrain might be rocky, hilly, or swampy. **Laticia enjoys hiking the rocky** *terrain* **in the state park.** *syns.* land, territory

terrain

Word Origins

terrain The word *terrain* can be traced back to the Latin word *terra,* meaning "earth." The word was later used by the French as *terrain.*

ACADEMIC LANGUAGE

textbook *Textbooks* are organized by chapter titles and headings within chapters. Textbooks provide information without giving the authors' opinions.

---

throng [throng] *n.* A throng is a crowd of people. **The shouts became louder as the** *throng* **waited for the doors to open.** *syns.* crowd, mass

---
ACADEMIC LANGUAGE

time line A *time line* shows information about events in the order in which they happened.

---

tran·quil·i·ty [trang·kwil′ə·tē] *n.* A feeling of tranquility is a feeling of calm and peace. **Jessica finds** *tranquility* **in sitting beside the pond and observing nature.** *syn.* serenity

tur·bu·lent [tûr′byə·lənt] *adj.* Something that is turbulent, such as air or water, has strong currents which change direction suddenly. **The captain of the airplane turned on the seat-belt sign and announced that the weather had become** *turbulent.* *syn.* unsettled

a	add	e	end	o	odd	o͞o	pool	oi	oil	th	this		a in *above*
ā	ace	ē	equal	ō	open	u	up	ou	pout	zh	vision	ə =	e in *sicken*
â	care	i	it	ô	order	û	burn	ng	ring				i in *possible*
ä	palm	ī	ice	o͝o	took	yo͞o	fuse	th	thin				o in *melon*
													u in *circus*

U

un·der·ly·ing [un′dər·lī′ing] *adj.* Something that is underlying is located below or beneath something. **An ant mound's underlying soil has a network of tunnels made and used by thousands of ants.**

un·fath·om·a·ble [un·fath′əm·ə·bəl] *adj.* If something is unfathomable, it cannot be understood or known. **Without an understanding of basic arithmetic, college algebra would be *unfathomable*.** *syn.* incomprehensible

un·im·ag·i·na·ble [un·i·maj′ə·nə·bəl] *adj.* If something is unimaginable, it is impossible to think that it might happen or exist. **A summer without sunshine is *unimaginable*.** *syns.* unthinkable, inconceivable

un·in·hab·it·a·ble [un·in·hab′it·ə·bəl] *adj.* A place that is uninhabitable cannot be lived in. **This place will be *uninhabitable* until the water can be made clean and safe to drink.** *syn.* inhospitable

ur·gent·ly [ûr′jənt·lē] *adv.* If you urgently tell someone to do something, it is important that it be done right away. **Phillip's father *urgently* needs him to help make all the deliveries before dark.** *syn.* immediately

V

van·ish [van′ish] *v.* To vanish is to disappear suddenly. **The magician made the tiger seem to *vanish* and then appear again.** *syn.* disappear

veto [vē′tō] *v.* **ve·toed** If someone has vetoed something, he or she has rejected it. **Congress passed the bill, but the President *vetoed* it.** *syn.* reject

FACT FILE

veto During government sessions in ancient Rome, elected members, called tribunes, yelled "*Veto!*" if they did not want a law to pass. *Veto* is Latin for "I forbid."

vi·tal [vīt′əl] *adj.* Something that is vital is necessary for life. **Food, air, and water are *vital* for survival.** *syn.* essential

ACADEMIC LANGUAGE

voice The term *voice* is used to describe a writer's tone, attitude, or personality. A reader might perceive a writer's voice as formal, confident, or mischievous.

W

wisp·y [wisp′ē] *adj.* Something that is wispy is thin, lightweight, and easily broken. **Rosa's china doll was so fragile and *wispy* that she was afraid to play with it.** *syn.* delicate

wist·ful [wist′fəl] *adj.* You are wistful if you feel as though your wishes probably won't come true. **Sheila felt *wistful* knowing she wouldn't be going to music camp this summer.** *syn.* melancholy

with·ered [with′ərd] *adj.* Something that is withered is dried up and faded. **The fallen leaves were brown and *withered*.** *syn.* wilted

withered

ACADEMIC LANGUAGE

word choice A writer may choose sensory, vivid, and precise words to help the reader imagine people, places, and events. *Word choice* helps writers express a personal voice, or personality, in their writing.

Y

yearn·ing [yûr′ning] *n.* A yearning is a great desire to have something that you may never be able to get. **Gracie has a *yearning* to travel to the Amazon rain forest to see the many flowers that she has only read about.** *syns.* desire, longing

Index of Titles and Authors

Page numbers in green refer to biographical information.

Acknowledgments

For permission to reprint copyrighted material, grateful acknowledgment is made to the following sources:

Atheneum Books for Young Readers, an imprint of Simon & Schuster Children's Publishing Division: From *Ultimate Field Trip 3: Wading into Marine Biology* by Susan E. Goodman, photographs by Michael J. Doolittle. Text copyright © 1999 by Susan E. Goodman; photographs copyright © 1999 by Michael J. Doolittle.

Curtis Brown, Ltd.: "Summer Hummers" by Linda Sue Park. Text copyright © 2001 by Linda Sue Park. Originally published in *Cricket* Magazine, November 2001 by Carus Publishing Company.

Candlewick Press, Inc., Cambridge, MA: From *Interrupted Journey* by Kathryn Lasky, photographs by Christopher G. Knight. Text copyright © 2001 by Kathryn Lasky; photographs copyright © 2001 by Christopher G. Knight.

Carus Publishing Company, 30 Grove St., Suite C, Peterborough, NH 03458: "Got a Problem? Get a Plan!" by Karen Bledsoe from *APPLESEEDS: Kids Can Change the World,* September 2005. Text © 2005 by Carus Publishing Company. "Central Park" by John J. Bonk from *COBBLESTONE: New York City,* June 1995. Text © 1995 by Cobblestone Publishing. "Voyage into the Past" by Ann Collins from *APPLESEEDS: American Places, San Diego,* May 2000. Text © 2000 by Cobblestone Publishing. "Journey on the Silk Road" by Luann Hankom from *APPLESEEDS: Children of China Long Ago,* October 2002. Text © 2002 by Carus Publishing Company. "Sourdough" by Jane Scherer from *COBBLESTONE: The California Gold Rush,* December 1997. Text © 1997 by Cobblestone Publishing.

Children's Press, an imprint of Scholastic Library Publishing, Inc.: From *Lewis and Clark* by R. Conrad Stein. Text © 1997 by Children's Press®, a division of Grolier Publishing Co., Inc.

Chronicle Books LLC, San Francisco, ChronicleBooks.com: From *The Man Who Went to the Far Side of the Moon: The Story of Apollo 11 Astronaut Michael Collins* by Bea Uusma Schyffert. Text and illustrations copyright © 1999 by Bea Uusma Schyffert; translation © 2003 by Chronicle Books LLC.

Clarion Books, a Houghton Mifflin Company imprint: From *Project Mulberry* by Linda Sue Park, cover illustration by Debora Smith. Text copyright © 2005 by Linda Sue Park; cover illustration copyright © 2005 by Debora Smith.

The Cricket Magazine Group, a division of Carus Publishing Company: "Ninth Inning" by Anna Levine from *Cricket* Magazine, June 2004. Text © 2004 by Anna Levine. "Take a Bow!" by Anna Levine from *Cricket* Magazine, January 2005. Text © 2004 by Anna Levine.

Darby Creek Publishing, a division of Oxford Resources, Inc.: "Line Drive" by Tanya West Dean from *Sport Shorts: An Anthology of Short Stories.* Text © 2005 by Tanya West.

Dial Books for Young Readers, a Division of Penguin Young Readers Group, A Member of Penguin Group (USA) Inc., 345 Hudson Street, New York, NY 10014: "On Top of the World" from *A World of Wonders: Geographic Travels in Verse and Rhyme* by J. Patrick Lewis, illustrated by Alison Jay. Text copyright © 2002 by J. Patrick Lewis; illustration copyright © 2002 by Alison Jay.

Farrar, Straus and Giroux, LLC: From *Chang and the Bamboo Flute* by Elizabeth Starr Hill, cover illustration by Lesley Liu. Text copyright © 2002 by Elizabeth Starr Hill; cover illustration copyright © 2002 by Lesley Liu. From *Chester Cricket's Pigeon Ride* by George Selden, illustrated by Garth Williams. Text copyright © 1981 by George Selden Thompson; illustrations copyright © 1981 by Garth Williams.

HarperCollins Publishers: From *When the Circus Came to Town* by Laurence Yep, cover illustration by Suling Wang. Text copyright

© 2002 by Laurence Yep; cover illustration copyright © 2002 by Suling Wang.

Highlights for Children, Inc., Columbus, OH: "When Our Family Bands Together" by Teresa Bateman from *Highlights for Children* Magazine, August 2003. Text copyright © 2003 by Highlights for Children, Inc. "The Alligator Race" by Karen Dowicz Haas from *Highlights for Children* Magazine, August 2004. Text copyright © 2004 by Highlights for Children, Inc. From "The Artist's Eye" by Joan T. Zeier in *Highlights for Children* Magazine, March 2004. Text copyright © 2004 by Highlights for Children, Inc.

Houghton Mifflin Company: "Steam" from *Splish Splash* by Joan Bransfield Graham. Text copyright © 1994 by Joan Bransfield Graham. From *The Top of the World: Climbing Mount Everest* by Steve Jenkins. Copyright © 1999 by Steve Jenkins.

Alfred A. Knopf, an imprint of Random House Children's Books, a division of Random House, Inc.: From *The Daring Nellie Bly: America's Star Reporter* by Bonnie Christensen. Copyright © 2003 by Bonnie Christensen. "Stormalong" from *American Tall Tales* by Mary Pope Osborne. Text copyright © 1991 by Mary Pope Osborne. From "How Beaver Stole Fire" in *In a Circle Long Ago* by Nancy Van Laan, illustrated by Lisa Desimini. Text copyright © 1995 by Nancy Van Laan; illustrations copyright © 1995 by Lisa Desimini.

Lerner Publications Company: From *Nellie Bly's Book: Around the World in 72 Days* (Retitled: "A Proposal to Girdle the Earth"), edited by Ira Peck. Text copyright © 1998 by Ira Peck.

Little, Brown and Co., Inc.: From *Into a New Country: Eight Remarkable Women of the West* (Retitled: "Klondike Kate") by Liza Ketchum. Text copyright © 2000 by Liza Ketchum.

Mary Anne Lloyd: Illustrations by Mary Anne Lloyd from "Kids in Action" by Elizabeth Schleichert in *Ranger Rick®* Magazine, September 2005.

Gina Maccoby Literary Agency: "Ice Cycle" by Mary Ann Hoberman from *Once Upon Ice,* selected by Jane Yolen. Text copyright © 1997 by Mary Ann Hoberman. Published by Boyds Mills Press, Inc.

National Geographic Society: From "The Zoo Crew" by Laura Daily in *National Geographic WORLD* Magazine, February 2000. Text copyright © 2000 by National Geographic Society. From *Inventing the Future* by Marfé Ferguson Delano. Text copyright © 2002 by National Geographic Society.

National Wildlife Federation®: From "Kids In Action" by Elizabeth Schleichert in *Ranger Rick®* Magazine, September 2005. Text copyright 2005 by the National Wildlife Federation®.

North-South Books Inc., New York: Sailing Home: A Story of a Childhood at Sea by Gloria Rand, illustrated by Ted Rand. Text copyright © 2001 by Gloria Rand; illustrations copyright © 2001 by Ted Rand.

G. P. Putnam's Sons, A Division of Penguin Young Readers Group, A Member of Penguin Group USA (Inc.), 345 Hudson Street, New York, NY 10014: From *Leonardo's Horse* by Jean Fritz, illustrated by Hudson Talbott. Text copyright © 2001 by Jean Fritz; illustrations copyright © 2001 by Hudson Talbott.

Marian Reiner, on behalf of August House Publishers, Inc.: "Paul Bunyan Makes Progress" from *Sweet Land of Story: Thirty-Six American Tales to Tell* by Pleasant deSpain. Text © 2000 by Pleasant deSpain. Published by August House Publishers, Inc.

Scholastic Inc.: "The Night of San Juan" and cover illustration from *Salsa Stories* by Lulu Delacre. Text and cover illustration copyright © 2000 by Lulu Delacre. From *Any Small Goodness: A Novel of the Barrio* by Tony Johnston, cover illustration by Raúl Colón. Text copyright © 2001 by Roger D. Johnston and Susan T. Johnston as Trustees of the Johnston Family Trust; cover illustration copyright © 2001 by Raúl Colón. Published by

The Blue Sky Press. "Rain, Dance!" from *Splash! Poems of Our Watery World* by Constance Levy. Text copyright © 2002 by Constance Kling Levy. Published by Orchard Books. From *In 1776* by Jean Marzollo. Text copyright © 1994 by Jean Marzollo. "The Ant and the Dove," "The Lion and the Mouse," and cover illustration from *Aesop's Fables,* retold by Ann McGovern. Text and cover illustration copyright © 1963 by Scholastic Inc. Published by Apple Classics. *Nothing Ever Happens on 90th Street* by Roni Schotter, illustrated by Kyrsten Brooker. Text copyright © 1997 by Roni Schotter; illustrations copyright © 1997 by Kyrsten Brooker. Published by Orchard Books. From *A Drop of Water* by Walter Wick. Text and photographs copyright © 1997 by Walter Wick. Published by Scholastic Press.

Brian Selznick: Cover illustration by Brian Selznick from *The School Story* by Andrew Clements. Illustration copyright © 2001 by Brian Selznick.

Simon & Schuster Books for Young Readers, an Imprint of Simon & Schuster Children's Publishing Division: When Washington Crossed the Delaware by Lynne Cheney, illustrated by Peter M. Fiore. Text copyright © 2004 by Lynne Cheney; illustrations copyright © 2004 by Peter M. Fiore. From *The School Story* by Andrew Clements. Text copyright © 2001 by Andrew Clements.

TIME For Kids: "Tree Houses for Everyone" by Tiffany Sommers from *TIME For Kids* Magazine, September 24, 2004. From "Evren Ozan, Musician" by Harsha Viswanathan in *TIME For Kids* Magazine, October 27, 2003.

Albert Whitman & Company: From *Rope Burn* by Jan Siebold, cover illustration by Layne Johnson. Text copyright © 1998 by Jan Siebold; cover illustration © 1998 by Layne Johnson.

Photo Credits

Placement Key(t) top; (b) bottom; (l) left; (r) right; (c) center; (bg) background; (fg) foreground; (i) inset.

17 (b) Peter Bennett/Ambient Images; 17 (tr) Scala/Art Resource; 18 Images.com/Corbis; 22 (b) Joe Atlas/PictureQuest; 23 (tr) VStock LLC/Index Stock; 24 (b) Zoran Milich/Getty; 44 (l) Peter McBride Photography; 45 (tr) Peter McBride Photography; 53 (b) Brandon D. Cole/Corbis; 56 (b) Brandon D. Cole/Corbis; 57 (tr) Larry West/Bruce Coleman, Inc.; 77 (tr) Jon Shireman/Getty; 79 (bl) Lester Lefkowitz/Corbis; 80 (br) James Marshall/Corbis; 81 (tr) Siede Preis/Getty; 83 (tr) Tim Hawkins/Getty; 85 (b) Wright State University; 86 (bl) Wright State University; 86 (br) Wright State University; 87 (bl) Henry Ford Museum & Greenfield Village; 87 (br) Wright State University; 88 (br) National Air and Space Museum; 89 (tr) Bettman/Corbis/Magma; 91 (b) LIbrary of Congress; 92 (b) LIbrary of Congress; 93 (t) Library of Congress; 93 (br) Smithsonian Institution; 94 (bl) Library of Congress; 95 (c) Library of Congress; 95 (bl) Library of Congress; 97 (b) Wright State University; 98 (b) Library of Congress; 98 (bl) Wright State University; 99 (b) Wright State University; 102 Corbis; 109 (b) Jerry Cooke/Corbis; 112 (bl) Bettmann/Corbis; 113 (tr) Tony Duffy/Allsport/Getty; 128 (t) Stephen Dalton/Photo Researchers Inc.; 129 (c) OSF/Howard Hall/Animals Animals; 131 (tr) Jim Vecchi/Corbis; 150 Anna Pugh/Lucy Campbell Gallery; 157 (tr) Stockdisc/Superstock; 179 (b) David Stoecklein/Corbis; 180 (b) Michael Wells/Getty; 181 (tr) Bigshots/Getty; 182 (b) Michael Cogliantry/Getty; 201 (br) Comstock/Superstock; 201 (bcr) Thinkstock/Superstock; 205 (bl) Robert Dowling/Corbis; 206 (bl) Ludovic Maisant/Corbis; 207 (tr) Tom Nebbia/Corbis; 208 (bl) Bettmann/Corbis; 208 (br) Hulton-Deutsch Collection/Corbis; 209 (tr) Bettmann/Corbis; 224 (bl) Standard Insurance Company; 225 (l) Paul A. Souders/Corbis; 225 Standard Insurance Company; 228 (b) Kevin R. Morris/Corbis; 230 (b) Gordon Whitten/Corbis; 231 (tr) Ed Kashl/Corbis; 234 Ben Klaffke/Millbrook Press/Lerner Publishing Group; 236 (t) Ben Klaffke/Millbrook Press/Lerner Publishing Group; 237 (r) Ben Klaffke/Millbrook Press/Lerner Publishing Group; 238 (tl) Ben Klaffke/Millbrook Press/Lerner Publishing Group; 238 (b) Ben Klaffke/Millbrook Press/Lerner Publishing Group; 239 (tr) Ben Klaffke/Millbrook Press/Lerner Publishing Group; 239 (br) Ben Klaffke/Millbrook Press/Lerner Publishing Group; 240 Ben Klaffke/Millbrook Press/Lerner Publishing Group; 241 (b) Ben Klaffke/Millbrook Press/Lerner Publishing Group; 242 (l) Ben Klaffke/Millbrook Press/Lerner Publishing Group; 243 (tl) Ben Klaffke/Millbrook Press/Lerner Publishing Group; 243 Ben Klaffke/Millbrook Press/Lerner Publishing Group; 244 (t) Ben Klaffke/Millbrook Press/Lerner Publishing Group; 245 (b) Ben Klaffke/Millbrook Press/Lerner Publishing Group; 248 (l) Setboun/Corbis; 249 Ed Kashi/Corbis; 250 (l) Justin Sullivan/Getty; 251 (r) Barry Smith/Scholastic; 253 (tr) Dan Lamont/Corbis; 267 James L. Amos/Corbis; 268 James L. Amos/Corbis; 271 (l) Tom Bean/Corbis; 272 Christie's Images/Corbis; 275 (b) Paul A. Souders/Corbis; 276 (b) Royalty-free/Getty; 277 (tr) MedioImages Inc./Index Stock; 278 (b) Norbert Wu/Minden Pictures; 279 (tr) Bill Curtsinger/National Geographic Image Collection; 281 (t) Bill Curtsinger/Tilbury House; 282 (tl) Bill Curtsinger/Tilbury House Publishers; 282 (bl) Bill Curtsinger/Tilbury House Publishers; 282 (c) Bill Curtsinger/Tilbury House Publishers; 283 (tr) Bill Curtsinger/Tilbury House Publishers; 284 (tl) Bill Curtsinger/Tilbury House Publishers; 284 (cr) Bill Curtsinger/Tilbury House Publishers; 286 (tl) Bill Curtsinger/Tilbury House Publishers; 286 (bl) Bill Curtsinger/Tilbury House Publishers; 286 (br) Bill Curtsinger/Tilbury House Publishers; 287 (br) Bill Curtsinger/Tilbury House Publishers; 289 Bill Curtsinger/Tilbury House Publishers; 290 (t) Bill Curtsinger/Tilbury House Publishers; 290 (b) Bill Curtsinger/Tilbury House Publishers; 291 (c) Bill Curtsinger/Tilbury House Publishers; 292 (tr) Bill Curtsinger/Tilbury House Publishers; 292 (br) Bill Curtsinger/Tilbury House Publishers; 292 (tl) Bill Curtsinger/Tilbury House Publishers; 293 (b) Bill Curtsinger/Tilbury House Publishers; 294 (b) Bill Curtsinger/Tilbury House Publishers; 296 (br) Lester V. Bergman/Corbis; 296 (t) Tom Brakefield/Getty; 297 (tr) Lester V. Bergman/Corbis; 299 (tr) Steve Terrill/Corbis; 300 (b) Ludovic Maisant/Corbis; 301 (br) National Geographic/Zuma/Corbis; 301 (b) Wolfgang Kaehler/Corbis; 303 (b) Peter Adams/Zefa/Corbis; 305 (tr) Theo Allofs/Corbis; 306 (b) Darrell Gulin/Corbis; 307 (b) Veer; 308 (cr) Galen Rowell/Corbis; 308 (bl) Galen Rowell/Corbis; 309 (r) Galen Rowell/Corbis; 324 Tilbury House Publishers; 325 (t) Jason Stemple/Boyds Mills Press; 325 (b) Jason Stemple/Boyds Mills Press; 327 (tr) Kennan Ward/Corbis; 329 (b) P. Wilson/Zefa/Corbis; 332 (b) Hulton Archives/Getty; 333 (tr) Bettmann/Corbis; 364 (b) Royalty-free/Corbis; 365 (tr) Lew Robertson; 367 (r) Royalty free/Corbis; 404 Bettmann/Corbis; 406 (bl) Royalty-free/Corbis; 406 (cr) Royalty-free/Corbis; 406 (t) Royalty-free/Corbis; 407 (bl) Royalty-free/Corbis; 407 (cl) Royalty-free/Corbis; 407 (cr) Royalty-free/Corbis; 408 (b) Royalty-free/Corbis; 409 (r) age fotostock/Superstock; 410 (b) HIP/Art Resource; 411 (r) Fine Art Photographic Library, London/Art Resource; 428 Calder Foundation/ARS; 429 (br) Art Resource; 429 (cl) Calder Foundation/ARS; 430 Art Resource; 430 Art Resource; 430 Art Resource; 430 Art Resource; 430 (bl) Calder Foundation/ARS; 431 (b) Calder Foundation/ARS; 431 (t) Calder Foundation/ARS; 433 (tr) Royalty-free/Corbis; 434 (br) Ingo Boddenberg/Zefa/Corbis; 440 (b) Royalty-free/Corbis; 441 (cr) Comstock/Superstock; 441 (tr) Royalty-free/Corbis; 442 (b) Image Source Photography/Veer; 461 (b) Royalty-free/Corbis; 463 Images.com/Corbis; 464 (b) Denis Scott/Corbis; 465 (r)